Yale Historical Publications

H. CLARK JOHNSON

Gold, France, and the Great Depression, 1919–1932

Yale University Press
New Haven &
London

Published under the direction of the Department of History of
Yale University with assistance from the income of the
Frederick John Kingsbury Memorial Fund.

Printed in the United States of America.

Johnson, H. Clark.
    Gold, France, and the Great Depression, 1919–1932 / H. Clark
Johnson.
        p.   cm. — (Yale historical publications)
    Includes bibliographical references and index.
    ISBN 0-300-06986-3 (cloth : alk. paper)
    1. Depressions — 1929 — France.   2. Inflation (Finance) — France —
History — 20th century.   3. Gold — France — History — 20th century.
4. Economic stabilization — France — History — 20th century.
5. International finance — History — 20th century.   I. Series.
II. Series: Yale historical publications (Unnumbered)
HB3717   1929.J64   1997
330.944'0815 — dc21   97-168
                                                                 CIP

A catalogue record for this book is available from the British Library.

The paper in this book meets the guidelines for permanence and durability
of the Committee on Production Guidelines for Book Longevity of the
Council on Library Resources.

10 9 8 7 6 5 4 3 2 1

To Margaret and Lisa

Contents

Acknowledgments   ix

Introduction   1

1   Deflation and Depression   11

2   The Prewar Gold Standard   27

3   The Postwar Undervaluation of Gold   44

4   The Postwar Gold Exchange Standard   63

5   The French Inflation, 1921–26   73

6   German and French Capital Inflows, 1924–31   90

     Appendix to Chapter 6: The Reparations Controversy   108

7   The British and German Deflations, 1924–27   111

8   The French Stabilization, 1926–28   120

9   The French Deflation, 1928–32   135

10   The American Deflation, 1928–32   159

11   Why Did the Great Depression Happen?   177

Appendix: Gold in Central Banks and Treasuries,
December 1926–June 1932   190

Notes   195

Glossary   239

Bibliography   245

Index   261

Acknowledgments

I owe an essential argument to Robert Mundell, who called my attention to the post–World War I undervaluation of gold as a cause of the interwar deflation. I also thank the late Harry Miskimin and Willem Buiter, William Parker, Gail Makinen, Scott Sumner, Diane Kunz, Kenneth Mouré, Barbara Sands, Lester Taylor, Adam Klug, Felippo Cartiglia, and Mundell (again) for reading and commenting on drafts at various stages. David Weir, Barry Eichengreen, Harold James, Stephen Schuker, Eugene White, T. N. Srinivasen, and Alan Reynolds also offered useful advice. John Covell at Yale University Press has been encouraging from our initial meeting and has done me the huge favor of believing in my effort. I also owe a large debt to my wife, Margaret Loss, and to my daughter, Lisa, who were supportive throughout.

I am grateful for permission to cite or reproduce material from the archives at the Federal Reserve Bank of New York, the Bank of England, the Bank of France, the Fondation nationale des science politiques (FNSP), Yale and Columbia universities, the Harvard Business School, Amherst College, the Archives économiques et financières, and the Archives nationales. A number of archivists made unusual efforts to accommodate me. I particularly acknowledge Rosemarie Lazenby at the Federal Reserve Bank, Henry Gillett and Elizabeth Ogborn at the Bank of England, William Massa at Yale, Luc Nemeth at the FNSP, Marie Dijou at the Archives économiques et financières, and Brigitte Maymard at the Bank of France.

The Yale Center for International Studies provided a grant for travel to France in the summer of 1990. Yale University also provided a fellowship during the spring and fall terms of 1992. University Seminars at Columbia University supported my preparation effort with a subvention in 1995. Material drawn from this work was presented to the University Seminar on Economic History.

Martha Buckwalter did a thorough job of proofreading, and Stephanie Malewski advised me repeatedly in the use of my word processor. I thank Brian Call for preparing the index.

Translations from French and German sources are mine unless otherwise indicated. In the interest of reaching as broad an audience as possible, I have included a glossary.

Gold, France, and the Great Depression,
1919–1932

Introduction

A great deal has been written about the origins of the Great Depression of 1929–32. This book makes extensive use of insights developed elsewhere but may nevertheless be controversial. It advances the view that essential portions of the history of these years have seldom been incorporated into a coherent account.

Why does this matter? The Great Depression marked the sharpest international business contraction of modern times. Worldwide manufacturing production (excluding the USSR) dropped by almost 40 percent in a span of three years.[1] Unemployment rose to nearly a quarter of the total workforce in the United States and Germany and remained there for several years. It was only slightly lower in other leading countries. The volume of world trade declined by fully two-thirds from early 1929 to mid-1932.[2] The economic distress suggested by these figures dwarfs that of any downturn in the decades after 1945. The contraction no doubt contributed to the rise of national fascisms and the spread of international aggression and war in the following years.

Issues

The Great Depression of 1929–32 originated in a sustained decline in prices, which ushered in widespread default on fixed-payment contracts. This resulted in dominolike reductions in investment and consumption and consequently in widening cutbacks, bankruptcies, and growing unemployment. General price decline, however, has sometimes coexisted with approximate equilibrium in employment and real output growth; it does not always give rise to depression. The difference between these generic experiences turns on the nature and extent of real redistribution that follows upon the deflation — a task at hand is to explain why this deflation brought disaster.

The price declines themselves were caused in large part by avertable malfunctions of the interwar gold standard. American, British, and French leaders, including central bankers in all three countries, wanted to reestablish an international gold standard after World War I. Much of the period of the prewar gold standard — from about 1880 to 1914 — saw relatively stable prices and consistent growth in world output, international trade, and cross-national investment. The functional weakness of the interwar gold standard was that it rested on an inadequate real quantity and a historically low real price of gold. The inadequate supply of gold meant there was no cushion for error in the management of the world's monetary reserves. Should a country or group of countries absorb a disproportionate amount of gold, the amount available for central banks in other countries would be restricted and hence force a contractionary monetary policy. The undervaluation of gold mattered further because it increased the demand for nonmonetary uses of gold, while simultaneously lessening incentives for new exploration and production.

Restriction or suspension of gold convertibility in much of the world during and after World War I led to an international currency inflation (that is, an inflation in which prices are measured in units of currency). Meanwhile, a flow of gold into the United States, where gold convertibility was maintained throughout, facilitated a gold-backed expansion of the currency here. Dollar prices of most goods and services rose greatly, but the dollar price of gold remained fixed at its prewar level, $20.67 per ounce. The international commodity-exchange (that is, "real") value of gold therefore declined sharply to nearly the lowest level in modern history by the early 1920s. The physical quantity of the world's gold increased only moderately during these years because production trended downward after 1915. The decline in the real value of gold thus gave rise to a gold shortage by traditional gold-to-paper money and gold-to-credit measures. This shortage has been neglected by most post–World War II scholars of the depression, including W. Arthur Lewis, Kenneth Galbraith, Murray Rothbard and other Austrian School economists, Milton Friedman and Anna Jacobson Schwartz, Stephen Clarke, Jacques Néré and Peter Temin, and nearly so by Charles Kindleberger.[3] Barry Eichengreen considers but rejects a gold shortage as a cause of the depression.[4] Yet emphasis on the quantity of gold has precedents in the literature. Ralph Hawtrey, Charles Rist, and Gustav Cassel in the 1920s and 1930s and more recently Jacques Rueff and Robert Mundell have stressed the shortage and undervaluation of gold during the twenties.[5] Irving Fisher, Ragnar Nurkse, and (beginning in 1928) John Maynard Keynes also noted the shortage but were less clear about the undervaluation.[6]

Hawtrey, Cassel, and Keynes argued that proper management of limited international reserves could prevent deflation. This argument was concretized in the fledgling postwar "gold exchange standard," in which gold reserves were supplemented with foreign exchange in central bank stocks. Rist and Mundell have argued, to the contrary, that the reserve shortage made a large measure of deflation nearly certain. In their view, had the reserve management failure not occurred as it did, a similar failure might have come soon afterward. Whether a deflation was certain or not is, I think, unknowable; here I want to concentrate on how it in fact took place.

The systemic tendency toward severe currency price deflation began to be realized in 1929. To account for the timing of the deflation, however, one must also identify more immediate influences. Beginning in 1929, the price declines were triggered by the rapid concentration of gold in a small number of central banks, where it was partly or entirely sterilized (that is, the increase in reserves was not permitted correspondingly to increase the amount of currency or deposits). The Federal Reserve drew large amounts of gold from abroad starting in early 1929 and continuing through the summer of 1931, which contributed to the deflationary process; but this movement was exceeded by a larger amount flowing concurrently to the Bank of France. In addition, the gold inflow to France began earlier and persisted after the flow to the United States was reversed.

Had there been no general reserve shortage, the movement of gold to France would not have given rise to systemic deflation. Because this reserve shortage is neglected in most of the literature, the role of the French gold absorption has been deemphasized. Of the writers cited above who overlook the reserve shortage, none has treated the role of France as more than a second-order causal factor.[7] In contrast, Hawtrey saw French deflationary policies as the critical cause of the world deflation, and Keynes and Cassel were only slightly less categorical. Nurkse attributed the subsequent end of the gold exchange standard to adoption of the French Monetary Law of June 1928;[8] this law required that new Bank of France reserves be absorbed in gold rather than foreign exchange. Keynes and Cassel quickly identified this law as a trigger for systemic deflation.

The de facto stabilization of the franc in 1926 left the price of goods and services in France below international parity. The de jure stabilization in 1928 maintained the undervaluation. Damage followed not from the undervaluation itself but from the subsequent sterilization of reserve inflows that maintained it.[9] From December 1926 through June 1932 the proportion of the world's moderately growing stock of monetary gold held by the French central bank rose from 8 percent to 28 percent.[10] Slightly more than a tenth of the increase, or nearly 3 percent of the world's total, came from either the return of gold pledged to the Bank of England during World War I or from French private hoards in exchange for banknotes;[11] the remaining increase came from the share that would otherwise have been held by other central banks. In the absence of sterilization, the French money stock might have grown more rapidly and hence satisfied the demand for francs. In consequence, French prices might have risen toward the world level, at which point the gold inflow would have slowed or stopped. Instead, the sterilization and the gold movement to France continued, and with them the downward pressure on prices and output persisted.

This interpretive framework permits an integrated account of a variety of economic events that are usually treated in isolation. The war debt and reparation issues appear different viewed in the context of a systemic gold shortage from what they do in a neoclassical equilibrium model. The restoration of sterling prewar parity in 1925 is discussed here for its impact on the world economy as well as for its effect in Britain. The French inflations of the early and middle 1920s influenced and in turn were influenced by events in the broader world economy. At different intervals during the predepression decade, Britain, Germany, France, and the United States each saw large inflows of capital. The reasons for these capital movements differ strikingly, however, and are related to extended recessionary deflations in Britain and Germany but to periods of expansion in France and the United States. Particularly vivid capital movements surrounded the New York stock market boom and crash of 1928 and 1929. All of these events must be understood in relation to the dominant fact of the world economy: the attempt to reestablish a gold standard on an inadequate supply base. A detailed narrative of events within this framework has not before been available.

American writers on the Great Depression tend either to assume or briefly justify the premise that the worldwide downturn was caused in large part by events in the United States.[12] French scholars are equally parochial, but with opposite effect; it is rare to find a French historian or economist who acknowledges any French contribution to the international depression.[13] Similarly, studies of the deflationary mechanism in the United States are often technically detailed and quantitatively sophisticated. Nevertheless, they typically lack adequate explanation of how American developments related to the international deflation. Studies that posit non-U.S. origins of the depression are sometimes opposite in their methodology. Explanation shifts away from technical economics to treat the deflation as a fundamentally political or diplomatic phenomenon.

Where economic and diplomatic history are fused, the tendency arises to treat diplomatically interesting or complicated events as those with the greatest economic impact. The effort of Heinrich Brüning's government to revise reparation demands, followed by the collapse of the Austrian Creditanstalt in May 1931 and the German banking crisis, is illustrative. Stephen Schuker thinks that these events set in motion a tightening round in the economic downturn.[14] Kindleberger and Eichengreen make much of the subsequent failure of other central banks to support the Reichsbank adequately.[15] From a systemic monetary perspective, however, German and Austrian events appear less important. Germany did not draw world reserves after 1928; indeed, had Germany been in a position to attract reserves, the Reichsbank would have been able to resist demands for deflationary measures from central bankers in New York and London. More coordination among central banks might have prevented the sharp rise in German discount rates that occurred in the summer of 1931 and that preceded defensive rate adjustments elsewhere. However, this does not begin to explain why Reichsbank reserves were so short when the crisis hit.[16] It also minimizes the importance of a string of events dating back to 1927 that threatened sterling convertibility and involved suspensions of convertibility elsewhere.

Focus on diplomatic controversies also leads us to overlook nondiplomatic events that contributed to the deflation. Even in the case of the banking crises of 1931, emphasis on the issue of international lending distracts us from the Reichsbank's misguided discounting policy — that is, its failure to act as the *domestic* lender of last resort. Earlier developments were still weightier. For example, had the Federal Reserve unilaterally raised the dollar price it would pay for gold in the early 1920s by 30 or 40 percent, the systemic cause of the deflation would have been removed at a stroke; yet I have found no evidence that such action was ever officially considered. Furthermore, events in France are almost never examined in the context of the world depression: which French decisions were crucial? why were they made? were there alternatives? These questions have remained unasked. My book seeks to fill this gap.

Organization

The book demands theoretical underpinnings as well as a recounting of decisions and data. Prominent work in economic theory during recent decades has reasserted the typical pre-1930s view that monetary and price changes should be neutral in their effect on real output. This view postulates that the redistributional consequences of deflation are minimal. In contrast to that view, I explain in chapter 1 under what circumstances price declines bring profit disequilibrium and how one can measure these effects. These conclusions are bolstered with historical illustrations.

The "Keynesian revolution" grew out of its author's attempt to understand the interwar economy. Although Keynes has remained among the most influential writers on the causes of the depression, the popular view of him is deceptively narrow. I deemphasize the Keynes who argued that demand is chronically anemic and that the private economy is routinely unstable and hence that government must undertake frequent action to boost demand. In his place is Keynes the theorist of the causes of economic disequilibrium, and here analysis begins with changes in the relation between economy-wide costs of investment capital and anticipated returns. Keynes identified specific (and probably avoidable) reasons for the rise in the real cost of capital in the years before the depression.

Chapter 2 considers recurrently advanced explanations of the relative success of the international monetary framework during the decades before 1914. There is little evidence to support claims either that the prewar gold standard worked according to a classical price-specie flow mechanism, that central banks regularly responded to signals provided by international gold movements, or that international cooperation played more than a secondary role. However, most central banks did adjust policy depending upon their reserve levels; and they usually kept at least one eye cast for profit opportunities.

The key to the operation of the prewar system during most of its life, and especially after the middle 1890s, was an adequate and growing supply of monetary gold. This ensured that domestic objectives (that is, expansion of output and avoidance of price deflation) and systemic requirements under a fixed-rate régime (that is, approximate cross-national uniformity of price changes) were seldom in conflict. An important contributory factor was the stabilizing role of the Bank of England. The bank's reserve management rapidly affected international conditions because of Britain's position as an international creditor and the role of London as the world's banking center. That the bank did not use its market power to accumulate excess reserves helped to ensure that international monetary gold remained reasonably well distributed. The international depression of 1891–96, similar in its causal dynamics although milder in its consequences than that of 1929–32, marked a failure of the prewar gold standard. It occurred when gold supplies were short and when the Bank of England for a while augmented and sterilized its reserves.

Chapter 3 describes the wartime and postwar inflation-induced undervaluation of gold and its resultant international shortage. The undervaluation diminished the worth of existing gold stocks and discouraged new production. This analysis is reinforced by evidence of an increase in demand for nonmonetary uses of gold, both in the West and spectacularly in India. (The tendency in the literature to overlook the postwar gold shortage is accompanied by almost total neglect of Indian absorption.)[17] An orchestrated rise in the currency price of gold in the early 1920s might have drastically changed the world's interwar economic history and probably the political and diplomatic history of the century as well. But such action would have been inconsistent with contemporary understanding of the way a gold standard should work.

Chapter 4 looks at the context and outcome of early efforts to restore gold convertibility after World War I. Unusual power accrued to the world's central bankers during the 1920s, a consequence of postwar monetary chaos. In the face of the failure to adjust the price of gold and its consequent shortage, the use of gold as a reserve had to be supplemented with foreign exchange, including especially sterling and dollars. Monetary leaders in the United States, France, and Germany, however, never embraced the "gold exchange standard" as more than a temporary expedient. Indeed, concern over renewed inflation led central banks in France and Germany to increase their reserve ratios above their pre-1914 levels. This introduced another rigidity into the interwar system.

In chapter 5, I examine the causes and effects of price inflation in France in 1921–26. What domestic impact did they have, and what was their interaction with sterling-area deflation beginning in 1924? Identification of the causes of the inflation is preliminary to understanding action that would be taken to reverse it during and after 1926. The inflationary episode demonstrates both obstructionist and passive behavior on the part of the French central bank and Treasury that would paradoxically anticipate the stance of a different group of French leaders a few years later in the face of heightened international deflation.

In the late 1920s, gold movements often followed capital movements. Some capital flows are deliberately short term and seek high guaranteed returns, while others follow longer-term investment opportunities and anticipated returns. Chapter 6 distinguishes between the capital movement to Germany, which began in 1924, and that to France, which started two years later. The capital flow to Germany followed high interest rates and coexisted with depressed domestic economic conditions. Because it was offset by a passive trade balance and transfer (that is, reparation) demands, the increase in German reserves was very moderate. When the capital in-movement slackened in 1929,

Germany lost both foreign exchange and gold reserves. One might posit that rigidities in the Weimar economy led to inefficient use of reserves and investment capital, hence that German economic performance acted as a (probably limited) drag on the world economy. It is hard to see this as a factor that would trigger a systemwide turn for the worse in 1928 or 1929.

A more serious failure was the Reichsbank's restrictive discounting policy during the banking crisis of 1931, a policy reinforced by demands from potential creditors at the Federal Reserve and the Bank of England. Reichsbank actions led to massive note withdrawals from commercial banks, which immediately raised the German currency-to-deposit ratio. This rise put pressure on official reserves and threatened the gold standard in Germany.

The French capital inflow was only slightly offset by a trade deficit after 1927 and was reinforced by positive balances on tourism and intergovernmental transfers. This produced a heavy inflow of reserves to France, first in sterling and dollars, then in gold. Growing monetary constraint in other countries increased the attractiveness of franc-denominated investment assets. Because most of France's new reserves were sterilized, this capital movement contracted effective world reserves.

Chapter 7 outlines the deflationary impacts of the German stabilization in 1924 and the British return to gold in 1925. Both contributed to the pressure upon international reserves. Through at least 1927, however, the Federal Reserve was able to offset systemic contraction by releasing gold reserves from its enormous stockpile. The rise in influence of the American central bank in part reflected the overvaluation of sterling; this left the Bank of England in a permanently defensive position and hence weakened its ability to affect world monetary conditions.

Chapter 8 details the return to stable prices in France. The key to stopping the French inflation was to end the Treasury's policy of maintaining submarket interest rates, while changing tax laws to encourage repatriation of capital. A Committee of Experts report in mid-1926 advocated stabilization of the franc while permitting domestic prices to rise toward a level of international purchasing power parity, but, in the event, domestic inflation was not allowed to occur. Instead, both a budget surplus and the reserve inflow were used to strengthen the central bank's balance sheet by paying down advances to the Treasury. The new governor of the Bank of France, Emile Moreau, and the new prime minister (and finance minister), Raymond Poincaré, played crucial roles in this policy reversal; the reversal, in turn, played an essential — but seldom remarked upon — role in generating the world deflation. In the spring of 1927 the Bank of France converted a portion of its sterling into gold, which so pressured the British reserve position that continuation of gold convertibility was threatened. This offered a foreglimpse of events that would force sterling off the gold standard in 1931.

An enormous movement of gold reserves to France occurred during the three and one-half years following the adoption of the French Monetary Law of June 1928. In chapter 9 I deal with the causes and international consequences of this shift. France at the time had a rising poststabilization demand for currency, accentuated by a restrictive discounting policy at the Bank of France that forced commercial banks to increase their cash holdings sharply. The Monetary Law authorized the issue of new francs against gold only, rather than against foreign exchange as before, and thereby made certain a drain on the monetary gold of the rest of the world. During 1929–30 these gold movements brought international wholesale prices toward the lower French level. After the sterling devaluation of September 1931, the Bank of France converted its remaining foreign exchange holdings to gold. This aggravated deflationary pressures in economies whose currencies maintained gold convertibility — including France's, whose prices were by then at approximate parity with those elsewhere.

I next consider the effect of reparation and war debt payments upon this deflationary process. When transfers are allowed to affect aggregate demand in the receiving countries, they should have no effect on systemic prices or output. When the payments are sterilized in the receiving countries, as they were in France and the United States at different times beginning in the late 1920s, world prices and output adjust downward.

Three different U.S. contributions to the world deflation are discussed in chapter 10. The first is high short-term interest rates in the United States during 1928 and 1929, associated with both the demand for margin credit in the then-booming stock market and the restrictive Federal Reserve policy to dampen that boom. Interest rates consequently rose in much of the world during 1929, with deflationary consequences. A second factor was the contractionary policy pursued by the American central bank after the boom ended in October 1929. (The postcrash rationale for tight money was distinct from the rationale during the market boom.) The final contribution was the Smoot-Hawley tariff of 1930, which heightened reserve flows to the United States. It was thus disequilibrating in a way comparable to reparation and war debt payments after 1928.

The volatile behavior of the stock market deserves attention. Much of this book follows the conventional (at least in the financial economics literature) presumption that financial asset prices reflect relations between the cost of and return on capital — based on a reasonable understanding of economic fundamentals. This is approximately what is meant when markets are described as being efficient. There is strong evidence, however, that Wall Street investors simply ignored an impending systemic deflation during the late stages of the bull market. If one follows this evidence, the behavior of the stock market *independently* contributed both to an overheating of the economy and to a run-up of short-term interest rates. After the market crash, investors withdrew from call market lending and banks sought to rein in credit on numerous fronts, which forced contraction of output and unemployment. The associated instability contributed to the early stages of the international downturn. This argument is close to that popularly understood as Keynesian, in which the free market is unstable and requires steady direction through government intervention.

If the behavior of unstable financial markets is to account for the deepening depression after October 1929, one must posit that the subsequent bear market reaction was also beyond what reasonable estimates of costs and returns warranted. The Federal Reserve, however, implemented a protracted contractionary policy after the crash. Evidence that might link self-generated financial market volatility to the longer course of the depression is thus weak. The etiologies of the crisis of 1929 and of the subsequent depression are distinct.[18]

The concluding chapter presents a recapitulation of the events that produced the depression. It summarizes the sequence of causative factors and offers not only a view of their relative weights but also estimates of the historical responsibility of different individuals in bringing about the deflation.

Deflation and Depression

This book joins a growing consensus that the Great Depression had predominately monetary causes.[1] Implicit in this view is the argument that the international price deflation that began in 1929 had real effects on employment and output. This convergence of opinion nevertheless masks puzzlement over the source of the monetary disruption. Further, the theoretical underpinnings of this argument are seldom identified.

A Theoretical Framework

Neoclassical economists have often argued the case for monetary neutrality, which asserts that price inflation or deflation does not bring a sustained change in economic performance. They posit that markets clear rapidly, hence that supply and demand will not long stay out of balance. They indicate that, following an exogenous shock, equilibrating forces will surely turn the economy toward a full employment path. An approximately opposite view, summarized in what is known as the Phillips Curve, suggests a direct correlation between the rate of change in general prices and the level of employment and output. This view is sometimes identified as Keynesian, although Keynes almost certainly would have rejected it (see below).[2]

There are two generic channels through which a decline in prices might

bring a protracted decline in employment and output. One posits an exogenous price or monetary shock or perhaps a series of such shocks, followed by
slow adjustment in the real economy. Friedman and Schwartz, for example,
seem to have this causality in mind when they point to repeated failures of
central banking policy in the United States from 1928 through 1932.[3] This
argument is loosely consistent with a neoclassical framework, in which the
economic system is presumed to tend toward equilibrium of output and employment, even if disequilibrium prevails at times.[4]

The second channel through which price deflation might bring real disequilibrium proposes that market-driven adjustments do not always move a system
closer to full employment of resources. Endogenous tendencies may amplify
rather than counteract the effects of exogenous disturbance.[5] For example, a
decline in end-prices combined with a rigid cost structure might reduce aggregate profits. This, in turn, could amplify unemployment rather than bring a
downward adjustment of labor costs. Another example might be a shift in
expectations for future profits and consequently a shift in systemwide equity
prices combined with a change in the public's desired liquid holdings. Neoclassical models generally assume that financial markets respond to external
stimulus and hence that prices efficiently reflect information. But if causality *in
some instances* works in the opposite direction — from changes in asset prices
(and therefore in the cost of capital) to levels of investment and consumption —
then the neoclassical framework becomes unsuitable.

This distinction between exogenous shocks and endogenous amplification
of those shocks is important in economic theory. For my empirical purpose
here, however, it will be sufficient to establish that, for whichever reason, price
inflation (deflation) has sometimes correlated with expanding (contracting)
employment and sometimes has not. I shall describe instances of each in the
decades before 1929. The deflationary experience of the early 1930s undermined the view of some neoclassical economists that price trends had only
mild effects on output or employment. The stagflation of the 1970s, in which
prices and unemployment rose almost synchronously, in turn badly damaged
the credibility of the Phillips Curve model. Indeed, the experience of the 1970s
gave impetus to the rapid development of the rational expectations school,
which advanced an extreme version of the neoclassical "general equilibrium
point of view."[6] The premise that equilibrium is a normal condition, in turn,
has been undermined by the persistence of high unemployment during portions of the 1980s and 1990s in the United States and Europe.[7]

What is needed is a theoretical middle ground. Paul Krugman, in part with
this doctrinal history in mind, recently concluded that "in the long run, Keynes
is still alive."[8] He means that economists now widely believe that monetary

and price changes affect real economic performance and hence that money is not neutral. Keynes's most extensive treatment on the effects of inflation and deflation appears in his seldom-read *Treatise on Money* of 1930. The *Treatise*'s "fundamental price equation" divides determinants of the price level into a cost term and a profit term. The first (cost) term reflects a "money-neutral" relation between costs and prices and hence incorporates a corresponding steady-state rate of profit for investors. The second (profit) term indicates the contribution to end-prices of aggregate profits or losses; a value of zero represents a steady-state, or equilibrium, rate of return on investment.[9]

Inflation (deflation) in the second term arises when investment exceeds (falls short of) savings.[10] Keynes explained the following year:"The costs of the entrepreneurs are equal to what the public spend plus what they save; while the receipts of the entrepreneurs are equal to what the public spend plus the value of current investment. It follows . . . that when the value of current investment is greater than the savings of the public, the receipts of the entrepreneurs are greater than their costs, so they make a profit."[11] Equilibrium in this framework requires that systemwide investment match systemwide savings.[12] The schedule of marginal efficiencies of capital (which always represents a schedule of *anticipated* returns) is then balanced against the schedule of risk-adjusted costs of capital so that full employment of resources results. The value of the profit term changes from zero in step with change in the aggregate investment–savings relation.

Keynes was interested in the divergence between savings and investment as an inducement to profit inflation or deflation; he was less concerned from a policy perspective about changes in the price level as such.[13] This distinguishes him from both monetarists and Phillips Curve advocates, for example, as both resist acknowledging theoretical distinctions among causes of inflation. It also distinguishes him from classical economists more broadly, who argue that price changes only briefly disrupt economic equilibrium.[14]

This summary provides evidence for rejecting the new classical argument that monetary non-neutrality is "irrational."[15] The rational expectations framework deals inadequately with changes in the second term of the price equation; it assumes that the value of the second term does not depart from zero. If price changes affect input costs but not the level of enterprise profitability, then only the first term is affected.[16] In some instances, "rational" analysis can generate fairly uniform forecasts about what the first term will be; this is the portion of price change that businesses and consumers might reasonably anticipate, and against which they may to some extent hedge themselves. However, only movements in the second term correlate with profit inflation or deflation — and without the second term we have an inadequate picture of the price level. Yet forecasting the value of the second term is a task different in kind from forecasting the first term; indeed, it requires several subsequent levels of analysis. It is the difference between (1) anticipating what input prices will be at some point in the future (which is hard enough to do); and (2) anticipating the effect of those input costs on economy-wide consumption and investment spending, on desired savings and liquidity rates, and consequently on profits. Analysis may bring a variety of forecasts for the future value of the second term, some of them mutually contradictory, but perhaps most of them rational. Keynes wrote in 1937 that this kind of "knowledge" is "a particularly unsuitable subject for the methods of classical economic theory."[17]

Robert Lucas, the most prominent advocate of rational expectations theory during the 1970s and 1980s, has grudgingly acknowledged that the assumption of rationality in adjustment to price fluctuations is conceptually inadequate to explain the depression. To save the postulate that behavior is rational, he proposes that the experience of 1929–32 be treated as a statistical outlier:

> A perhaps ultimately more influential feature of post–World War II time series has been the return to a pattern of recurrent, roughly similar [business] "cycles." . . . If the magnitude of the Great Depression dealt a serious blow to the idea of the business cycle as a repeated occurrence of the "same" event, the postwar experience has to some degree restored respectability to this idea. If the Depression continues, in some respects, to defy explanation by *existing economic analysis* (as I believe it does), perhaps it is gradually succumbing to the Law of Large Numbers.[18] [emphasis added]

Lucas manifestly identifies "existing economic analysis" with arguments drawn from the new and neoclassical canon. If one is less rigid, Lucas's conclusion about the Great Depression may serve instead as a reason to challenge the new classical paradigm. It plainly invites consideration of monetary non-neutrality as a cause of the depression.

The fundamental equation also connects price dynamics with capital movements in a way that sheds light on the economic history of the 1920s. Capital moves across borders in response to relative national differences either in interest rates or in capital's anticipated marginal efficiencies. Capital movements may (if not offset by current account imbalances) bring reserve movements. When capital follows interest rates, as it then often did in moving to Britain, Germany, and the United States, the effect is likely to be contractionary and may induce or aggravate profit deflation in the world economy. When capital flows in response to higher expected profitability on investment, as in the case of the inflow to France during 1927–30 and on occasion in the inflows to the United States, the result may be systemic expansion.

It also helps one sharpen focus on the puzzle of the link between the downturn of output and the price declines in the years leading to the depression. Price declines can certainly cause profit deflations. The second term, however, also can turn negative autonomously of changes in costs and indeed can cause broader price changes. Both mechanisms were at work during 1929–32.

MEASURING PROFIT INFLATION AND DEFLATION

The practical drawback in the above framework is that the level of profit inflation or deflation is hard to measure. Whereas interest rate data are available, the cost of equity capital and the schedule of marginal efficiencies of capital can only be estimated.[19]

Tobin's q, the ratio of an equity share price index divided by the price level of newly produced capital goods, offers a rough measure of the extent of profit inflation or deflation.[20] When returns and expected returns on capital are higher (lower) than their cost, Tobin's q rises (declines) from an initially profit-neutral position. When the initial position reflects either profit inflation or deflation, movement in Tobin's q suggests a relaxation or intensification of the non-neutrality; in these circumstances, a rise (decline) in Tobin's q may be consistent with continued profit deflation (inflation). Alternatively, if replacement costs of assets — reflecting input costs — increase by more (less) than the change in their market values, stock prices and Tobin's q will decline (increase). Movement in this indicator reflects change in investor expectations; more exactly, it reflects change in expectations about the future distribution of economy-wide revenues between costs and profits. If one posits that investors respond to price incentives, a shift in Tobin's q will bring — with some time lag — a parallel shift in economy-wide investment activity.[21]

If markets become "inefficient," in which case share prices might represent something other than a consensus regarding economic fundamentals, then a change in Tobin's q might not bring a change in real outlays. Equities markets appear (although I do not test this) to have been reasonably efficient in most countries during much of the period under study. The outstanding exception to the premise of market efficiency in the 1920s involves the New York stock market of 1928 and 1929; I offer evidence of inefficiencies in that market in chapter 11.

Historical Instances

An income inflation, induced by change in the first term of the equation, can coexist with flat or declining profits — a phenomenon dubbed stagflation during the 1970s. Similarly, price declines in the first (cost) term can coexist with stability in the profit term. Below I examine instances of income deflation in the United States in the 1870s and internationally during 1920–21. Inversely, a profit inflation (deflation), when accompanied by downward (upward) pressure on factor costs, may be accompanied by near stability in overall price indexes.[22]

A profit inflation benefits producers and, often, speculators—those in a position to shift resources to take advantage of anticipated price changes. Higher profits encourage easier financing, hence new investment, which generates new employment. Relative losers during a profit boom include wage earners and functionaries, whose incomes do not keep up with price increases, and rentiers on fixed incomes. But losses to wage earners are qualified by higher employment levels in the short period and by greater productivity from higher capital investment in the long period. Also, a profit inflation may upset traditional economic relations and create new concentrations of wealth and power. This process can engender misgivings about the legitimacy of the economic system and even of the political system. Irving Fisher argued, for example, that the two decades of rising prices that preceded World War I contributed much to the contemporary agitation for socialism.[23]

A profit deflation, especially when it leads to a lower general price level, brings opposite conditions. Aggregate investment contracts because the cost of capital tends to exceed its anticipated return. Liquidity preference increases on the part of individuals, enterprises, and lenders. Those with secure employment as well as holders of high-quality rentes gain relatively and often absolutely. Middlemen, that is, holders of inventory, are squeezed as pressure for price reductions builds. Business failures become more frequent, as does unemployment. Political sentiment against the capitalist system may grow, but for different reasons than during a profit inflation. Fisher attributed the growth of the Populist movement in the United States in the decades before 1896 to the pressures of deflation.[24] Similarly, it seems likely that the political success of the New Deal in the United States, of the Popular Front in France, and of National Socialism in Germany would not have occurred but for the prolonged profit deflations that preceded them.

I want to consider three deflations that occurred during the decades prior to 1929. The 1870s in the United States and 1920–21 internationally saw large price deflations with only modest impacts upon aggregate real income. In contrast, the 1891–96 period saw more marked profit deflation, with high unemployment and protracted stagnation of output. More than other downturns, its effects were comparable to (although milder than) those of the 1929–32 downturn. The task is to explain why it differed from the aforementioned income deflations.

THE INCOME DEFLATION OF THE 1870S

In the case of the post–Civil War price deflation in the United States, aggregate real income appears to have expanded, even on a per capita basis. Friedman and Schwartz challenge some high-end estimates of the level of output growth, especially after 1873; but they note that "whichever estimate of output one accepts," the rate of its growth was "unusually rapid."[25] This period is sometimes highlighted as evidence that price deflation may coexist with rapid growth.[26] Nevertheless, events of the 1870s were atypical.

In 1862, official gold convertibility of the dollar was suspended, which ushered in the Greenback Era and wartime price inflation. After the war, prices began a steady decline, anticipating resumption of convertibility at prewar parity, which came in 1879. This pattern calls to mind that of sterling's return to prewar parity in 1925 (discussed in later chapters). But several factors make the deflation of the 1870s unusual.

The 1870s was a period of dual currencies; gold continued to circulate. In much of the country, prices were quoted in greenbacks, but gold was accepted for payment at its current greenback exchange value. On the West Coast, by contrast, gold was the *numéraire,* but greenbacks were accepted at their current gold value.[27] Greenback price changes thus never worked their way through the economic system to affect returns and expectations in the way that price changes do in single-medium systems. Gresham's law, which posits that an overpriced money will not circulate, did not operate.[28] The two media could co-circulate, as their exchange rate was market-determined.

Interest and principal on Treasury debt were almost always paid in gold at pre–Civil War monetary value. Some private debt was contracted in gold.[29] In particular, most long-term railroad debt was marketed in the form of gold bonds, by which both interest and principal were payable in the values of gold contracted at issue date.[30] Greenback deflation had only limited redistributive consequences among these segments of debtors and creditors — a huge difference from what occurred in many countries during deflations of the 1920s and 1930s. International payments were made in gold, which provided another form of price indexing in the U.S. economy; greenback price changes had little direct effect on export markets or international input prices.

Although this argument explains some of the paradox of rapid growth coexisting with declining prices, it does not explain all of it. Greenbacks appreciated against gold by about 26 percent from 1866 to 1879, about half of this rise occurring from 1872 to 1879.[31] Gold indexation protects contract-holders only to the extent that the real value of gold itself is stable. After 1872 the value of gold itself rose against other commodities. Roy Jastram's figures indicate a rate of increase in the real value of gold during 1873–79 of nearly 5.0 percent annually in Britain and 4.5 percent per annum in the United States. These numbers are sensitive to the precise years selected for measurement and hence should be interpreted cautiously. In Britain from 1870 to 1880, the increase in the real value of gold was only 0.9 percent per annum. In the United States from 1869 to 1880, the increase was only 1.1 percent per annum. These numbers suggest that the gold deflation (that is, the decline in gold-denominated prices) during these years was fairly modest. Also, the real value of gold in the United States was higher on average during 1861–64, when much of the Civil War debt was incurred, than at any time during the subsequent two decades except for the years 1878 and 1879.[32] The burden of *this* debt upon taxpayers (the ultimate debtors) was eased, despite subsequent deflation.

A common stock index shows a decline from the average level in 1872 to the average level in 1879.[33] The decline in greenback prices was probably somewhat greater than this, and the decline in gold-denominated prices somewhat less.[34] Tobin's q thus appears to have been fairly stable during that decade, which suggests that this was a period of approximate profit equilibrium. This supports Friedman and Schwartz's aforementioned skepticism about claims of extravagant output growth during that decade. To return to Keynes's price equation, the first term absorbed most of the price decline, which left the profit component in prices relatively unaffected.

Trend line data for money aggregates, prices, and both real and nominal income turned up beginning in 1879, presumably a consequence of the resumption of gold convertibility.[35] Whatever expansionary influences operated in the deflationary environment of 1873–79 were evidently strengthened by an upward turn in prices. The common stock index surged by more than 50 percent from the average in 1879 to that in 1881, perhaps impelled by an upward bump in wholesale prices in the 10–15 percent range.[36] One cannot run an extended comparison, however, for price indexes again turned downward in 1882.

THE POST–WORLD WAR I INCOME DEFLATION

The 1920–21 currency deflation was especially pronounced. Price indexes in the United States, Britain, France, and elsewhere dropped by one-third or more.[37] Jastram's index for the purchasing power of gold in Britain shows a 53 percent increase for 1921 over 1920 (equivalent to a 35 percent deflation in a sterling price index) and only a slightly higher 58 percent increase for the *three* years of deflation from 1928 to 1931. Similarly, in the United States the exchange value of gold rose by 58 percent from 1920 to

1921, but only by 48 percent during 1928–32.[38] Depressed conditions accompanied the price collapse in much of the industrial world during 1921. Monetary ease brought rapid recovery in France and the United States in 1922, although not in Britain; British monetary constraint continued as part of an ongoing effort to raise the value of the pound.

But there was less to the 1920–21 deflation than met the eye in France and the United States. Wholesale and retail price indexes in both countries show that the deflation canceled only the unusual inflation from November 1918 to about May 1920. For the United States, the GNP price deflator of 1921 was slightly below that of 1919, and for 1922 was slightly below that of 1918.[39] The same pattern appears in the wholesale price indexes of the United States, France, and Britain.[40] The period 1918–20 saw a rapid profit inflation based on postwar restocking, the end of price controls, and the opportunity for gain through speculation on where shortages would arise.[41] Sliding-scale contracts, which indexed wages to price changes, were introduced in many countries during the war and remained common afterward.[42] The higher price level of 1919–20 was not institutionalized (so as to make input costs inflexible downward), as it would have been given an extended period of stable prices and more long-term contracts.

Based on contemporary estimates, the British price index moved to a level 35 percent higher than the unit wage index by the beginning of 1920 (using a prewar base). The subsequent (mild) profit deflation was absorbed in significant measure just in bringing prices and input costs back into historical alignment. Even in Britain, where the subsequent upturn was weakest, profits began to recover by the second quarter of 1922. The 52 percent peak-to-valley drop in wholesale prices was offset by a 35 percent drop in the nominal wage index and a slightly greater drop in the unit wage index. For only seven quarters was the unit wage index above the price index by more than 10 percent (relative to the same prewar base).[43] Even more important, because prices in 1921 remained above the levels before and during the war, the deflation did not injure creditors on contracts entered prior to 1919. Keynes later wrote that "only a small portion of the banks' loans had been based on such values and these values had not lasted long enough to be trusted."[44] For the United States, recent estimates show a decline in real GNP of only between 3 percent and 4 percent from 1919 to 1921.[45] Tobin's q was roughly steady over the same interval; it may even have risen somewhat, depending on the beginning and ending months used for comparison.[46] This does not rule out the occurrence of temporary profit deflation during that period, but it does mean that any occurrences were short.

Dramatic price shifts seldom occur without redistributional consequences;

the deflations of the 1870s and 1920–21 brought increased mortgage foreclosures and increased unemployment.[47] But the effective indexation of costs,
including much of the cost of debt, left large parts of the economy protected in
both cases. Broadly considered, both were income deflations.

THE PROFIT DEFLATION OF THE 1890S

The international deflation of 1891–96 directly compressed profits. The
extent of actual price decline was less than for the two income deflations
considered above. From 1890 through 1896, Sauerbeck's British wholesale
price index declined by 18 percent and *The Economist's* index dropped by 14
percent. British money wages, however, actually rose by several percentage
points, so the rise in real wages was striking. The rate of investment dropped
sharply; new capital issues averaged £102 million during 1880–89 and £154
million during 1889–90 but fell to an average level of £70 million during
1891–96. (These data depict a trend; investment need not be financed through
new issues.) The rate of saving was high and increased from perhaps £150
million annually in 1880 to £200 million annually in 1896. Aggregate savings
deposits grew greatly during the 1890s, both at the Post Office and at private
banks.[48] As investment declined despite the increase in savings, the second
term of the price equation turned negative, while the first term increased
slightly but steadily — reflecting the rigidity of input costs.

The pattern in the United States was similar. During 1893–96, the wholesale price index declined by 2.4 percent annually, compared to a decline of 1.1
percent annually during 1879–92.[49] Unlike wages during the deflation of the
1870s, hourly wages were steady in nominal terms and hence rose in real
terms.[50] (Evidence on British and American wage levels during the 1890s
undermines frequent assertions that wages were flexible during the period of
the prewar gold standard.) Whereas the (nominal) volume of New York City
bank clearings was steady during the deflation of the 1870s, it decreased
abruptly during 1892–94.[51] Tobin's q declined moderately from 1892 through
1896, which was significant in part because it followed a full decade of stagnation in real stock prices. The annualized stock index level of 1881 was not
exceeded until 1899.[52]

The 1890s saw intense agitation for inflationary policies, and a central
plank of William Jennings Bryan's Democratic party platform of 1896 was
that the gold standard should be abandoned in favor of bimetallism. When the
Republicans won the election, the gold standard was again perceived as being
secure. This conclusion was soon reinforced by rising world gold output and
the beginning of a mild international inflation, which weakened the political
attraction of bimetallism. Bond yields declined slightly during the 1891–96

period, presumably a result of the slump-induced decline in demand for credit. However, they declined further as output and the domestic price level began to rise in 1897.[53] This is evidence that debt capital was expensive (for issuers) during 1892–96, just as was equity. Fear of the inflationary consequences of bimetallism helped keep long-term interest rates high and slowed real activity. Thus *anticipation* of U.S. inflation within the context of an international deflation through 1896 in fact aggravated domestic deflation.[54] The expectation of higher prices also accentuated the profit deflation by hindering downward adjustment of the first term of the fundamental price equation. The cost of debt service and labor remained high; price compression was absorbed in the profit term.[55]

Keynes argues in chapter 19 of his *General Theory* that declining money wages might suppress aggregate demand, which in turn may further lower prices and aggravate a profit deflation. But this well-known argument holds only in a closed-economy analysis. In an open-economy analysis — typical of much of the earlier *Treatise on Money* — end-product prices are set at least in part through international arbitrage. In an open-economy framework, a reduction in (for example) British money wages would not affect most British end-product prices. It would, however, shift resources in Britain from factor costs to profits.[56]

Profit Deflation after 1928

The profit deflation of 1929–32 was severe. By 1932, industrial unemployment reached 36 percent in the United States, 44 percent in Germany, 22 percent in Britain and Sweden, 25 percent in the Netherlands, more than 30 percent in Norway and Denmark, and 28 percent in Australia. Industrial unemployment in France and Belgium was relatively low, 15 percent and 19 percent, respectively.[57]

The extent of this profit deflation is indicated further by the behavior of Tobin's q, which plunged almost everywhere, dwarfing its decline during the 1890s. A U.S. stock index dropped by 85 percent from September 1929 to June 1932; the deflation-adjusted decline in Tobin's q exceeds 75 percent.[58] A French stock index declined 63 percent from February 1929 to December 1931, recovered slightly in 1932, but fell further for a total decline of 73 percent by November 1934. French wholesale prices fell by perhaps a third from early 1929 to late 1931, and by a quarter from the new level to their low point in early 1935.[59] The decline in Tobin's q was thus approximately 45 percent by the end of 1931, and it continued generally downward through

1934. German stocks declined by 69 percent from June 1928 (at which point they had already declined by 15 percent from their high in April 1927) to June 1932. The four-year decline in Tobin's q was nearly 50 percent — from an already depressed level. A British stock index dropped by 48 percent in nominal terms from January 1929 to September 1931, when convertibility was ended. The decline in Tobin's q in Britain was relatively mild but, as in Germany, occurred from an already depressed level. To carry the comparisons to smaller countries, stock indexes declined by 80 percent in the Netherlands, 70 percent in Sweden, 60 percent in Switzerland, and 84 percent in Canada.

AN EXPLANATION

This brings me directly to Keynes's explanation of the Great Depression. He argued that the depression would not have occurred without a protracted international price deflation. The 1922–29 period saw price stability and sustained capital investment in the United States and, although less consistently, in much of Europe. This generated a large volume of (unindexed) medium- and long-term financial commitments. These were built upon a large substructure of national debts and cross-national war debt and reparation obligations.[60] When prices fell rapidly beginning in 1928, the compression came in profits.[61] Liquidity preference subsequently rose on several fronts. More investors adopted bear positions, that is, held cash in anticipation that asset prices would decline. This reduced stock prices, which meant that the cost of capital increased relative to expected returns. Among the consequences were less investment, fewer jobs, and attempts to de-stock. Banks increased reserves in anticipation of depositor withdrawals. Individuals, uncertain of their futures, increased their cash holdings and demanded more — in either goods or interest return — to part with it. Fewer capital outlays appeared remunerative to enterprises, which already were strapped to meet interest and other fixed costs.

Rising capital costs were reinforced by other events. Keynes identified three unusual sources of demand for capital during the 1920s, each of which pushed up market rates. All three were artificial, meaning that their demand was not influenced by anticipated returns on investment. One motive for borrowing was to build official liquid balances in order to defend currencies against reserve losses during a period of international resumption of gold convertibility. The need to conform to an international monetary standard blocked purely national efforts to keep the market interest rate and marginal efficiency of capital in balance.[62] Another was the large demand for capital to meet war debt and reparations payments. In addition to these long-term, government-affiliated borrowers, a sizable group of commercial borrowers sought short-term funds to speculate on stock price movements. A consequence was that so-called genuine borrowers were forced to pay higher rates, which thereby discouraged investment.[63] This drove the value of the second term downward and hence amplified the price deflation.

In this form, the argument is incomplete. First, then-rising stock markets made equity capital more accessible, even if debt capital was becoming dearer. Second, in a steady-state analysis, increased borrowing simply shifts liquid resources among individuals or groups without increasing or decreasing aggregate liquidity. New groups of borrowers (including issuers of equity) drive up interest rates only when a consequence of the borrowing is to redistribute monetary resources in a way that increases aggregate liquidity preference — and this was indeed the mechanism Keynes had in mind.

When a central bank raises interest rates to protect its gold stock, this is unlikely to generate offsetting rate declines or enhance investment prospects elsewhere. Higher interest rates induce a flow of money to the country (in national accounting terms, the country borrows) at the same time that they discourage investment of real resources. When reparations are paid to a country whose residents demonstrate relatively high liquidity preference and low propensity to consume, then the transfer may result in less international spending and hence in contraction of international trade and income. Under these circumstances, borrowing to meet reparation payments is disequilibrating. In the case of short-term speculative borrowers, a steady-state analysis suggests that purchase of new shares would increase spending capacity on the part of the sellers. If, however, the sellers are bearish, they will demand higher interest returns for parting with their cash.[64] A purpose of this book is to explain how the activities of these groups of artificial borrowers induced high interest rates and protracted disequilibrium.

Alongside the rise in market rates was the decline in the marginal efficiency of capital. This decline followed a downturn in prices when, as at the end of the 1920s, the profit term absorbed much of the downturn. But the deterioration in expected returns also mirrored the separate rise in demands for liquidity that further reduced spending. An aggregate profit decline for either reason creates more distress borrowers, which in turn aggravates price declines.

REMEDIES

Whether a profit contraction was caused directly by price declines or in fact gave rise to them, it might be countered by action to raise — or at least to stabilize — the general price level. In 1930, Keynes proposed open-market operations *à outrance*. The idea was to saturate the demand for liquidity preference and thereby to lower interest rates. This would encourage investment. Also, by raising the supply of money relative to its demand, the demand for goods would rise, any prior increase in liquidity preference would be neutralized, and prices would be pushed upward.[65]

Keynes's argument for open-market operations in 1930 sanctioned more aggressive central bank action than Friedman and Schwartz would propose thirty years later! Friedman and Schwartz sought steady growth in monetary aggregates and have always deemphasized shifts in the demand for money as a factor that might vitiate the impact of a quantity rule.[66] Keynes urged monetary expansion sufficient to offset rising demands for liquidity (sometimes manifested in a growing "financial" circulation) regardless of how much this might swell monetary aggregates. He wrote, "Central Banks have always been too nervous hitherto — partly, perhaps, under the influence of crude versions of the Quantity Theory — of taking measures which would have the effect of causing the total volume of bank money to depart widely from its normal volume, whether in excess or in defect. But this attitude . . . forgets the financial circulation in its concern for the industrial circulation, and overlooks the statistical fact that the former may be quite as large as the latter and much more capable of sharp variation."[67]

Keynes believed that determined monetary expansion would bring economic recovery in most circumstances, and particularly within a national, closed-economy framework. An exception occurs when a rise in the domestic money supply drives interest rates below an internationally sustainable level. This would provoke an outflow of capital, followed by an outflow of gold or foreign exchange reserves. To meet this circumstance, Keynes proposed in 1929 that the government directly undertake domestic investment. He had in mind that public works, financed by deficit spending, might permit an expansion of domestic demand without prior banking action to lower interest rates. The government might undertake projects with anticipated returns below the market rate of interest — projects that no profit-seeking enterprise would accept. The government would become a guaranteed domestic borrower.[68] Such action would generate increased economic activity and a growing domestic money stock without lowering interest rates and hence without causing reserve losses.[69]

The international marginal efficiency of capital was low in 1930, while real interest rates were high, because of declining prices and the growing demand for liquid balances. The British economy could be sheltered from this dismal plight only by protecting its domestic investment function. Keynes at different times also proposed tariffs, restrictions on foreign lending, and floating the pound to achieve the same goal. The reasoning behind the call for tariffs was that they might improve the trade balance and hence increase reserves, so that interest rates could be lowered or open-market purchases undertaken. The purpose of proposed restrictions on foreign lending, similarly, was to improve the capital balance. Increased public spending was an alternative route to sheltering the domestic economy, one that would not require direct controls on the movement of goods or capital.[70]

But even when the international economy is beyond influence, "fiscalist" relief was not Keynes's first recommendation. Immediately prior to Britain's return to gold in 1925, he recommended to Montagu Norman, governor of the Bank of England, and Winston Churchill, then chancellor of the Exchequer, that sterling continue to be floated against the dollar.[71] This advice was monetary and was rejected.

Anticipated and Indexed Price Changes

I can reinforce my claim that price deflation during 1929–32 had real economic consequences with specific empirical evidence. Ben Bernanke argues from a new classical premise that attributing deterioration in real economic performance during these years to price changes is to adopt the postulate that economic life is pervaded with irrationality. To maintain the premise that economic behavior is fundamentally rational, he proposes a nonmonetary explanation for the economic downturn.[72]

James Hamilton challenges the claim that systemic price deflation during the Great Depression was anticipated. Proceeding from the rationalist premise that futures market prices incorporate available information, he compares commodity market spot and futures prices for cotton during the 1922–29 period. He concludes that "the futures price embodies a better forecast of cotton price inflation than would be obtained by just using the historical average rate of cotton inflation [that is, a form of "adaptive expectations"], though not a whole lot better; speculators were able to forecast only 20 percent of the variance in cotton price inflation rates during 1922–1929." He then extends his analysis into the period 1929–32 and finds that commodity markets then predicted an average change in cotton prices of +9.4 percent annually. The actual change in prices turned out to be −39.0 percent annually, for a huge average forecast error of −48 percent annually. Similar errors were found for other commodities.[73] Futures markets were thus either irrational or lacked information. Most likely they lacked information; much of the 1929–32 deflation was not anticipated.

On a theoretical plain, the effort to separate expected from unexpected price changes is misdirected. The difference between a profit and an income deflation (or inflation) does not turn on whether the price movement is anticipated. Deflation can depress economic activity even when it is anticipated, and sometimes especially then. Keynes noted on a related matter that if wage reductions led to the possibility or expectation of further decline in wages and prices, it would "diminish the marginal efficiency of capital and [would] lead to the postponement both of investment and of consumption."[74] Cassel wrote similarly of the damage that *any* deflation would do in the midst of depression, even if anticipated and deliberate: "[Deflationists want] necessary equilibrium . . . by forcing down all prices to the level of the lowest. They disregard the great social evils, labor struggles, and political disturbances, unavoidably connected with a restrictive policy of such severity as would be required for the purpose. And, what is still more important, they do not understand that such a restrictive policy would inevitably expose the low prices to new pressure and cause them to fall still more."[75] Both anticipated and unanticipated price declines contributed to the depression.

The key to the impact of price changes lies in the extent to which they are indexed, deliberately or by accident, so as to reduce their redistributive consequences. Indexing occurred to some extent in the 1870s in the United States and in 1920–21 internationally. The deflation of the late 1920s and early 1930s was in large measure not anticipated in financial markets, and even when it was, its effects were softened scarcely at all by indexing.

The Prewar Gold Standard

In a common view, the pre-1914 gold standard succeeded because it functioned automatically, in contrast to the managed interwar standard. This argument usually assumes one of two somewhat contradictory forms. In one version the price-specie-flow mechanism automatically raised prices (and then output) in surplus countries and lowered them in deficit countries.[1] A second version stresses the role of central banks operating according to rules. Through this mechanism central banks adjusted their discount rates in response to changes in their gold reserves, which in turn kept price and output changes roughly uniform with systemic averages. Parallel to the arguments stressing automaticity stood the claim that the operation of this mechanism was blocked under the interwar gold standard. As I shall show, neither of these linkages occurred consistently before 1914. A weaker automatic mechanism may well have been at work, however, during both the prewar and interwar periods — in which case one must look elsewhere to discover why the interwar system failed.

A contrasting cluster of interpretations of the prewar gold standard points to institutional and diplomatic dynamics that extended beyond the activities of central banks. Kindleberger stresses the prewar leadership of Britain and contrasts it with the financial weakness of Britain and the unwillingness of the United States to lead during the late 1920s and early 1930s. Eichengreen argues that central banks and national treasuries cooperated during monetary crises before 1914 but failed to do so in 1931. I shall argue that these explanations are inadequate because they obscure economic contrasts between crises before and after World War I.

Still another explanation, one advanced by Cassel, Rist, and more recently Mundell, points to adequate supplies of international monetary gold before World War I contrasted with a shortfall in the 1920s. If these commentators are correct, then prewar success represented price and demand responses in the gold market, however incomplete they may have been.

Did the Prewar Gold Standard Function Automatically?

The classical price-specie-flow mechanism proposes that a transfer of gold from one country to another brings a price decrease in the specie-losing country and a price increase in the specie-receiving country. The specie-losing country is then positioned to increase exports, hence to balance its trade account and preserve its remaining specie. The specie-gaining country imports more until trade balances, at which point specie movements stop. Benjamin Strong, the president of the Federal Reserve Bank of New York from 1914 until his death in 1928, argued that the prewar gold standard worked according to this mechanism. He explained in a letter of 1924:

> Shipments of gold *had the effect of depleting bank reserves in the country where prices had advanced too rapidly* and overtrading and speculation had developed, thus forcing advances in the rate of discount of the bank of issue and of interest rates generally, which in turn induced borrowers to liquidate stocks of goods in order to pay loans, so again reducing prices and restoring world price equilibrium. *Comparatively slight but rapid advances of prices in one country* were automatically corrected by these means and a fairly stable level of world prices resulted.[2] [emphasis added]

A weakness in the price-specie-flow argument is that it posits an intermediate adjustment of prices between the movement of gold and the subsequent adjustment of trade movements — what Strong above calls the "comparatively slight but rapid advances of prices." In fact, pre-1914 transfers show but minor traces of nationally differentiated price adjustment. The trade economist Frank Taussig wrote in the mid-1920s, "The recorded transactions between countries show surprisingly little transfer of the only 'money' that moves from one to the other — gold. It is the goods that move, and they seem to move at once; almost as if there were an automatic connection between these financial operations and the commodity exports or imports. . . . The presumably intermediate stage of gold flow and price changes is hard to discern, and certainly is extremely short."³ Subsequent work in monetary economics reinforces the conclusion that prices typically adjusted through arbitrage under the prewar gold standard; hence, the effect of gold flows themselves upon prices was secondary.⁴

The other automatic mechanism, that by which central banks should respond to international reserve flows according to rules, was identified by Walter Bagehot in *Lombard Street* in 1873.⁵ Bagehot observed that in the case of an external drain the Bank of England should raise its discount rate and continue to increase it in steps until the drain ended. Through discount rate changes, prices and output might adjust automatically, but without large gold movements. The two notions of automaticity were fused in the Cunliffe Committee *Report* of 1919, which appended an effective Bank of England discount rate policy onto the specie-flow mechanism.⁶ (Bagehot and the Cunliffe Committee neglected to define appropriate action for the event of a reserve *inflow*, although the notion of rules suggests an inverse procedure.)

The League of Nations' *Second Interim Report of the Gold Delegation* of January 1931 affirmed the conclusions of the Cunliffe Committee *Report*, then extended their application to central banks in general and made explicit that gold-receiving countries should ease discount rates. But the league noted that "this tendency towards automatic alterations of the bank rate was neither absolute nor universal."⁷ The Bank of England had perhaps an even stronger view of reciprocal obligations under the prewar standards. A bank memorandum from 1927 concisely stated what came to be known as the rules of the game:

> A country which is on the Gold Exchange Standard will adapt its internal credit policy to the course of its international balance of payments as indicated by the fluctuation of its foreign exchange reserves, just as the Gold Standard country [gold center countries were understood to be Britain and the United States] will adapt its credit policy to the movements of its gold reserves. Since these fluctuations are ordinarily a reliable index of the need for expansion or contraction of the domestic currency, maladjustments of the international balance of payments will be automatically and rapidly put right. A surplus or deficit can seldom be large and can never be cumulative, under a properly working Gold Exchange Standard, without bringing into play the required correctives.⁸

In a common British view, the interwar gold standard failed because other central banks, including especially the Bank of France but also the Federal Reserve Bank, did not observe the above rules in the event of gold inflows. In subsequent chapters I shall show that French and American gold accumulation would indeed have sharply deflationary consequences for the world economy. But the author of the memorandum was inaccurate if he meant that other prewar central banks in practice adjusted their monetary policies in response to international reserve flows.

In his earliest book, *Indian Currency and Finance,* Keynes stressed that prewar central banks would take action to prevent gold losses, while omitting mention of symmetrical action in the event of gold inflows.[9] He appears to have been the first (in 1925) to use the phrase "the rules of the gold standard game," in reference to the contractionary policy that must be followed to prevent a gold outflow, but not, again, to expansionary policies in gold-receiving countries.[10] He repeated the phrase in the *Treatise on Money,* but there he specifically defended the United States and France against the "accusation . . . that they [were] breaking the rules of the 'Gold Standard game'" by not adopting expansionary policies in response to gold influxes in 1930.[11] In Keynes's view the only prewar central bank inclined to adjust monetary conditions in response to gold in-movements was the Bank of England. He wrote in the *Treatise,* "During the latter half of the nineteenth century the influence of London on credit conditions throughout the world was so predominant that the Bank of England could almost have claimed to be *the conductor of the international orchestra.* By modifying the terms on which she was prepared to lend, aided by her own readiness to vary the volume of her gold reserves *and the unreadiness of other Central Banks to vary theirs,* she could to a large extent determine the credit conditions prevailing elsewhere"[12] (emphasis added). Cassel similarly argued that prewar creditor countries other than Britain were not inclined to export capital to avoid accumulation of gold reserves. Indeed, prewar central banks other than the Bank of England often kept more gold than their laws required and acted to maintain such a position.[13]

Subsequent analysis by Arthur Bloomfield and Nurkse to determine whether the rules were in fact observed under the prewar and interwar gold standards nevertheless includes data for a spectrum of central banks, not just the Bank of England[14] — and thus tested for the opposite of what Keynes and Cassel asserted to be the case! Bloomfield's research corroborated evidence that the Bank of England was indeed more inclined than other central banks to adjust domestic discounting policy, hence to adjust the volume of its domestic assets, in response to international gold movements.[15] Even the Bank of England sometimes had to struggle to make its bank rate effective in the market.[16]

While specie-flow mechanisms and adherence to "rules of the . . . game" played only a minor role under the prewar gold standard, another kind of automatic mechanism does appear to have been important. Bloomfield points to considerations of central bank reserve management and profitability that induced predictable behavior. In Britain, France, and Germany, gold coins were often used because of the absence or shortage of small-denomination notes. Business upswings brought higher demand for domestic credit and internal drains of specie (that is, withdrawal of gold coins from central bank vaults for use in hand-to-hand circulation), both of which reduced reserve ratios.[17] When ratios approached legal minimums, bankers would raise discount rates, increase gold premiums, or employ other mechanisms to attract and maintain reserves. During business downswings, for inverse reasons, reserve ratios tended to rise. Central banks would then lower discount rates to encourage discounting and thereby to maintain earnings.[18]

This automatic pattern does not require international reserve flows as a signal or trigger mechanism. According to the monetary theory of the balance of payments, gold flows to economies in which the domestic demand for money exceeds the domestic supply.[19] But if a central bank accommodated the rising domestic demand for money by permitting an internal drain from its reserve stock in the case of a business upswing, no international in-movement of gold would occur. External reserve movements occurred only when changes in domestic demand and supply for money were not synchronized. In a typical upswing, increased discounting raised a central bank's domestic assets. Only incidentally did this correlate with an increase in a central bank's holdings of external assets (gold or foreign exchange).

The priority assigned to profit-making activity and the mechanisms involved in bringing it about varied among central banks. Almost every central bank stressed public service as its paramount goal, which meant that profit-maximizing behavior was usually constrained.

NATIONAL PRACTICES

We may now see why changes in the Bank of England's levels of domestic and international assets were positively correlated more often than were those of other central banks. Because of the huge size and depth of London's network of finance houses, funds could shift rapidly between local and foreign deployments.[20] A British discount rate change — because of this depth and Britain's creditor status — would immediately affect the direction of short-term capital movements.[21] Also, changes in Britain's domestic money supply were closely correlated with changes in the international asset holdings of the Bank of England — which differed from the pattern elsewhere.[22] Other central banks found it easier to manage their reserve ratios through attention to *internal* drains and refluxes of gold.

The contrast between the British experience and that of Germany and

France is instructive. Changes in the Bank of England's discount rate had only mild effects on domestic business conditions before the war, and this encouraged its frequent use. A rise in London's bank rate forced primary producers to liquidate stocks, which meant lower input costs for British manufacturing; this somewhat offset the depressing effects of higher interest costs.[23] Greater sensitivity of German and French economies to discount rate shifts and a relatively smaller effect of rate changes on their capital flows were among the factors that led their central banks to manage reserves differently.

The prewar Reichsbank followed some reserve rules, although not those proposed later by the Cunliffe Committee or the League of Nations. It targeted both the sterling exchange rate and its own reserve ratio. Evidence for the first is that the gold import and export points were rarely reached and rarely altered through premiums (although both happened frequently elsewhere) during 1879–1913. A further indication is the absence of correlation between business cycles and gold imports over the same period.[24] Evidence for the reserve target is that changes in Reichsbank liquidity ratios correlate with 60 percent to 70 percent of the variability in the discount rate during the same prewar years.[25]

By the Bloomfield and Nurkse tests mentioned earlier, the rules of the game required that international and domestic asset levels of central banks change in the same direction. The German central bank did not follow this rule and, indeed, might not have recognized it. Insofar as more than two-thirds of Germany's monetary gold was in circulation rather than in the central bank, a Bloomfield- or Nurkse-type rule focused on cross-border movements to and from the central bank would have done little to block overall Reichsbank gold absorption.

France held nearly 20 percent of the world's monetary gold immediately before World War I, an amount second only to that of the United States. By 1914, only American and Russian central banks had more gold reserves, and no country had more gold in circulation.[26] The Bank of France resisted raising its discount rate for fear of the damage this might bring to commerce and industry and sometimes instead sterilized gold losses.[27] The bank's discount rate changed only 30 times during 1880–1913, against 116 times for the Reichsbank and 194 for the Bank of England.[28] The use of gold premiums, the typical alternative to discount rate adjustments, also became rare by the late 1890s because of criticism from those who needed to make payments abroad; however, premiums were used briefly in 1901 and 1903.[29] The Bank of France thereafter often chose to moderate its external gold losses by helping foreign centers, especially London, keep their discount rates low. It would accomplish this by either lending gold or discounting paper.[30]

The question remains as to why France attracted so much gold during this period; in both population and industrial expansion, it grew slowly relative to Germany, the United States, and Russia. A plausible explanation is that heavy reliance upon currency (due in part to an underdeveloped use of checking facilities) reduced the superstructure of credit that might be constructed per unit of monetary gold in France.[31] A given monetary expansion thus required more gold than in other countries. This fundamental characteristic of the French monetary system would remain in place during the 1920s and 1930s.

The ratio of official gold reserves to notes and total deposits at the Bank of France never dropped below 63 percent during 1885–1912, despite the absence of formal reserve requirements. Given the unusual reliance upon circulating currency in France, this implied an enormous concentration of gold holdings. The French central bank, unlike the Bank of England and the Reichsbank, was content to hold nonearning gold assets beyond legal requirements. This was consistent with profit-seeking behavior by the Bank of France because of the importance of discounting privileges — which were open only to banks, enterprises, and individuals who held bank balances. The high gold reserves were the bank's guarantee to customers that its notes were completely secure and that its discounting would always be available.[32]

The prewar Bank of England and Reichsbank were economical in their own use of gold, behavior at least partly motivated by profit considerations. Both, however, either encouraged or were indifferent to the buildup of gold in circulation. In contrast, large official reserves were essential to the Bank of France's policy for sheltering the domestic economy from discount rate fluctuations while maintaining a strong franc.

During the period of the interwar gold standard, the role of gold coins was much smaller than it had been before 1914. Postwar reserve levels were therefore no longer determined by influxes from and refluxes to domestic circulation. A parallel mechanism operated, however. Economic expansion raised the demand for money in circulation relative to gold in official stocks and thereby brought pressure upon central bank reserve ratios — most often, as I shall point out, in Britain and Germany. The task is to determine why concern for reserve positions became deflationary as 1930 approached, when it generally was not before 1914.

The Influence of the Bank of England

Conceptually distinct issues concerning the prewar gold standard are often jumbled. One concerns the institutional machinery of the prewar standard, or of the respective roles of central bank policy and self-equilibrating action in the commercial sector. A corollary issue here is the importance of the role of the Bank of England relative to other central banks. Closely related is the influence of monetary policy in the "center" upon countries farther out — and influences in the opposite direction. A second and separate issue concerns how currency price levels were determined, both systemically and in specific countries. A description of how central banks behaved does not itself explain how systemic price levels were set — prices may have been determined largely independently of central bank activity. Both issues, furthermore, are distinct from the question of whether the prewar gold standard succeeded sufficiently that it might provide a model framework for later economies, including that of the interwar period.

Keynes addressed the first of these issues in his remark, quoted earlier, that the prewar Bank of England was "almost . . . the conductor of the international orchestra." He noted that France, a large-scale international creditor, was the only other country in a position to influence reserve flows through discount rate policy before 1914 — but, in fact, seldom did.[33] Donald McCloskey and Richard Zecher, adopting the monetary approach to the balance of payments in the 1970s, took direct aim at the orchestra conductor metaphor. They argued that the Bank of England could affect the world's price level only by accumulating or disbursing securities or gold. Since the bank held less than 1 percent of the world's stock of either, they continued, its power in this context was very limited. They argued forcefully that prewar prices of goods and services were set through cross-national arbitrage and that central banking policies of individual countries permitted little divergence from this pattern.[34]

McCloskey and Zecher shifted too quickly from evidence of price arbitrage to conclusions about the impact of interest rate changes and the management of reserve ratios. They proposed that the Bank of England's discount rate influenced world prices only as it shifted international reserves into or out of Britain. This inference presumes (1) that the English discount rate changes did not influence foreign interest rates directly and (2) that external money stocks would not change unless the external supply of reserves did. Neither premise is sustainable. First, changes in the British discount rate did affect the systemic cost of money. For example, a closer empirical correlation existed during 1890–1907 between the Bank of England's discount rate and the parallel rates in France and Germany than between the discount rates of the latter two countries.[35] Ralph Hawtrey, a British Treasury economist, argued further that the dominant role of sterling in international trade finance to some extent led British interest rates to influence external conditions.[36] Another mechanism by which British banking policy affected international money market conditions derived from a high level of international capital mobility before 1914; a rise in remuneration on short-term placements in London could bring downward adjustment of working capital investments abroad. A. G. Ford later noted the damaging effect of rises in the British bank rate upon investment in the world's economic periphery.[37] Wide holdings of sterling as a reserve currency before World War I also increased the leverage of English bank rate policy over systemic conditions.[38]

McCloskey and Zecher's second premise, which identifies determinants of the world's "supply of money" with determinants of the world's monetary "reserves," is even more problematic. An increase in the systemic relation between central bank credit money (defined as currency and whatever categories of deposits one chooses to include for comparison) and gold may result from a Thornton effect. The early-nineteenth-century economist Henry Thornton argued that the substitution of credit for gold in the domestic money supply would lead to an export of gold, which ceteris paribus would increase the world money supply — without any change in the world's reserve base.[39] McCloskey and Zecher implicitly posited that no important Thornton or (opposite) reverse-Thornton effects occurred during the prewar period.

During the 1870s and 1880s, Germany, France, Italy, the Scandinavian countries, and the United States adopted or readopted gold standards. In the 1890s they were joined by Austria-Hungary, Russia, and Japan. The spread of the gold standard meant rising demand for gold both in circulation and by central banks, as currencies previously backed by silver or without metallic backing now required gold reserves. Corresponding out-movements of gold from established gold standard countries led them to slow credit expansion in order to protect reserves. Contrary to McCloskey and Zecher's premise, a reverse-Thornton effect occurred as the superstructure of world credit per unit of the world's gold declined.

In addition, McCloskey and Zecher overlook channels by which the Bank of England might have affected prewar money-to-reserve ratios and through them the general world price level. An important factor in the success of the prewar standard lay in the management of Britain's position as the world's premiere creditor. Cassel wrote, "[The] strength of the sterling bloc lay in Britain's unbroken adherence to the principles of free trade and willingness to export capital, *and her abstention from using her position as a creditor country to accumulate an unnecessary amount of gold*"[40] (emphasis added). In the late 1920s, Britain's position as a long-term creditor would be compromised by a growing volume of short-term debts — an effect of the overvalued pound, high sterling interest rates, and a passive trade balance. The dominant creditors would become the United States and France, and both would accumulate unnecessary gold.[41] McCloskey and Zecher's conclusions neglect the potential of the world's leading creditor to disproportionately amass gold and other reserves.

McCloskey and Zecher's view of the causality of long-period changes in the world's price level was in fact similar to Keynes's. Keynes wrote, "The pre-war system did not do much to stabilise world prices or to ward off Credit Cycles — with such acts of God it did not consider itself in any way concerned."[42] And "The International Gold Standard has no views on Inflation or Deflation as such. Its business is to ensure that no Central Bank shall inflate or deflate at a pace very different from that of its neighbors."[43] Where Keynes and the monetary approach differ is in the distinction between the way prices are set in the short period, that is, in response to temporary disequilibria, and in the long period, in which steady-state conditions are more closely approximated.

Keynes argued that most short-term price changes depend directly upon the relation between interest rates and the marginal efficiency of capital, which *were* subject to the influence of central banks. He explained, "The most disastrous price fluctuations of modern times have been those associated with Profit (or Commodity) Inflations and Deflations; and these, whilst they have been indirectly connected with fluctuations in the supply of metal gold, have directly depended on the combined effect of the policies of the world's Central Banks taken as a whole on the market-rate of interest in relation to the natural rate."[44] McCloskey and Zecher's monetary approach specifically assumes that equilibrium of employment and output is maintained despite price changes.[45] The followers of this approach, in common with rational expectationists, monetarists, and others, often disregard the distinction between income and profit inflation, or between the first and second terms of the fundamental price equation. Their effort to link world prices with world reserves neglects the price changes stemming from short- and medium-period variability in aggregate profits that sometimes most affect general economic welfare.

One should proceed empirically: the characteristics of some economic environments approximate long-period steady-state assumptions, while those of others do not. In the international economy of 1929–32, pressures toward disequilibrium were overwhelming. During much of the period before 1914, the real importance of Bank of England policy was that it avoided greatly influencing the world price level — although the years from 1891 through 1896 marked an exception. The assumptions of the monetary theory — that the world's economy was unified by price arbitrage and, especially, that world prices were proportional to the amount of world reserves — are otherwise warranted in part for the prewar period precisely because of the British trade and discount rate policies.

Prewar Cooperation and Disruption

My account has emphasized the role of the stabilizing influence of the prewar Bank of England upon the international monetary system. The picture of the prewar mechanism is misleading, however, without discussion of three other economies — those of France, India, and the United States. French and Indian reserves regularly provided a cushion for the Bank of England. The French practice of lending from its vast gold stock during crises has been noted. India typically ran a trade deficit with Britain and a trade surplus with the rest of the world. Its surplus was treated as a British reserve. Basil Blackett, then a British Treasury economist, explained in a memorandum of 1914 on gold reserves,

> Here then in the conversion funds of the South American Republics, and the Gold Standard Reserves of India, the Straits Settlements, etc. are new stores of gold which exist for the direct purpose of being available at times of need for export to the older monetary centers of the world. . . . For good and sufficient reasons in their own interest, these countries have, in fact, relieved London's Gold Reserves of part of their former burden, and *pro tanto,* these new reserves take the place of corresponding additions to our reserves and furnish a strong presumption that our present reserves are adequate, seeing that they have increased, if but slightly, above the figures of twenty years ago when none of these new external reserves existed at all.[46]

The Indian reserve was by far the largest of those mentioned. The so-called contribution of India was less in its official gold holdings, which were minor, than in the compulsory use of its sterling surplus for the purchase of London Council Bills — to a total of more than £240 million in the ten years before 1914, in spite of maximum Home Charges (that is, charges on India to support the British presence) of perhaps £15 million annually and against Bank of England gold reserves averaging £35 million. Interest earned on Council Bills was automatically reinvested, which prevented exports of gold to India and kept the British bank rate lower than it otherwise would have been. London's use of the Indian reserve also led to nationalist agitation for a true gold standard in India, rather than the prevailing de facto sterling standard.[47] The present-day observer knows that India's days as a willing provider of British backup reserves were limited. Although the Gold Standard Reserve balance remained at £40 million in the mid-1920s, beginning in 1923 interest on reserve investments was credited directly to the Indian government.[48] This development would increase pressure on the already weakened interwar Bank of England.

The largest source of prewar monetary disruption was the United States. Cassel noted that "a metallic standard always runs the risk of losing its stability if a Power with vast economic resources sets its mind on accumulating great stocks of that metal."[49] Absorption by the United States continued up to World War I. Gold in circulation nearly trebled, from $639 million in 1890 to $1,753 million in 1910. By 1914 the United States had 25 percent of the world's total monetary gold and nearly a third of official reserves.[50] It also had the world's largest economy by a sizable margin; nevertheless, it had a huge bank-deposit-averse agricultural population, a many-tiered private banking structure with complicated gold reserve requirements, and no lender of last resort. Deposits were not easily convertible into currency. Currency consisted of national bank notes, specie, and silver certificates; these items also served as bank till money and reserves. Gold coin was regularly withdrawn from the banking system during the fall harvest and spring planting seasons. Surges in demand could be satisfied by drawing specie from abroad—this was the only rapidly flexible item of the nation's currency stock.[51] A large portion of U.S. foreign trade was financed in sterling, which provided a lucrative business for acceptances and discounts in London.[52] It thus served the interests of London banks and the Bank of England to rescue the American banking system whenever a seasonal reserve shortage loomed.

Eichengreen's explanation of the mechanics of the prewar monetary standard emphasizes international cooperation. He notes that in 1890, 1895–96, 1906, 1907, 1909, and 1910, convertibility crises involving the dollar or sterling were relieved, usually with the assistance of the Bank of France and occasionally with that of the Reichsbank.[53] All of these except the Baring Brothers banking crisis of 1890 began with gold drains to the United States. He moves from this evidence to conclude that more active cooperation in 1931 might have prevented runs on the mark and the pound and thereby saved the interwar gold standard. The comparison is inexact. In January and February 1895, the American Treasury borrowed $60 million of gold from foreign countries. Another major support operation came in 1907, when the Bank of France discounted foreign bills for F65 million ($13 million) in March and sterling bills for F80 million ($16 million) in November.[54] Against these amounts, Reichsbank President Hans Luther requested up to *$1 billion* in May 1931 from the central banks of the United States, Britain, and France to replenish reserves.[55] (The purchasing power of the prewar dollar was almost double that of the 1931 dollar.)[56]

The noncomparability of cooperation under the prewar standard and what would have been needed in 1931 goes beyond the larger lending requirement for the later date. Germany's reserves in 1931 were nearly exhausted, and its budget was in disarray. Sharp German deflation (including profit deflation) had been under way for two years. Pre-1914 rescue operations occurred in a different context. Gold drains from the United States before 1914 reflected an irrational domestic banking system, not the underlying production and budget and reserve weaknesses of late–Weimar Germany.

Gold Reserves and the Prewar Gold Standard

The pertinent danger in a gold standard — or in any fixed–exchange rate system — is that the requirements of external equilibrium will conflict with those of domestic equilibrium; for example, a rise in the discount rate to protect gold reserves may induce a domestic profit deflation. Keynes observed that in prewar England the separate equilibrium demands were seldom in conflict. A decline in the domestic bank rate tended to generate a capital outflow from Britain. This in turn might increase foreign demand for British goods and thereby improve the trade balance so as to offset the weakening capital balance. But Keynes thought achievement of this balance would some-times bring disequilibrium among prices, income, and employment.[57] Why was equilibrium usually maintained during the decades before 1914?

In Keynes's view prices were set by a combination of changes in reserve levels and the effect of systemic central banking policy:

> The long-period price-level depended — after allowing for secular changes in other monetary factors — on whether the new gold available for the reserves was increasing faster or slower than the trade of gold-standard countries, which, in its turn, depended on the rate of the discovery of gold mines, the proportionate use of gold in circulation and the number of gold-standard countries, as well as on the growth of population and of trade per head; whilst the short-period price-level depended on whether the fluctuations in the second term of the Fundamental Equation were set in the direction of inflation or deflation.[58]

Charles Rist, the leading French interwar economist, also distinguished be-tween long-period influences resulting from gold production and short-period influences upon prices from the banking system; this distinction is not contro-versial.[59] Keynes differs above by attributing profit inflation and deflation — shifts in the second term of the price equation — to central bank action rather than to changes in the quantity of reserves. Keynes's argument rests on the important theoretical point that price changes caused by profit disequilibrium can proceed independently of changes in the money supply.[60] But the sugges-tion that change in the quantity of gold does not affect profit equilibrium contradicts his reasoning elsewhere. He wrote in 1911 and again in 1936 that growing supplies of gold would bring lower interest rates, which could increase output and employment.[61]

Underlying reserve adequacy (inadequacy) may reinforce episodes of profit inflation (deflation). Robert Marjolin, a French economist writing at about the same time the *General Theory* was published, explained:

> The movement over the long-period represents the underlying trend comprised by a series of short-period cycles, it provides the general "climate" within which these cycles unfold. To say that prices during a certain period are buttressed by an ascendant long-period movement, for example, means that price declines are less deep and of shorter duration than they would be during a long-period depression. Further, during a long-period ascent, the rate of price increases is greater and the upward trend lasts longer than otherwise; each short-period cyclical price peak is higher than the previous one.[62]

Consistent with Marjolin but in contrast to Keynes's equivocation, Bloomfield drew out the connection between reserve adequacy and banking policy. He noted that central banks could pursue countercyclical policies — and hence ease monetary conditions in order to moderate cyclical downswings — only when reserves were adequate.[63]

During 1850–71, world gold production averaged nearly 6.3 million troy ounces annually. For 1872–90, during which time much of the economically advanced world adopted the gold standard, annual production dropped to about 5.4 million troy ounces. Jastram's index for Purchasing Power of Gold in Great Britain declined from 127 during 1849–51 to 88 during 1872–73 (indicating sterling price inflation), then rose to 156 during 1894–97 (indicating sterling price deflation). After the mid-1890s, the world's gold production increased rapidly: from 7.5 million troy ounces in 1893 to 13.9 in 1898 and to 20 in 1907.[64] The world's stock of gold money nearly doubled from 1896 to 1914.[65] By 1912–14 gold's purchasing power had declined to 114 on Jastram's index.[66]

None of the leading prewar central banks hindered the buildup of gold in their domestic circulations; to the contrary, they preferred that gold circulate internally rather than leave the country. The United States, which did not have a central bank until 1913, also had a growing circulation of gold coins. The Bank of England and the Reichsbank were economical in their use and accumulation of reserves, but the Bank of France, the Bank of Russia, and the United States Treasury accumulated large official reserves. The relative success of the gold standard during 1896–1914 is thus only secondarily attributable to effective monetary management — although note is due the Bank of England for not using its leadership role to accumulate more gold. The key to the prewar success was the growing systemic supply of gold, which permitted rising prices and—except during short-term crises induced by periodic surges in the American demand for currency—an absence of serious pressure upon official reserves.

This evidence also explains the greatest failure of the prewar gold standard, the systemic deflation of 1891–96, the prewar event with the closest similarity to the 1929–32 depression (see chapter 1). The underlying cause of the 1891–96 depression was the ongoing contraction of the world's money and credit caused by the rising demand for gold consequent upon the geographical expansion of gold standards and matched with only slow increases in gold production. In 1890 the United States passed the Sherman Silver Purchase Act, which required official purchases of silver. This brought uncertainty about gold backing for the dollar and gave rise to an external drain. Consequent deflationary pressure led to runs on banks and the Panic of 1893, hence to an internal drain as well. Doubts about the viability of gold convertibility heightened the demand for gold coins. The decision in mid-1893 to repeal the silver purchase clause in the Sherman Act halted the external drain of gold, which somewhat eased conditions in the United States but perhaps tightened them elsewhere.[67] Silver price oscillations brought losses to agrarians in Austria-Hungary, who then demanded gold-backing for their currency. The separate Hungarian and Austrian parliaments passed the Currency Reform Bill in 1892, which called for replacement of official silver with gold. Russia adopted an official gold standard in 1896, which followed years of anticipatory official gold purchases—hence its systemic contractionary effects predated 1896.[68]

World gold production hit a cyclical bottom in 1883 at 4.7 million ounces, but even in 1891 at 6.4 million ounces was only as high as the average annual level for the 1850s. Production rose significantly to 9.7 million ounces in 1896, after which it surged.[69] However, despite production increases in the early 1890s, the relative quantity of world gold fell in 1896 and 1897 to its lowest point vis-à-vis the 1850–1910 supply trend line. The years 1896 and 1897 also marked the low point for world price indexes, whether denominated in gold or in currency; in this instance, the correlation between the relative gold supply and the level of world prices is startlingly close[70] (see fig. 2, p. 52). A growing international economy required ever-expanding gold production just to maintain a constant gold-to-total-money ratio; Cassel called this the "gold standard paradox," which he thought "a fundamental difficulty connected with the use of gold as a standard of value."[71]

Inadequate monetary management also contributed to the depression of 1891–96. The first instance was the Baring Brothers bank crisis of 1890 following the collapse of Argentine bonds, which brought a severe shock to confidence; this shock may be compared to the New York Stock Exchange crash in 1929 or to the Austrian and German bank crises of 1931 for their roles in triggering the 1930s depression. The shocks to confidence of 1890 and 1893 brought declines in aggregate investment outlays paired with increases in desired savings. Thus a negative turn in the profit term of the price equation led to the decline in general prices.

A consequence of the crisis was a falloff in the export of British capital, which led to growing accumulation of gold in London. Fears about foreign lending were aggravated by the Australian bank crisis of 1893. The futures of the American and Indian currencies were then in serious doubt, a consequence both of the bank crises and the long-term systemic deflation associated with low gold production and the rising demand for gold tied to the spread of gold standards.[72]

This crisis was the one significant occasion during the prewar era in which Britain's gold-to-credit ratio expanded and hence aggravated the systemic reverse-Thornton effect initiated by the spread of gold convertibility. The Bank of England's gold reserves and deposits doubled between 1890 and 1896, while deposits of other British banks rose by 20 percent—in spite of significant price deflation. Notwithstanding the domestic monetary expansion, this was a period of declining investment and rising unemployment in Britain. Keynes remarks that this evidence is hard to reconcile with the "quantity theory" (by which price changes correlate with changes in the quantity of money).[73] In a one-country analysis, the quantity theory may indeed explain little. However, British deflation is easier to understand in the context of systemic monetary constraint—in which the world economy is understood as an integrated whole. Britain's position in the 1890s was comparable to that of France and the United States around 1930. Keynes wrote,

> If Great Britain [in the 1890s] had been a closed system, the excess of saving over investment might have been enough by itself to account for a [moderate] fall . . . in the Consumption Index. But in fact the phenomena were international—the same things were also happening elsewhere, with complicated interactions both in the primary and in the secondary phases on international wholesale prices. Moreover, in the later stages the drain of gold to London caused by the cessation of foreign investment probably induced an Income Deflation abroad, as well as a Profit Deflation, which operated as a further depressing influence upon international prices; just as at the end of 1929 the French and American price-levels felt the effect of the international deflation caused by the drain of gold *into* those countries earlier in the year.[74]

Many expected a domestic gold inflation following the avalanche of metal toward the Bank of France after 1928.[75] They would have been less surprised by the French deflation that ensued after 1930 had they been reminded of this precedent.

As I noted earlier, prewar central bank cooperation occurred in response to temporary reserve disturbances. The period after 1896, during which most of the prewar rescue operations occurred, was one of systemic reserve adequacy and gold-backed inflation. It is unlikely that any sustained deflation would occur under these circumstances, no matter how misguided central bank policy were to be. The post–World War I monetary environment would be quite different.

3

The Postwar Undervaluation of Gold

The roots of the world deflation of the 1930s lie in the international liquidity crisis induced by the price inflation during and after World War I. The issue of uncovered notes to finance wartime spending in European countries gave rise to systemic monetary expansion (and to an expansive Thornton effect), hence to price inflation. United States exports grew to fill both the commercial demands of neutral countries — whose markets had been vacated by Europe's traditional exporters — and the war-related demands of the belligerents. The U.S. gold stock grew from $1.8 billion in 1914 to $3.2 billion in mid-1917.[1] This represented an increase in the American share of growing world reserves from 34 percent to 45 percent in three years.[2] The pressure of gold losses elsewhere had by then led much of the world to end convertibility. From April 1917, when the United States entered the war, through 1919, the Federal Reserve's gold stock plateaued, as American war materials were then transferred to European allies on credit. The American military buildup was financed through budget deficits and an expanded note issue, much of it backed by the new gold. During the war, U.S. monetary expansion and price inflation were restrained by the public's liquidity-seeking increase in currency holdings relative to deposits.[3] After the armistice in November 1918, the public increased its deposit holdings, permitting the money supply and prices to inflate rapidly. By one standard index, dollar wholesale prices rose from 116 in 1914 to 258 in 1920.[4]

The Gold Shortage

The dollar price of gold, however, remained fixed at $20.67 per ounce. The real value of gold thus dropped sharply, to some 40 percent of its level in 1914 and to less than 50 percent of its average purchasing power during the period 1778–1914.[5] This decline in purchasing power reflected a drop in the systemic central bank demand for gold brought on by the removal of much of the world from the gold standard. The concentration of gold in the United States, which maintained gold convertibility throughout, nourished the wartime and postwar dollar inflation there. The worldwide demand for gold would increase anew as gold standards were restored during the 1920s; this would put upward pressure on the real price of gold by giving impetus to currency deflation in gold standard countries.

An important price adjustment occurred with the recession of 1920–21. Dollar wholesale prices dropped quickly, from an index level of 258 to 167. (The wholesale price figures somewhat overstate the postwar inflation and partly reflect speculative purchases on the part of distributors. See also chapter 1.) The price deflation was initiated by U.S. discount rate hikes beginning in November 1919, following concern over the drop in gold stock from $3.2 billion in mid-1919 to less than $3.0 billion. Free gold, or that available above reserve requirements, dropped to $176 million. American officials were concerned that without rapid deflation, the dollar would be forced off gold. Assistant Treasury Secretary Russell Leffingwell said that, were a credit panic to break out in New York, he would be "glad of it."[6] The U.S. unemployment rate rose from 1.4 percent in 1919 to 5.2 percent in 1920 and 11.4 percent in 1921.[7] Almost simultaneously, the Bank of England raised its discount rate to contain a price explosion; one result was a short-lived increase in unemployment among British union members from 1.4 percent to more than 16 percent.[8] The price deflation shored up American reserves. In 1921, the U.S. gold stock began rising anew and reached $4.6 billion by mid-1924; some of this increase reflected expansion of the world's gold supply. But the purchasing power of gold remained at least 35 percent below the level of 1914 and 25 percent below the average level of the previous 135 years. The pressure on the American gold stock in 1919 was a warning of reserve pressures to come as other countries would restore convertibility; at its postwar reduced real value, nearly half of the world's gold stock was barely sufficient to support a gold standard in one country. Restoration would put renewed upward pressure on the commodity value of gold and thereby threaten more deflation.

The outlook for the supply of monetary gold in the 1920s was also discouraging from the standpoint of the stability of the real value of gold. World gold production dropped by about 13 percent from the peak levels of 1912 and 1915 to the late 1920s, or from 22.6 million ounces annually to 19.3 million ounces annually (the 1924–29 average) and was virtually stationary after 1923.[9] Some 53 percent of production in 1929 was in the Transvaal, where volume was fairly stable, but output elsewhere fell by more than a third after 1915. By the 1920s more than a quarter of the world's gold output required the cyanide process, which was first applied in South Africa in 1891. There was no reason to expect either another Transvaal-like discovery or another technological breakthrough in the 1920s.[10] This was particularly so in view of the depressed real price of gold.

In the face of this supply constraint, trends in the nonmonetary demand for gold offered little relief. Indian consumption of gold increased rapidly. Strong identified this as a "disturbing factor" for international prices.[11] Gold in India was used primarily for jewelry, which was a means of private hoarding. The Indian share of world output rose from $5 million per annum in 1890 to $50 million per annum in 1910 and to over $90 million in 1915. By the early 1920s, approximately one-tenth of the gold ever produced had found its way to India.[12] In 1924, Indian absorption was estimated at $230 million, or more than 60 percent of the total output that year. A portion of this extraordinary inflow followed from fluctuations in the dollar/sterling and rupee/sterling exchanges, which created arbitrage opportunities for which gold was a natural vehicle. The British restoration of fixed-rate convertibility in 1925 brought some stability. But speculation that the rupee would be devalued against sterling continued into 1926 and to a lesser extent into 1927, contributing to demand for new gold imports.[13]

Over medium and long periods, however, Indian hoarding demand was largely an inverse function of gold's real price. During the 1860s, a period of rising nominal prices internationally, hence of a declining real value for gold, gold absorption by India totaled about £5.9 billion.[14] During the following decade, one of currency price deflation and parallel increase in gold's real value, Indian absorption dropped approximately by half. In the years before World War I, Indian absorption rose again as the real value of gold declined. The historic undervaluation of gold following World War I led to still larger movements to India.[15] In 1920 and 1921 there were poor harvests in India, hence reduced Indian resources and a virtual halt to the gold inflow; more successful harvests in subsequent years permitted Indians to outbid central banks (which paid a fixed currency price) for gold (see fig. 1).[16] During the decade of 1919–28, India absorbed 27 percent of the world's gold output. (Only 49 percent of total production during this decade was available for monetary uses.)[17]

From the standpoint of the world economy, the spectacular rise in Indian

Fig. 1. Indian Consumption of Gold 1859 to 1929

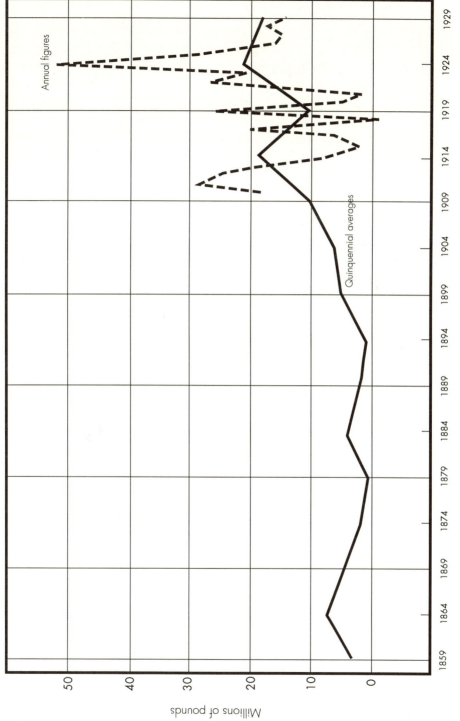

Source: Interim Report of the Gold Delegation of the Financial Committee, League of Nations (1930).

gold consumption during this decade was endogenous — it was a response to independent price incentives. Were the real price of gold to return to a more traditional (higher) level, Indian gold consumption would presumably decline. The onset of world deflation in 1929 led to severe declines in the prices of Indian export commodities; harvests could be sold only at heavy loss. The value of gold expressed in terms of these Indian commodities rose correspondingly. A further disincentive to the purchase of gold was the rapid decline in the real price of silver that began in 1929, due in part to famine and political disturbances in China. Some Indian demand for precious metals was diverted to the cheaper silver. During 1929 and 1930, Indian gold consumption indeed fell by roughly a third from its 1926–28 average. Yet even this reduced level of absorption was misleadingly high; Indian dealers overestimated consumer demand. Internal demand for gold collapsed by 1931, and India became a net exporter; a London gold advisory letter wrote of "distress" sales from the Indian "up-country."[18]

Industrial use of *new* gold in the West appears to have leveled in the 1920s at $70–75 million annually, an amount somewhat lower than estimates for pre-1914 use owing to reuse of old gold following wartime melting of jewelry and coins.[19] The overall demand for industrial gold increased — as one would expect, given the decline in its real price. Indicative figures are available for the United States and France. In the United States during 1911–13, new gold was employed in more than 80 percent of gross industrial use; by 1925–28 this proportion had declined to 55 percent. Average industrial use of gold in the United States rose from $44 million annually during the earlier period to $63 million annually a decade and a half later.[20] In France, the prewar peak for industrial use came in 1910, at about forty tons of gold. This amount was exceeded every year from 1919 through 1927 and reached a peak in 1920 of ninety-four tons. Industrial use of gold in France might have been yet higher but for legal sanctions against the fabricating of jewelry introduced in 1921.[21] Cassel wrote in 1920 that "the use of gold in the arts is growing rapidly. This consumption threatens, indeed, to absorb a large part of the diminished annual production of gold. What is left for monetary use will then be very insufficient for the necessary regular increase in the world's monetary stock."[22]

Similarly, the reduced use of gold coins augmented central bank reserve stocks without absorbing current production. From 1913 to 1929 gold monetary reserves worldwide increased by nearly $6 billion, of which more than $2 billion came from gold in circulation before the war. Eichengreen has pointed to this source of reserves as alleviating any general shortage of monetary gold.[23] Some of the gold savings from coins withdrawn from circulation, however, were offset by reserve requirements on the increased paper circulation.

(For example, if one assumes a 33 percent cover ratio, one-third of the gold withdrawn from circulation would have been immediately immobilized as a reserve.)

A conceptual flaw in Eichengreen's argument is that it overlooks the fluid movements of gold between circulation and central bank reserves before World War I. The Bank of England viewed gold coins as potential reserves and took steps to maintain a large circulation. In this respect, it did not introduce national frugality in the use of gold. The governor explained in 1910, "Our objection [to the issuance of one-pound notes] is based principally on the opinion that if there were £1 notes in circulation they would take the place of gold in the pockets of people and thus tend indirectly to drive gold from the country."[24] The Reichsbank also viewed circulating gold as a backup reserve. In July 1913 it was authorized to issue twenty- and fifty-mark notes to absorb gold and silver coins in circulation, hence to increase international reserves at the disposal of the Treasury should hostilities occur.[25] A German government investigative committee in the late 1920s noted that gold in circulation was generally available to reinforce Reichsbank reserves before 1913, and that this should be kept in mind when lower prewar reserve levels were compared with those maintained later.[26]

The French experience was similar. In the summer of 1914 the Bank of France distributed five- and twenty-franc notes to all of its branches to be used to absorb gold coins.[27] During 1880–1901, an amount equivalent to the average French specie inflow regularly found its way within a year to the coffers of the Bank of France. The price level declined somewhat during this period, thus reducing the demand for hand-to-hand currency; in addition, the prestige of the central bank — and hence of its banknotes — was high. The circulation of notes doubled. During 1901–13, this pattern changed completely. Only 10 percent of new specie was absorbed by the Bank of France, while 75 percent went into circulation. (The remaining amount was consumed by industry.) The period 1901–13 saw significant franc price inflation. Harry Dexter White argued that increased prosperity led to a greater hand-to-hand circulation that could as easily be met by gold and silver coins as by banknotes. The Bank of France meanwhile did not issue lower-denominated notes. The bank was unconcerned by the decline in its cover ratio, so long as gold went into circulation rather than out of the country.[28]

The portion of the world's gold money stock held by central banks and treasuries rose from 62 percent to 92 percent between 1913 and 1929.[29] In part because of the reduction of circulating gold, reserve ratios on currency issue and central bank deposits were raised relative to prewar levels in Germany and France. Beginning in 1925 the Reichsbank maintained minimum gold reserve requirements of 40 percent, against a 33 percent prewar minimum (see chapter 7). The Bank of France justified its enormous gold holdings in the early 1930s by comparing them with the *combined* level of its reserves and gold coins in circulation before 1914.[30]

Finally, any relaxation of demand for new gold through recirculation of old gold was destined to be short-lived. These potential reserves as well as this source of supply for industrial gold were nearly exhausted by the end of the decade. The undervaluation of gold would ensure continued high demand for nonmonetary uses, both in the West and in Asia, while providing little incentive to develop new supplies.

The 1913–29 period saw gold supply increases of 2.5 percent annually, and for the early 1920s about 2 percent annually — below the 1850–1910 average of 3.1 percent annually. As price indexes at the end of this sixty-year period were at about the same level as at the beginning, 3.1 percent came to be seen as the gold expansion rate that would roughly assure stable prices.[31] These numbers suggest that the 1920s might have seen some deflation, but hardly a catastrophic amount. In fact, data focusing on the new supply of gold greatly understate the extent of the gold shortage. The 1914–20 period was one of sharp currency price inflation. Hence a postwar decline of 13 percent in the rate of gold produced, expressed in dollars (or ounces), was a much sharper decline in the real (or commodity-equivalent) rate of production. If one adjusts the production figures to reflect a 39 percent decline in gold's purchasing power — as reflected in a U.S. price deflator index — then the value of the gold produced in the mid-1920s was only 53 percent of what it had been in 1914.[32] Further, one must adjust the real value of existing stocks of gold reserves and coins downward by the same 39 percent factor. The key to the concept of a gold shortage is in the relation between the value of gold supplies and the value of other assets, not in the raw amount of gold relative to the amount at another point in time. If the value of gold is set arbitrarily low and maintained at that level by the world's central banks, then — absent extraordinary measures to reduce demand — the supply will fall short.

The Golden Constant and the Supply of Gold

The real purchasing power of gold often shifted prior to 1914. During the 1870s and 1880s, with the spreading adoption of gold convertibility, gold's purchasing power in England rose by some 30 percent. It rose further during the depression of the 1890s. Much earlier, during the sixteenth-century price revolution and its aftermath, the purchasing power of gold in England declined by some 30–50 percent over several decades.[33] That price inflation reflected both an increase in the volume of specie and the broader use of fiat money — effectively a specie substitute, analogous in its price effects to the use of foreign exchange reserves in the 1920s.[34] Again, following the surge in South African gold production during the 1890s, the real value of gold dropped some 25 percent by 1914. Yet the trend level purchasing power of gold changed little from the seventeenth century into the middle of the twentieth. Jastram's series shows gold price indexes in England of 106 in 1646, 104 in 1694, 105 in 1726, 104 in 1763, 103 in 1790, 104 in 1822, 104 in 1842, 103 in 1859, 103 in 1877, 114 in 1912, and 100 (the base level) in 1930.[35] Jastram concluded in 1977, "Gold does not match commodity prices in their cyclical swings. The record of the centuries . . . is very clear and is broken only by recent events. . . . This is due to the Retrieval Phenomenon. *Commodity prices return to the index level of gold over and over.* This is one of the principal findings of my study."[36]

The commodity value of gold during the 1920s was comparable to that during the Napoleonic Wars and the 1960s, the lowest values in modern history except for those of 1917–20. From 1795 through 1814 the index ranged from 66 to 87; in 1919 and 1920 it fell to 50 (the lowest on record) but then rose to the 71 to 80 range during 1921–28. Later, during 1956–71, the gold price index ranged from 62 to 79. During the Puritan Wars three hundred years earlier, from 1647 to 1658, the value was only slightly higher, ranging from 88 to 99. In none of these instances was the low gold value sustained — the aftermaths of the Napoleonic era and the 1920s saw currency deflation, and the aftermath of the 1960s brought the formal breakdown of gold convertibility. This pattern suggests that the gold value of the 1920s also would be difficult to maintain. (Figure 2 shows a gap developing during World War I and persisting into the late 1920s between the world's "relative stock of gold money" and "wholesale prices," whereas these two lines tracked each other very closely during the prior hundred years. The deflation of 1929–32 would restore the historical gold supply/wholesale price relation.)

The supply of gold is also price-sensitive. When currency price deflation brings a higher gold value, resources are redirected to the exploration and production of gold. Much of the expansion in prospecting in the middle and end of the nineteenth century resulted from price incentives. The discovery in California in 1848 appears to have been an exception, an accidental by-product of the expansion of agriculture into the interior of the state. But discoveries shortly afterward in Australia and New Zealand corresponded with periods of high unemployment, which shifted labor resources into prospecting.[37] Even the California discovery was preceded by prospecting elsewhere and by a smaller discovery near Los Angeles in 1842. The availability of

Fig. 2. The Relative Stock of Gold Money as Compared with Wholesale Prices

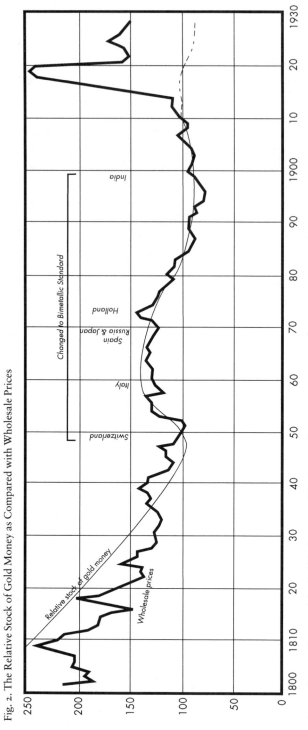

Source: Interim Report of the Gold Delegation of the Financial Committee, League of Nations (1930).

a large number of miners able to work alluvial deposits was thus partly at-tributable to gold's higher real value. The discovery in the South African Rand in 1886 was a result of intense prospecting, again correlating with a period of high and rising real gold prices. Subsequent discoveries in Colorado and Alaska occurred during the depressed 1890s.[38]

The discovery of the cyanide process, also in 1886, resulted from a commer-cial venture to extract gold from ore. Evidence suggests that a number of metallurgists were close to perfecting the same process when the breakthrough occurred. A similar process was already known in the jewelry trade; the inno-vation was a matter of technology and engineering, not pure science. Hugh Rockoff finds it "hard to escape the conclusion that this activity was the result of the high real price of gold."[39]

This kind of evidence has led some economists to wax lyrical about price-induced, exploration-driven monetary equilibrium. Jacques Rueff wrote of the way a free market might deal with a (Keynesian-style) decline in the de-mand for goods:

> If there really is an offer of an increment of employment on the market, and if only increases in cash holdings are desired by the persons for whom the increase of employment will provide an increase of income, the labor forces offered will find themselves spontaneously but inevitably directed by the force of the price mechanism alone towards the production of the additional cash holdings desired. Thus, the increment of production associated with an in-crease of employment will not have lacked a market, since it will have taken the form in which the owners of the additional incomes wished to absorb it. . . . The considerable variations in the rate of gold production between periods of boom and periods of depression clearly showed the sensitiveness of the productive apparatus to price movements.[40]

The weakness in this argument is its casual treatment of the time lapse neces-sary to generate a supply response to a gold shortage. The supply response to the 1870s deflation certainly came, but it took two decades.

The supply response appears to have been faster during and after World War I. Leffingwell, by then a partner at the Morgan Bank, wrote in 1922,

> The world [gold] output which in 1913 was about 95 millions sterling, in 1922 had sunk to about 65 millions sterling, or nearly 33%, [and] the esti-mate for 1924 is less than 80 millions sterling.
> . . . [T]he war inflation made gold mining unprofitable, or relatively so, by increasing the cost of mining gold and increasing the cost of the things that gold would buy. But already in response to the deflation of 1920 gold produc-tion has regained about half of what it lost. Further deflation will tend to increase the value of gold, in terms of goods and services, and stimulate the

production of gold. Thus the situation will work its own cure, though after some delay.[41]

Perhaps more striking is the output response following the rise in real gold prices (the world currency deflation) after 1929. World gold production rose from 19.6 million ounces in 1929, a figure only trivially higher than in any of the years 1924 through 1928, to 20.9 million ounces in 1930, 22.3 million ounces in 1931, and 24.3 million ounces in 1932. The rate of increase accelerated somewhat after the U.S. dollar price of gold was raised to $35 per ounce in 1934, and production reached 39.6 million ounces in 1939 and 42.2 million ounces in 1940.[42] Production expanded in all gold mining countries, which makes it unlikely that the increase can be explained through isolated or chance events.[43]

Even those less sanguine about the self-restorative capacity of free-market equilibrium must acknowledge that supply responses do occur in the gold market. A crucial reason for the relative success of the prewar gold standard, particularly in the two decades before 1914, is that the real value of gold in Great Britain in the early 1890s was at its highest level since *Elizabethan* times.[44] This encouraged the prewar exploration of gold, while decreasing its nonmonetary demand. The depressed real gold price after World War I and in the 1920s hampered the development of any comparable supply response. After World War II and post–1945 price inflation, gold was equally undervalued against the dollar by the early 1950s.[45] In both cases, gold reserves were inadequate and had to be supplemented with foreign exchange and, in the later episode, with "special drawing rights" issued by the International Monetary Fund. As in the case of sterling in the late 1920s, however, the international appetite for designated currencies is self-limiting. Failure to absorb this lesson from the 1920s would plague the international monetary system during the 1950s and especially the 1960s, when dollars would glut international markets much as pounds did earlier.

Economists and the Undervaluation of Gold

Three prominent contemporary economists identified and then drew quite different conclusions from the undervaluation of gold. Hawtrey saw the problem at the time of the Genoa Conference of 1922 as one of both a shortage (as a consequence of undervaluation) and a maldistribution of gold. He noted the "fall since 1914 in the value of gold in comparison to other commodities."[46] In the absence of a coordinated central bank response, he anticipated a rise in the value of gold as European countries reestablished gold convertibility.[47] He therefore proposed, first, that foreign exchange, principally sterling and dollars, be used next to gold as a monetary reserve (hence: "gold exchange" standard) so as to "economize" on the use of gold. Second, he wanted a dollar price inflation to permit restoration of gold convertibility at prewar (dollar) parity without further British and Continental deflation.[48] He was implicitly critical of American policy for the severity of the 1920–21 deflation. Third, he advocated that European countries with greatly devalued currencies restore convertibility at a level below prewar parity.[49] Hawtrey's recommendations would have had the effect of somewhat alleviating the systemic supply pressure on gold, through the economization of reserves. Dollar inflation, however, would simultaneously increase the demand pressure on existing stocks by aggravating gold's real undervaluation.

Cassel, too, proposed economization of gold. He advocated the withdrawal of gold coins from circulation and the lowering of reserve ratios as well as the use of foreign exchange as a reserve. He noted that the undervaluation of gold would be aggravated by a new dollar area inflation. Where Hawtrey sought U.S. inflation, Cassel therefore urged U.S. price stability.[50] Cassel agreed with Hawtrey that Britain and other European countries should restore convertibility at below prewar parity to make the transition less deflationary. In the absence or breakdown of efforts to stabilize the value of gold, Cassel in early 1928 accurately predicted world depression:

> The post-War superfluity of gold is, however, of an entirely temporary character, and the great problem is how to meet the growing scarcity of gold which threatens the world both from increased demand and from diminished supply. We must solve this problem by a systematic restriction of the monetary demand for gold. Only if we succeed in doing this can we hope to prevent a permanent fall in the general price level and *a prolonged and world-wide depression* which would inevitably be connected with such a fall in prices.[51] [emphasis added]

Rist saw deflation as inevitable to the restoration of gold's historic purchasing power. This was especially so because demand for gold would rise in the face of some twenty countries in Europe and elsewhere returning to gold and others planning to adopt it for the first time. He thought the world price level in 1925 "completely artificial." For Rist, any effort to maintain stable price and credit conditions—as attempted by American and British policy during 1924–29—would only delay the necessary adjustment of a credit-inflated production to a level sustainable by long-period consumption patterns. Long-term prices were determined by the supply of monetary gold; central bank efforts to overturn this historical regularity through economization of reserves were destined to fail. Rist argued later that the U.S. effort to maintain prices in the face of reserve losses sustained a sort of inflation that served mainly to intensify the subsequent deflation.[52]

Fisher had little to say about the specific postwar undervaluation of gold, but he worried that instability in gold's purchasing power would bring economic distress — as it did in bringing extended periods of deflation and inflation before 1914. He proposed that the gold weight of the dollar be adjusted regularly to maintain the dollar's stable real purchasing power.[53] Fisher's plan was more radical than anything sought by his trans-Atlantic peers, for it proposed an end to the role of precious metals as a standard of value. He had in mind that other postwar currencies would choose to stabilize against the dollar rather than against gold. Fisher's plan, had it been implemented, might well have prevented depression; but the analysis behind it was disconnected from the specific undervaluation of gold that helped bring a collapse of world prices a decade later.[54]

Hawtrey's proposal to stabilize the purchasing power of gold would work only if the supply effects of using nonspecie reserves outweighed the demand effect on (undervalued) gold of renewed American inflation. Rist, in contrast, sought no official action on the gold price from either the demand or the supply side. He would accommodate the increased demand for gold by letting its price rise — that is, by acquiescing in a currency deflation. This prophecy would be self-fulfilling, given the pattern of French monetary policy in the late 1920s (see chapters 8 and 9). Cassel sought to reduce the demand for gold through economization in its use, while maintaining stable prices to avoid increasing demand from this direction. Of the three, Cassel offered the conceptually most consistent method for avoiding a major worldwide price decline.

A Lost Opportunity to Prevent Deflation

Gold producers noted the shortage of gold during the 1920s and recommended a systemic increase in the currency price of gold. This obviously self-interested advice gained no discernable contemporary following.[55] Nevertheless, raising the price of gold might have increased world liquidity at a stroke. It would have restored gold's historic relation with other commodity prices, thereby obviating recourse to gold substitutes in the form of expanded use of sterling and dollar reserves and avoiding what would be the insurmountable diplomatic and ideological obstacles that this recourse would create. A higher real price of gold would have encouraged expanded prospecting and production. It would also have reduced the portion of gold absorbed into nonmonetary uses in the West and in India. (That the producers' viewpoint was self-interested did not make it wrong.)

When Franklin Roosevelt raised the dollar price of gold to $35 per ounce in 1934, he paved the way to stabilizing exchange rates in 1936 and again after World War II on a nondeflationary basis. Mundell has called the gold price increase "one of the most important events of the century."[56] In principle, the dollar price of gold could have been raised at the time of the Genoa Conference in 1922 in anticipation of higher demand for gold following convertibility restorations. It might even have been raised in 1919, so as to avoid the 1920–21 deflation. Or it might have been raised via joint devaluations of all major currencies against gold in 1930 or 1931, as proposed by Pierre Quesnay, who was by then general manager of the Bank of International Settlements.[57]

The purpose of raising the dollar price of gold would have been to stabilize dollar prices of goods and services, not to trigger a new round of inflation. First, it would have protected payor nations against fluctuations in the real value of war debt and reparation obligations, both of which were denominated in gold-convertible currencies.[58] The 1920–21 deflation theoretically helped the United States, the leading creditor country, which would be paid back in more valuable (gold-linked) dollars. However, the diplomatic history literature for this period scarcely mentions the role of the 1920–21 deflation in raising the value of gold relative to other currencies. I have found no evidence that American officials reckoned on further deflation after 1921 — yet this would be the only route by which a creditor nation could have acquired a further advantage. Even this route was closed by the Dawes Committee of Experts in 1924, which proposed that war debt payments be adjusted "automatically in correspondence with changes in the general purchasing power of gold, whenever, by the decision of an impartial authority, such changes amount to more than 10 per cent."[59]

The U.S. World War Foreign Debt Commission quietly negotiated greatly reduced war debt settlements with Britain, France, Belgium, and Italy during the early 1920s.[60] Subsequently, the Dawes Plan of 1924, which formalized German reparation requirements, demanded that Germany stabilize the reichsmark — a task that would have been facilitated had the deflationary bias been removed from the international monetary system. Strong, for one, was emphatic that collection on war debts was a secondary matter:

> It has always been my opinion that our country has a greater interest in the success of the Dawes Plan generally than it has in the collection of the moderate amounts of money which the Dawes Plan might produce for the liquidation of indebtedness directly to be repaid by that means to the United States. This is, indeed, a small consideration compared to the great importance of financial and monetary reconstruction in Europe and the reestablishment of normal facilities for the conduct of trade between our country and the European countries affected by the Dawes Plan.[61]

Second, international price deflation could force systemic contraction of output. Preventing this would be welcome even in the absence of international transfer obligations; but economic stability was especially important as a *diplomatic* goal in the postwar environment, in which fears of Bolshevik and, later, fascist upheavals were widespread.

Economic understanding at the time did not encourage the revaluation of gold. Alteration of the currency price of gold was thought alien to the spirit of the classical gold standard.[62] Leffingwell wrote in 1922,

> The question of whether a country shall when it can restore the pre-war value of its currency does not, however, seem to be properly one of expediency or justice. Such questions should not arise in the case of any country which *can* restore its currency to pre-war mint parity. In this respect the instinct of the business community is just. It is based not so much upon vague notions about prestige, as upon the sound principle that promises are made to be kept. Little importance would attach to re-establishing any gold standard, if it were done as part of a program which recognized the right of government to determine its course in respect to such a matter according to theories of social justice as between classes or of the relative benefits to be derived by the state, by the proletariat and by the bourgeoisie by one course or another . . . [T]here cannot be prosperity without confidence, nor confidence without a fixed measure of values and medium of exchange.[63]

Judging from Leffingwell's view of the likely ramifications should Britain fail to restore prewar gold parity for sterling, one can imagine what he (or another banker) might have said had the United States deliberately — and without immediate evidence of crisis — abandoned the dollar parity it had hitherto maintained.

A revaluation of gold would in addition have ratified the inflation-induced shift in wealth in favor of preinflation debtors and against preinflation creditors that occurred in most belligerent countries. This was politically delicate, as the creditor category included purchasers of wartime savings bonds. Meanwhile, devaluation of the dollar would have been domestically unpopular in the early 1920s, in part because American gold reserves were so substantial. By most accounts the American public was then in no mood to take on so internationalist a task.

Another reason action was not taken to counter systemic deflationary pressure was that the sharp 1920–21 deflation had relatively mild effects on real output (see chapter 1). This reinforced the "liquidationist" view that purging the effects of inflation could be salutary and only somewhat painful. In a similar vein, the Austrian School economist Ludwig von Mises wrote of the gold shortage on the eve of the depression:

One popular doctrine blames the crisis on the insufficiency of gold production. The basic error in this attempt to explain the crisis rests on equating a drop in prices with a crisis. Businessmen have become accustomed to a relationship of the demand for, and supply of, gold from which a slow steady rise in prices emerges as a secular (continuing) trend. However, they could just as easily have become reconciled to some other arrangement — and they certainly would have if developments had made them necessary.[64]

Rist argued similarly that "a decline in prices . . . does not appear to us as baneful. . . . Indeed, a gradual decline in prices has heretofore been considered desirable by all economists, that is, as a normal consequence of an expanding volume of production."[65] This view might have been correct had 1929–32 been marked by an income deflation triggered by declining unit input costs.

Rist elsewhere acknowledged that this deflation was impelled by a rise in liquidity preference. Rist used evidence that savings exceeded investment in Britain in early 1931 to demonstrate that money and credit were abundant.[66] He evidently imagined that growing liquidity demands and declining investment would bring a decline in production to a level in sustainable balance with long-period levels of consumption. In this context he perceived deflation as an equilibrating mechanism. However, as Keynes proposed, an increase in economy-wide savings above the level of investment outlays might be an endogenous and deviation-amplifying *response* to deflation — which in turn aggravates price declines. Profit deflation, unlike what might occur with a deflation driven by declining input costs, is *dis*equilibrating.

Meanwhile, such luminaries as Strong and (until 1928) Keynes, both of whom sought to avoid price declines, denied that a gold shortage existed.[67] Both argued that central banks had the power to maintain stable prices even if reserve levels were below historic levels. Keynes asserted in 1925 that the "amount of gold" was "devoid of importance." He anticipated that central banks would adjust their reserve ratios if gold stocks fell short.[68] In fact, as Keynes understood but Strong may not have, this argument was inconsistent with traditional understanding of the gold standard. Cassel explained, "We now [in the middle 1920s] know that the value of gold can be controlled by a suitable regulation of the world's monetary demand for gold. This alters the whole relation between currency and gold."[69]

As traditionally conceived, the stability of the real (commodity exchange) value of gold conferred stability upon the value of currencies. Strong and Keynes argued to the contrary that central banks could stabilize the commodity value of gold — which otherwise, in the deflationary postwar environment, was likely to increase greatly. Fisher went a step further, as I showed, arguing that the stability of money should no longer rest on the purported stability of gold.

Had gold been revalued against the dollar by, for example, 30 percent in 1922 — which would have removed systemic deflationary pressure — monetary adjustment might have remained precarious. With only the United States among leading economic countries on a gold standard, huge quantities of gold would have been offered to the Federal Reserve from both internal and foreign sources. The United States would have needed to sterilize much of the inflow, most likely through large-scale open-market sales, in order to stabilize dollar prices. (A new American inflation would have lowered the real value of the gold stock once again, hence defeating the purpose of the currency-to-gold realignment.) The drain of gold to New York would have aggravated the imbalance between American and European gold supplies. This imbalance would have lasted until European currencies were stabilized at the new (higher) currency: gold parity. A combination of U.S. capital outflows and an open trading system might then have gradually shifted reserves to Europe. This would have required unusual leadership and monetary management on the part of the new American central bank. Nevertheless, it is hard to envision any other action that might have so directly alleviated the world's gold shortage.[70]

Beyond discussion of what central bankers thought or what diplomats believed possible lies a fundamental issue about the nature of money. Alteration of the currency value of gold — even if done in an effort to stabilize the real value of gold — could be a large step down the road to removing the golden anchor from the international monetary system. Fisher proposed exactly this and managed to garner support for his views among a variety of government officials, academic economists, and bankers. This suggests that a more resourceful American leadership might have found support for the more moderate step of making a one-time adjustment in the gold-to-currency price.[71] Cassel, however, recoiled from advocating a non-gold-based system in the 1920s. Keynes went slightly further down that road than did Cassel: Cassel argued that before World War I gold determined the value of currency, but Keynes questioned even that. For Keynes, the switch from a silver standard to a gold standard that occurred over much of the world during the nineteenth century was a switch from "commodity money" to "representative money."[72] The gold standard maintained the "mystique" of an automatic system but was in fact managed ever more by central banks. Keynes argued that gold in the 1920s had been reduced from its former position of "sun . . . stationed in heaven" to the "sober status of constitutional king with a cabinet of Banks."[73] But he too stopped short of boosting a monetary system in which gold would be stripped of its sheen.

To summarize, those most ideologically committed to the gold standard (for example Rist, Leffingwell, and von Mises) were only slightly distressed by the prospect of currency price deflation, which they believed the banking system would be in the end powerless to resist. Meanwhile, those more concerned about the potential consequences of deflation (for example, Strong, Keynes, Hawtrey, and Cassel) believed that central banks could stabilize the purchasing power of gold and currencies, hence that adjustment of the systemic currency/gold price relation was unnecessary. Fisher argued that the value of currencies should not be anchored in gold, regardless of its current real value. Consequently, almost no one proposed action to correct the real undervaluation of gold.

As I have shown, the low real gold price aggravated the shortage of monetary gold from the directions of both demand and supply. Melted-down coins provided a respite on the supply side, but this source of gold was almost depleted by the end of the 1920s. Nonmonetary demand for new gold would consequently rise, hence the expansion of gold available for monetary use would follow a slower pace. Meanwhile, by the "paradox of the gold standard," an expanding gold base required accelerating absolute growth in the quantity of monetary gold merely to maintain existing paper-money-to-gold ratios. Those who wanted to manage the value of gold needed a system that would increase the systemic paper-to-gold ratio, perhaps inexorably, if they intended to maintain stable prices. It may have been unrealistic to hope for this.

The imperative here is to explain in its particulars how the stability was broken. The spreading of gold convertibility from the 1870s to the 1890s was accompanied by gradual deflation and recurrent hard times and high unemployment, but never by epochal depression. The previous instances of comparably low gold values in Britain, during the Puritan and Napoleonic wars, were followed by extended rather than time-compressed deflations. The decade-long nadir-to-peak increase in the value of gold during 1658–69 was perhaps 41 percent. The level of gold's real value during the 1780s—which was at a level typical for the eighteenth century—was not sustained after the French wars until the 1840s.[74] The undervaluation of gold in the late 1950s and through the 1960s was managed by the Federal Reserve, through sterilization of reserve outflows, so as to avoid systemic deflation; this worked for more than a decade but was breaking down even before the financial and diplomatic pressures that arose from the Vietnam War.[75]

A persistent but gradual deflation following gold restorations in the 1920s might have led to less disastrous events in the 1930s. Resumption per se does not explain the *abrupt* collapse of prices that began in 1929. The index of the real value of gold in the United States rose by 44 percent over the three years from 1929 to 1932.[76] Nonmonetary uses of gold, although at a high level, had plateaued for the time being; no systemic change is to be found here. Production of gold was lower than before or during the war, but in the short period this would exert only a mildly depressive influence on prices. The shift came in the demand for gold within the monetary framework and in the largely unanticipated way the new international gold standard would function. What happened was much closer to the deflation that Rist forecast than to the central bank action that others advocated to prevent it.

The Postwar Gold Exchange Standard

The Genoa Conference of 1922 called for cooperative central bank action to maintain the value of gold at its current purchasing power level. It proposed that gold centers, then understood as London and New York, should hold some gold reserves and maintain convertibility of their currencies into gold. Other participating countries might hold a large portion or all of their reserves in the form of foreign exchange. Resolution 9 was vague about the extent to which gold center countries, too, should hold reserves in foreign exchange.[1] Hawtrey, the dominant British economist at Genoa, indicated subsequently that he had in mind that gold centers should supplement their reserves with foreign exchange — so as to economize further in use of the world's monetary gold.[2] He noted carefully that exchange reserves should increase only to a point consistent with price stability and were not to become an engine of reserve-backed currency inflation. The gold exchange standard should not become "too effective" in the economization of gold.[3] Years later, in 1928, the Executive Consultative Committee of the League of Nations adopted a resolution that called for avoidance of "undue fluctuations" in the purchasing power of gold.[4] This essentially upheld the Genoa Conference conclusions.

The Genoa resolutions were short on diplomatic support from the beginning. They were put through by an influential British delegation. The French delegation carried little clout, and the United States did not attend the conference. French officials came to view the resolutions both as a British power play and as inflationary. They and Belgian central bankers were inclined to reject a system that designated pounds and dollars as gold equivalents but denied this status to other currencies.[5] The postinflation Reichsbank began replacing exchange reserves with gold as early as 1925.

Strong said that America had enough gold to support a worldwide gold standard, if distributed properly. (Strong ignored Hawtrey's claim that gold was undervalued relative to historic levels.) Strong's argument for U.S. leadership was at variance with another position he often advanced, namely, that a gold standard should operate automatically; interference in the gold market, he thought, would introduce speculative excesses. On this ground, he rejected central bank–managed price stabilization as a long-term objective.[6]

Still a third Strongian position was that the Federal Reserve was a *national* central bank and thus ought to place the furtherance of domestic stability and prosperity above international objectives. Shortly after the Genoa Conference he wrote to Governor Norman of the Bank of England, "The domestic functions of the bank of issue are paramount to everything (*sic*)." A few months later he added, "You may be sure that inflation has no charms which have not been examined by the Reserve Bank men and rejected as spurious."[7] But to conceive of the Federal Reserve as having a "paramount" domestic function contradicts both of Strong's other objectives: that the United States should assume a leadership role in distributing the world's limited gold stock and that the gold standard should be automatic. Domestic policy is necessarily subordinated to an automatic gold standard.[8] A working premise might be that Strong attempted to pursue all three goals and was repeatedly forced to compromise.

Strong also feared that as the main lender nation in a postwar world of borrowers, the United States might be isolated on every issue at an international conference.[9] In fact, U.S. policy was to avoid attendance at such conferences on the expectation that other countries would attempt to join war debts and reparations in negotiations. This would be unacceptable in American domestic politics, regardless of a central banker's wishes.

The United States nevertheless was to encourage European monetary recovery. In 1924, the Federal Reserve lowered interest rates, risking a new cycle of U.S. asset speculation, in order to assist European central banks in their efforts to increase gold reserves.[10] Strong concluded in 1928 that his bank's objective of bringing monetary reorganization to Europe had been met.[11] Cassel, too, believed that Federal Reserve policy succeeded into 1928, as evidenced by a stable general price index in the United States, with only mild wholesale price declines through 1928.[12]

In 1927 and 1928, as reserves flowed into France, Strong expressed concern and urged that the use of gold be economized. One mechanism for realizing this economy might be a reduction in the French gold reserve ratio.[13] Strong was also consistent in urging that American interest rates be monitored with regard to their effect upon European economies.[14] Finally, he argued that heavy transfer payments from Europe to the United States (connected with war debts) could depress European markets for years. He wanted to moderate these effects.[15] Friedman and Schwartz praise Strong as a central banker and find his death an important factor in the deflation and crisis that set in soon afterward.[16] Even Hawtrey praised him years later for his wise regulation of credit during the 1923–28 period.[17]

This praise is the reverse side of an important criticism: although Strong believed in the gold standard as an automatic system, under his direction it was carefully managed. Although he rejected the "real bills" doctrine (which restricted discounting of financial bills), a doctrine that was put to deflationary uses after his death, he used his influence on this issue only in private (see chapter 10). Strong handicapped his successor by refusing to acknowledge that the effective countering of systemic deflation might require more than tinkering.[18] He objected to participation in any commission that might advance "the views of Keynes, Cassel and Fisher regarding an impending world shortage of gold and the necessity of stabilizing the price level." In 1928 he offered the view that maintaining a stable domestic price level had probably been a mistake, as it had led to wild speculation in New York stocks.[19] He had also by then joined forces with those challenging the legitimacy of the gold exchange standard.[20]

At his death, the only automatic force was deflation, which would restore the historic price relation between gold and other commodities. The Genoa framework came to be seen as an arrangement transitory to a full gold standard. This attitude was reinforced by new central bank statutes in Austria, Germany, and Hungary, worked out in conjunction with the League of Nations, that permitted direct convertibility of notes into gold. The German Bank Law of 1924 even limited the amount of foreign exchange that the Reichsbank might include in its minimum reserves.[21]

The Genoa resolutions also encouraged restoration of convertibility at levels below prewar gold parity.[22] The goal was to avoid domestic deflation as part of financial reconstruction. But whereas other countries resisted the call for gold economization and central bank cooperation, Britain was most prominent in choosing deflation to restore prewar parity. The effort to raise the external value of the pound would leave sterling prices with a protracted downward bias. This decision left British monetary needs at odds with those of other countries, especially France's. British policy demanded external price stability or even inflation so as to ease conditions at home; France, in later undervaluing the franc, would actually welcome some systemic deflation as a check to an upward adjustment of home prices.

The United States set international monetary cooperation as a policy priority only where it did not greatly conflict with its two other goals, thus undermining one support of the Genoa framework. Britain undermined another by not adjusting prewar parity. France eventually toppled a third by deliberate undervaluation followed by refusal to treat sterling as an official reserve. These actions were a formula for systemic breakdown.

Gold Reserve Ratios in the 1920s

Another development in the 1920s that contributed to systemic inflexibility was the percentage reserve system adopted by most central banks on resumption of convertibility. The percentage system required that a fixed ratio be maintained or exceeded between reserves and the note issue and (sometimes) sight deposits at central banks. Alternatives were the fixed fiduciary system, which permitted a specified note issue beyond the amount of reserves, and the fixed maximum system, which limited the total note issue regardless of the amount of central bank reserves. Both alternative systems were more widely used before World War I; they typically required fewer reserves and left more discretion to central bank management, particularly when the level of reserves declined rapidly. They were also flexible in practice because allegedly fixed levels could be changed by new legislation. The Bank of England continued to use a fixed fiduciary system after the war. However, the Bank of France, which had used a fixed maximum, switched to the percentage cover system in 1928. The Reichsbank's policy was to maintain gold reserves equal to at least 40 percent of its portfolio after 1925, whereas the actual levels during 1891–1914 had varied from 32 percent to 39 percent.[23] A League of Nations study in 1930 confirmed this as an international trend; legal reserve requirements were typically higher in 1928 than before the war.[24]

Meanwhile, the worldwide percentage level of official gold reserve cover against notes and central bank sight liabilities declined from 48 percent to 41 percent between 1913 and 1928.[25] If one sets these levels against typical legal requirements in the 30–35 percent range (a problematic hypothesis because cover requirements varied greatly), then the free reserve ratio was nearly halved over this period. If this estimate for the generally higher reserve requirements in the 1920s is adjusted, the proportionate reduction of central bank cushion was yet greater. In late 1928, only 36 percent of the gold in the world's central bank stocks was excess, or beyond that needed to meet legal reserve requirements, slightly more than half of which was in the United States. Keynes estimated that, leaving aside the Federal Reserve, the free gold reserves of the central banks of the rest of the world were on average equivalent to only about 10 percent of their note and deposit liabilities.

I noted earlier that gold in circulation was often treated as a contingent central bank reserve prior to World War I; higher central bank reserve ratios during the 1920s to some extent compensated for the decline in circulating gold. If one includes circulating gold as part of the monetary substructure, then the international gold-to-money ratio (that is, the sum of gold in central bank reserves and in circulation divided by the sum of gold and notes in circulation and central bank sight deposits) declined from 84 percent in 1913 to 44 percent in 1928.[26]

Eichengreen nevertheless points to central bank reserve ratios in 1928 that were only moderately lower than those in 1913 as evidence that a shortage of gold was not a serious constraint on monetary policy during the 1920s.[27] However, even if gold-reserve-to-money ratios remain steady, this can as well reflect new compression on the side of bank deposits as continued ease in the availability of reserves. The *quantity* of reserves can influence money and credit conditions, which in turn affect output; higher (lower) output might then increase (reduce) the demand for money, which in turn lowers (raises) the overall reserve *ratio*. For example, monetary contraction might give impetus to higher demand for currency on the part of the public, perhaps for hoarding purposes.[28] Cash withdrawals would compress banking deposits, both at the central bank and in the private sector, and hence the aggregate ratio of gold to money (including sight deposits) would increase. This would occur in a manner conditioned by economic contraction. (Eichengreen's conclusion assumes opposite causality — that a stable or rising gold-reserve-to-money ratio demonstrates absence of a reserve constraint.)

In this vein, evidence from France over the period from 1820 through 1914 indicates that systemwide reserve (gold and silver bullion) ratios against M1 (defined to include notes and both central and private bank sight deposits) actually increased during periods of general price deflation and decreased during periods of price inflation. In 1825, during a period of mild deflation, the ratio was 44 percent. In 1864, following years of economic expansion after the gold discoveries in California and Australia, the ratio dropped to 27 percent; it fell further to 22 percent following the Franco-Prussian War. By 1885, during the long international deflation, the reserve ratio rose to 51 percent. In the years of relatively abundant gold reserves that followed, the ratio fell to 45 percent in 1907, and 35 percent in 1913. If one looks at the ratio of reserves to the narrower measure of central bank liabilities — as Eichengreen does in comparing 1913 and 1928—the pattern is more erratic. Even here, the reserve ratio trended generally upward from the Napoleonic Wars through 1838, downward from 1838 to 1871, and upward again from 1871 through 1903, following which it stabilized or moved slightly lower. In broad strokes, this ratio too moved in directions inverse to the level of currency-denominated prices. These data offer no support for the hypothesis that high reserve ratios reflect monetary ease.[29]

There is evidence that this prewar pattern recurred in the mid-1920s. As commodity price deflation gathered force, money-to-reserve multipliers contracted in Germany and France. Strong wrote of Germany in 1925,

> The monetary and credit system of Germany is such that the use of checks has almost disappeared and any expansion of credit by the Reichsbank will be accompanied by an expansion in its note issue. If the policy of the Reichsbank, as outlined by Dr. Schacht, is continued, and the ratio of its reserve should become greatly reduced because of expansion in its note issue, a continuance of his policy would require a still further rationing of credit in order to effect a reduction in the note issue to offset increases caused by loans of the Reich.[30]

Money had to remain tight in Germany to keep reserve ratios suitably high.

Developments in France soon afterward were parallel. From the time of the tax and currency reforms of 1926 through 1928, during the period of de jure stabilization, the economy-wide sight-deposits-(at both the central and private banks)-to-currency ratio rose from 0.85 to 1.17.[31] Greater willingness to hold deposits indicated growing confidence in French financial institutions, concomitant with the rising franc and stable prices. Hoarding of currency increased subsequently, perhaps in direct response to deflationary fears; the deposit-to-currency ratio fell again, to less than 1.00 in 1931.[32] Coincidentally, the French Monetary Law of 1928 exempted sight deposits in commercial banks from cover requirements, although gold reserves were required against deposits in the central bank; the Bank of France's gold rose from 39 percent of liabilities at the end of 1928 to 82 percent in 1932. This ratio would have moved yet higher had the earlier public proclivity to hold commercial bank deposits been maintained. The contraction of sight deposit totals in commercial banks meant that the ratio of gold reserves to total M1 (the broader measure of money) thus rose proportionately even more, from 22 percent to 49 percent.[33] As in Germany, a strong official reserve ratio was coincident with a growing preference for currency in place of deposits. The high reserve ratios appear indeed to reflect compression on the side of bank liabilities at least as much as ease in the availability of reserves.

Thus—paralleling the experience after the Napoleonic Wars and in the

1880s—stable money-to-gold ratios in the late 1920s in part reflected monetary constraint. The intensified use of currency in Germany and France in the late 1920s aggravated a reverse-Thornton effect internationally. Had aggregate income and broader measures of money been higher, while aggregate gold reserves were unchanged, then central bank gold ratios would have fallen to levels far below those of 1913. Rigid gold reserve management by central banks, often under legal requirement, did not permit such relaxation.

This issue sits at the heart of the conclusions of my book. If the gold shortage of the 1920s was the essential precondition for the 1929–32 deflation, then much recent literature is off target. Perhaps the central argument in Eichengreen's *Golden Fetters* is that the interwar gold standard failed because of lack of central bank cooperation, a situation with roots in the diplomatic tensions arising during and after World War I. He argues accordingly that reserve adequacy was not a constraint in the late 1920s, or at least was only slightly more constraining than it had been before 1914. Kindleberger similarly explains the breakdown of the world's monetary system in terms of economic diplomacy and passes very lightly over the issue of the supply of monetary gold.[34] Whereas Eichengreen proposes that the Great Depression occurred because of a lack of cooperation, Kindleberger stresses a lack of leadership.

For Cassel, by contrast, international cooperation was imperative during the 1920s because of the post–World War I gold shortage, which fundamentally changed the gold standard framework.[35] If one finds the postinflation reserve constraint to have been greatly aggravated, then the weight of my interpretation must shift away from the failure of central bank cooperation and other matters of high diplomacy and toward those of the systemic monetary framework and the use and absorption of reserves in particular countries.

Central Banks in the 1920s

Central banks and their governors played an unusually prominent role in the developments of the 1920s, a prominence not again approached until the 1970s and early 1980s, another period of monetary turmoil. In part, the turmoil of the 1920s reflected the aftermath of the wartime and postwar international inflations. But the instability was also the result of inept analysis and banking decisions in one country after another. Monetary instability in turn threw more power into the laps of central banks, which were expected to restore order.

I have already mentioned the Federal Reserve's postwar neglect of the undervaluation of gold, which created the framework for a systemic deflation.

The Bank of England and the Reichsbank subsequently took actions that added local deflations to the systemic deflation. Instead of stabilizing the pound against the dollar at the exchange level reached in 1923 or 1924, the Bank of England forced the pound up to the prewar dollar parity of $4.86 per pound. Basing themselves on an inaccurate understanding of the prewar gold standard, the British inferred that other central banks would not put Bank of England reserve ratios under pressure through undue accumulation of gold. However, French, German, and American monetary policies before 1914 were not responsive to international gold movements, and they would not become so after gold convertibility was restored during the 1920s (see chapter 2). Consequently, Bank of England reserves were usually under pressure after 1925, hence domestic bank-rate policy moved to centerstage in economic discussions.

Hjalmar Schacht was appointed president of the Reichsbank in December 1923 in the aftermath of a calamitous hyperinflation. Paradoxically, in view of his later connections with German right-wing nationalists, Schacht was appointed with the support of Foreign Minister Gustav Stresemann and with the active encouragement of Norman and other foreign central bankers.[36] The Dawes Plan of 1924 placed restrictions upon the Reichsbank, forcing it to keep its reserve ratios high and its discount rate firm in times of pressure against the new reichsmark. Bolstered by the new Bank Law, Schacht set the Reichsbank on a path that was often at loggerheads with the Treasury. One of his important initiatives was to implement restrictive discounting, which was demanded in principle in the 1924 statute.[37] This marked a reversal from prewar Reichsbank practice, in which discounting policy was directed toward stabilizing internal gold flows; the macroeconomic impact of prewar Reichsbank policy was usually countercyclical. The new restrictions would be used to particular procyclical—and deflationary—effect by Schacht's successor, Hans Luther, in 1930 and 1931 (see chapter 6).

The domestic popularity and prestige of the Bank of France were high after World War I. The emotional desire among much of the population to restore the status quo ante led naturally to support for a restoration of gold convertibility and a return to an earlier price level. Toward this end the François-Marsal Convention in 1920 between the Treasury and the Bank of France promised a liquidation of wartime and postwar bank advances to the government. The public myth that prewar prices might be restored made rigid the preexisting limits on circulation and advances. Rather than acknowledge that these limits were unsustainable, the bank and a succession of governments avowed their support for them ever more tenaciously. This reduced their public credibility and blocked solutions to the ever more acute French stagflation of 1924–26 (see chapter 5). French banking policy changed rapidly when Emile Moreau became governor of the Bank of France in the summer of 1926. His central bank soon replaced the Federal Reserve as the one with the greatest influence upon international prices.

My account deemphasizes the role of specific central bank governors—excepting Moreau, who reversed previous policy. Strong's role as the dominant figure at the Federal Reserve, especially regarding international policy, was already established through his leadership in arranging conferences with the Bank of England and the Bank of France in 1916.[38] There is no reason to believe that a different Federal Reserve leader would have taken action to adjust the dollar price of gold—or even that such action would have been a central banker's prerogative. Norman became governor of the Bank of England in 1921; but the decision to restore the prewar sterling/dollar (and sterling/gold) parity had been set in motion by the Cunliffe Committee *Report* of 1919 and was reinforced by the Bradbury Committee *Report* of 1924. Churchill at the Exchequer was genuinely puzzled about what the consequences of an overvalued pound might be, but he accepted the consensus.[39] The German return to gold after the hyperinflation occurred under international pressure. Schacht modified the German gold standard but did not change its integration into a deflationary systemic framework.

The key to the power of the central banks was in the international attachment to gold not as part of a reasoned economic doctrine, but as a public myth—indeed, as a fetish. Signals from the gold market, especially changes in gold's real price, production level, and nonmonetary demand, should be heeded. In the postwar climate, gold was not allowed to serve this regulatory function; consequently, these signals were ignored. Instead, the gold shortage was allowed to drive systemwide prices and production. The British psychoanalyst Ernest Jones wrote the following in 1917, before any prominent banker or economist anticipated the consequences of a postwar return to gold:

> Modern economists know that the idea of wealth means simply "a lien on future labor," and that any counters on earth could be used as a convenient emblem for it just as well as a "gold standard." Metal coins, however, and most of all gold, are unconscious symbols for excrement, the material from which most of our sense of possession, in infantile times, was derived. The ideas of possession and wealth, therefore, obstinately adhere to the idea of "money" and gold for definite psychological reasons, and people simply will not give up the "economist's fallacy" of confounding money with wealth. *This superstitious attitude will cost England in particular many sacrifices after the war, when efforts will probably be made at all costs to reintroduce a gold currency.*[40] [emphasis added]

Jones was most familiar with his native Britain. Parallel forecasts might have been offered for other countries. The Bank of France had the impact that it did upon world prices in the late 1920s because Moreau rejected the public revalorization myth — thereby releasing France from deflationary pressure in the short period — while tenaciously clinging to the view that the value of money derived from its attachment to gold.

5

The French Inflation, 1921–26

Price inflation often eased economic recovery and postwar reconstruction in the early 1920s. In a cross-country study, Eichengreen finds this connection especially pronounced when market participants, if anything, expected deflation as part of a return to prewar price levels.[1] He tests price shifts against the obvious alternative explanation, that high aggregate demand associated with reconstruction efforts (and independent of price changes) was the vital variable. He concludes that during 1921–27 "different price-level trends account for approximately twice as much of the [change in output] differential as differing reconstruction requirements."[2]

Eichengreen's study stops short of answering the more difficult question of when inflation facilitates growth in output and when it instead means only higher prices and paves the way for shifts in asset preferences. He does not, for example, attempt a statistical correlation between price inflation and output growth on a sequential basis within countries. He notes, however, that when rapid inflation continued in France and Italy in 1924–25, industrial production growth stopped in both; in view of the conclusions in his study, he terms this "perplexing."[3] Yet if one cannot account for the mid-decade stagflation, one's explanation of why some economies were susceptible to output contractions when deflation set in after 1928 will lack force.

Reconstruction in France

Eichengreen understates the role of postwar reconstruction in producing the high growth rate in measured output in France. From late 1921 through the end of 1922, the French industrial production index rose from 49 to 88 (1913 = 100).[4] This was by far the largest upward burst in his index during the years of his study. Yet 1922 saw stable French domestic retail prices and less than a 10 percent rise in general wholesale prices (including import prices) over the course of the year. This followed the 1920–21 deflation, which was perhaps the most abrupt in modern history.[5] On average, prices in 1922 were slightly below the level for 1921 and far below those of 1920; this growth spurt cannot be attributed to any balm of rising prices. Rather, the jump in the production index in 1922 came because three years of reconstruction were completed, which brought new capacity on-line. Reconstruction efforts were not measured as industrial output during 1919–21.[6]

Other evidence nevertheless supports the conclusion of the existence of a link between inflation and French economic growth in the early 1920s. The trend in Tobin's q indicates that profit expansion was somewhat more likely given conditions of general price inflation.[7] The following are annualized French index data for 1919–26:

	Stocks	WPI	Tobin's q	Ind Prod
1919	100	100	100	62
1920	123	143	86	66
1921	92	97	95	62
1922	97	92	105	88
1923	140	118	119	98
1924	169	137	123	113
1925	163	154	106	117
1926	190	197	96	120[8]

The Tobin's q data suggest that the sharp 1920–21 price decline generated only mild profit deflation, which is consistent with conclusions offered earlier for this period in the United States and Britain. Albert Sauvy notes,

> Never subsequently, not even during the Great Depression, did prices fall so rapidly. . . . Wholesale prices fell by 48 percent, a veritable collapse, which brought large losses, including bankruptcies, to agrarians and others. But the also sizeable decline in retail prices (from 20 percent to 30 percent, depending on the index used) gives rise to an important phenomenon: *despite its magni-*

tude, the price decline scarcely aroused public opinion. Households were
scarcely affected, and the press treated the decline with irony or indifference.[9]

A mild profit inflation, as measured by Tobin's q, began in 1922, gathered
strength through 1924, then faded in 1925 and 1926.[10] Evidence also suggests
that wages and salaries did not maintain pace with price increases, either
during the profit inflation or after 1924 (see table below). One consequence of
this inflation was to shift resources in favor of producers.[11]

Wages:	Average	Unskilled	WPI
February 1921	411	430	387
October 1924	478	504	510
October 1925	502	540	586
October 1926	584	612	772
(1913 = 100)			

Another redistributive consequence of the inflation involved debt. Old industries, which were usually large net debtors, benefited from its partial era-
sure. Newer industries, on the other hand, were hampered by the high (inflated) interest cost of new long-term debt. This led to a sharp increase in the
issue of corporate stock relative to bonds in 1924–25. The squeeze on newer
industry was aggravated after 1924 as, according to the trend of Tobin's q, the
real cost of raising equity capital also rose slightly.[12] Electricity, to cite a new
industry, was set back.[13]

The most evident losers in the French inflation were bondholders. At the
end of 1913, some 69 percent of the securities traded on the Paris Bourse were
fixed-interest debentures. An index of bond values shows a loss of 40 percent
of paper value and 91 percent of real value by 1926. During 1919–26 alone,
bonds lost 60 percent of their real value.[14] Holders of real estate often lost also
because values were depressed by unlapsed wartime rent controls. These controls were even strengthened to protect existing tenants in 1922 and 1923,
which nearly halted new building. Toward the end of the decade, the government undertook public housing construction.[15] Farm production appears not
to have benefited from the inflation, in part because agricultural price increases lagged behind those for manufactured goods. Keynes noted that peasant producers sold their output "much too cheap."[16] Growth of agricultural
output was slower than in either the United States or Britain.[17] Inflation-
induced losses on peasant bond holdings may have contributed to sluggishness
in this sector.

The French Stagflation after 1924

If one considers the groups that lost through the French inflation —
rentiers, workers, landlords, farmers — it comes as no surprise that industrial
producers gained. The 1922–24 profit inflation was a significant boon for
output and employment. (From the standpoint of employment security, workers also benefited.) During this period of high debt-overhang, deflation would
have hindered industrial recovery. The pertinent question is why, in this environment, producers did not gain *more*. This was a period of French recovery
but hardly of explosive profit or output growth.

THE THREAT OF NEW TAXES

One important factor inhibiting more rapid profit growth during this
period was the high level of marginal taxes. General taxes ran to as much as 60
percent at the margin on income, and the tax on corporate profits ranged from
46 percent to 77 percent before taxing of the remaining amount as income.
Marginal taxes on inheritances were as high as 55 percent.[18] Keynes wrote in
early 1926 that France was "one of the most heavily taxed countries in the
world."[19] In the United States, by contrast, income and other taxes were lowered repeatedly. By 1923, the top marginal tax rate on income in the United
States was only 23 percent. When Strong visited Governor Moreau in July
1926, he stressed that lower tax rates should be part of a French recovery
program.[20]

French public spending was high in the mid-1920s principally because of
outstanding war and reconstruction debt. By 1925 and 1926, debt service
accounted for 40–50 percent of government spending.[21] France faced a financial crisis in 1924, a consequence of the failure of the Ruhr occupation and the
realization that German reparation payments would remain insufficient to
solve the French budget problem. President Raymond Poincaré and the right-
leaning Bloc national–dominated legislature imposed a 20 percent increase on
nearly all taxes. This action aggravated the high-marginal-rate bias of the
French tax system, but it averted a capital levy.

The Bloc national was defeated by the Cartel des gauches in elections in May
1924; discontent over rising prices, the sinking franc, and new taxes played an
important role in the outcome.[22] The cartel was a loose grouping of Center and
Left parties that lacked a consensus on either fiscal or monetary policy. The
Socialist party, led by Léon Blum, refused to participate in the first cartel
ministry, which was headed by Edouard Herriot. Nevertheless, the cartel's
assumption of power implied a new threat of taxes punitive toward capital

and enterprise.[23] During a volatile all-night session in March 1925, the cartel-dominated Chamber of Deputies voted to remove the exemption on double taxation of foreign property and to double the tax rate on profits on venture capital and on the transfer of registered securities. A contemporary observer wrote, "These plans may indeed follow from admirable intentions and be made in response to real abuses. Their defect is their tendency to mix finance and politics, and to bring doctrinal disputes into the drafting of a law that should have the narrow object of assuring an adequate budget. Even in a rich country, this is the wrong way to legislate. In the current French situation, it is dangerous."[24] In July, the more conservative Senate accepted the double taxation on foreign property but rejected doubling of the other taxes. The tax controversy persisted, however, as did the tendency to "mix finance and politics."

Keynes generally favored a capital levy (on both enterprise and individual assets) to offset the redistributive effects of a wartime and postwar profit inflation. His argument had a political dimension, as he noted that unchecked war profiteering could have a corrosive effect on public legitimacy. He urged in January 1926, however, that the key to economic recovery in France lay in "coolly consider[ing] . . . how best to reduce the claims of the rentier." He advised against a capital levy in France — advice that Finance Minister Joseph Caillaux cited in support of his own view later that year.[25] Keynes had not yet presented his *Treatise* schema dividing price changes into profit and income components, but one might apply that framework post hoc. French rentiers certainly lost during the years through 1925, but Keynes thought it best that they should lose further, in order that agricultural and industrial producers might gain.[26] A French capital levy administered in a way that might spare small rentiers would have been for Keynes especially objectionable.

During the middle 1920s, the Socialist leader Blum, the leading advocate of a capital levy, was perhaps more closely aligned with small rentiers than with workers.[27] At least rhetorically, Blum viewed a capital levy as an alternative to inflation, which he opposed.[28] Blum asserted even that a capital levy might bring deflation — an assertion in which he was either confused or disingenuous; his conclusion neglected the effect that fears of new capital taxes had upon the franc exchange.[29] Socialist demands for a capital levy thus followed a logic almost opposite to that which Keynes advocated. More capital taxes would hurt producers and weaken confidence in the franc; this is the wrong medicine when the malady is income inflation or stagflation rather than excessive profit inflation.[30]

Even in the absence of a still-threatened capital levy, a state-appointed Committee of Experts drew the following conclusion about French taxes in 1926:

The nominal rate of 60 percent (with an additional premium of 25 percent for the unmarried), is in itself very high. Without doubt, the full amount is never paid because of a variety of deductions, but the high rate discourages savings and the spirit of initiative; it hinders capital formation; it encourages tax fraud and capital flight. The tax rate should be reduced: this would undoubtedly bring impressive results, including more honest declarations of income, and would gradually bring an increase in revenue. This has already been demonstrated in a variety of countries.[31]

Their report also argued that the high tax on profits discouraged savings and productive investment in favor of speculation.[32] Finally, the registration of government securities had similar effects: "The imposition of these formalities on small holders otherwise not liable for income taxes simply serves to damage the savings motive that is so necessary to France's economic recovery. [It] can only provoke the exportation of securities' holdings and capital."[33] The Committee of Experts pointed to a kind of Laffer Curve *avant la lettre* in its claim that lower tax rates on income and profits might, by increasing investment and transactions, yield more revenue.[34] Strong, in a meeting with Moreau and Rist the following month, indicated that reductions in the rate of direct taxation in the United States during the 1920s actually increased revenues.[35]

THE BANK OF FRANCE

The Bank of France conjointly fueled inflation during 1924–26. Bank regents, led by François de Wendel — who was also a steel magnate and a deputy — and Baron Edouard de Rothschild, dominated a weak governor, Georges Robineau, during 1920–26.[36] The regents demanded full revalorization of the franc and thought themselves uncompromising anti-inflationists, but the practical effect of their efforts was to obstruct exchange-rate management. They supported the François-Marsal Convention, which committed the Treasury to a gradual reimbursement of wartime and postwar bank advances. They opposed any increase in the legal ceiling on the issue of banknotes.[37] (France then had a fixed maximum.) Bank regents shared two postwar French public myths: first, that the franc could be restored to its prewar parity against sterling and the dollar; and second, that Germany would pay for postwar reconstruction. Further, monetary and fiscal matters aside, the regents, Wendel in particular, were associated with the political Right and were inclined to use banking issues to discredit the cartel, which they opposed on a broad range of diplomatic and social issues.

The magnitude of the French wartime and postwar inflation made restoration of prewar parity unrealistic. The franc fell to one-third of its 1914 dollar-parity value by 1920, recovered to one-half of parity in early 1922, then fell to

less than a quarter of its prewar par during an exchange crisis in early 1924. It
then recovered somewhat but fell steadily through 1925 and the first half of
1926.[38] The industrial retrenchment and high unemployment associated with
restoration of parity in Britain—where depreciation of the pound was much
less than the concurrent franc depreciation—offered further testimony against
a return to prewar franc parity. Furthermore, after the Ruhr occupation in
1923 failed to significantly increase net transfers from Germany, the cry "The
Hun will pay" demonstrably reflected wishful thinking.[39]

Two incidents highlight bank-inflicted damage. During the exchange crisis
of March 1924, the Bank of France borrowed $100 million from the Morgan
Bank and £5 million from a British syndicate in order to defend the franc.
Through the direct employment of the investment firm Lazard Frères to manage its foreign exchange intervention, the bank quickly brought the franc from
F123 per pound on March 8 to F84 per pound, which was then a level of
approximate purchasing power parity, by March 18. Lazard and Morgan then
urged the central bank to stabilize at this level by using francs to purchase
foreign exchange. The bank agreed in a halfhearted way to sell francs but did
so in a quantity insufficient to prevent the franc from rising further—to F63
per pound by April 23. At this point the market turned against the franc, and
Lazard urged the bank to let the franc fall at least to F80 per pound before
expending more foreign exchange in its defense. Instead, the bank expended
$30 million in recently realized foreign exchange profits by defending the
franc at F68 per pound well into May.[40] The bank's commitment to revalorization made it unwilling to buy foreign exchange at a level above prewar franc
parity, hence unwilling to stabilize.

As early as March 1924, demands for *bon* reimbursements forced the Treasury to turn again to the bank.[41] Governor Robineau publicly opposed any
increase in the ceiling on bank advances. The Treasury instead took advances
from commercial banks, which in turn quickly discounted their Treasury
IOUs at the Bank of France. These so-called indirect advances prevented technical violation of the legal limit on direct advances to the Treasury; but new
bank notes issued against the IOUs soon pushed against the legal circulation limit. In July 1924, Robineau formally notified Finance Minister Etienne
Clémentel that the bank would no longer discount Treasury IOUs and urged a
tax increase to balance the budget. On December 18, Robineau acknowledged
to the board of regents—which had until then been uninformed—that over
the past several months the bank's public statements of the total circulation
had been falsified.[42] When made public in April 1925, this revelation brought
down the Herriot-Clémentel ministry, and it damaged confidence in the policies and integrity of the central bank. Bon reimbursements increased over the

rest of the year, and currency issued against the bons led to an increase in the note circulation; fears of accelerating inflation heightened capital flight.

Pierre de Mouÿ, a permanent Treasury undersecretary, recommended a sharp break with the Bank of France's monetary management policies. In a report on June 27, 1924, he urged Herriot to tell the country the truth about France's financial and monetary situations: that German reparations would not balance the French budget and that denunciation of inflation would not roll back price increases that had already occurred. He proposed instead that the note and advance limits be raised and that the François-Marsal Convention be terminated.[43] Over a longer period, these changes would pave the way for stabilization of the franc at a realistic level. He recommended that the central bank be confronted publicly and directly: "I want to believe that the Bank of France will itself discover that it would be imprudent under current conditions to persevere in its deflationary policies. Those policies were conceived when it was possible to have hopes — which, unfortunately, have since been dashed — for the evolution of French finances. It will surely deduce that in assenting to now-inevitable modifications in the schedule of *bon* reimbursements . . . it will be able to help calm public opinion when these measures are announced."[44] De Mouÿ's views anticipated what the Committee of Experts would recommend two summers later.

Had the cartel embraced these views in 1924, the outcome of the French stabilization might have been quite different; but important figures within the cartel were no more realistic on the matter of inflation than was the Bank of France. For example, Herriot, Clémentel, and Robineau swore together on December 16, 1924, that each would resign before demanding an increase in the legal limit on circulation — at which point the limit had already been secretly violated![45] Blum wrote in July 1926, in language similar to Robineau's of 1924, "The mortal threat of inflation is only to be averted by acts of will and heroic resolution, by announcing: from this day, from this hour, not one more banknote will be printed by the central bank."[46] Blum also concurred with Robineau, as I have shown, in the view that the way to break the monetary impasse was through higher tax rates. The bank's insistence that ceilings be frozen and that the François-Marsal Convention be respected raised uncertainty about the liquidity of short-term government debt — hence increasing demands for reimbursements. Rather than confront this public mismanagement, as de Mouÿ recommended, the cartel compounded investor fears by repeated discussion of forced consolidation of short-term bons.[47] Much of the political motivation for the cartel's economic policies — doctrinaire deflationism and the threat of a capital levy — came from the power of rentiers. However, rentiers also held bons in large quantities, so the prospect of illiquid bons was a political nonstarter. By the time the Committee of Experts' *Report* appeared in July 1926, the cartel's public credibility was exhausted.

THE PARADE OF CARTEL MINISTRIES

The Herriot ministry rejected a capital levy but, as noted, fell in April 1925 following disclosure of secret advances and falsified records by the Bank of France. The disclosure further weakened Governor Robineau but strengthened the position of those regents who had been unaware of the doctored statements. The second cartel ministry, led by Paul Painlevé, was equally moderate but included the more experienced — and controversial — Caillaux as finance minister.[48] More left-leaning factions in the cartel were alienated by Caillaux's opposition to either a capital levy or a forced bon consolidation and by Painlevé's military response to a colonial rebellion in Morocco. Forces on the Right, led by Wendel, agreed to support Caillaux on financial issues so as to forestall formation of another Herriot, perhaps even a Herriot-Blum, ministry.[49] Goaded by Wendel, the Painlevé-Caillaux ministry proposed an exchange consolidation bond, indexed to sterling, in an effort to avoid a rush of reimbursements. Paired with this, the government sought an increase of F6 billion in the limit on advances. Herriot- and Blum-led forces in the cartel objected to the financial package both because it violated their doctrinaire views about blocking inflation and because it was offered as an alternative to their preferred capital levy. The package was nevertheless approved in the Chamber of Deputies on July 12, in a vote that split the Left and saw a majority of cartel deputies vote against the government.[50]

Subscriptions for the consolidation offer totaled less than F6 billion; the government had hoped for at least three times that much.[51] The issue failed largely because its yield was too low. The interest was more than one-and-a-half percentage points lower, for example, than the level at which short-term French government notes had been issued in Britain the previous year.[52]

The weakness of the response to the exchange bond rekindled interest in a capital levy and enabled the Left to regroup politically. In September, Caillaux sought to negotiate a war debt settlement with the United States, a step preliminary to the acquiring of another loan. Negotiations broke down in early October because of American opposition to a safeguard clause that would have tied French payment obligations to receipt of German reparations. The franc exchange fell, but the Bank of France refused advances to the Treasury for intervention against the pound.[53] The French Right was displeased with what it perceived as a threat to French independence in debt negotiations, and bank regents were especially disturbed that a debt agreement might restrict their freedom of action. It was no longer in their interest to cooperate with a cartel government. Meanwhile, a Herriot-led Radical-Socialist congress in October 1925 endorsed a capital levy, which brought down the Painlevé-Caillaux ministry. A second and more left-leaning Painlevé ministry followed, with Painlevé as his own finance minister. This ministry fell less than a month later after losing a vote on its proposal for a forced consolidation.[54] The following eight months saw four more cartel ministries and five finance ministers.[55] Most of the ferment centered on the budget, the sinking franc exchange, and the floating debt.

The turmoil generated capital flight. A Belgian bank issued a circular to its investment customers in late 1925 that was soon quoted in *Le Quotidien:* "Large and small French capitalists, you cannot place confidence in French credit; disorder is everywhere. . . . You must defend yourselves against the uncertain future, and Belgian banks are prepared to aid you in gathering your indispensable treasure for the difficult times ahead. However, to do this is not merely a prudent precaution but will be profitable in its own right: French taxes are heavy, while ours are comparatively light."[56] One might expect that with such a barrage of pressure against its currency, French monetary authorities would have attempted either to rein in the supply of francs or to raise domestic interest rates.

The Control of French Interest Rates

The Bank of France had limited influence on the domestic money market. The rate on three-month government bons, set at 4 percent in January 1923, was unchanged until July 31, 1926—despite the monetary and political precariousness of this three-and-a-half-year period.[57] Leffingwell drew the following consequence in June 1925: "France has adopted the perfectly untenable position of having a dear money policy at the Banque de France and a cheap money policy at the Treasury. This was bound to have precisely the effect it has had, namely of a falling off of renewals of Bons de la Defense Nationale and increased borrowing by the French Treasury from the Banque de France, with increased currency inflation."[58]

As I pointed out earlier, Caillaux's exchange bonds, issued a few weeks after Leffingwell wrote the above, also offered below-market interest rates. French bankers and financiers usually argued publicly, consistent with Leffingwell's taunt, that bons-holders were not interest-rate sensitive. But in a candid exchange the following year, the Federal Reserve official Robert Warren heard a different viewpoint:

The best man I met [at the Credit Lyonnais] was the head of their Portfolio Department, with whom I had a long and very enlightening conversation on the rate structure of the market. I asked him about the position of the Bons in the market. At first he took the position — the usual one here — that the floating debt floated on confidence *and not on its yield;* but when I quoted to him the 1923 report of the Credit Lyonnais itself, *which stated flatly that the floating debt would not float after the demand for commercial credit expanded,* he turned his position and agreed with me that that was just about what had happened during the last two years and was more or less what was happening now.[59] [emphasis added]

Rist had described the same phenomenon a few months earlier:

We persist in believing that the Treasury's problems can be easily resolved as soon as the budget is balanced or moves into a slight surplus, *provided only that the State offer its lenders a rate of interest that corresponds to actual market conditions.*

However, because *this has not heretofore been attempted,* the Treasury must now anticipate — beyond current budgetary outlays — that it will have to meet "massive" reimbursement demands, which, according to published data, will total around two-and-a-half billion francs in December.[60] [emphasis added]

When repayments on maturing bons exceeded renewals and new subscriptions, the Treasury turned to the central bank. During 1925 alone, bank advances to the Treasury rose from F27 billion to F41 billion, which nearly matched a F15 billion reduction in outstanding Treasury and Defense bons.[61] Three times during the year, the legal limits on both advances and the note circulation were increased.[62]

Treasury bon policy was stifled by the same public myths and political maneuvers that formed the backdrop for other aspects of French monetary policy. Higher bon rates, it was observed, would have raised the cost of debt service and thereby increased the budget deficit. With the ceilings mentality then prevalent in both the Bank of France and the cartel, this alone might have blocked rate adjustments. Leffingwell thought the politicization of monetary policy had driven out the best permanent Treasury officials, including de Mouÿ and his like-minded predecessor Jean Parmentier, hence demoralized those remaining.[63] I might emphasize that such a budgetary focus represented a false economy. An increase of, for example, 2 percent in the interest rate on bons would have added just more than F1 billion in the course of a year (the national total of bons stood at F57 billion in 1924) to the total of bank advances — in the event that all of the additional interest payment was financed in that manner.[64] This amount is trivial next to the above-mentioned rise in advances during 1924–26.

The French currency issue expanded by F13 billion, or 30 percent, and M1 (which also includes sight deposits) by F27 billion, or 34 percent, from the second quarter of 1924 to the second quarter of 1926.[65] At about the same time, the French wholesale price index rose by 70 percent, and the external value of the franc fell by about half.[66] The greater correlation between domestic prices and the franc exchange in part reflected price arbitrage — the impact of higher prices for imported goods on the domestic cost structure. It also reflected a common cause of both: declining confidence in the franc and a run on franc-denominated financial assets. The correlation between changes in the money supply and in the price level is less close here than a quantity theorist might anticipate; indeed, the French money supply grew approximately as fast in the years after the de facto stabilization of December 1926 as in the previous years of inflation and a declining franc.[67] The expansion in the currency issue between 1924 and 1926 nevertheless mattered because it signaled that the Bank of France had lost control over the French money market in the face of demands for reimbursements of Treasury bons.

Beginning in 1924, commercial banks could open interest-bearing deposits at the Treasury. This quickly became a popular option, in spite of the relatively low (2½ percent) interest paid, as it offered protection against forced bon consolidation. Deposit withdrawals — like bon reimbursements — could force the Treasury to the Bank of France, up to the limit of legal advances. The bank, however, was not authorized to undertake open-market sales to offset unwanted expansion of the money supply. The bank could induce contraction only by either raising its discount rate or protesting signatures presented for discount. In the face of the rapidly growing money supply occasioned by deposit withdrawals and bon reimbursements, discounting at the central bank became unnecessary.[68] Adjustment of the bank rate and protesting signatures — the usual central bank policy levers — thus lost effectiveness for controlling market interest rates. As the Treasury (through its bon rates) rather than the central bank effectively came to dominate money market conditions, short-term rates were steady or declining despite a dropping franc exchange and rising prices. An inflationary liquidity preference developed. (The confluence of rising prices with rising liquidity preference betokens the coexistence of income inflation and profit deflation.) Warren summarized of the French money market, "A threat of repudiation, a scramble for cash or something convertible into currency, a low rate on a type of paper convertible into currency at need, a high rate on any other kind of bank credit, and capital in the form of fixed interest securities unobtainable at any price." He also noted the possibility of a "bear" squeeze through a business downturn connected with a franc stabilization that might freeze payment on any but the shortest period Treasury paper.[69] This fear, too, encouraged liquid holdings.

Cash holdings of the four largest commercial banks nearly doubled from F1.6 billion in January 1924 to F3.1 billion at the end of 1925.[70] Growing liquidity preference drove the premium on illiquid instruments very high, so that rates on less liquid *reports* rose briefly to 8 percent in June and July of 1926 and to double-digit levels in September.[71] This suggests that the rising demand for liquidity raised the level of interest necessary to induce bonholders to forego reimbursement.

More often, however, market-determined rates for other short-term securities offered little indication of the level that might assure rollover of French government securities. During 1925 and the first few months of 1926, the rate on *reports* stayed below 5½ percent. On a number of occasions, the *report* rate actually fell below the 4 percent bon rate. For several months in 1926 the average commercial paper rate fell to the bon rate, and rates on high quality paper at times went still lower. Over this somewhat longer period, the problem was that *all* French short-period rates were too low, not that some were too low relative to others.[72] While bon rates were frozen, British treasury bill rates more than doubled from 2 percent in early 1923 to 5 percent at times in late 1925 and mid-1926.[73] The main effect of too-low French rates was capital flight, which in turn lowered the franc exchange. The preference for liquid financial instruments was complemented by a rush to tangibles and real estate as inflation hedges.[74] Only in 1926 did the low bon rates have the secondary effect of generating a dichotomized domestic rate structure.[75]

From another perspective, interest rates were a subordinate issue. Had the franc been stabilized earlier, sustainable French interest rates would have been closer to international averages. Nevertheless, the impression that the exchange level of the then-floating franc was independent of interest paid on government debt has persisted. Alessandro Prati, for example, cites contemporary French newspaper reports to demonstrate that fears of forced consolidation — rather than low interest rates — made investors reluctant to hold bons. He also notes contemporary reports that high rates offered on longer *rentes* actually encouraged fears of inflation, thereby diminishing investor confidence.[76] But this argument is circular. Had bon rates been high enough earlier, the pace of reimbursements would have slowed, and forced consolidation would not have become an issue. Similarly, the long-term rate on *rentes* was below the rate of domestic inflation from 1922 through much of 1926.[77] Had long-term rates been set at a margin above the expected rate of inflation, the demand for French bonds would have risen.

One's reasoning remains circular as long as management of the currency and management of the government debt are not coordinated. The central bank might prevent a decline in the exchange level of its currency only if its discount rate is effective in the market (or, alternatively, if it can undertake open-market sales). If Treasury rates are set without regard to market conditions, then the central bank loses control over interest rates and the exchange level alike. Even when the Treasury issues long-term bonds above the market level, it may signal either that it (perhaps under a future finance minister) will default directly or that it expects the central bank to inflate. Keynes wrote in early 1924, prior even to the journalistic accounts that Prati cites, that the French discount rate should be raised to probably 10 percent or even higher, "in view of the high rate of interest now available on [long-term] French government securities." Only in this way might the Treasury have supported the Bank of France's effort to regain control over a sinking franc.[78] In 1925 and 1926, furthermore, the weakness of the franc was caused by the pattern of the Treasury and the Bank of France working at cross-purposes. Given this pattern, bon rates were set too low during much of 1924 through 1926.

A closed-economy model of France in the middle 1920s would suggest that workers, bondholders, landlords, and farmers lost, while producers gained. But the French economy was not closed; in spite of legal restrictions, both banks and individuals exported capital.[79] The shift of resources to domestic producers was offset by a flight from French currency. The rush to liquidity raised the effective cost of capital. The flight from the franc brought exchange rate–driven uncertainties, which raised the cost of capital for new outlays. Both effects dampened domestic investment. French savings, including expatriated savings, now matched or exceeded French investment. The profit inflation was over.

Events abroad contributed to the capital outflow and changed the domestic consequences of the French inflation. Some of the movement away from France during 1924–26 was induced by high interest rates in countries in which stabilization was then under way, notably Britain and Germany (see chapter 8). This restricted demand outside of the stabilizing countries by siphoning away capital and savings; meanwhile, contraction in the stabilizing countries prevented offsetting demand growth from that quarter. France was able to avoid some of the consequences of the mid-1920s systemic deflation precisely by permitting its own inflation to continue.[80]

This inflationary solution is necessarily self-limiting. The higher external interest rates rise and the stronger the induced capital flow that results from it, the greater will be the drop in the exchange rate of the currency in which those rates are not matched. (This is comparable to the dynamic that forced U.S.

interest rates upward in the 1890s; high rates were then necessary to overcome investors' resistance in the face of concerns that bimetallism might be adopted with inflationary consequences — see chapter 1.) In France in the middle 1920s, the drop in exchange rates moved just ahead of domestic price increases. But France was spared the squeeze on debtors and the rise in bankruptcies common elsewhere. Industrial unemployment rates in France averaged 3 percent during 1924, 1925, and 1926, while concurrent rates in Britain were 10.3 percent, 11.3 percent, and 12.5 percent, and in Germany, 13.1 percent, 6.8 percent, and 18.0 percent.[81]

France suffered from the inflation in other ways. Exported capital is estimated at F10 billion in each of 1924 and 1925, and F17 billion in 1926, much higher than in previous years.[82] Tobin's q turned downward because the costs and risks of French investment rose relative to their returns. A consequence of this no-longer-benign inflation was a social crisis and a potential political collapse. Days before Poincaré formed a new ministry on July 23, 1926, Moreau wrote in his diary, "The franc is falling with alarming speed: the pound opened this morning at 220 francs, reached 234.50 before noon, and fell back to 225 at the stock exchange. The dollar is now worth 46.42 francs. By order of the administration of the P.T.T. [the Post, Telegraph and Telephone service] radio broadcasting of financial or commercial rates and prices has been forbidden until further notice. Crowds are demonstrating their hostility to the parliamentary regime. The situation is very serious."[83]

French policy changes beginning in 1926 under Poincaré would bring a coordinated interest rate policy, procapital tax reforms, approximate price stability domestically, and — notwithstanding the new international gold standard — a respite from systemic deflationary pressure. France was able to end its inflation without suffering the near-depression conditions that prevailed in some other countries.

Profit Inflation and Deflation Elsewhere

In his book on inflation during 1921–27, Eichengreen deliberately excluded the German hyperinflation, but elsewhere he adduces evidence that shows a pattern in Germany conceptually similar to that in France.[84] Tobin's q for Germany increased from the 55 to 70 range during the first half of 1920 to more than 140 by the end of 1921 (the level of January 1921 is base = 100).[85] In addition to its balmlike effect on real input costs, including debt servicing, the German inflation reduced the real tax burden on capital. The scope for appealing against tax assessments was broad, while actual payments were often deferred.[86] (German tax revenue during the hyperinflation fell far below government expenses, partly from a deliberate effort to undermine the reparation transfer mechanism.) Research has corroborated that this period of accelerating inflation saw unusual capital expansion. Gerd Hardach indicates that Germany's aggregate capital stock reached 90 percent of its prewar level by 1924, despite the loss of Alsace-Lorraine and Upper Silesia.[87] Claus-Dieter Krohne notes that the inflation dramatically shifted resources in favor of industrial investment.[88]

The boost from inflation ends when uncertainty comes to outweigh the redistributive effects of price increases. In Germany, this was subsequently reinforced by an inflation-induced liquidity preference in the form of a flight from the currency and domestic investment securities. By the end of 1922, Tobin's q in Germany had dropped to less than a quarter of its level at the end of 1921, indicating economy-wide profit deflation. Industrial unemployment rose from 1.5 percent in 1922 to 10.3 percent in 1923, the year of the hyperinflation.[89]

Britain saw moderate but fairly steady price declines after 1920, impelled by the decision to raise the value of sterling to its prewar parity. During 1921–26, only 1923 and 1924 saw small increases in the sterling wholesale price index. Because of rigidities in wage and interest costs, while many end-prices were set through international arbitrage, the price compression was concentrated in the profit term of the fundamental equation. Britain's annual rate of increase in industrial production trailed France's in five of six years during 1921–26.[90] British real interest rates began to rise in mid-1923 and stayed high through most of the decade.[91] The average rate of unemployment during 1924–29 was more than double that for 1899–1913.[92]

Norman insisted that there was little conflict between achieving an external goal for sterling and maintaining a desired level of domestic business activity. Several years later he somewhat modified his view in testimony: "I think that the disadvantages to the internal position are relatively small compared with the advantages to the external position."[93] Under questioning by Keynes, however, Norman acknowledged that raising the bank rate worked through the mechanism of curtailing domestic demand and employment and lowering prices.[94] He also observed that Britain's return to gold had become problematic after 1925 because France and Belgium stabilized their currencies at a level too low (that is, below purchasing power parity) relative to sterling.[95] Tobin's q in Britain rose only 20 percent from the 1926 level to its 1929 peak, during a period in which French and American levels would more than double.[96]

The chronic profit deflation in Britain during the 1920s aggravated diplomatic tensions between London and Paris. During much of the decade, French domestic demand was robust and unemployment was low. Even during the stagflation of late 1924 through the middle of 1926, the weakness in the French economy could only in part have been aided by more rigorous demand growth abroad; the external value of the franc was declining faster than the internal value, and exports were growing rapidly.[97] In contrast, the British economy faced chronic trade deficits and related monetary constraint. The strategy for restoring and maintaining sterling parity thus required vigorous demand growth abroad to absorb British exports; hence it needed a strong German economy.[98]

6

German and French Capital Inflows, 1924–31

Keynes distinguished between "spontaneous" and "induced" capital movements.[1] A spontaneous capital flow occurs because the marginal efficiency of capital is perceived as being higher in the receiving country. An induced capital flow, by contrast, is propelled by differential interest rates, independent of changes in the marginal efficiency of capital. (A third variant, not mentioned in the *Treatise on Money* — but which Keynes surely would have recognized — is a capital flow driven by concern for safety, for example, fear of principal loss through bankruptcies or confiscation. Such fears would drive capital flows at times during the 1920s and 1930s.) In an open-economy framework, an attempt to counteract the contractionary effect of an induced outflow through monetary expansion will bring reserve losses (given fixed exchange rates) or a decline in the value of the currency (under floating rates). A spontaneous outflow will have milder effects on domestic conditions in the capital-losing country insofar as it contributes to a systemwide increase in demand.

Induced capital inflows of themselves move the world economy in the direction of systemic profit deflation. When capital follows rising interest rates, the consequence is an increase in the open-market cost of capital without an offsetting increase in expected returns on capital. A related contraction of world credit follows as capital flows from economies with monetary environments of relative ease to those with relative constraint. This process can be reversed if monetary policy is subsequently relaxed in the capital-receiving country — hence ending the induced inflow. Systemic ease is also more likely to result if the capital-receiving country has an advanced banking system, as was the case during the interwar period in Britain and the United States, such that deposit-to-reserve ratios can expand rapidly. Expansion can then occur without further movement of capital or reserves.

The effect of a spontaneous capital movement upon world prices and credit depends on circumstances. If demand rises in the capital-receiving country without affecting demand in the capital-losing countries, then world demand — hence output and employment — should also increase. This can raise systemic demand and move the international economy in the direction of profit inflation. The increase in demand can be offset, however, if capital-losing countries raise interest rates to prevent reserve drain. Then the systemic effect of the spontaneous capital flow depends upon whether the demand expansion in the capital-receiving country is greater than the demand contraction in the capital-losing countries. If the capital-receiving country sterilizes its reserve inflow, so as to choke off domestic monetary expansion, this usually brings a contractionary reverse-Thornton effect. The conclusion is complicated by the relative credit-to-reserves ratios in the capital-receiving and capital-losing countries. If reserves flow from a high-leveraged to a lower-leveraged economy, partial sterilization of international reserves and systemic deflation may result even if the reserve-receiving economy maintains its traditional credit-to-reserve ratio.[2] On the other hand, if reserves follow a spontaneous movement to the economy with the higher credit-to-reserves ratio, systemic expansion is probable.

I have already discussed the induced capital inflow to Britain that occurred during and after the stabilization of sterling. The United States had a better-known capital inflow during 1928 and 1929, some portion of which was induced by high call money rates (see chapter 10). I want to look now at the induced capital flow to Germany during and after stabilization in 1924 and at the largely spontaneous flow to France after 1926. Both proved deflationary for the international economy.

The Induced Capital Flow to Germany, 1924–28

Germany absorbed capital (net) even as it paid reparations resulting from World War I. This fact has generated controversy and has given rise to the charge that the German economy thrived while others were constrained.[3] On a related matter, Temin and Schuker have written that German economic downturns after 1925 and 1928 were self-induced rather than a consequence of international credit contraction.[4]

INTEREST RATES AND NATIONAL ACCOUNTS

During 1924, 1925, 1927, and 1928, years of relative prosperity, Germany ran trade deficits ranging from RM1.3 billion to RM3.0 billion. During the near-depression year of 1926, when industrial unemployment averaged 18 percent, the trade surplus was a modest RM0.8 billion.[5] During 1929, another year of rising unemployment, the trade account was in balance; during the depression years of 1930 and 1931, German trade surpluses were RM1.6 billion and RM2.8 billion, respectively. Capital movements followed an approximately inverse pattern. If one excludes the amount paid out in reparations, the net capital inflows were RM2.6 billion, RM2.1 billion, minus RM0.6 billion, RM2.2 billion, and RM2.1 billion for 1924 through 1928, respectively. This net figure was in balance for 1929 and negative afterward; 1931 saw a massive net outflow of RM2.7 billion. The current account balance (including payments for services, interest, and reparations as well as merchandise trade) was negative every year except during 1924–30 and turned positive only in 1931. Germany nevertheless had significant net reserve inflows in 1924, 1926, and 1928, approximate balance in 1925, and only moderate outflows in 1927, 1929, and 1930. Not until 1931 did a large loss of reserves occur.[6]

Temin argues that the falls in German net capital imports were endogenous—they merely offset the declines in net merchandise imports.[7] However, his demonstration neglects the role of interest rates. Higher German rates—or, more specifically, a rise in interest rates relative to returns on capital—reduces domestic investment and lowers the trend of change in output and income. This in turn lowers German imports, which ceteris paribus stimulates a positive movement in the trade balance. But it merely reflects a bookkeeping identity that the current account balance is inversely related to combined capital and reserve flows. What affects the level of investment and income is the cost of foreign and domestic capital vis-à-vis expected returns, not the relative amount of each kind of capital invested. Why were German interest rates high in 1925 and again in 1928? This is the factor that drove net capital imports.

Temin makes no distinction between an induced capital inflow, which would indicate relative constraint in German money and capital markets, and a spontaneous inflow, which might indicate robust domestic demand. Because Germany in 1925–26 was in a near-depression, we know that demand was weak, hence that the capital inflow was not spontaneous. As the Dawes and private loans came on line, the Reichsbank discount rate was reduced to 9 percent in February 1925, a level then close to short-term domestic market rates.[8] The British gold standard restoration and the cyclical recovery of the American economy pushed discount rates up in both countries in early 1925. If German interest rates were high in order to restrain an induced outflow to London or New York, then constrained German credit conditions at least in part reflected systemic conditions.

International rates were pushed up again in 1928 and early 1929, directly by conditions on Wall Street and Federal Reserve discount rate policy and indirectly by the French Monetary Law of June 1928. Temin argues that a flow of capital from the German stock market to the American stock market need not have affected the level of investment in Germany.[9] He is surely correct that a shift of stock ownership from one country to another does not in itself involve an allocation of real resources.[10] Once again, however, he overlooks the effect of an induced capital outflow on German monetary reserves and hence on interest rates and credit conditions.[11] (In the previous chapter, I described the effects of an induced capital outflow on French investment during 1924–26.)

Schuker focuses on relative money stock and price inflation levels to argue that the German economy did not meet external constraint during the middle and late 1920s. He notes that, despite Schacht's public anti-inflationary rhetoric, the broad money supply grew at 16 percent annually from 1924 through 1930, and even high-powered money increased by 9.2 percent annually through 1927. He then cites evidence that German consumer prices rose (cumulatively) 8.5 percent between 1925 and 1929, while they fell by 2.3 percent in the United States. Meanwhile German wholesale prices were down by 3.2 percent, while U.S. wholesale prices dropped by 8.0 percent. German export prices fell by only 1.7 percent over the four years, compared with declines of 12.8 percent in the United States and 10.7 percent in industrial Europe as a whole.[12] Schuker cites other evidence to show that German wages rose quickly and that German spending on public works and social welfare was too high for an international borrower.

Schuker's conclusions from the record of German money stock growth in the 1920s overlook the legacy of hyperinflation. The restoration of stable money invariably leads to an increase in real money balances. The German experience occurred after similar increases in the money stocks of Austria and Hungary, which followed hyperinflations in those countries.[13] The same happened after de facto stabilization in France in 1926, even though the mid-1920s price increases there never approached hyperinflationary dimensions. M2 (a broad quantity measure) in France rose from F126.1 billion to F223.7

billion from the fourth quarter of 1926 through the fourth quarter of 1931, for a 12.1 percent annual growth rate. Currency in circulation rose by 8.6 percent annually over the same period, despite significant declines in wholesale price indexes and only slight increases in cost of living indicators over the five-year period.[14] One can deduce that the demand for money in Germany could rise greatly following stabilization even absent "inflationary" behavior on the part of the German banking system.

Similarly, the relative German price increases reveal little about economic conditions in Germany. The mark was stabilized at a low purchasing power level, particularly in relation to the level of sterling's stabilization the following year. Exchange rate–adjusted prices were also higher in the United States, Switzerland, the Netherlands, and the Scandinavian countries; prices were lower only in France and Belgium. Cassel noted that international price arbitrage should have brought relative German price increases following the stabilization of 1924.[15] By 1929, divergences between German and external prices were in fact much smaller.[16] The evidence above shows stronger divergence between German and other export price changes than appears in the broader domestic price indexes. This adds weight to the conclusion that crossnational arbitrage, rather than easy money, drove mid-Weimar German price increases.

The above illustrates that both cyclical downturns and price trends in the German economy were influenced by external factors. Temin and Schuker are nevertheless accurate in their sense that something about the German economy in particular was troubled. The essential problem was that the cost of capital was too high relative to returns on capital. For example, ten-year domestic paper of the highest quality produced an average pretax profit yield of 8.24 percent during 1925–29. Yet during the nearly parallel period 1926–29, the average reported pretax profit ratio (the income-to-book value of capital) of German corporations was only 5.67 percent. A mere four out of twenty-six industry groups saw returns on book value equal to the cost of long-term debt capital.[17]

These data are not entirely convincing. Coming after years of upheaval, including war and hyperinflation, corporate financial statements doubtless contained badly skewed estimates of equilibrium-level costs. Raw profit numbers themselves are no better than accounting decisions regarding which assets to depreciate and at what rate and which to record as current expense. However, the behavior of Tobin's q reinforces the conclusion that profits were generally anemic. It more than doubled from a near-depression low in early 1926 to April 1927 but fell steadily afterward.[18] Aggregate private sector investment figures also demonstrated weakness. The 1925–29 index average was 72, against a 1910–13 base of 100.[19] This suggests profit deflation. Additional evidence, less theoretical, is that the German unemployment rate for 1925–30 averaged about three times its level of 1904–12.[20]

DETERMINANTS OF HIGH GERMAN INTEREST RATES

German interest rates were high relative to international standards—notwithstanding the generally depressed domestic economy. Short-term rates were usually more than 3 percent higher than in New York; in 1925, the differential rose to more than 5 percent. German discount rates for 1924–30 averaged 273 basis points higher even than in London.[21] Extremely tight short-term money conditions brought frequent bankruptcies in Germany in the middle 1920s.[22] German long-term rates in 1928 exceeded the international average by 64 percent.[23] An important cause of the British profit deflation during the middle and late 1920s was that sterling was stabilized at too high a level. However, the German profit deflation cannot be explained in these terms, for the new mark was stabilized in 1924 at a level below international purchasing power parity.

One reason for high German interest rates was the postinflation demand for restoration of real balances. The banking system was weakened by the hyperinflation; banks, as creditors, saw their resources depleted.[24] Enterprises, in the aggregate, also suffered a shortage of working capital. The rush to tangibles during the hyperinflation turned to a rush for liquidity following stabilization.[25] Another reason was Germany's postwar current account deficit. An essential cause of this deficit was the decline of German manufacturing and invisible exports as a result of expropriations under the Treaty of Versailles.[26] Had the demand for imports in other countries risen proportionately to their new resources, German exports in time might have recovered. But the demand shortfall was made rigid by protectionist measures in France, in the successor states of the former Hapsburg Empire in Central Europe, in the United States with passage of the Fordney-McCumber tariff in 1922, and through a variety of actions in the British Commonwealth.[27] Rist noted in 1923 that French imports actually declined in real terms from their prewar level and wrote of "the opposition between our rigorously protectionist commercial policy, and the notion inherent in reparations that foreign merchandise shall enter France unpurchased."[28] By the end of the decade, Britain, the United States, and France would adopt restrictive monetary policies, which again blocked any systemic increase in demand for German exports.

Reparation obligations separately drove German interest rates further upward. Transfer payments added from 7 to 12 percent to consolidated government expenditures during 1925–30.[29] The contractionary effect was reinforced by the Dawes Plan. The point of the plan's "transfer protection" was to protect the gold standard in Germany, by high rates if necessary, and only incidentally to shelter the German economy from economic distress.[30] In one instance Parker Gilbert, the reparations agent, resisted efforts by the German government to diffuse the Reichsbank's control over borrowing conditions in 1925. He feared this would bring lower interest rates and thus reduce the inflow of hard currency needed to meet transfers. He thought an effort to do this "dangerously near" to the sort of maneuver prohibited by the Dawes Plan.[31] Formal testimony in Germany in the late 1920s also emphasized the link between reparations and high interest rates.[32]

In its effect upon national accounts, reparations forced adjustments identical in kind to those implicit in restoring liquid balances and in moving toward a positive trade balance. A key to all three adjustments was more savings — which might be achieved through higher interest rates. In the event, high German interest rates also attracted foreign savings to supplement domestic savings, which permitted both German savings and interest rates to move lower than otherwise. Indeed, the elastic response of foreign lenders to high German interest rates permitted domestic savings to remain at a low level through much of the decade.[33] German interest rates, however, remained relatively high.

In a more rapidly expanding world economy — perhaps one like that of 1896–1914 — the German requirement for higher savings might have been met more easily. However, systemic reserve constraint during the 1920s, which was aggravated by currency stabilizations and combined with the deliberate narrowing of foreign markets through protectionist measures, made it unlikely that both aggregate foreign demand for German imports and aggregate foreign savings might increase simultaneously. As it was, to bring savings — foreign or domestic — to a level sufficiently high to restore and maintain equilibrium in both the German goods and the money markets, while also financing reparations, put uncommon pressure on German interest rates. (The high German rates do not by themselves tell us which among the trade, illiquidity, and transfer factors had the largest effect.) When foreign lending slowed after 1928, higher domestic savings filled the gap, further damaging domestic consumption and employment.

Yet another factor driving up interest rates, although probably a minor one, was the effort by Reichsbank president Schacht to augment German reserves. The legal reserve minimum, including gold and foreign exchange, was 40 percent of the note issue. During the seventy-nine months between January 1925 and July 1931, the actual ratio fell below 50 percent during four months only and below 60 percent in seventeen months only. On its face, it appears there was room for ease, although one cannot know how much lower the Reichsbank discount rate might have been set without bringing a loss of reserves to below the legal minimum. In January 1927 the discount rate was lowered from 6 percent to 5 percent, and in January 1929 from 7 percent to 6½ percent; both moves were followed by rapid reserve losses. But these were not fair tests; in both cases independent factors reduced the inflow of long-term capital. (In early 1927, foreign bondholders' exemption from German taxation was suspended, and in early 1929 the net American capital outflow largely stopped because of both the soaring stock market and high call rates at home.) Reichsbank reserves might under these circumstances have come under pressure even in the absence of discount rate changes.[34] German short-term rates might have been lowered somewhat without major reserve loses, but the Reichsbank's freedom of maneuver was surely limited.

DETERMINANTS OF LOW CAPITAL EFFICIENCY IN GERMANY

Although German interest rates were unusually high during these years, other factors lowered the efficiency of invested capital. Rising wages played a role. Per capita real earnings data show a 16 percent increase in Germany from 1925 to 1929, during which time the same measure rose by no more than 5 percent in France, Britain, or the United States.[35] Schuker's figures show relative rises in German labor costs and declines in the average number of hours worked compared with 1913. Knut Borchardt shows an economy-wide 24 percent increase in real wages from 1913 to 1928. Unit wages declined in Britain and the United States but actually rose in Germany.[36] Wage increases probably reflected the political power of labor during the middle Weimar years. By 1925, some 75 percent of labor disputes went to Labor Ministry arbitration, and in 83 percent of cases the union side requested that the ruling be compulsory.[37]

Nevertheless, one should hesitate to hold labor responsible for the weakness of the Weimar economy in the midtwenties. Carl-Ludwig Holtfrerich argues, contrary to the implication above, that unit wages in Germany in fact declined from 1913 to 1928.[38] Heinrich Auguste Winkler agrees with Theodore Balderston and Schuker that German real wages increased but offers evidence that German national income per head was significantly lower in 1928 than in 1913.[39] A rise in labor's share of national product may be symptomatic of general weakness in investment and output, rather than evidence that too large a share for labor is the source of the weakness. Real wages are relatively high at the trough of cyclical downturns; and the portion of German national income going to labor reached a historic peak in 1932.[40] The issue of Weimar-era wages stirs passion to this day; however, relatively little is at stake regarding one's understanding of the international economy in the 1920s. Complementary explanations for the troubled Weimar economy are close at hand.

Agriculture received enormous direct and indirect subventions from the state during much of the Weimar period. The Rentenbank often guaranteed both international and domestic loans to agriculturists. Agricultural producer prices in Germany declined by nearly 15 percent during 1925–30, in spite of widespread protectionist tariffs. In these circumstances, and with the high cost of capital in Germany, few agricultural investments were remunerative.[41] Yet by the end of 1928, German agriculture had borrowed about RM7.5 billion, of which the minister of agriculture estimated that 80 percent was used unproductively. By late 1930, short-term agricultural debts exceeded those of German cities and the Reich combined.[42] Those in agriculture were usually hostile to Weimar's democratic institutions and to industrialization generally. One-third of the German working population was employed in agriculture, hence their political acquiescence was indispensable.[43]

Still another cause of misallocation of resources, hence of anemic aggregate returns on capital, was the growing cartelization of German business during the 1920s. Vertical integration was common even before the war, but horizontal integration was adopted to protect market shares and profit margins in the face of international price declines that appeared in 1925. This movement met little political opposition in Weimar. The Marxian economist and Socialist party leader Rudolf Hilferding embraced the concentration of capital as a "historic necessity," a step along the way from anarchistic capitalism to "democratically organized commerce."[44] But (unfortunately for Hilferding's argument) as the German economy was a part of an "unorganized" world economy, the effort to organize it slowed adjustments of prices and output.[45]

William McNeil argues that "the Weimar Republic led the way toward a modern welfare capitalism backed by a powerful and interventionist government."[46] Schuker notes that Weimar Germany's social welfare benefits were rivaled during the 1920s only in Britain, while its municipal amenities "commanded the wonder of the world."[47] Gilbert reported in 1927 that public sector largess distorted development by directing limited capital away from private sector investment and raising the market cost of borrowing.[48] This effect was reinforced as higher interest rates perversely favored public expansion at the expense of the private sector, by making public credit more attractive on the international market. Bertil Ohlin noted in 1928, "Thanks to the old debt having disappeared as a result of the collapse of the mark, the municipalities, for instance, are now in possession of a considerable unused tax-power and have no difficulty in finding the wherewithal to pay interest and amortization in even very substantial fresh loans."[49]

Aside from the resources directly absorbed in social welfare spending, the German tax structure depressed returns on capital. Germany had higher marginal personal and corporate rates than Britain, the United States, or France during the late 1920s.[50] The Reichsbank called, unsuccessfully, for replacing taxes on inheritances and capital gains with consumption taxes to stimulate savings and investment.[51] A conference of economic and financial leaders called for income tax cuts to increase capital formation and discourage capital flight.[52]

It is instructive that this damaging spending and tax regime was introduced largely under right-leaning governments; it occurred defensively and reflected the political weakness of the state. Von Kreudener argues that without this commitment to social welfare the Weimar government lacked legitimacy.[53] Weimar needed the appearance of shared sacrifice among groups and classes; Finance Minister Heinrich Köhler was explicit about this in 1928.[54] The need for consensus aside, the cost of reparations, social welfare, and interest group subventions also increased revenue requirements. (Reparations would theoretically permit somewhat lower taxes, hence higher returns on capital, in receiving countries; on this probably unrealistic steady-state assumption, world income would have been unchanged.)

Germany's capital inflow, induced by high interest rates, was accompanied by a spontaneous capital outflow — inspired by high taxes, concern about a resurgence of inflation, and fear of social or political disruption. The modes of outflow ranged from big business's investment abroad to small farmers', artisans', and pensioners' savings packed in suitcases. During 1927–29, perhaps RM4–4.5 billion ($1–1.1 billion) left the country as flight capital.[55]

To summarize, Germany experienced a profit deflation during 1924–29, with most of its usual symptoms: a relatively high cost of capital, high taxes, and low returns on investment — and consequently, reduced outlays and persistent unemployment coupled with rising real wages for those remaining employed. Prices, on the other hand, were fairly stable. Herein lies a cautionary tale for what is paradoxically called Keynesianism. Germany had an unusually heavy dose of government-led demand for goods and services during these years; the government budget was often in sizable deficit. Yet this did not end the profit deflation and may indeed have worsened it by shifting resources away from market-oriented producers.

German Alternatives after 1928

Keynes in the *Treatise on Money* proposed government pump-priming as a mechanism for escaping a deflationary open-market environment (see chapter 1). Prior to 1929, the German credit cycle was surely influenced by international monetary conditions. However, *sustained* profit deflation was geographically confined (inter alia, to Germany) rather than systemic. Action taken to isolate the German economy from systemic influences during 1924–29 would therefore have been misdirected.

What course of action might have succeeded during the middle years of the Weimar economy? The answer did not lie in easier monetary policy. German market rates were high partly owing to fears of inflation, which such a policy would have aggravated. Even a policy of mild price inflation, in order to relieve downward pressure on the profit term of the price equation, might not have been sustainable. From a strictly economic point of view a better strategy would have been to reduce government investments and transfer payments. Such a reduction might have shifted aggregate resources into profit margins, which in turn could have raised stock prices and private investment. But this was probably impractical, as it would have undermined the social welfare network and the group interest compromises at the center of the strategy to stabilize Weimar.[56]

Monetary policy became a more disturbing factor after 1928. Before 1914, Reichsbank policy was deliberately countercyclical (see chapter 3). In a response to the hyperinflation of the early 1920s, however, the German Bank Law of 1924 prohibited further Reichsbank advances to the Treasury. Open-market purchases of government securities were also prohibited. The law required high discount rates (5 percent and rising progressively) whenever reserves fell below 40 percent of the note issue. The restrictions hampered expansionary action by the Reichsbank during downturns. The binding quality of the Bank Law was reinforced during negotiations for the Young Plan in 1929 and 1930. (The discretionary instruments that remained available to the Reichsbank were setting rediscount rates and making qualitative and quantitative selections of commercial bills.)[57]

After the failure of the Austrian Creditanstalt in May 1931, German depositors grew wary, first of the security of bank assets and only later of the safety of the currency itself. Accordingly, the subsequent German bank crisis began with a *domestic* drain; Berlin banks, for example, lost 2.6 percent of their deposits in May, well before any withdrawal of foreign deposits. The weakest banks were not those with the highest ratios of foreign deposits. Foreign deposits comprised 66 percent of the total at the Berliner Handelsgesellschaft, yet it gained deposits during May from the Darmstädter Bank, the Disconto Gesellschaft, and the Commerzbank, whose foreign deposits were only 42, 43, and 44 percent of their totals.[58] In the early stages of the crisis, the 40 percent reserve limit on the note issue was threatened by internal hoarding, rather than by a cross-national movement of short-term money. The Reichsbank estimated in October 1931 that RM1 billion, about one-fifth of the currency notes in the country, had been withdrawn from active circulation.[59]

The Reichsbank, seemingly indifferent to the hoarding-induced deflation, then threatened to let banks fail as a warning against "inflationary" credit expansion.[60] Governors Harrison at the Federal Reserve and Norman at the Bank of England reinforced this message, demanding that Hans Luther, who succeeded Schacht as Reichsbank president in 1930, restrict private domestic credit in order to conquer fears of inflation and thereby diminish capital flight. Because Luther hoped to obtain loans from the American and British central banks, he heeded their demands. But his motives were complicated both by his personal belief in old-time deflationary medicine and by a German diplomatic strategy to demonstrate that reparation transfers brought disastrous economic consequences and should be suspended. Luther urged banks to ration credit, and the Reichsbank fortified this demand by asserting a procyclical agenda, one that restricted discounts even on commercial bills.[61] The idea was to spare legitimate business from high borrowing rates while punishing speculators — a formulation that denies a legitimate economic role to speculation. In early July 1931 the Dresdner Bank failed; the bank's management attributed the demise to the Reichsbank's failure to stand as lender of last resort.[62] This policy should be set against Bagehot's classic prescription: "The best way for the [central] Bank ... to deal with a drain arising from internal discredit is to lend freely. . . . A panic . . . is a species of neuralgia, and according to the rules of science you must not starve it. The holders of the cash reserve must be ready not only to keep it for their own liabilities, but to advance it most freely for the liabilities of others."[63] As it was, at points of crisis the German public demonstrated an inflation mentality. Precautionary orders for rolled steel surged after the Nazi party election advances of September 1930 and again after the banking crises of May and June 1931.[64] These were further destabilizing consequences of starving Bagehot's "neuralgia."

The foreign central bankers' demands rested in part upon overemphasis on the external drain vis-à-vis the internal drain.[65] Similarly, focus on the external drain led Luther and others to overrate the importance of a foreign loan. But even if their diagnosis had been correct, their deflationary medicine would have worsened matters. From Bagehot's classic formulation, again:

> We must look first to the foreign drain, and raise the rate of interest as high as may be necessary. Unless you can stop the foreign export, you cannot allay the domestic alarm. The [Central] Bank will get poorer and poorer, and its poverty will protect or renew the apprehension. And at the rate of interest so raised, the holders . . . of the final Bank reserve must lend freely. Very large

loans at very high rates are the best remedy for the worst malady of the money market when a foreign drain is added to a domestic drain.[66]

A more liberal discounting policy (perhaps at a penalty rate) might have contained the German banking crisis and hence prevented the rise in the currency-to-deposit ratio, the concomitant threat to the legal reserve ratio, and the external drain.

The sharp German downturn preceded the banking crisis; the industrial unemployment rate exceeded 22 percent in 1930.[67] When the world depression came in 1929, Germany (in theory) might have continued its government spending pattern of the middle Weimar years, with the modest goal of sheltering its domestic economy from aggravated systemic deflation, much as Keynes then proposed for Britain. Balderston indeed identifies the collapse of public fixed investment after 1928 as the "distinctive feature of the depression in Germany."[68] However, in the later years of Weimar Germany, government stimulus was foreclosed in practice because investors would no longer absorb Treasury securities.[69] Banks with large holdings of public sector debt were believed to be at risk.[70] If commercial banks nevertheless squeezed their commercial portfolios harder so as to make room for Treasury bills, the effect of the Reichsbank's private sector discount restrictions would be magnified.[71] It is plausible that a more accommodative rediscounting policy for commercial bills at the Reichsbank would have increased the banking sector's ability to digest government paper. However, because the Reichsbank was prevented by statute from either making advances to the Treasury or purchasing government paper, an expansive German public works program was foreclosed during the downturn.

President Herbert Hoover of the United States announced a one-year moratorium on intergovernmental payments on debt and reparations on June 20, 1931. On July 8, a political objective of his monetary stringency achieved, Luther reversed policy on commercial rediscounting; domestic bills in the Reichsbank's portfolio trebled within six months.[72] The switch came only after the Bank of International Settlements and three other major central banks extended a loan of $100 million to shore up the Reichsbank's reserve position. In 1932, the deposit-to-currency and deposit-to-reserve ratios rose — that is, liquidity preference declined. "Standstill agreements" negotiated in July 1931 and renewed the following year froze most foreign deposits in German banks. Exemptions in the agreements, however, permitted the withdrawal of more than RM4 billion in foreign deposits over the following fourteen months. Some of the decline in the German money supply occasioned by the outflows was offset by domestic monetary expansion; if foreign deposits alone had influenced the money supply, the nominal decline would have been 20 percent. With the domestic expansion, the decline was held to 12 percent. Harold James concludes, "The main factor in halting the decline of the money supply in 1931 was the increasing confidence of bank depositors and bank willingness to reduce the reserves that the banks had been forced to build up in the uncertainty of 1931."[73] A further mechanism to partially isolate the German economy was the negotiation of bilateral trade agreements. These are usually associated with the National Socialists during or after 1933 but in fact were initiated before Hitler came to power and before Schacht returned to the Reichsbank.[74] By most measures of production and output, the recovery began during 1932,[75] although unemployment continued to rise.[76]

A course of floating or formally devaluing the reichsmark would have sheltered Germany from systemic deflation — and in itself this might have helped to stabilize expectations. To succeed, the strategy would have required parallel guarantees against another independent Reichsbank inflation. After the banking crisis, Leffingwell suggested to his partners at the Morgan Bank that devaluing the reichsmark might be preferable to alternative outcomes. This contradicted the stance of fiscal rectitude with which Morgan was usually associated and suggests that a German devaluation might have found international support.[77] Calls within Germany for fiscal and monetary expansion were common during the second half of 1931 and 1932.[78] Whether such a course was politically practicable before the banking crisis of 1931 is hotly debated;[79] my narrower goal is to indicate what might have worked economically.

Isolation or partial isolation of the German economy would not, however, have ended the milder (and geographically limited) profit deflation of the 1924–28 period. Change in the earlier period would have required the sort of resource redistribution of which the Weimar state was probably incapable. A few years later, however, the National Socialist government set removal of labor bottlenecks — a legacy of the Weimar era's group compromises — as a high priority.[80] In 1933, unions were abolished and their assets incorporated into the régime-controlled German Labor Front. Similarly, the Nazi thrust against "interest slavery" resulted in controls over the cost and availability of credit. Sustained profit deflation can indeed bring political upheaval.

The German economy's aggregate credit-to-reserve ratio tended to be low, as its banking system was less developed than those of Britain and the United States. Yet while the potential credit superstructure per unit of reserves in the United States was greater than in Germany, much gold held at the American central bank was deliberately sterilized. On balance, gold flows to the Reichsbank during 1924–28 probably had little effect on the world economy's credit superstructure (see also chapter 7). After 1928, Germany lost gold reserves, in part from fears of monetary breakdown generated by the accelerating German deflation. A more liberal Reichsbank discounting practice, had it succeeded in stabilizing internal conditions, might have reduced capital flight. However, most of the *systemic* effects of a contraction induced in Germany could have been offset by expansionary policies undertaken in gold-receiving countries. In this broader context, Germany's role was largely passive.

The Spontaneous Capital Flow to France, 1926–31

A capital outflow can be reversed by generating an offsetting capital inflow, either an induced or a spontaneous one. There is evidence that France received both types of capital flows following the reforms of July and August 1926. The franc rose from a low point of more than 240 per pound in July 1926 to about 122 per pound in December, approximately the 124 per pound level at which de jure stabilization occurred in June 1928. The rate on three-month government bons was raised from 4 to 5 percent in August 1926, which set it briefly above the comparable British and American rates.[81] French long-term interest rates were much higher; Norman identified this as an important cause of the subsequent capital inflow.[82] Industrial production dropped to 107 in mid-1927, from a high of 128 in October 1926.[83] French industrial unemployment rose to 11 percent for 1927, the only year during the decade after 1922 for which the rate exceeded that in either Britain or Germany.[84] The slowdown in activity discouraged merchandise imports. The French contraction of 1926–27 induced an inflow of funds from abroad but without generating an increase in aggregate demand; hence it was (probably to a small extent) contractionary for the world economy.

From July 1926 until de jure stabilization, tens of billions of francs came to France, a large portion of them repatriated. This capital movement was in part similar to (although larger than) the speculative flow to Britain in anticipation of a higher pound in 1924. Parallel to the capital flow to France induced by higher rates and a rising currency, other French policy changes encouraged a spontaneous capital movement by increasing real returns on investment in France. Maximum marginal tax rates on income were reduced from 60 percent to 30 percent, and estate taxes were also reduced. A very moderate tax on capital was imposed, a once-and-for-all assessment of 7 percent on the first sale of real estate or a business; the threat of a more extensive capital levy was thereby removed. Indirect taxes, including user fees and customs duties, were raised in nominal terms, often by enough to roughly adjust upward for previous years of inflation. This generally shifted taxes toward middle-class consumers and small proprietors and away from capital formation. The tax changes were consistent with recommendations in the Committee of Experts' *Report* of the previous month but the opposite of what the Cartel des gauches had promised on taking power more than two years earlier.[85]

The fiscal reforms of 1926 are sometimes credited with solving the French budget problem, hence permitting subsequent economic growth.[86] Keynes and others argued more convincingly that the essential budget problem had been resolved by the French inflation of the early and middle years of the decade, which much reduced the real value of the government debt even before the arrival of the Poincaré ministry at the end of July 1926.[87] The inflation thus facilitated the transfer of resources from rentiers to producers. Government outlays as a portion of national income fell from 31 percent to 18 percent from 1922 to 1925; some of the decline reflects shrinkage of real debt service costs.[88] However, investment as a portion of national income rose but slightly during this period, from 13.9 to 15.2 percent. Only in 1928 did the investment rate rise substantially, to 18 percent. Over the period from 1925 to 1928 the portion of national income spent by the government nevertheless declined but modestly, approximately from 18 to 16 percent.[89] The budget reforms of 1926 scarcely affected these multiyear patterns. The data only awkwardly correlate either reduced government deficits or the decline in total government spending during 1922–25 with the investment spurt that began in 1928.[90]

The budget changes would have accomplished less without monetary reform. The French stabilization succeeded because it left the franc undervalued against most currencies, including the dollar and sterling. This released France from the monetary constraints that hampered economies elsewhere. The undervaluation of the franc persisted until at least late 1930.[91] Growth in French output during 1927–30 was robust, especially relative to other parts of the world.[92] Tobin's q in France reached two and a half times its 1926 level by early 1929, a much higher level than was reached during the inflationary growth years of 1923 and 1924.[93] During 1928–30, industrial unemployment in France averaged 3 percent. In Britain, in contrast, unemployment exceeded 10 percent during 1928 and 1929, then rose to 16.1 percent in 1930. In Germany, the comparable annual averages were 8.6 percent, 13.3 percent and 22.6 percent.[94]

At no point after 1926 were high short-term interest rates a factor in drawing capital to France — although from August through December of that year, higher short-term rates did contribute to the recovery of the franc.[95] French short-term rates were among the lowest in the world during most of the late 1920s. In January 1928, the Bank of France discount rate was reduced to 3½ percent, at which time the U.S. rate was raised to 4 percent, the Bank of England rate was at 4½ percent, and the Reichsbank at 7 percent. Subsequently, the Reichsbank rate was raised in steps to 7½ percent in April 1929, the U.S. rate to 6 percent in July, and the British rate to 6½ percent in September. In contrast, the Bank of France rate was steady at 3½ percent until January 1930, when it was reduced to 3 percent. In April 1930, the Federal Reserve lowered its discount rate to 3 percent, making this the first time in more than two years that the Bank of France rate was not alone as the lowest among the four major central banks. The next month, the French and American central banks lowered their discount rates to 2½ percent.[96] On December 24, 1930, the Federal Reserve lowered its discount rate to 2 percent; the Bank of France followed a week later. Only in May 1931 did the Federal Reserve reduce its rate to a level below what the Bank of France would match.[97]

The Bank of France wrote of "the easy terms" on which money was available in Paris in 1930.[98] During most of this period, private discount rates were even lower than the Bank of France rate; from the spring of 1930 on, they were much lower.[99] Relatively low French rates induced an outflow of short-term money after June 1928, particularly to London but also to other centers, including New York and Berlin.[100]

The two years from 1926 to 1928 saw an impressive change in the French bond market. In 1926 and 1927 French long-term rates were unusually high, which — as in Germany — reflected uncertainty about future inflation. In early 1927, for example, a fifteen-year, 6 percent government issue was sold discounted at 92. This was nevertheless an improvement over earlier flotation efforts; the Treasury noted with satisfaction that it was fully subscribed.[101] The international market for French government securities improved gradually during 1927.[102] Coincident with de jure stabilization in June 1928, the *Economist* reported a "widespread revival of [French] economic and industrial activity." Prior to this, the combination of high long-term interest rates, uncertainty about the currency, and various fiscal charges drove many enterprises to borrow short-term from commercial banks.[103] Almost within days of the adoption of the Monetary Law, a large postal and telephone development issue was quickly oversubscribed.[104] The volume of all long-term bonds issued on the French market more than doubled between January and October 1928, while the average yield fell from 7.25 percent to 6.30 percent.[105]

Improvement in the French bond market ran counter to developments elsewhere, further evidence of the spontaneous nature of this capital inflow. High quality bond prices declined in the United States after the first quarter of 1928, then continued downward through the third quarter of 1929. German bond prices declined through 1927, stabilized in 1928, then moved downward again in 1929. Total German flotations declined sharply in the second half of 1928 and did not recover the following year.[106] The movement of capital to

France in the late 1920s occurred despite relatively and absolutely declining short- and long-term domestic interest rates.

The French boom of 1927–30 was led by *domestic* investment; it was not export-driven. Investment rose from 14 percent of gross national product in 1927 to 21 percent in 1930. Investment grew in virtually all sectors of the economy, especially in 1928 and 1929. Yet export volume declined after 1928 and dropped in 1930 by a fifth relative to national product from a peak in 1927. The current account surplus fell from 3 percent of national product in 1926 to balance by 1930. The ratio of nontraded prices (that is, on goods produced and consumed only in the domestic market) to traded prices (that is, on goods traded internationally, regardless of where they were produced) rose by a third from 1926 through 1930, an indication of relative increase in domestic demand.[107] Particularly as world deflation began to accelerate after 1928, the French domestic market was sheltered by easy money, stable prices, and expanding demand.

Just as France escaped the stabilization-induced deflations of the middle 1920s by allowing the franc to drop, it escaped the early effects of the Great Depression a half-decade later because its central bank did not have to defend an overvalued currency. In 1924–26 the French economy grew less than it might have because of a tax system becoming punitive toward capital and fears that inflation would hurtle out of control. For a while after 1928, France thrived while the rest of the world economy deflated. Because the franc by then was tied through its new gold standard to world prices, while the latter were undergoing deflation, France was able to avoid inflationary consequences from its rapid growth in demand and output.

The impact of French stabilization and reforms was often misunderstood at the time. The view from the Bank of France was that de jure stabilization would bring an outflow of speculative capital and then of reserves.[108] The often insightful Leffingwell anticipated about the same.[109] The typical error was to explain the capital movement to France as being motivated mostly by the prospect of appreciation in the value of the franc. In fact, the induced capital movement to France was shifting to a spontaneous movement that would be sustained after de jure stabilization. The inflow of gold intensified after passage of the Monetary Law.

The investment-led rise in French demand spilled into demand for imports —which offered a way to recycle capital out of France again. The rise in French aggregate demand might through this channel have contributed to an increase in world demand. However, this potential boost was canceled by French sterilization of new reserves. This softened any rise in French prices, domestic demand, and imports. It forced other countries to react to France's spontaneous capital inflow as though it were *induced* by high long- or short-term interest rates. Hence capital-losing countries adopted contractionary monetary policies to avoid further reserve losses.

Appendix: The Reparations Controversy

German adjustment to reparations demands could be smooth only if foreign consumption expanded enough to absorb German exports and foreign savings increased enough to make up a shortfall in German liquid balances. In a steady-state analysis all of these adjustments would take place, presumably rapidly. However, Keynes, an "elasticity pessimist," repeatedly expressed doubt that the assumption of rapid adjustment was realistic. He wrote in 1929, for example,

> Historically, the volume of foreign investment has tended, I think, to adjust itself — at least to a certain extent — to the balance of trade, rather than the other way around, the former being the sensitive and the latter the insensitive factor. In the case of German Reparations, on the other hand, we are trying to fix the volume of foreign remittance and compel the balance of trade to adjust itself thereto. Those who see no difficulty in this — like those who saw no difficulty in Great Britain's return to the gold standard — are applying the theory of liquids to what is if not a solid, at least a sticky mass with strong internal resistances.[110]

Keynes's argument in the following year's *Treatise on Money* links his doubts about collecting reparations to the world deflation that by then had become evident. He noted that reduced consumption in Germany as a result of transfers might be matched by increased demand elsewhere "given an appropriate [that is, expansionary] credit policy in the receiving countries."[111]

Rueff, who was more committed to equilibrium models, objected to Keynes's metaphor that economic transfers involved a "sticky mass." He instead asserted "the principle of the conservation of purchasing power."[112] Rueff's argument is tantamount to asserting that the value of the second term of Keynes's fundamental equation never long departs from zero, a position he implicitly shares with many monetarists, rational expectationists, and others (see chapter 1).

Ohlin, Keynes's other opponent in the celebrated 1929 debate on the transfer mechanism — and, like Rueff, an "elasticity optimist" — acknowledged that trade rigidities might block adjustment. He wrote, "If the policy of protection and of preference to home-made goods, which has been growing so much after the war, is intensified when German exports begin to grow, and is used consistently to prevent such exports, then the reparation payments may become impossible."[113] Ohlin oddly failed to mention the possibility that sterilization and, hence, systemic monetary contraction might block adjustment. He then looked in the wrong place to find evidence of profit disequilibrium. He asked, "Is it not surprising that one has heard so little of transfer difficulties during the last five years, when one single country has had a net import of capital (over and above its own payments to other countries) of six or seven milliards of marks? That country is Germany."[114]

Etienne Mantoux eagerly embraced Ohlin's example in his influential response to Keynes nearly a generation later.[115] In spite of Ohlin's — and Mantoux's — implication, however, the direction of the flow of capital in itself tells us nothing about the presence or absence of equilibrium conditions. The relevant question concerns the effect of the flow of capital on output, employment, and interest rates in both the capital-losing and capital-receiving countries. Here the evidence (above) indicates that the German economy saw extended profit deflation — probably in part because of reparations demands. When foreigners loaned less to Germany, as occurred after 1928, a negative capital flow worsened this disequilibrium. Yet an initially positive German capital account balance also coexisted with a profit disequilibrium.

Mantoux noted that large transfers were made in reparation by France after the Franco-Prussian War and in loans by the United States during World War I. He observed that neither had damaging consequences for the transferor. However, both of these transfers occurred during periods of systemic adequacy of gold reserves, that is, each instance followed two decades of historically high real levels of gold production (see chapter 4).

A transfer-paying country must either save more than it invests domestically or procure savings from abroad. If foreign countries increase their savings so as to lend to the transfer-paying country, they must reduce either domestic investment or consumption. If foreigners invest or consume less, then their appetite for the transfer-paying country's trade exports decreases. A country can increase its own savings but cannot thereby increase systemwide savings. When systemic saving exceeds investment, a decline in spending results, followed by systemwide downward adjustment in investment and output. The only escape from this unpleasant arithmetic is through action that might raise the marginal efficiency of capital relative to the cost of capital, which would raise investment outlays and, hence, aggregate demand. The most obvious such action is taken through the banking system, in which expansion of the money supply reduces capital costs; taxes and regulatory, technological, and perhaps other kinds of changes, though, might independently shift the marginal efficiency of capital.

The German banking system, however, was tied to the international gold standard and could not affect systemic reserves or the systemic money stock, except very marginally. Mantoux cites Keynes's *General Theory* to the effect that it should be possible to increase consumption and savings simultaneously whenever excess capacity exists.[116] But Keynes offered that advice for a closed-economy framework, that is, for states in which the government does not have to worry about the central bank's reserve position.

7

The British and German Deflations, 1924–27

Keynes and others have focused attention on the British return to prewar parity in 1925 at the cost of sustained deflation. In the early 1920s, Keynes's emphasis was that a particular country — Britain — not be constrained in its internal banking policy by the vicissitudes of another country's monetary situation. In his *Tract on Monetary Reform* of 1923, he set maintaining of the stability of sterling prices as the primary goal of British monetary policy, while proposing that cooperation with the U.S. Federal Reserve be a secondary objective. He suggested that the Bank of England regulate, rather than peg, the price of gold in terms of sterling.[1] The idea was to avoid the rigid link with U.S. monetary trends that a gold standard would demand. The international slump of 1920–21 was fresh in his mind.[2] He could as well have mentioned volatility in the patterns of American demand for gold before World War I;[3] it was far from clear in the early 1920s that the recently established Federal Reserve System would convert the United States into a force for world monetary stability.

Keynes argued that by waiting for a dollar price inflation, sterling might return to prewar parity without domestic deflation. This would have brought a temporary respite; it would also leave the British economy exposed to further American-instigated inflation as well as to deflation on the downswing. His objection to reestablishing prewar sterling parity was in the context of a cyclical deflation and unemployment, as in Britain during the 1920s; he accurately forecast that a pound restored to par would leave British unit wages above international levels and bring a loss of export markets and protracted domestic unemployment.[4] Keynes did not then contemplate a thirties-style world depression involving a general collapse of prices, in which case even America might suffer profoundly.

Keynes omitted mention of the systemic undervaluation of gold following the wartime and postwar inflation, which would be aggravated by another American price inflation. This oversight reflected his repeated neglect of the importance of the price and supply of the world's gold. Keynes's view of the pre-1914 gold standard exaggerated the role of the banking system in generating profit inflations and deflations, while underestimating the importance of changes in the world's gold stock (see chapter 2). Had he instead taken the gold shortage seriously—as Rist would soon do in discussions on French stabilization—he would have noted the potential for protracted rather than merely cyclical deflation.[5] This would have strengthened his case against return to an overvalued $4.86 sterling parity.

The Resumption of Sterling Convertibility

The restoration of sterling parity added a local deflation to the systemic deflationary pressure arising from the postwar undervaluation of gold. But unlike the 1920–21 deflation, which had the salutary systemic effect of raising the commodity value of gold, the British deflation actually lowered it slightly. Lifting of the value of sterling against the dollar (and thereby against gold) made British goods more expensive in world markets and might through arbitrage have raised world prices somewhat.[6] To the same extent, it also reduced the commodity-exchange value of Britain's stock of gold reserves, which thereby somewhat reduced the real value of the world's gold reserve stock.[7] If one posits a constant world money-to-gold ratio, the British revaluation would force a small reduction in the world's money supply. Hence the immediate inflationary pressure of sterling's revaluation would be countered subsequently by its greater systemic deflationary influence.

Quantitative evidence for an initial inflationary effect from sterling's upward valuation is suggestive. Gold-equivalent wholesale prices rose by an average of 13 percent in Britain, France, Germany, and the United States from the end of 1923 to the end of 1924. Britain had the greatest increase, at 23 percent, which partly reflects a rise in the sterling exchange of nearly 10 percent over the same period. For this latter portion of the price increase, it is plausible that prices elsewhere were arbitraged upward by the rise in the exchange value of sterling.[8]

Short-term inflationary consequences of British policy were soon to be exceeded — as suggested above — by its systemic pressure in the opposite direction. During May–November 1924, the Federal Reserve deliberately eased credit conditions, thereby granting British policy-makers a temporary respite. The New York discount rate was lowered from 4.5 percent in April to 3.0 percent in August, while the Open Market Investment Committee called for liberal open-market operations. Nationwide demand deposits expanded at the fastest rate for any six-month period from 1924 to 1931.[9] But in early 1925 American banking policy turned more restrictive, which forced sterling rates upward. The U.S. discount rate was raised to 3.5 percent in March 1925. British government three-month bill rates rose from as low as 2 percent in 1922 and 1923 to more than 4 percent during most of 1925 and all of 1926, occasionally rising to nearly 5 percent.[10] As British domestic price indexes were generally flat or declining after 1924, this was an unusually high real rate. (German interest rates went even higher, but they were less important as regards international money market conditions.) Norman's extended policy was to keep the British bank rate high in order to protect the new sterling exchange.[11] His tactics were defensive — British gold reserves stayed in the $650–850 million range (less than 10 percent of the world's total) from 1925 through the first months of 1931.[12] High rates helped bring overvalued sterling prices down to the world level through the process of slowing British borrowing and lending.

High rates in London had three other effects. For countries already on the gold standard, they exerted upward pressure on interest rates beginning in perhaps mid-1924. This international impact of British rate changes mirrored in part the ability of the London money market to absorb short-term capital flows and in part the volume of international trade financed through sterling acceptances. This volume greatly exceeded that for dollar or franc financing.[13] Hawtrey noted, "If you examine the position of any one country you will immediately find a number of factors affecting industry in that particular country which are of greater immediate importance than the London discount rate. If you take the world as a whole you will find the London discount rate acquires a very special importance."[14] He concluded that the 1924–26 slump in world prices was due to the high Bank of England bank rate.[15]

Second, the British decision to revalue sterling reduced capital exports to the usually agricultural countries on the world's so-called periphery. Before 1914, Britain was the world's largest capital exporter. But the forcing of sterling upward aggravated Britain's postwar current account deficit, which had to be offset by a capital account surplus. One way to balance accounts was to raise interest rates. In November 1924, this was reinforced by an embargo on foreign lending in London.[16] The withdrawal of foreign lending to nonindustrial countries slowed their development, which in turn further reduced international demand for industrial products. Leffingwell wrote that the embargo tended "to retard the recovery of the world's trade in general, and British trade in particular."[17]

Third, high sterling rates gave impetus to funding crises in countries in which government borrowing rates were not adjusted to market conditions, for example, in France, Belgium, and Italy. Where the same countries also had floating exchange rates, a collapse in external purchasing power ensued, which caused accelerating national inflations. (This was marked in France and Belgium, less so in Italy.)[18] But external loss of purchasing power was more rapid than internal inflation. In these economies, gold would soon cease to be undervalued—the decline in a currency's external purchasing power would increase the domestic purchasing power of gold.[19]

Were these currencies to be restored to convertibility at this sharply devalued level, either they would require catch-up internal inflations to restore international purchasing power or the higher-priced gold standard countries would have to deflate. In the absence of the sterling appreciation and interest rate increases, the floating-rate countries might never have faced this dilemma on returning to the international gold standard. In the event, France and Belgium later restored convertibility at below purchasing-level parities and in the process aggravated systemic deflationary trends (see chapter 9). The overvaluation of sterling, high British rates, the undervaluation of floating currencies, and renewed world deflation were seamlessly linked.

Had sterling returned to convertibility at a devalued level to reflect purchasing power parity against the dollar, hence raising the real value of gold within the sterling area, Britain might have avoided the deflation associated with the return to prewar par. The British economy would have seen more growth and less unemployment in the 1920s. The systemic undervaluation of gold would have persisted but without the separate British contribution to it. On the other hand, had sterling been devalued to the point of undervaluation against the dollar, some American deflation might have occurred—until dollar and sterling prices were arbitraged to a new purchasing power parity. (This would have again raised the value of gold, much as the 1920–21 deflation did.) During an adjustment period, Britain might have seen a measure of monetary ease, coexistent with tighter conditions in and perhaps reserve losses by the United States. Deliberate undervaluation of sterling would have reduced somewhat the undervaluation of gold in Britain. Only a much greater undervaluation of sterling could have eliminated the undervaluation of gold within the sterling area, and then only by forcing systemic deflation in overvalued dollar prices.

Had sterling been undervalued, the Bank of England might have absorbed large amounts of gold reserves, thereby much increasing its policy discretion. A stronger Bank of England would have been in a position to offset deflationary impulses originating elsewhere. The eclipsing of the Bank of England's ability to influence systemic conditions must be judged the highest (although an indirect) cost of the overvaluation of sterling. This cost, or potential cost, seems not to have been discerned by anyone at the time.[20] The irony is that the restoration of sterling's prewar gold parity, which was intended to save London as the world's premier financial center, could be accomplished only through the restricting of capital movements and the weakening of the Bank of England.

But even in the revalued pound, weakness was not inevitable. In order to keep sterling at par after 1925 without greatly increasing the bank rate, the British counted on some American monetary accommodation and general acceptance of sterling as a gold substitute. They did not anticipate that a third country might devalue by four-fifths, leaving sterling again overvalued against a major currency, and that that country would finally refuse to accept pounds as a reserve.[21] American accommodation was fitful over the next few years. But French monetary policy would force outright deflation all over again.

The German Stabilization

At approximately the same time Britain was restoring parity, the Reichsbank enforced a restrictive monetary policy in Germany. The German Bank Law of 1924 required cover of at least 40 percent against notes in circulation; of this, at least 75 percent had to be in gold and as much as 25 percent might be in foreign exchange. Schacht then independently stiffened these requirements. At a central committee meeting at the Reichsbank in July 1925, he announced that the partial foreign exchange cover allowed by the Bank Law was merely an expedient, while in the future he would seek to hold all required reserves in gold.[22] The *Frankfurter Zeitung* immediately recognized this decision as a challenge to the gold exchange standard and to the stability of the international monetary system. The newspaper anticipated that "the conduct of the Reichsbank will stand as an example of the practice for central banks to follow when their currencies are similarly stabilized."[23] Undermining the gold exchange standard would aggravate the international reserve shortage and increase deflationary pressure. The newspaper suggested also that Schacht's decision, by making central bank cooperation more difficult, could jeopardize Germany's access to credit in the future.

From the end of 1924 to the end of 1928, German reserves rose from $491 million to $776 million, of which the share held in gold rose from 37 percent to 84 percent. Over this period, the Reichsbank's gold reserves rose from $181 million to $650 million, or from 2 percent to 6.5 percent of the world's total. German foreign exchange reserves correspondingly dropped from $310 million to $126 million during a time that aggregate Continental exchange holdings trebled.[24] In April 1928, Schacht again confirmed the Reichsbank's intention to adopt a pure gold standard.[25] This announcement preceded adoption of the similarly intended French Monetary Law by two months.

Schacht's reasoning was in large measure tied to his handling of the reparations question in domestic politics. He anticipated that, given large German borrowings abroad as well as sizable transfer obligations, pressure on the reichsmark at some point was nearly certain. Were this to come in the form of gold losses, Schacht would be in a stronger political position should he wish to take stringent action, whether to raise interest rates or to place controls on domestic borrowing. If, by contrast, the Reichsbank lost only foreign exchange (most likely sterling), his hand would be weaker.[26] A senior American official at the Office for Reparations Payments endorsed this logic and noted by analogy that the Bank of England would be more likely to endorse a contractionary policy if its gold — rather than merely American credit — was at risk.[27]

Schacht offered two narrower economic motives for accumulating gold reserves. As did Rist and other French economists, Schacht expected the gold exchange standard to collapse. In an interview in October 1925, he opined that the real price of gold was likely to rise in the future, hence it was wise to purchase it then rather than wait.[28] But another consideration was probably more important. Schacht believed that a higher gold reserve backing would increase confidence in the mark and thereby help to reduce German interest rates.[29] In the context of Germany's recent hyperinflation, this argument is not easily dismissed.

Germany's actual gold accumulation was nevertheless moderate, which reflected deliberate policy. In the October interview, Schacht indicated that the Reichsbank wanted to increase its holdings by only another RM100 million (less than $25 million), and he would prove consistent in this. In 1927, Schacht deliberately avoided taking in more gold, in spite of heavy foreign lending to Germany, by temporarily lowering the gold import point.[30] He also avoided buying foreign exchange. This left Germany short of reserves when foreign credits were reduced in 1928 and 1929.[31] One can identify two of Schacht's motives. First, he may have feared that a reserve inflow would produce inflation and more stock market speculation, which central bankers almost everywhere then sought to dampen. Second, and more important, a large cache of reserves would have made it harder for Germany to get reparation amounts revised downward.[32]

As was true of the British restoration of convertibility, the effect of German policy was to increase demand for monetary gold, while — by substituting gold for foreign exchange — reducing the supply available for the rest of the world economy. In the short period this somewhat tightened world monetary conditions, which made it more expensive for Germany to borrow internationally to meet transfer demands. Over a somewhat longer period, a policy undertaken for national advantage contributed to a worldwide deflation that would damage Germany as much as any country. By 1932, Germany's entire reserve base was exhausted — its economy would have benefited had foreign exchange reserves been widely accepted as a gold substitute.

In the absence of reparation demands the Reichsbank might have been willing to hold more reserves. Had the Reichsbank concentrated additional reserve holdings in gold, it would have aggravated the world's reserve shortage. But one should tread cautiously with counterfactuals. The gold-to-money ratio in Germany in the late 1920s already exceeded prewar levels (see chapter 4). In a calmer domestic and international environment, the Reichsbank might have held more of its reserves in the form of foreign exchange. Perhaps more to the point, absent reparations pressures, German interest rates would have been lower and the induced inflow of capital to Germany correspondingly less.

The Federal Reserve, the Bank of England, and World Prices

The British and German resumptions contributed immediately to a moderate world deflation. British prices turned downward in January 1925, a few months prior to resumption of convertibility in April. Cross-national data show that the downward turn in world prices was concentrated in the early months of 1925.[33] The wholesale price index in the United States dropped from 161 in February 1925 to 144 in April 1927.[34] The decline in international commodity prices that accelerated after 1925 is further evidence of deflation; a general world commodity price index fell by a third to 1928.[35]

Identification of causality in monetary history is often slippery. British and German actions had deflationary consequences but probably not irreparably so. Few doubted that the United States, with the Federal Reserve's enormous gold stock, had the capacity to offset local contractions and hence to control world prices in the middle years of the 1920s. The views of Cassel and Strong regarding this point have already been noted (see chapter 5). Keynes, too, viewed Federal Reserve management during 1923–28 as a triumph.[36] Ohlin wrote in 1927,

> The influx and efflux of gold in the United States has thus lost influence upon the monetary purchasing power and the price level in that country. The ques-

tion of granting credit is instead determined by what the Federal Reserve Board considers suitable from an economic point of view.

This implies nothing less than a revolution in the monetary system not only of the United States but of all countries with a gold standard. *The control of the development of the world price level has passed entirely into the hands of the Federal Reserve Board and Governors.*[37]

And at the beginning of 1929, Ohlin concluded,

The reason for the fall in prices since 1925 is probably to be ascribed largely to this gold policy of the European central banks following upon the restoration of the gold standard some years ago. This does not of course mean that the Federal Reserve System might not easily have been able, by means of a more liberal credit policy, to bring about a flow of gold to Europe such as would have made this restrictive credit policy superfluous and have prevented deflation. The responsibility for the unnecessarily restrictive policy thus lies primarily with the Board and banks of the Federal Reserve System.[38]

The newfound influence of the Federal Reserve was in some measure a result of the overvaluation of sterling in 1925. The pound went from its prewar position as a usually strong currency to a post-1925 position as chronically weak. Before 1914, the Bank of England could attract or lose gold by adjusting its discount rate with only mild consequences for domestic business conditions. This was an important stabilizing mechanism for the prewar gold standard (as I argued in chapter 2). The overvaluation of sterling from 1925 onward aggravated a domestic profit deflation, which made foreign investment relatively attractive to Britons. A spontaneous capital outflow combined with chronic British trade deficits left large quantities of sterling in foreign hands. Inducing of capital back to Britain thus required higher domestic interest rates than it did before the war.[39] It also left the Bank of England's reserves vulnerable to export in the case of any change in financial sentiment. Keynes noted in 1930 that British reserves were startlingly small.[40] The Bank of England was thus scarcely in a position to lower its discount rate so as to encourage systemic ease, even when on occasion it did receive new gold reserves.[41] Influence on the world's credit-to-gold ratio passed to the United States and later to France, where currencies and reserve positions were stronger.

A lower pound would have left the Bank of England in a position to attract gold more easily. It might thus have blocked or slowed the subsequent accumulation of gold in France and the United States, as either the franc or the dollar might then have been overvalued against sterling. However, the analogy to the period before World War I does not really fit. The prewar Bank of England performed a stabilizing function when this was fairly easy to do, during an era of adequate and expanding reserves. Such a role would be difficult for any central bank to assume during an extended period marked by an insufficient supply of gold. One can speculate that a stronger Bank of England might have slowed the rate of systemic deflation in the late 1920s and early 1930s, but it seems unlikely that this would have restored an environment so conducive to growth of employment and output as that of 1896–1914.

The 1925–28 deflation, the most obvious cause of which was the British and German resumptions of gold convertibility, was fairly mild. Economic conditions ranged from on-and-off recession in Britain and Germany to on-and-off boom in France and the United States. Stock markets were up almost everywhere, to differing degrees. Cassel argued that the stability following convertibility resumptions was an essential factor in restoring economic progress for the remaining years of the decade. International trade grew 20 percent during 1925–29, and world nonagricultural production went up by 25 percent. Even agricultural production grew by perhaps 6 percent.[42] Kindleberger concludes that the agricultural situation "was not so desperate that it could not have been rectified if prices had not collapsed in 1929, followed by the collapse of the banks and the money supply."[43] Something else had to happen to bring on the Great Depression.

The French Stabilization, 1926–28

During the years of a declining franc, from 1922 to July 1926, French capital was exported in bulk; capital holders sought relief from both inflation-sensitive French financial assets and French taxes.[1] Capital export took form in the purchase of non-French securities, loans of francs against foreign exchange, deposits in banks abroad, and investments of all varieties in Europe's financial centers. Much of this capital settled in London, almost without condition as to date of repayment or interest rates. This foreign demand for sterling eased otherwise tight British credit conditions and buoyed the pound. Leffingwell noted that because of the flight from the franc, "France, instead of competing with the others for gold and money, is thus contributing to easy money in other centers."[2] A Bank of France economist observed similarly a few years later,

> It appears to be almost certain today that this exportation of capital was probably the most powerful factor in the appreciation of the international value of sterling. . . . The last 20% in the depreciation of the pound, which, whatever be the position, are always the most difficult to reabsorb, only appeared to be child's play to the English Government and the Bank of England, nothing more in fact than a monetary parade in accompaniment of the merely nominal support of the American market.[3]

Just as some British observers, including Hawtrey and Keynes, hoped for American inflation to ease sterling's return to parity in the early 1920s, others now hoped for an appreciating franc to raise French gold-equivalent prices at least to a level of purchasing power parity with sterling. Were the franc to be stabilized at too low a level, the capital flow to London of 1924–26 might be replaced by a reverse flow to France.

Following the collapse of the currency in the summer of 1926, the external purchasing power of the franc was far under international parity, which introduced a theoretically unsustainable disequilibrium. As Keynes had explained a few months earlier, France had either (1) to let its currency rise until franc prices reached a level of international parity, or (2) to stabilize the franc at its current level, then permit an internal inflation to raise franc purchasing power to the world level. Keynes argued that a sharp revalorization of the franc would bring on a British-style stagnation, which might reduce tax revenues and throw the budget back into deficit. It would also wreak havoc with French export industries, an economic bright area during 1924–26, when the external value of the franc declined more rapidly than the internal value.[4]

Keynes suggested instead that the franc's external exchange be stabilized by committing the Bank of France's gold to its defense and that a rise in French domestic prices to the level of international parity be accepted as inevitable. The bank's gold reserve was worth roughly 40 percent of the note issue if its value were adjusted to the current exchange level. Keynes argued that investors would be more inclined to hold French bons in the event of a gold-backed stabilization, and thereby discourage the export of capital, if the franc's external value were guaranteed.[5] Keynes had previously stressed that the Treasury and the central bank must coordinate interest rate management in order to stabilize the franc successfully; however, he did not emphasize this in his articles of 1926.[6]

The suggestion that France commit its gold reserves to the stabilization of the franc drew support elsewhere. Leffingwell wrote,

> The plan for a gold currency . . . [is] intended to enable France to avail of the resources she already has in order to enable her to float at home in France the necessary loans to take care of her internal debt. . . . The whole point of the gold plan is to throw the vast resources of the Bank of France, some eight hundred million dollars of gold [at market value; book value — expressed in prewar franc-to-gold parity — was lower], into the scales, and use those resources freely if need be (and at first undoubtedly the necessity will arise) to support the new gold value of the franc. . . . The existing resources of the Bank

of France are so stupendous that they make any possible foreign loans or credits look trivial.[7]

The Bank of France's rigid advocacy of revalorization continued to block the use of gold for stabilization, and this was reinforced by the weakness of Cartel des gauches ministries. The combination of low interest rates and fears of forced consolidation brought reimbursement of the floating debt, hence more bank advances and higher note circulation. "Bracket creep" tax increases and threats of a capital levy further undermined confidence and hastened capital flight. The franc declined persistently from F94 per pound in May 1925 to F130 per pound in December, to F166 per pound in June 1926.[8]

The Committee of Experts

The Committee of Experts was appointed by Raoul Peret, the finance minister in the second Aristide Briand ministry of the cartel (Briand's tenth ministry, dating back to 1909), and met from late May through the beginning of July 1926. Peret was prodded by American bankers who wanted a portion of the Bank of France's gold as security for a new loan.[9] The idea for a Committee of Experts had been in the air for some time, however, and had been recommended in the *London Times* as early as November 1924.[10] The committee had thirteen members, including six private sector bankers (Moreau, then director general of the Banque d'Algérie, and Raymond Philippe among them), three representatives of industry, one current (Paul Ernest-Picard) and one former deputy governor of the Bank of France, and two professional economists (Rist and Gaston Jèze).[11] Ernest-Picard had limited influence with the other experts; indeed, the Bank of France was not consulted concerning appointment of the committee, and Wendel quickly forecast conflict between the regents and the experts.[12] Many on the committee were close politically to Caillaux, who returned as finance minister on June 23 in a third consecutive Briand cabinet.[13]

The experts, probably influenced by Keynes's argument, followed in the framework of de Mouÿ's report of June 27, 1924 — that is, they concluded that a domestic inflation should accompany a stabilized and devalued franc.[14] Their *Report*, issued on July 4, 1926, called for stabilization at a value low enough to avoid domestic deflation and the industrial crisis that might accompany it. The experts proposed that the bank buy and sell gold and foreign exchange at their current market prices, a veiled acknowledgment that prewar parity would not be restored. They indicated that expansion of the currency might be welcome if it were backed by international reserves, rather than by more central bank advances.[15] They suggested that bank advances to the Treasury be reimbursed slowly and that not all need be reimbursed, while those that were might be replaced by commercial advances and discounts: "The only problem is that of the gradual amortization of what remains of the advances to the State. The Committee believes that this reimbursement should continue at a slow pace, in order to gradually replace banknotes backed by a State credit with those backed by commercial credits."[16]

This qualified embrace of inflation was balanced with a call for a Fund for Debt Amortization and Management of National Defense Bons (hereafter, the Amortization Fund), one of whose duties was to adjust bon rates biweekly to reflect market conditions. The experts called for management of outstanding bons, not their complete consolidation into longer-dated issues; they intended also that shorter-dated securities would continue to be discountable at the Bank of France.[17]

The experts took direct aim at the taxation ideas of the Cartel des gauches. Contradicting the cartel's election platform of 1924, they endorsed increases in indirect taxes to balance the budget but recommended that this be combined with reductions in direct taxes to encourage repatriation of capital. They also called for eliminating bon registration, which had been introduced for tax records and collection, because it discouraged renewals and encouraged capital flight.[18] This change was intended to benefit small bon-holders, including rentiers. The experts further recommended that the bank undertake a foreign loan that would constitute a working balance for exchange operations. As a condition for loan approval, they indicated that the Assembly should ratify the Caillaux-Churchill and Mellon-Bérenger agreements in order to settle war debt issues with Great Britain and the United States.

The budget situation in itself was only a minor worry when the experts wrote. The budget deficit was enormous in the early part of the decade, but essential balance was reached by 1926. The ratio of internal public debt to net national product declined from 1.65 in 1920 to 1.14 in 1926.[19] The experts found the budget situation "in sum, satisfactory."[20] During 1925 the budget deficit was less than F5 billion, yet bank advances to the Treasury increased by 14 billion; most of the increase was driven by bon reimbursements.[21]

The arguments advanced by Keynes and the Committee of Experts in favor of domestic inflation and against a capital levy were nevertheless politically vulnerable. Debt-holders were well represented politically; some of the era's leading politicians, including Poincaré, Herriot, and Blum, were closely identified with them. Rentiers—those who had sunk their savings into support of the war effort—had already been large losers through inflation during the previous ten years. An economic solution would not come easily at their expense. Yet aside from the proposal to eliminate bon registration, the experts offered little to assuage rentier concerns.

On June 23, 1926, at the formation of the Briand-Caillaux ministry, the franc exchange stood at F169 per pound. The next day, Caillaux asked Moreau to replace Robineau at the Bank of France; within days, Moreau, his chosen under governor Rist, and a new director of economic research, Pierre Quesnay, were in place. Caillaux endorsed the experts' *Report* as the foundation of his economic policy on July 6.[22] He also endorsed ratification of the debt agreements and requested authorization to rule by decree through November. The Mellon-Bérenger Agreement with the United States was unpopular because it lacked a safeguard clause tying French transfer obligations to receipt of German reparation payments — a clause included in the parallel accord on British debt. (The United States would not accept a safeguard clause because of a long-standing public insistence that American war loan obligations were independent of other transfer obligations (see chapter 4). Caillaux remained suspect to the Left because of his economic orthodoxy and his embrace of the experts' antirentier measures.[23] He was unpopular with the Right because his career-long foreign policy views were thought to be soft. Right-leaning bank regents were especially unhappy about the Mellon-Bérenger Agreement, although for broadly political rather than monetary reasons. In Caillaux's troubles they saw a way of restoring Poincaré to power. On July 17, in a 288 to 243 vote, Wendel's allies in the Chamber of Deputies voted with the Socialists to block Caillaux's request for decree powers, and the ministry fell.[24]

The franc declined rapidly from F194 per pound on July 14 to F226 when Briand and Caillaux resigned on July 19.[25] The succeeding Herriot-(Anatole) de Monzie ministry lasted only three days; on July 20 the franc fell to F243 per pound. The franc began its recovery on anticipation of Herriot's resignation, rising somewhat to F225 per pound on July 21. Memories of the Bank of France's secret advances and illegal violation of its note limit during the first Herriot ministry probably did more immediate damage to the franc than did concern about a proposed capital levy.[26]

Appointment of a Poincaré Ministry of National Union on July 23 brought a burst of reassurance and an improvement in the exchange rate to F210 per pound. The new ministry was drawn from a cross section of French politics and included Briand, who would remain influential as foreign minister; it excluded only Socialists and close allies of Caillaux. Real power on economic issues rested with Poincaré, who was his own finance minister. On July 28, however, following announcement of Poincaré's fiscal program on July 27, which included establishment of the Amortization Fund, higher indirect taxes, and a lower marginal rate on direct taxes, the franc weakened from F197 per pound to F204. Moreau wrote in his diary on July 29 that Poincaré apparently expected fiscal action alone to bring a return of confidence and recovery of the franc.[27] Pierre Frayssinet similarly noted the market's disillusion with Poincaré's failure to propose a monetary remedy.[28] Poincaré thus far had failed to confront his erstwhile allies on the bank's board of regents regarding revalorization, debt ratification, or rigid limits on advances and circulation.

The impetus to more extensive recovery of the franc was the Law of August 7 (1926), which authorized the purchase of foreign exchange at market value (rather than at prewar par values) in order to manage the franc's exchange level, combined with a coordinated rise in interest rates by the bank and the Treasury. These measures opened the way to linking French prices and monetary policy to those elsewhere.[29] (The bank did not actually use its authorization to buy foreign exchange until December.) Authorization to issue francs against foreign exchange would bring the supply and demand for the currency into alignment and hence remove one source of demand for bon reimbursements. In a stroke, the bank was released from the ceilings on debt and note issuance that had heretofore stymied monetary management. The decision to coordinate a rise in interest rates would reverse the bon-rate-directed policy failure maintained throughout the inflationary 1924–26 period. Moreau summarized in his diary on July 30, 1926,

> I suggested to [Poincaré] that he should have a law passed which would permit the Bank of France, in carrying out the plan of the experts, to purchase gold coins and foreign currency with notes issued beyond the maximum set by law. Mr. Poincaré accepted this proposal.
>
> He also approved my proposal of simultaneously raising the discount rate of the Bank of France and the interest rate on National Defense bonds in order to attract money to Paris and to replenish the treasury.
>
> I left this meeting satisfied. This is *the first time since I became governor of the Bank of France that I am beginning to see the possibility of bringing the country out of its quandary.*[30] [emphasis added]

On the same day, July 30, the Chamber of Deputies passed the Candace Resolution, which limited the legislature's right to amend proposed legislation — hence granting Poincaré some of the authority that had been denied to Caillaux two weeks earlier. On Saturday, July 31, the bank's board of regents adopted Moreau's proposal to raise the discount rate from 6 percent to 7½ percent, and the rate on advances from 8 percent to 9½ percent; on the same day, the Treasury announced smaller increases in the rates on three-month, six-month, and one-year bons.[31] The franc strengthened immediately to F184 per pound on Monday, August 2. Creation of the Amortization Fund, Poincaré's commitment to a higher franc (without indicating how much higher), and the Law of August 7 were then announced during August 3 through August 6, by which time the franc had risen to F159 per pound.

The history of the Cartel des gauches raises an intriguing historical conjecture. On two occasions Caillaux as finance minister proposed solutions that might have led to successful stabilization of the franc. In 1925, the exchange consolidation bond might have worked had it paid sufficient risk-adjusted interest. In 1926, in a different ministry, Caillaux sought to implement the Committee of Experts' proposals. Had he been a less controversial figure or had the cartel not by then lost most of its public credibility, his request for temporary decree powers might have been granted. Following this double failure the way was open to Poincaré, under whom the experts' proposals were modified in important ways — and with serious deflationary consequences for the world economy.

The Moreau-Poincaré Policy Reversal

The collapse of the Briand-Caillaux ministry made it unlikely that a debt agreement ratification would be a part of any economic recovery program. Philippe argued that the debt agreements posed no threat to French interests because American leaders would not demand payments in the event of a reparations breakdown — even in the absence of a safeguard clause.[32] Poincaré accordingly indicated to Moreau in late July 1926 that he intended to push for debt agreement ratification.[33] Regardless of the likely American attitude regarding obligations in the face of a reparations breakdown — the agreements were finally ratified in 1929 — the issue carried large symbolic weight in 1926. Louis Marin, a right-wing deputy closely aligned with Wendel, threatened to resign as minister of pensions should Poincaré endorse ratification — a step that might have brought down the coalition ministry.[34] Yet opposition to debt ratification came from the Left also. Blum opposed a foreign loan as a "bankers' solution" and urged France to "save itself."[35] Faced with opposition from both directions and with the fate of the recent Briand-Caillaux ministry in mind, Poincaré looked for alternatives to the debt agreements and to a foreign loan.

The unifying theme of Poincaré's effort was to restore confidence. Four supports to this effort were in line with the experts' recommendations of a few weeks earlier. A Government of National Union was formed with the intention that, unlike any of the cartel ministries, it would endure and hence bring consistency to fiscal and monetary policy. The limitation on the Assembly's right of amendment enabled the government to act quickly, and Poincaré reinforced this with his insistence that rapid action was crucial — as demonstrated in the legislation passed during the early part of August 1926.[36] The tax changes were meant to encourage the return of expatriated capital; the elimination of bon registration was meant to reassure small merchants, peasants, and rentiers. The rise in both discount and bons rates brought French money market levels closer to international averages, which facilitated holding of franc-denominated financial assets.

Poincaré also proposed measures that were not recommended in the July *Report* and that indeed contradicted what the experts intended. He deliberately left uncertain the extent to which he hoped to revalorize the franc, in order to encourage a continued inflow of speculative foreign exchange. In his most far-reaching change, he shifted the primary mission of the Amortization Fund from that of managing the national debt — thereby assuring resources adequate to guarantee bon liquidity without recourse to a moratorium or a forced consolidation — to amortization of the short-term debt. The financial integrity of the new fund was buttressed by endowing it with revenues from the tobacco monopoly and from inheritance and real estate transfer taxes, rather than funding it through an allotment in the national budget, as the experts had proposed. The purpose was to build confidence that the floating debt would be reduced.[37] In further contrast to the experts, Poincaré wanted external stabilization without domestic inflation. Blocking domestic price increases would reinforce confidence, hence remove the need for resorting to a foreign loan. In political terms, Poincaré's program was a blend of the experts' calls for removing circulation limits and lowering marginal taxes and the anti-inflationism of rentiers and the regents of the Bank of France.

Poincaré succeeded in sharply limiting the size of the floating debt and extending the maturity of what remained. Issuance of one-month bons was discontinued after December 16, 1926, of three-month bons after January 13, 1927, of six-month bons after January 29, and of one-year bons after June 3.[38] During December 1926 and January 1927, interest rates were lowered on remaining bons. A two-year bon was issued beginning on January 1, 1927, at 6 percent, but to discourage large placements the rate on subsequent issues was lowered on February 4 to 5 percent.[39] At the end of July 1926, the floating debt stood at F44 billion; by June 1928, all bons of shorter than two years' maturity were withdrawn. Of this total, F10 billion was converted into long-term amortizable bonds in October 1926 and May 1927.[40] This left a large pool of liquid assets, much of which was placed on deposit at the Treasury.

Whereas Poincaré's recovery program was broadly political in its goals, Governor Moreau's was narrowly concerned with the quality of assets on the Bank of France's balance sheet. It was largely an accident that the two rose to power only weeks apart; as Moreau was Caillaux's ally while Poincaré was his career-long enemy, each was routinely suspicious of the other. Nevertheless, their separate agendas dovetailed.

Moreau resisted initial pressure from both Poincaré and some regents for accommodative discounting on behalf of the Treasury.[41] He also restricted commercial discounts in the summer of 1926. Moreau's instructions to a branch manager, recapitulated in his journal entry for August 30, 1926, summarize his new direction: "I gave him instructions which I am going to repeat to all the directors who come to see me: give broad acceptance to statutory paper which is strictly commercial, take agricultural paper in moderation, reject without mercy any real estate borrowing, do little direct discounting in competition with credit institutions, and only for first class firms, wait for improvement of the bond market before making advances on securities."[42] Moreau easily gained the support of the regents Wendel and Rothschild for restricting commercial discounts.[43] But Moreau's initiative flew in the face of the experts' recommendation that commercial discounts and advances be *expanded,* so as to offset an anticipated contraction of advances to the Treasury. This new discounting policy was widely unpopular and drew criticism.[44] Moreau was committed in addition to reducing bank advances to the Treasury; the contractionary consequences of his discounting policies are thus unmistakable.

Subsequent to fiscal and monetary reforms in late July and August 1926, much of the French wealth that had been expatriated in previous years was converted back to francs. A large amount was placed in government securities or sight deposits at the Treasury, where it augmented liquid amounts separately generated from bon consolidations. A portion of this was then paid by the Treasury to the Bank of France to liquidate advances; also, greater Treasury ease led to lower market rates and less discounting at the central bank. By this process, which came to be known as the monetary circuit, most of the inflow of foreign exchange was sterilized. From December 30, 1926, to May 19, 1927, the Bank of France bought more than F13 billion in foreign exchange, but circulation actually declined by F750 million; bank advances to the Treasury were reduced by F8.5 billion.[45]

French central bankers reasoned that they could have no control over money market interest rates as long as some of the bank's assets were immobilized. One internal memorandum explained: "The existence of advances to the State immobilized our central bank, and left it powerless regarding all of the fiduciary circulation that corresponded to the advances. It blocked the ability of the Bank to reduce any portion of the very large amount of currency issued against the credit of the State."[46] The premise was that the reduction of advances would force the market to the bank's discount window.[47] Because the French central bank did not perform open-market operations, discounting was its only lever of control.

Such logic is flawed because the discount rate affects the availability of credit at the margin, regardless of the total stock of credit or money or of the central bank's supply of international reserves. In early 1927, valuing the Bank of France's gold at market levels, the "immobilized" portion of French circulation — that covered only by advances — was 39 percent, lower than in England, for example, where central bank advances offset 47 percent of currency.[48] The British discount rate could nevertheless be effective in the market.

In 1927 the Bank of France discount rate was not effective, in spite of the theoretically sufficient gold cover ratio, because excessive liquidity kept French market rates low. As another internal bank memorandum stated, in June 1928,

> *The international inflation of credit* which has manifested itself during recent months, and which has to a large extent reduced the Bank's discount portfolio, *has denied the central bank almost every means to affect the volume of circulating francs,* at the same time it has confirmed precisely the pressing necessity of undertaking this regulatory action.
>
> The commercial portfolio of the Bank, which rose in 1913 to 1.655 billion francs, and which in normal monetary conditions (i.e., in view of the 80 percent devaluation of the franc) should consequently reach more than 8 billions today, instead oscillates only around 2 billions.[49] [emphasis added]

Borrowers could again be forced to the discount window only if market liquidity were drained.[50] But a policy of making the official discount rate effective by strengthening the bank's asset mix would succeed only by arbitraging world prices down to a new equilibrium level at which gold, sterling, and dollars would stop coming to France. Whether the French gold reserve ratio was 30 percent or 90 percent was in theory irrelevant to the effectiveness of the discount rate. French reserve levels mattered in practice because a change in the Bank of France's reserve ratio immediately affected reserves and prices outside of France. As long as French prices were below international parity, reserves would pour into the central bank and domestic liquidity would be high. This would help keep French interest rates low and shelter the Bank of France from the pressures then being felt at the Bank of England and the Reichsbank.

This returns us to the options identified by Keynes and the Committee of Experts and to their conclusion that franc-denominated prices should have been allowed to rise. Keynes and the experts thought stable franc prices possible only if joined to a sustained revalorization of the franc — which they op-

posed, as it would have damaged French export industries. It seems not to
have occurred to anyone in mid-1926 *that a consequence of stabilizing franc-
denominated prices might be to force other international prices downward.*
The French policy that paved the way for this systemic contraction was the
liquidation of bank advances to the Treasury.[51] Moreau's role was crucial; he
wanted a full pay-down of advances even after — indeed, because — the financial position of the bank and the Treasury had improved greatly. In February
1927 his under governor Rist, consistent in spirit with the experts' *Report,*
proposed that the advances be mobilized (that is, be made security for a bond
issue) rather than liquidated. Moreau objected:

> Mr. Rist, who would like to see the stabilization take place as soon as possi-
> ble, discussed a proposal with me, interesting in certain respects, but which
> would result in obliging the Bank of France to renounce for practical purposes
> repayment of the advances it has granted to the state. As representation of
> these advances, the bank would receive bonds from the treasury which would
> be put into circulation or withdrawn depending on monetary conditions. For
> a while, I was in favor of this proposal. But now that the financial situation
> has improved beyond all expectations, I have the duty to demand from the
> treasury that it repay as much as possible the advances by the bank to the
> state.[52]

The advances would not have been liquidated to the extent they were without Poincaré's support. At least twice during the fall of 1926, Poincaré indicated that he supported repayment of bank advances. In one case he avowed
this over the specific objection of Clement Moret, a senior Treasury official
(and Moreau's successor as governor of the Bank of France).[53] He formalized
his administration's commitment to repaying at least some advances in the
convention of June 13, 1927, between the Bank of France and the Treasury,
which was negotiated pursuant to the issuing of a new consolidation bond. In
February 1928, Poincaré indicated that the Treasury's commitment in the
1927 convention followed the framework of the often-criticized François-
Marsal Convention.[54] H. A. Siepmann wrote in June 1928 that "no one but
Poincaré would have agreed to the repayment in full of the Government debt
to the Bank."[55]

Poincaré also accepted the logic of devaluing the franc more rather than less.
According to Rist, the advocacy of the labor leader Léon Jouhaux in late 1926
was decisive.[56] Poincaré sought to determine where the franc might be set
without damaging export markets or loss of employment. But while French
leadership chose to stabilize at the lower exchange level, no corresponding
decision was taken to permit the domestic value of the franc to drop (through

price inflation) to the level of the external franc. Instead, French policy effectively sought to bring world prices down to the level of French internal prices. French rejection of the existing international gold-to-commodities price ratio amounted to rejection of the never-quite-established interwar gold standard. France launched what was in fact the first of the competitive ("beggar-thy-neighbor") devaluations that would become common in the early 1930s. Contemporary financial and journalistic observers were uniformly impressed by the management of the French economy after July 1926. Yet evidence was accumulating that the franc was so low as to be destabilizing.

According to a purchasing power index provided in the *Statistique Générale*, the exchange-adjusted purchasing power of the franc was 15 percent and 16 percent less, respectively, than that of the pound and dollar at the end of 1926 (at which point the franc was de facto stabilized). By the end of 1928, the undervaluations remained 10 percent and 15 percent. Vis-à-vis the reichsmark, the franc's undervaluation increased slightly from 5 to 7 percent.[57] The *Economist* more pointedly estimated in early 1928 that French prices were 25 percent below the world level.[58] This fundamentally explains why French assets, including French currency, were in demand following the financial reforms of 1926.

This in-movement of gold could have been self-limiting, by inducing price increases that would eliminate the franc's special attractiveness. Rather than permit this adjustment to occur, the French sterilized gold and foreign exchange inflows, as I observed earlier. French monetary officials understood their options. Rist wrote in late 1926, "The pound exchange must be fixed at a rate that permits a certain delay between the point where stabilization is achieved and that where French prices rise to the world level — should they reach it. This implies a certain margin for increase in prices in the French domestic market. *But this adjustment can be limited.* It is always easier to block a price increase than to induce a reduction" (emphasis added). And again, on both the importance of keeping French prices below the world level and how to stop them from rising later: "The most serious consequence would be the *failure of the stabilization* [emphasis in original], *that appears certain if French prices were brought in one stroke to the world level.* If, on the contrary, one wishes to maintain some margin of difference in price levels, the ill consequence would be a period of [internal] price increase for some time to come, *an increase that could be effectively blocked by an appropriate discount policy*" (emphases added).[59] The Treasury also understood its options, as indicated by the circumstances under which the large consolidation bond was issued at the end of June 1927. Following Poincaré's successful effort to reduce outstanding bons, banks placed large deposits with the Treasury. These deposits could be withdrawn on short notice, thereby flooding the market with liquidity and perhaps driving up prices. In effect, the old floating debt consisting of bons had been converted into a new floating debt consisting of deposits at the Treasury. In the middle of 1927 this presented no liquidity danger for the Treasury, whose current level of advances from the Bank of France was well under the legal limit.[60] The avowed purpose of the new issue was to block a rise in prices by shifting short-term funds on deposit in Treasury accounts to longer-term, less liquid investments. The Treasury explained, "If this movement from money market instruments [that is, bons] to Treasury accounts should end, it would result in overly abundant market liquidity. This would imply a new expansion of money and credit that would give rise to speculation in securities and merchandise, and would probably cause *price increases*."[61]

This issue appropriately came to be called the "deflation bond."[62] In view of the ongoing effort to prevent equilibration between the internal and external values of the franc after 1926, a recently revived debate about whether the franc was deliberately undervalued *initially* is somewhat off focus.[63]

In April 1927 the Bank of France demanded gold (in exchange for sterling) from the Bank of England in order to force a discount rate increase in London and slow the flood of foreign exchange moving to Paris. In the first half of 1927, both the Bank of England and the Reichsbank were forced to sterilize gold outflows to avoid domestic monetary contraction; gold held in central bank portfolios against note liabilities left both countries and was replaced by open-market purchases of domestic securities. Governor Norman told French central bankers in May, "Any transfer to the Bank of England tending to a conversion of sterling into gold succeeds not so much in diminishing credit on the London market as it does in diminishing the proportion of English cover, since the Bank of England must deliver pounds to the market. The Bank of France has enough pounds to enable it in this way to create at a given moment a situation *endangering the gold standard* and delighting all the enemies of the gold standard."[64] Norman added that any effort to keep British reserves intact by constricting credit would strain industry to the breaking point and probably "cause a riot."[65] Germany, too, lost reserves in 1927. This was attributed in the financial press partly to French monetary policy but also to reparations and French trade restrictions.[66] Here was an early view of the pattern that would bring world depression.

Moreau's diary easily impresses.[67] He recounts instances in which he told ministers not to badger him for confidential information or to offer him self-interested advice. Following years during which French central bankers accommodated French governments' cash needs, Moreau flatly refused to do so and instead demanded a coordinated program along the lines of the Committee of Experts' *Report*. He could be dismissed at the discretion of the prime minister and traded simply on his public credibility as the governor of the Bank of France. In July 1926 and again in June 1928, he icily offered to resign. This evidence of direction and independence aside, Moreau showed little sensitivity to the fact that central banking requires international accommodation. He put too high a priority upon his obligation to advance the narrrow interests of his bank. On the matter of liquidating advances through the convention of June 13, 1927, for example, he wrote, "We are, in effect, in the situation of a creditor to whom a bad debtor offers a partial repayment in advance in exchange for a lowering of the interest rate. It is certainly more advantageous for the bank to accept the proposal than to reject it."[68] On this crucial issue, Moreau was more concerned about the quality of bank assets than about what his policies would do to price levels in France and abroad. In historical perspective, this was an unfortunate focus.

The Eclipse of the Monetary Power of the Federal Reserve

Central bankers soon understood the power of the Bank of France to force contraction on the rest of the world. Moreau wrote in his diary in May 1927,

> I instructed Mr. Siepmann [of the Bank of England, then visiting Moreau in Paris] to explain to Mr. Norman: " . . . you [the Bank of England] have actually opened credits abroad. You could call them in, obliging the speculators who annoy you to cease their maneuvers in Paris. They would then have to sell their francs by taking gold in Berlin, Amsterdam, Bern and Stockholm. You, the Bank of England, have decided to be a clearinghouse and to make London into a world money market. You have to live with the consequences of your ambitions. To get at the German, Swiss, Dutch and other speculators, we must necessarily pass through the intermediary of the pound. . . ."
>   Mr. Siepmann is writing to Mr. Norman to explain our point of view, but he is not concealing distress or anxieties caused to the Bank of England *by the brutal revelation of the power of the Bank of France upon the London market*.[69] [emphasis added]

A few months later Siepmann expressed parallel views in a Bank of England memorandum: "If a country decides to revert to the Gold Standard, it may lay claim to more gold than there is any reason to expect the gold centre to have held in reserve against legitimate Gold Exchange Standard demands. What is then endangered is not merely the working of the Gold Exchange Standard, but the Gold Standard itself. Such a violent contraction may be provoked that gold will be brought into disrepute as a standard of value."[70]

Norman noted in May 1927 that potential credit from the United States was "inexhaustible as a well."[71] In June 1927 the United States sterilized gold losses to France so as not to upset domestic credit conditions.[72] But the ability of the American central bank to control world prices would soon be tested. Strong wrote privately that "the Bank of France has skimmed all of the loose dollar exchange and all of the free gold off the markets so that the usual accumulation of both New York exchange and gold for use in the fall has not been possible in London." He thought the widespread return to the gold standard responsible for the recent decline in the price level. At the Long Island Conference of July 1927, the Federal Reserve agreed to lower its discount rate from 4 to 3½ percent and hoped that this would lead to rate reductions on the Continent. Strong wanted an alibi so that responsibility for world price declines could not be laid at his or any other American door.[73] The rate reduction brought some buoyancy in prices. Irving Fisher's weekly price index number rose from 135 on August 11, 1927, to 146 on October 13, 1927, a movement Cassel attributed to the drop in the U.S. discount rate.[74] It led also to a sizable U.S. gold loss, and monetary ease brought renewed share price increases on the New York Stock Exchange.

The French foreign exchange inflow accelerated following specific sterilization measures in France. For instance, at the beginning of May 1928 the Treasury issued another long-term loan, this one subscribed to F10.3 billion, proceeds of which were used in part to reduce advances from the Bank of France by F6.0 billion. The contractionary effect of this loan and pay-down of advances immediately induced a new inflow of foreign exchange. In May alone, F5.0 billion of new foreign exchange was presented at the Bank of France — up from a monthly average of about F2.0 billion earlier in the year. The bank's annual report causally linked these events.[75]

9

The French Deflation, 1928–32

French action during 1926–28, the period of de facto stabilization, had already damaged the Genoa framework. The F35 billion increase in gold and foreign exchange in the two years up to June 1928 was used to increase currency by only F3½ billion and to increase M1 by only F24 billion.[1] Reserves are normally assumed to support money expansion by some multiple of their growth rate. (For example, a 33 percent reserve requirement would support an increase of three units of currency and deposits for each unit increase in reserves.) The amount of sterilization of foreign exchange reserves from 1926 to 1928 thus appears to have been enormous. Moreau, indeed, denied sterling's reserve status even before the Monetary Law of 1928, in spite of the pivotal role of exchange reserves in the Genoa resolutions. Repeated references in 1927 and 1928 make clear that French central bankers viewed the gold exchange standard as inflationary because it permitted a fairly small amount of British gold to serve as a base for both British and foreign monetary expansion. Shortly after the Monetary Law was passed, Moreau wrote to Strong that he (hypothetically) might accept dollars as French monetary reserves based on the high gold cover ratio in the United States, but that he would not accept sterling.[2] He might still hold his current stock as an investment, however.

By the middle of 1928, 42 percent of Continental European reserves were held in sterling or dollars, and of this amount, half were held in the Bank of France.[3] France's decisions were manifestly critical to the future of the gold exchange standard.

The French Monetary Law of 1928

The Monetary Law of June 25, 1928, merely ratified current practice in not treating foreign exchange holdings as reserves — although it had been legally permissible under the law of August 7, 1926, to issue francs against foreign exchange. The new law's impact was to restrict further accumulation of foreign exchange as an investment.[4] Any further buildup in assets at the Bank of France would take the form of gold. A contemporary writer in the *Frankfurter Zeitung* concluded that the new Monetary Law represented the "negation" of the gold exchange standard.[5]

Action along the lines of the Monetary Law had been anticipated. Leffingwell wrote in July 1927,

> [Deputy Governor of the Bank of France] Rist agrees that the world's return to the gold standard after the war will be followed by falling prices as after the American Civil war and the Franco-Prussian war. But he doesn't see any alternative to the classically operated gold standard even as a transition measure. Heaven send he may! What will French peasants say to the Government or to the Banque de France if their policies are such as to accelerate the inevitable fall in prices?
>
> Ben[jamin Strong] has been full of plans to guard against the possibility of a flood of gold to France even after the adoption of a gold standard by France.[6]

The *Frankfurter Zeitung* noted concurrent speculation that the return to gold standards in Europe might lessen the capacity of the Federal Reserve to stabilize the world's price level. The newspaper also mentioned the pressure brought by French gold withdrawals from Britain upon the Bank of England's reserve base.[7] After adoption of the Monetary Law, the *Economist* concluded of French gold purchases, "The effect . . . will not only aid in bringing about a partial redistribution of the world's stock of gold, but should also lead to an appreciable fall in world commodity prices and help to restore some of the value which gold has lost since the war began."[8] Keynes wrote with some precision in January 1929 of the likely effect of the French Monetary Law:

> It is evident that we all survive, and the Bank of England in particular, by favour of the Bank of France. The Bank of France has used her position so far with an extraordinary considerateness, and there is no reason to suppose that she will act otherwise in the future. But it would be wholly contrary to French

mentality for the Bank of France to remain content with so little free gold at home. It is certain that she will use every convenient opportunity to increase her stock of gold; and no one can prevent her. The question of the sufficiency of the world's gold supplies and the abundance or scarcity of credit in the world's business lies, therefore, for the near future in the hands of the Bank of France. But however gradually and reasonably France draws her gold, there will be a continuing pressure of incipient scarcity on everyone else.[9]

Keynes was equally emphatic in the *Treatise on Money,* published the following year.[10] Cassel in 1928 — prior to passage of the French Monetary Law — predicted world depression if efforts to economize in central bank use of monetary gold did not bear fruit.[11] He revisited this theme in 1936: "In June 1928 France returned to the gold standard. . . . It would seem as if the international gold standard system ought to have been strengthened by the entrance of France into the system. The actual result was just the contrary. From that time on the gold standard began to show its inherent faults, and gradually a situation developed that could not but end in a complete breakdown."[12]

The Genoa resolutions of 1922 were intended to prevent systemic contraction of reserves and specifically to discourage any country from adopting a French-style "monetary law" that would undermine the status of "gold center" currencies as international reserves. The resolutions did not call for the unlimited use of sterling or dollars as a reserve, but instead for their use so far as necessary to maintain stable world prices. Hence, the extent of use of foreign exchange as a reserve was intended to be self-limiting.[13] The French instead targeted a stable domestic price level at below international purchasing power parity. French policy would either fail, resulting in domestic inflation, or "succeed" and bring a decline in world prices. In the event, it led to an enormous and theoretically unlimited accumulation of foreign exchange. A third possibility, an upward adjustment in the external value of the franc, was blocked repeatedly by the Bank of France, a resistance finally reinforced by Moreau's threat to resign in 1928.[14] French policy-makers appear to have only dimly understood the impossibility of maintaining an independent national price level given adherence to an international gold standard. In 1930 and 1931, as prices fell almost everywhere else, Bank of France officials feared that new gold inflow could cause a domestic "gold inflation."[15]

The adoption of the Monetary Law of 1928 has received little scrutiny from economic historians.[16] Sauvy offers a standard French judgment: "Of all the new economic and financial problems that appeared between the wars . . . *the monetary reform of 1928 was — along with Paul Reynaud's policies of 1938–39 — the only one that was sensibly solved.*"[17] Once given the sequence of events described in the previous chapter, in particular the decision to prevent either a decline in the internal value of the franc or a rise in its external value, adoption of something comparable to the Monetary Law was nearly certain. By the middle of 1928, the Bank of France had accumulated F36 billion (about $1.4 billion) of foreign exchange. Heretofore francs issued against pounds and dollars were used to liquidate advances to the Treasury, so that circulating currency grew only from F59 billion in the third quarter of 1926 to F62 billion in the second quarter of 1928.[18] There were widespread fears that indefinite absorption of foreign exchange would eventually bring an expanded money stock and price inflation. Henri Chéron, the general reporter of the Senate Finance Commission (he would become finance minister in another Poincaré ministry in November 1928), explained to the Senate immediately before adoption of the Monetary Law on June 25,

> But gentlemen, it is not now difficult to see ill consequences in the present system. If the pattern of demanding francs at the Bank of France continues, if it is forced to absorb foreign exchange indefinitely, we can fatalistically fore-cast — based on the increase in means of payment, on the issue of new bank-notes — that the increase in all prices will be exacerbated.
>
> . . . Foreign speculation . . . which has forced the Bank of France to absorb large amounts of foreign exchange, has made the intended working of the Law of August 7, 1926 [by which the Bank of France would sell francs against foreign exchange] impossible.[19]

Chéron deduced that to stop the in-movement of foreign exchange, and with it the threat of price inflation, "the Bank of France must convert its foreign exchange into gold." Then "foreign central banks, anxious to defend their metallic reserves, will be forced to end the practices that otherwise result in gold outflows."[20] The Bank of France elaborated several months later in its *Annual Report:*

> By leaving at the disposal of the markets in which they originated and without conversion into gold the foreign bills which it was obliged to purchase, the [B]ank [of France] actually increased the flood of tenders which it was en-deavoring to check. It was maintaining in these markets an artificial monetary ease which permitted them to continue their purchases of francs indefinitely without experiencing any corresponding reduction in their available funds. It was, in fact, working to facilitate the initiation and development of a world-wide credit inflation, which only actual purchases of gold could arrest or keep within bounds.[21]

This reasoning replays Moreau's arguments for forcing increases in the British and German discount rates to check speculation on a rise in the franc early in 1927. I conclude from these arguments that some measure of world deflation was both nearly certain and an understood consequence of adoption of the French Monetary Law.

The inflation of 1924–26 hurt rentiers, wage earners, and most producers; it led to capital flight rather than to profit inflation (see chapter 5). Partly as a consequence of this experience, almost no one in France in 1928 called for domestic inflation. The visible domestic opponents of the Monetary Law were the franc revalorizers. Revalorizers in France based their appeals upon patriotism, State responsibility toward those who purchased war bonds, and the integrity of money and contracts. They comprised an unimpressive group. Revalorizers tended to be the same people who stood in the way of effective central bank action against inflation during 1924–26, when they opposed adjustment of the circulation limit and blocked the use of the Bank of France's gold to stabilize the franc. Senator Gaston Japy spoke for them in the debate of June 1928: "Stabilization [of the franc] at 20 centimes would amount to absolving all the policy sins committed since the War. I am not ready to do this."[22] Wendel led their forces on the Right, but he lacked support even within the mining industry of which he was the acknowledged leader.[23] Revalorization also drew support from rentier interests on the Left, led without much enthusiasm on this issue by Painlevé and Herriot.[24] Poincaré was politically sympathetic to both the nationalist and rentier groups supporting revalorization. He was nevertheless persuaded by the economic arguments in favor of stabilization that a higher franc would mean deflation, bankruptcies, and unemployment. In a political maneuver, however, he invited his cabinet members to disagree with him and promised to resign should any other minister resign first.[25]

Moreau responded at the end of May 1928 that *he* would resign if the franc were not officially stabilized and the Monetary Law not passed by July 15.[26] He was appalled by Poincaré's political dance with the revalorizers. He wrote in his diary on June 8,

> This morning, Mr. Moret told me that Mr. Poincaré had just confided in him that he intended to present his resignation and that he would make a statement in which he described himself as a supporter of the stabilization in order to facilitate the task of his successor.
>
> Thus this man without courage will not dare to take a step himself which he considers vital for fear of losing his popularity. This indecision and lack of character show that, despite all his qualities, he is not a real statesman.[27]

Poincaré wished his supporters to believe that he forewent revalorization only under duress.[28] His equivocating tactics also affect historical judgment (as offered here); Poincaré's role in the adoption of the Monetary Law was smaller than Moreau's.

What really weakened the revalorizers' case were the nearly two years of price stability that predated the Monetary Law. This undermined political support for deflation, which had been strong during the years of inflation in the middle 1920s. The political strength of inflation-era losers blocked implementation of the Committee of Experts' 1926 program for external stabilization of the franc combined with a rise in internal prices. But the 1924–26 losers did much better during the 1926–28 stabilization; accordingly, the constituency for the price rollback that might accompany a further revalorization shrank. Beyond arguments of theoretical economics, this is why the franc was left undervalued.

One might reject one theory about French motives for stabilizing the franc at the low level of F124 per pound (about F25 per dollar). Paul Einzig argued in late 1931 that the franc was deliberately undervalued so that France might acquire a huge gold base that would give it diplomatic leverage over gold-depleted countries and hence make France "the financial dictator of Europe."[29] Prime Minister Pierre Laval certainly used France's new leverage in diplomatic *démarches* against Austria, Germany, Britain, Italy, and the United States during 1931;[30] but to deduce from this a prior motivation for banking policy during 1926–28 is to reason post hoc, ergo propter hoc. Nationalist French politicians, including the Germanophobic Alsatians Poincaré and Wendel, thought diplomatic advantage lay on the side of a *higher* franc. Meanwhile, Caillaux, who advocated debt ratification with the United States in 1926 and was associated through most of his career with accommodationist views toward Germany, argued for a *lower* franc. In the summer of 1927 he urged that the exchange rate be shifted quickly from F124 per pound to about F150 per pound to ease the cyclical downturn in France.[31] The labor leader Jouhaux, Rist, and other members of the Committee of Experts used plausible monetary arguments — not diplomatic ones — for a low franc; it was these that carried the day.

Interwar economic history would have been different had the revalorizers won. A higher franc might have ended the French profit inflation of the late 1920s, along with its associated capital inflow. The Bank of England would have gained systemic influence almost immediately; had revalorization of the franc been carried far enough, the relative power positions of the British and French central banks might have been reversed. (It is a historical paradox that both franc and sterling revalorizers of the 1920s, who were often to the right of center politically, proposed actions that, if enacted, would have weakened their countries' external balances and the systemic influence of their central banks. In Britain in 1925, they succeeded.) Had the Bank of France felt the pinch of the international reserve shortage, it might have been less inclined to undermine the use of foreign exchange as a reserve. Accidentally and in nationalist habit, revalorizers advanced an internationalist agendum.

The French Gold Sink

The French sterilization of foreign exchange reserves before passage of the Monetary Law in 1928 did not directly affect credit conditions in other countries; sterling reserves, for example, were generally held on deposit with London banks. However, the ceiling imposed upon foreign exchange after June 1928 did drain reserves from other central banks, as foreign exchange subsequently acquired by the Bank of France was exchanged for gold. (In fact, the central bank actually relinquished about $120 million in previously purchased foreign currencies in exchange for francs during the second half of 1928. Only the comparatively small amount of $34 million of previously held foreign exchange was converted to gold during this period.[32] Newly acquired foreign exchange was not converted to gold until 1929, when the new law began to have practical effect.)

From the end of 1926 through June 1928, the Bank of France gained some $335 million in gold, reaching an amount of $1.14 billion, and just over $1 billion in foreign exchange, reaching $1.44 billion. (These gold data include some $90 million that had been pledged to the Bank of England in 1917 and was returned to France during 1927 among holdings for *both* dates.)[33] In the subsequent three years, to August 1931, the bank lost about $350 million of foreign exchange, but added $1.160 billion in gold ($1.044 billion if one includes $116 million in gold coins turned in to the Bank of France from domestic circulation during this period among holdings for both dates.)[34] The net exchange loss understates the effect of French policy on the London market, for the French central bank actually increased its dollar holdings by some $80 million. The drain on British gold from sterling conversions exceeded $400 million.[35] Total French gold reserves rose from less than 8 percent of the world's stock (9.8 percent if one includes the other two above-mentioned categories of gold as "reserves" at the earlier date) in December 1926 to 11.6 percent (12.7 percent adjusted) in June 1928 and to more than 20 percent — over $2.2 billion — in August 1931 (see also Appendix, part C). Following the end of sterling convertibility in September 1931, the French gold inflow accelerated again through October 1932.

The concurrent movement of gold to the United States was only a secondary deflationary factor.[36] From the end of 1926 to the end of 1928, the U.S. *lost* $337 million in gold reserves, by which time the American stock was below its level for any month during 1924, 1925, or 1926. During 1929 and 1930, the

Federal Reserve gained $479 million in gold, most of it in 1930. Looking back over the high interest rates associated with the late stages of the New York equities boom, Hawtrey told the Macmillan Committee in April 1930, "[British] gold was going to France; the American demand for gold was not a very serious thing."[37] Rist, too, deemphasized the importance of the gold movement to the United States throughout 1929 and 1930. In February 1931 he told a London audience that the "mal-distribution of gold between continents" that had been an outstanding feature of the war and early postwar years was now "a thing of the past."[38]

The relative U.S. share of world gold reserves fell from 45 percent in June 1927 to 37 percent in June 1928, then rose to 41 percent in August 1931, after which the gold standard formally began to unravel. From December 1928 through August 1931, the period of maximum relative growth in U.S. monetary gold, the American share rose by $886 million, against a larger French increase of $1.042 billion.[39] If one measures only from the time the French Monetary Law was adopted in June 1928 through April 1931 — just before the banking crises began, which resulted in reactive shifts in reserves — France absorbed $1.044 billion ($928 million adjusted) and the United States $741 million.

Gold movements should be viewed in the context of the underlying postwar gold shortage. The consequences of shortages may not be coterminous with short-period gold movements. Gold losses during an earlier period may restrict freedom of action subsequently, perhaps after a financial crisis strikes. Hence one should examine gold movements over a longer period as well. From the end of 1926 through April 1931, France gained $1.469 billion in gold reserves ($1.264 million if the pledge to the Bank of England and gold from domestic circulation are excluded), while the United States gained only $290 million. Subsequent to the sterling devaluation in September 1931, U.S. gold reserves declined from $4.63 billion in August to $4.05 billion by the end of the year and to $3.466 billion in June 1932, before rising anew. The French gold stock continued to soar, to $2.699 billion at the end of 1931 and to $3.218 billion in June 1932. At this point, approximately the nadir for world prices, international trade, and production, the U.S. share was below 31 percent of the world total, while the French share exceeded 28 percent.[40] The French share of the world's official gold holdings outside of the United States rose from 15 percent in 1926 to 35 percent in August 1931 and to 42 percent in June 1932.[41]

Over the thirty-four months to April 1931, French and American gold reserves increased by 77 percent (68 percent adjusted) and 47 percent of the total world increase. Over the nearly four-and-a-half-year period from the end of 1926 through April 1931, France gained 78 percent (67 percent adjusted) and the United States only 15 percent of the world increase. From the end of 1926 through June 1932, French reserves increased by $2.507 billion ($2.302 billion adjusted), while world reserves increased by only $2.115 billion; the Federal Reserve finished with a five-and-a-half-year net *loss* of $617 million. The Bank of France gained 119 percent (109 percent adjusted) of the world increase over this longer period; that is, all other countries had $187 million less of gold reserves in June 1932 than in December 1926.[42]

Belgium, the Netherlands, and Switzerland, which along with France and some economically less important countries became known as the Gold Bloc in 1933, also rapidly accumulated gold. Their combined share of the world total nearly trebled, from less than 4 percent in mid-1928 to 11 percent in 1932. Most of their increases occurred during 1931 and began during the Austrian and German banking crises. Their accumulations — unlike that of the Bank of France — were therefore not factors in the systemic reserve constraint through April 1931. When the Central European banking crisis broke and foreign deposits were frozen, commercial banks in France and these smaller countries called in remaining deposits, especially from London, to reinforce their cash positions.[43] The combined increases of France and the smaller countries reached $2.964 billion ($2.759 billion adjusted) over the four years ending in June 1932.[44] This meant an absolute contraction in gold available to the rest of the world of $1.365 billion, or from $8.241 billion to $6.876 billion; if the U.S. stock is removed from this amount, the four-year shrinkage was $4.509 billion to $3.410 billion. The monetary and trade patterns of Belgium, the Netherlands, and Switzerland were inevitably intertwined with those of their large neighbor France. The deflation following upon their gold accumulation is thus not independent of events in France.

In 1930, the Federal Reserve eased conditions somewhat, which resulted in gold outflow to France. This should not have been a restraint on American policy, for the United States saw large concurrent inflows from Japan and Brazil and for the year had a net increase in official gold of $325 million.[45] Yet Harrison, obviously concerned, contacted Moreau at the Bank of France to learn whether he might expect any help from that quarter. He cabled as follows: "In view of our easy money program we are now witnessing a fairly substantial gold movement not only to France but to Canada. . . . Is there any information or comment which you might care to give me regarding your own position, the likelihood of continued further imports of gold, or the possibility of further foreign loans in Paris, which might be expected to supplement bond issues now being made here for foreign account?"[46]

Only during the first eight months of 1931 was the United States in the forefront of gold movement, with an inflow of $407 million; even here, France gained $196 million. Is there evidence during this period of unusual American-induced reserve pressures? The American gold in-movement was heaviest at $72 million in May and $148 million in June, that is, during the Central European banking crisis — yet it appears not to have instigated the crisis. From January through April, the inflow to New York totaled only $90 million.[47] A change in American monetary policy in 1931 or the Smoot-Hawley Tariff Act of June 1930, both of which aggravated systemic deflation over the long period, could have instigated a banking crisis only if the crisis had *followed* reserve outflows to the United States. But as I pointed out above, the German crisis began with internal drains from the banking system, not with a withdrawal of foreign deposits. When foreign deposits were later withdrawn, American banks were among the last to act.[48] Efforts to rescue the Austrian Creditanstalt were blocked by diplomatic tension surrounding the proposed German-Austrian Customs Union, which tension generated some of the flight of capital from Europe. The burst of gold movement to New York in May and June 1931 was therefore a consequence of the crisis.

To identify causality in gold movements, one must consider changes in the monetary demand for gold as well as the redistribution of its supply. When a gold-receiving country experiences a spontaneous capital in-movement, its demand for credit and reserves might rise without bringing contractionary pressure upon output or employment elsewhere. France indeed experienced a spontaneous capital inflow beginning around 1927 (see chapter 6). The capital movement to the United States during 1929 was in part spontaneous (that is, driven by share speculation), but probably in larger part induced by high call-money rates (see chapter 10). The gold flow to the United States during 1930 and much of 1931 was driven in some measure by a deflation-induced decline in American demand for merchandise imports combined with the adoption of new tariffs; together they made it harder for the rest of the world to balance its accounts with the United States.

At first glance, this suggests that new gold in France might have supported economic growth in a way that new gold in New York did not. However, the French economy was small relative to the world economy, while that of the United States was huge. In 1929, the French share of world manufacturing output was 6.6 percent, while the American share was about 43 percent.[49] The French economy grew relative to most other countries after 1927 — but to an extent proportionately far short of the increase in the French share of the world's monetary gold through August 1931, or of the even larger increase through June 1932. This increase can be set against a smaller gain in American gold reserves over the same three-year period. The U.S. economy shrank in both absolute and relative terms during the two years after the October 1929 stock market crash, and — to avoid sterilization and a reverse-Thornton effect — should have *lost* gold. But econometric evidence suggests that both countries had far more gold than they needed, hence from a systemic stand-point almost the entire inflows to both countries were sterilized.[50]

THE OVERHANG OF FOREIGN EXCHANGE RESERVES

Alongside actual gold movements, the threat of gold movements forced change in other countries' monetary policies. In June 1931, the Bank of France held F26 billion (more than $1 billion) in sterling or dollars, about 52 percent of European exchange reserves, almost a third of it in short-term instruments in London.[51] The Bank of England's short-term asset portfolio of gold and sterling acceptances had risen much less from prewar levels than had the London market's short-term foreign-held liabilities. The Macmillan Committee *Report,* issued in July 1931, noted that a rise in the bank rate might continue to draw short-term funds to London, but only by aggravating the excess of the Bank of England's short-term liabilities over short-term assets.[52] The (Sir George) May Committee *Report,* issued shortly afterward, noted Britain's worsening budget deficit;[53] it argued that raising the bank rate would aggravate the budget imbalance by lowering output, employment, and tax revenues. The Bank of England fully maintained its gold stock through most of 1930 and suffered only small net declines through September 1931 — in part by drawing distress shipments from Spain, Argentina, Brazil, and Australia.[54] A contemporary economist observed that reserve losses alone had not driven sterling off gold:

> The real reason for the abandonment of the gold standard may be seen not in the actual drain of the summer but in the long-run threat of the future weeks. For the net gold loss during the crisis, of only some 18 million pounds, seems a comparatively small amount to have forced the decision of September 21. That it did so, may have been because the Bank of England and the government, despairing of seeing the end of the "run" within any reasonable time, and unable to secure further adequate loans abroad, felt it wiser to preserve the gold stock than to permit its exhaustion to no purpose.[55]

When Britain left the gold standard, the Bank of England discount rate had been raised to only 4½ percent. Britain left gold because of a long-period problem in its international accounts, not because of an immediate crisis; this problem became apparent when the Bank of France demanded gold from the Bank of England in the spring of 1927. As Moreau noted then, the Bank of France could at any time demand enough gold to force an end to sterling convertibility.[56] French deflationary pressure after 1927 made the gold standard in Britain ever less tenable, even without actual withdrawals of gold.

REPARATIONS, WAR DEBTS, AND STERILIZATION

During most of the period 1925–28, reparation and war debt payments had only small systemic consequences. This matches steady-state assumptions; income gains in transfer-receiving France and the United States offset income losses in transfer-paying Germany. (The German economy was slowed in part by the higher interest rates needed to finance the reparation payments, while French and U.S interest rates were probably lowered somewhat by the capital inflows. See chapter 6.) Data on reserve movements reinforce the conclusion that the systemic effects of these transfers were mild. During 1925–28, France and the United States together received $1.364 billion (net) in transfers but actually lost $163 million in gold reserves.

During the following two and one half years, through June 1931, this pattern changed completely. France and the United States received another $898 million (net) in transfers but also received $1.683 billion in new gold reserves. Some of the increase in reserves at the Bank of France and the Federal Reserve represented a normal share of new gold that would go to two major central banks. Most of it, however, reflected sterilization of new reserves in France and the United States.[57] The dissenters in the League of Nation's 1932 *Report* concluded that the world deflation was the result of reparation and war debt obligations combined with the "unwillingness of the receiving countries to accept payment in goods and services, so that payment had to be made in gold."[58] This "unwillingness" need not reflect *trade* policies; the writers also identified *monetary* policies that restrict expansion of aggregate demand in receiving countries — which rendered it effectively impossible to make payment other than with gold.[59] What changed in 1928 and 1929 to bring about sterilization were French and American monetary policies. Without the reparation and debt transfers to France and the United States, the effects of the new policies would have been much milder.

Financial market developments following the Hoover Moratorium (on debt and reparation payments) of June 1931 support this view. The Dow-Jones Industrial Average rose 6.4 percent the day after Hoover announced his intention to put forward a plan for debt relief and another 4.9 percent the business day following disclosure of details. The *New York Times* noted that, except for the immediate recoil from the 1929 crash, the rally of the week following the announcement was the "swiftest advance during any corresponding period in a generation."[60] The link between transfer obligations and systemic contraction was not lost on investors.

DEFLATIONARY PRICE ARBITRAGE

While the United States did little to hinder the decline in world prices, especially after 1928, French policy can be charged with directly causing it. Cassel noted in early 1931 that the French price level had been too low and should have been allowed to rise to the world level; that this did not happen caused "a certain disruption to world commerce."[61] Evidence for this conclusion is striking. From January 1928 to November 1930, British domestic industrial prices fell by 27 percent, while French domestic industrial prices fell by only 4 percent. Over the same period the price of imported goods in France declined by 41 percent.[62] From the 1928 average to September 1930, a broader index of French domestic prices dropped only from 619 to 595 (base 1914 = 100), while that of imported products dropped from 660 to 428. Almost all of the decline came after March 1929.[63] In a revealing reference in its 1930 annual report, the Bank of France highlighted this deflationary mechanism: "Wholesale prices [in France] therefore followed for the most part the general decline of world prices on the important markets, although to a far less extent; this parallel movement *tends to prove that world prices have become fairly well adapted to the rate at which the legal value of the franc was fixed in 1928*" (emphasis added).[64] This formulation neglected the important distinction between domestic and imported wholesale prices — and was revised the following year: "Among the group indexes making up the general index, *the index of imported commodities declined more* than did the index of French commodities" (emphasis added).[65]

One mechanism for this convergence was price arbitrage, which can explain some of the sharp decline in the prices of goods exported to France. Another mechanism, one that would affect foreign nontraded prices as well as traded prices, worked through discount rate hikes and accompanying money and credit contraction forced by French gold conversions. One might argue the magnitude of these effects of French policy; their direction is clear.

Rist left no doubt that purchases of gold by the Bank of France following de jure stabilization in 1928 induced systemic deflationary pressure, which was offset by the Federal Reserve until 1929 — but not afterward:

> The inability of France to import gold during the period of *de facto* stabilization [from December 1926 until June 1928], and consequently, its inability to force credit contraction in foreign markets, in itself facilitated the rising in stock market indexes during 1927–1929. For a long time this obscured the impending decline in prices and delayed the outbreak of economic crisis by maintaining artificially high levels of consumption, especially in the United States.

> . . . The Open Market Policy of the Federal Reserve was formulated as a direct response to the first purchases of gold by the Bank of France [in the spring of 1927]. *It hindered the deflation of credit that should have resulted from these purchases.*[66] [emphasis added]

Evidence is strong for price level integration among countries on the gold standard in the 1920s. For example, a rising pound in 1924–25 was offset by declining internal British prices, so that by late 1925 almost exact purchasing power parity was restored with the dollar.[67] (However, one can infer from Britain's protracted profit deflation that its unit wages were higher and its profit levels lower than those in the United States.) The new reichsmark was somewhat undervalued in 1924, whereas price indexes reveal German prices to have been below those of the United States, Switzerland, the Netherlands, the Scandinavian countries, and Japan and higher only than those in France and Belgium; the overvaluation of the pound the following year somewhat increased the differential, at least temporarily.[68] By 1929, however, world prices dropped to restore parity. (I argue in chapters 6 and 7 that the Reichsbank played no more than a small role in inducing the moderate world deflation of 1925–29. By the end of this period Germany was losing reserves, which is further evidence that the deflation was generated elsewhere.)[69]

As world prices declined to the French level, the French economy lost its shelter from international deflation and depression; Sauvy estimates that French wholesale prices (on average) slightly exceeded international parity after October 1930.[70] By late 1930 prices in all gold standard countries, including those in France, would drop in a general liquidity squeeze. This development resulted from a cumulative process, as pressures built up at different intensities in different countries. From September of 1930, French domestic wholesale prices, which had fallen by no more than 10 percent over the previous eighteen months, fell another 16 percent by the time of the sterling devaluation a year later. French retail prices, which had been rising since late 1927, began to fall early in 1931.[71] An index for Paris Bourse shares lost over 30 percent of its value from August 1930 to August 1931; Tobin's q declined rapidly from its 1929 peak. French investment remained high in 1931, but it showed a decline in almost all areas from its level in 1930.[72] France continued to draw reserves through the first eight months of 1931, however, and it remained a motor of systemic deflation. The Tobin's q and investment data suggest that by 1931 capital moved to France less "spontaneously" than before and more in search of safety against devaluation and bankruptcy elsewhere.

The United States played a parallel role in 1931. The French price and investment data above suggest that this was the one interval during the years of severe deflation in which American gold exports — had they existed — might have been broadly distributed so as to ease systemic deflationary pressure, rather than merely fill vaults in the Bank of France. Prior to late 1930, subparity franc-denominated prices led to trade and capital arbitrage that brought gold to France. After September 1931, gold again went to Paris, most of it in exchange for pounds and dollars — neither of which any longer could be thought as good as gold. But during the final months of 1930 and the first eight months of 1931, an expansionary American policy might have helped to neutralize the reverse-Thornton effect of French policy and hence helped to stabilize world prices. This conclusion is conjectural; it posits that expansionary Federal Reserve action would have stabilized expectations, so as to slow the rush of world investors to the safety of heavily gold-backed franc-denominated assets. (The conclusion leaves another issue undetermined: whether, by 1931, the international gold standard was worth saving or was not better discarded as inexorably deflationary.)

International Deflation after September 1931

Had the worldwide recovery begun when the pound was floated in 1931, the Great Depression would not stand out as the historical catastrophe that it became. But the volume of world trade declined by another third between September 1931 and June 1932, and money supplies continued to drop sharply in much of the world through 1932.[73] In the United States and Canada industrial production dropped by nearly a quarter from September 1931 to the middle of 1932.[74] Industrial unemployment rates rose from 25 percent in 1931 to 36 percent in 1932 in the United States, from 17 percent to 26 percent in Canada, from 18 percent to 32 percent in Denmark, from 15 percent to 25 percent in the Netherlands, from 34 percent to 44 percent in Germany, and from 6½ percent to 15 percent in France; in Britain, by contrast, industrial unemployment was almost stable, rising only from 21 percent to 22 percent.[75] After the Bank of England floated sterling, the British economy was released from the constraint of international reserve flows and from the need to keep sterling tied to undervalued gold. This prepared the ground for British economic recovery.[76] Twenty-three countries, most of which did a heavy volume of trade in sterling, left gold by the end of the year. The devaluation of sterling changed price relations, making gold-linked currencies overvalued relative to those in the sterling area. This hurt exports from economies still on the gold standard, creating further balance of payments pressure, monetary contraction, and lower prices.[77] For the twenty-two countries that remained on the gold standard in 1932 — including the United States, the Gold Bloc countries, and, to a lesser extent, Germany, which had adopted exchange controls, bringing its partial isolation — the downturn worsened.[78]

The more important deflationary factor subsequent to the sterling devaluation was the accelerated contraction of the world's reserve base outside the sterling area — and the consequent higher interest rates. From the end of June 1931 to June 1932, the share of foreign exchange as a portion of central bank reserves declined in France from 32 percent to 7 percent, and elsewhere on the Continent from 32 percent to 12 percent;[79] most of this change came after Britain left the gold standard. In September 1931, about 30 percent of the Bank of France's foreign exchange was held in sterling and was henceforth rapidly liquidated.[80] The dollar, too, came under pressure. Over a period of nine months subsequent to the sterling devaluation, France alone converted more than $500 million of U.S. currency into gold. American free gold (that is, the gold available beyond the amount required to meet legal reserve requirements) dropped to about $350 million by early 1932, from a level more than double that in mid-1931.[81] In exchange for a slowdown in gold withdrawals, the French were able to demand higher interest rates on their dollar holdings in New York.[82] In response, the U.S. discount rate was raised from 1½ percent in September 1931 to 3½ percent by October 15. Deflation accelerated in the United States and elsewhere. During the latter part of 1931, the only sizable countries outside the sterling bloc to gain reserves were France, Switzerland, the Netherlands, and Belgium. In 1932, only France gained a significant amount of gold, but entirely through converting foreign exchange — most of it dollars. (The fact that France's new gold did not signify a net reserve gain is further evidence of a significant narrowing of price differences between the French and world levels.)

Paul Reynaud, the finance minister from March to December of 1930, acknowledged (while purportedly contesting it) in a quasi-official *Foreign Affairs* article of 1933 that the amount of sterilization was enormous.[83] He pointed out that of the increase of F54 billion ($2.2 billion) in the Bank of France's gold stock from June 1928 through October 1932, F26 billion ($1.05 billion) represented conversions of foreign exchange already held in portfolio.[84] Reynaud argues that the foreign exchange held by the bank was already "virtually gold," hence there was no requirement that it be monetized after conversion. However, the conversion of foreign exchange to gold drained reserves from elsewhere in the world economy. Also, most of the foreign exchange was absorbed between August 1926 and June 1928 and was sterilized then, as outlined earlier. About F20 billion ($800 million) of this amount was converted after September 21, 1931. From the third quarter of 1931 to the fourth quarter of 1932, French currency expanded by only F4 billion ($160 million), and M1 by only F1 billion ($40 million).[85] The financial impact of a two-step sterilization differs only in its timing from that of a one-step sterilization.

France might easily have inflated domestically after September 1931 to begin offsetting deflationary pressures at work elsewhere. Indeed, France was in a position to do this before the sterling devaluation and by doing so might yet have saved the gold standard. After September 1931, monetization of the more than $1 billion of gold acquired since the Monetary Law would have gone some way toward braking world deflation and might have ended the world's cycle of competitive devaluations. The Bank of France's gold cover rose in 1932 to nearly 80 percent of currency and central bank sight deposits, against a legal requirement of only 35 percent. The pursuit of central bank and Treasury policies with these drastic deflationary consequences was an avoidable mistake.

French Alternatives

French monetary practice during 1928–32 has been defended in recent years. Jean Bouvier points out that the Bank of France avoided converting its holdings of sterling into gold until after sterling left gold; further, it avoided raising its discount rate in late 1930 and early 1931 — which it wanted to do for domestic reasons — because this would have attracted more gold to France.[86] Eichengreen, in a different defense, acknowledges that the Bank of France sterilized a large amount of gold but believes that restrictions on its ability to undertake open-market operations meant that it had no choice.[87]

Bouvier's argument recalls those of the contemporary Bank of France and Treasury. For example, the bank argued in its *Annual Report* for 1932,

> Since 1928, in fact, the trend of exchanges has been almost constantly favorable to France. Under these circumstances the bank could not have realized any large portion of its foreign exchange holdings without deliberately provoking an enormous outflow of gold from foreign markets, in addition to the large withdrawals which had already resulted from *the natural orientation of international capital movements.*
>
> Your board of directors had no desire to increase by its own initiative the monetary difficulties of other countries. By retaining, therefore, the greater part of its foreign balances and especially its sterling assets, the Bank of France contributed greatly to the maintenance of the stability of British currency during the last three years.[88] [emphasis added])

This explanation — like Bouvier's — neglects the role of French policy in redirecting the "natural orientation" of capital movements toward France, that is, the sterilization of reserve inflows and the effort to keep French prices below international norms.

OPEN-MARKET OPERATIONS

The statutes of June 1928 provided two authorizations for open-market operations, both of which Moreau wanted.[89] First, article 3 of the June 23 convention between the bank and the Amortization Fund authorized the bank to sell and repurchase the fund's short-term paper "if it judges that to be of service in influencing the volume of credit and maintaining the volume of circulation."[90] Quesnay saw this paper as the main instrument for open-market operations.[91] Second, article 9 of a second convention of the same date between the Bank of France and the Finance Ministry gave the bank "the authority to undertake, for the account of such foreign banks of issue as have opened a current account on its books, the purchase of bills and securities."[92] The British economist Thomas Balogh proposed in 1930 that the Bank of France might grant credit to either foreign central bankers or to the Bank of International Settlements, which might then be used — following the above article — to undertake open-market purchases in France.[93] As discussed earlier, the bank often discounted foreign paper for other central banks before 1914, so any break with tradition here would have been small.

Kenneth Mouré argues that the bank could undertake open-market operations almost as it chose, in spite of a statutory restriction dating back to 1808 on transactions not specifically sanctioned.[94] He notes the opinion of the Bank of England official Siepmann in 1930: "The fact is that the elaborations of the jurists themselves destroy the efficacy of the material with which they work — with the result that, in practice, almost anything might be done and brought somehow within the four corners of the rules. . . . In order to overcome or circumvent the rules and regulations nothing more is needed than goodwill and an agreed plan."[95] Siepmann's opinion is not entirely reliable concerning the Bank of France, for he was inevitably influenced by experience in Britain, where the central bank was more interventionist. Even so, in view of Moreau's handling of demands from both bank regents and the Treasury from 1926 onward and of stabilization in 1928, it seems likely that, had he desired it, he could have obtained whatever authority he needed for expansionary open-market operations in 1930.

On January 23, 1930, the bank's council of regents approved Governor Moreau's request for authorization to sell Amortization Fund paper — action clearly within the scope of the convention of June 23, 1928 — but in the face of resistance from a number of regents. Their doubts were reinforced when Gaston Jèze soon afterward denounced the bank's embrace of "managed currency." The council reversed itself on January 30, 1930, almost certainly because of its members' continued skepticism about managed currency.[96]

This incident demonstrates that the Bank of France would not exercise even the powers clearly available to it. Also, that the bank considered undertaking open-market *sales* during the world deflation shows its attachment to orthodox liquidationist notions. Moreover, the bank remained committed to anti-interventionist monetary and orthodox deflationist policies into 1936, or for the entire period of the "franc Poincaré."[97] The bank, far from being somehow swept along by deflationary pressures generated elsewhere (as Eichengreen implies), was a significant source of pressure.

REDISCOUNTING POLICY

Emphasis on open-market operation policy diverts attention from striking changes in the Bank of France's rediscounting policies from the prewar and even the pre-1926 periods.[98] Before 1914, the bank played an important role as lender of last resort for other banks. Private banks were consequently able to reduce their own cash to a minimum. Governor Georges Pallain explained before the U.S. National Monetary Commission in 1910:

> It appears to us that for French private banks the proportion of cash to liabilities is less significant on account of the facilities offered by the organization of the Bank of France for rapid conversion — in a crisis — of a good portfolio into ready money. . . . The part which the Bank of France plays toward private establishments permits the latter, as has many times been proved, to reduce to a minimum their cash reserves, and to devote, without exceptional risk, a larger part than perhaps elsewhere to productive commercial operations.[99]
>
> The eminent founder of the Crédit Lyonnais, M. Germain, a very competent man in these matters, admitted frankly that if the Bank of France did not exist he would close the Crédit Lyonnais — in times of crisis, of course.[100]

When a banking crisis struck at the end of July 1914, the Bank of France made good on its promise of easy discounting, as its portfolio rapidly more than doubled from $1.6 billion to $3.4 billion.[101]

In 1930 and 1931 private banks no longer counted upon the support of the central bank. In early 1930, banks began increasing their holdings of cash, much of which they deposited at the Bank of France. Cash held by the four leading commercial banks (Crédit Lyonnais, Société Générale, Nationale d'Escompte, and Crédit Industriel et Commercial) grew from F2.66 billion ($106 million) in December 1929, to F3.96 billion ($158 million) in December 1930, to F5.50 billion ($220 million) in June 1931, and to F12.29 billion ($492 million) in December 1931. From December 1930 to November 1931, these banks' combined cash holdings rose from 10.8 percent to 32.6 percent of deposits.[102] By the end of 1931, slightly more than one-seventh of the total French currency issue was held in reserves by the four great banks.

This pattern indicates a direct causal connection between the buildup of bank cash reserves and the movement of gold to Paris. To some extent the cash buildup represented a postinflation restocking, following years of liquidity-averse portfolio choices.[103] Following the Oustric Bank crisis in the fall of 1930, French banks further increased their cash in anticipation of deposit withdrawals.[104] After the Austrian banking crisis of May 1931, accumulation of cash became more exigent.[105] French banks called back short-term deposits in London. Vicious circles of confidence breakdown were at work. Had private banks been confident that sterling would not be devalued, they might have held more of it; also, had French banks been confident that they might rediscount at the Bank of France in time of need, their reserve requirements would have been less.

An early postwar change was the Law of December 20, 1918, which extended Bank of France discounting privileges to small and medium-sized enterprises.[106] This in part reflected an effort to garner popular support for the bank in the immediate aftermath of the war.[107] Direct discounting soon became an important source of bank profit. It also expanded the area of direct competition between the central bank and private banks — a competition that became bitter when the depression struck. One result was that it became a matter of pride for the large private banks never to rediscount at the Bank of France.[108]

By the time the world depression struck in 1930, reduced central bank discounting also reflected specific public policy. At a time when the gold and foreign exchange backing of the French currency had increased to extraordinary levels, the "lessons" of Moreau's anti-inflationary effort of the middle 1920s were still being trumpeted. Jèze, then at the Academy of International Law, detailed a standard program for currency stabilization. He argued first that central bank advances to the Treasury should be prohibited except for the provision of working capital.[109] He then argued that central bank discounts should be limited to bills for "commerce and production" — the "real bills" doctrine:

> The mission of [the central bank] is to provide monetary "elasticity" as required for economic prosperity. It is thus expected that private banks will demand money creation for the needs of commerce and production.
>
> *But this money creation should occur only if it is necessary for the needs of commerce and production, and should be backed by very strong guarantees furnished by private banks.*

This is where the vigilance and independence of the central bank are indispensable.[110]

Real bills discounting policy is procyclical because commercial bills are abundant during upswings and scarce during downturns. Practiced faithfully, real bills–based discounting enfeebles the central bank as a lender of last resort. Jèze did not shrink from this consequence:

> [The] role [of the central bank] is to intervene only if it is required in the national interest. It is not sufficient [basis for intervention] that interested parties warn of a *crash*.
>
> . . . *In no case, under no pretext*, should the central bank create banknotes or open credits in a way that compromises the convertibility of its paper money. It is better to permit one, two or three banks, or even a large number of banks or large industrial firms to fail, *than to jeopardize the national currency*. The bankruptcy of certain banks or industrial firms brings only individual ruin. The consequence of compromising the national currency is the ruin and demoralization of the country. [emphasis in original]
>
> However, and this point is essential, *when private banks know that the central bank will not easily come to their aid, they will demonstrate more prudence*. [emphasis added]
>
> . . . The fact that the legal (reserve) percentage is maintained does not mean at all that the central bank is authorized to create paper money to save private banks or imprudent and badly positioned industrial firms. It is the task of central bank technicians, and theirs alone, to decide independently whether the public interest truly demands intervention, and to what extent the intervention should take place in view of the legal reserve requirement.[111]

In the world context of 1931, Jèze proposed exactly the wrong medicine. His counsel to disregard a rising reserve ratio was particularly inapt, as it overlooked the international character of the interwar gold standard, hence the effect that the accumulation of limited reserves by the Bank of France would have upon other central banks. What Jèze calls prudent behavior on the part of French banks, their cash buildups, was then aggravating the international gold movement to France. Sterilization of French reserves — a consequence of ignoring the Bank of France's rising reserve ratio — would aggravate systemic deflationary pressure.

Language in the Bank of France's *Annual Reports* offers a truncated version of Jèze's argument. The *Report* of 1932 (for activity during 1931) emphasizes the importance of "prudent" banking management and the subordination of discounting policy to maintaining the currency's metallic backing:

> The anxiety aroused by events abroad was further increased by a systematic and insidious campaign which endeavored to exploit certain isolated cases of

failure, *resulting from mistakes or unwise management,* in order to aggravate the lack of confidence and try to ruin the credit of the strongest and soundest houses . . .

. . . [The Bank of France] did not hesitate to support the market by assuming any risks which were compatible with its primary duty of preserving all the safeguards of the currency.[112] [emphasis added]

The findings of a commission appointed in November 1930 by the Chamber of Deputies are consistent. One expert explained, "An exclusive preference is granted for real bills of exchange or of commerce because they alone represent the products that consumers demand and can afford."[113] Further, the bank was disinclined to discount paper from troubled banks, regardless of the quality of specific assets. The minutes of a general counsel session in early 1932 indicate that the bank "accorded the most liberal help to all the houses whose situation was healthy."[114] A number of regional banks were allowed to fail; for some, profit prospects were weakened by the central bank's expanding role in direct discounting to small and medium enterprises.[115]

The portion of the four large credit banks' commercial portfolios rediscounted at the Bank of France was less in late 1930 at 36 percent of the total than in 1912 or 1913 at 58 percent and 46 percent of the totals, respectively. This is corroborating evidence for the bank's reduced role in this area. A portion of the rediscounting performed in the past by the bank was taken up in the interwar period by the Fund for Deposits and Consignations (hereafter Deposit Fund), whose task it was to invest money on behalf of savings banks. The Deposit Fund held a discounted portfolio of French bons, railway bills, and even British treasury bills of between F2 and F4 billion during 1930 and 1931.[116] French banks often turned to the Deposit Fund as an early source of supply for needed cash — that is, usually after withdrawal of funds from London but before recourse to the Bank of France.[117] The Deposit Fund's rediscounting differed from that of a central bank in important respects, however. First, it was undertaken strictly for the fund's own profit and safety, without concern for its effect on the money market. Second, it disposed only of deposited funds, hence it did not create new credit as do central bank discounting and open-market operations.[118] For these reasons it offered only a pale substitute for a central bank during times of distress.

The largest damage from restricted Bank of France rediscounting came not from financial bankruptcies but from doubts about the lender of last resort facility that had been available before 1914, and the consequent need to exercise caution in lending and to hold more idle reserves. The Bank of France may well have been a less restrictive lender than the contemporary Reichsbank and Federal Reserve Bank. Yet its policies did more systemic damage than those of the other central banks because the ensuing demand for cash led to larger flows of capital and gold to France than to anywhere else during 1930 and 1931.

Moreau, through the end of his governorship in September 1930, or Moret, who succeeded him, could surely have eased French monetary policy through the use of open-market operations or more liberal discounting. Such a course of action would have required acknowledgment of essential interconnections between the monetary policy of France and that of other countries on the gold standard. French bankers and politicians worried about domestic inflation; but once world deflation set in by 1929 or 1930, a significant gold-backed local inflation was no longer possible. The Bank of France failed to stop world deflation for doctrinal reasons.

SAVINGS BANKS

I discussed earlier how during the inflationary period 1924–26 the Bank of France lost control over interest rates because the Treasury set bon rates below a market equilibrium level. Beginning sometime in the late 1920s and aggravated by new legislation in March 1931, the bank's control over interest rates was again compromised; in this case, rentiers used their political influence to force rates above market levels on deposits at the Deposit Fund.[119] Siepmann, at the Bank of England, detected the problem even before the new legislation:

> [A] circuit has been formed or at least an eddy on the main stream of currency. It starts by a deposit of francs by a French national in a French Savings Bank. The Savings Bank is required by law to pass the deposit on to the *Caisse des dépôts et consignations* [the Deposit Fund] which invests the proceeds in rentes. These rentes are bought on the market in Paris but may come in effect from some reluctant seller ["reluctant" in the sense that he is a "natural" rente holder, who sells to take advantage of a good offering price] in the provinces who for lack of a better investment places his money in the Savings Banks and the process starts all over again. How much the stream of circulation is slowed down will depend on the time-lag between the deposit in the Savings Bank, the purchase of rentes and the next deposit. The process is probably slow.[120]

During the late 1920s and early 1930s, the French yield curve was sloped steeply upward. Through the auspices of the Deposit Fund, savings bank deposits were in large measure placed in government rentes — which paid higher long-period interest rates — even though balances were easily accessible for deposit-holders.[121] In March 1931, the amount that could be placed in a savings bank was raised from F50,000 ($2,000) to F100,000 ($4,000) for qualified organizations and from F12,000 ($480) to F20,000 ($800) for individuals; each family member could have an account. Through these changes, savings banks came to be used for idle cash balances — in which they competed directly with deposit banks — rather than for deposits that represented longer-dated savings.[122] From December 1930 to December 1931, the fund's deposits rose from F32 billion to almost F43 billion, and to almost F48 billion at the end of 1932.[123] Because this was a period of declining prices, the real increase in the fund's deposits was greater than these numbers suggest.

The easy availability of higher savings deposit interest rates lessened the influence of central bank discount rate policy upon market conditions. Had the Bank of France lowered its discount rate, commercial banks would have been constrained to follow, and this would have brought further deposit transfers to savings banks.[124] This is not exculpatory for the Bank of France, however. The legislative changes came at the end of March 1931, only a few weeks before the Creditanstalt crisis. Much of the damage had already been done. Also, open-market purchases or a more liberal discounting policy — the options theoretically open to the bank — would have worked through increasing the money supply and thereby improving expected returns on investment. These results might have been achieved even without first lowering the discount rate.

10

The American Deflation, 1928–32

The movement of gold to France played an essential role in ending the interwar gold standard and in wrecking international prosperity, but events elsewhere were not unimportant, and other monetary authorities did more than a little damage. Developments in the United States merit detailed attention, both for their contemporary impact and for the prominence they receive in most accounts of the period.

Heretofore I have treated the level of profit inflation or deflation as responsive to government fiscal and, especially, monetary actions. Where governments were unable to act, I have often identified external constraints, chiefly related to the workings of the interwar gold standard. Internal political constraints have also played a role. Interest group dynamics barred institutional restructuring of the German economy; a combination of ideological and interest-based opposition to inflation reinforced the French proclivity to burrow the world's gold in its central bank vaults.

From the standpoint of the performance of a market economy, the above influences were exogenous. What has scarcely appeared in my story is evidence of endogenously unstable financial asset price behavior, in which expectations about the marginal efficiency of capital become volatile and take on a life of their own. But if expectations are inherently unstable, then stock market prices may no longer reflect so-called economic fundamentals and can themselves exert a destabilizing influence. I shall consider evidence of such destabilization in the United States during the late 1920s.

Measurement of the impact of the Wall Street boom upon the U.S. and international economies is complicated by the effects of monetary and trade policies that were pursued either simultaneously or soon afterward. Monetary policy in the United States was contractionary both during and *after* the stock market boom. Furthermore, passage of the Smoot-Hawley Tariff Act in June 1930 raised duties on a wide array of agricultural and industrial products entering the United States. In estimating effects of the stock market boom and then of monetary and trade policies, I shall identify ways in which deflationary disequilibrium was induced or extended.

The Wall Street Boom

An index of U.S. common stock prices increased from 6.86 in 1921 to 11.15 in 1925 and 15.34 in 1927. From here the rise accelerated to 19.95 in 1928 and 26.02 in 1929.[1] In the sweep of history the increase was perhaps not the sui generis event that it seemed to some at the time; the rise in New York indexes during 1982–87 approached it in proportional terms, and the 1980s stock market boom in Japan exceeded it. Nevertheless, it was a constant concern to central bankers. Strong wrote to Norman in September 1925, "We all [at the New York Federal Reserve Bank] feel that the Stock Exchange speculation may reach a point where some action will need to be taken."[2]

The Federal Reserve lowered the discount rate in July 1927 in spite of fears that easier money would fuel the stock market boom.[3] Strong then viewed the harm that a tight money policy would have upon the real economy as a weightier consideration than the potential benefit it might bring by slowing the bull market in stocks. A gold outflow followed upon the discount rate reduction. During the last four months of 1927 the Federal Reserve lost $141 million in gold, and in 1928 — mostly in the first half of the year — it lost $388 million. The bank's *Annual Report* observed that this was "the largest gold outflow from the United States that has ever occurred."[4] This demonstrates (consistent with my earlier narrative) that contractionary pressure was generated outside the United States and was already strong by 1928.

Gold losses by themselves did not motivate American policy at this point; as noted earlier, Strong sought to redistribute gold away from North America. But when the financial boom continued and even accelerated after the middle of 1927, Strong reversed priorities.[5] Between December 1927 and July 1928, the Federal Reserve adopted sharply tighter monetary policies. It reduced securities holdings by nearly four-fifths through open-market sales and reduced its discounted securities by more than half. The discount rate was raised from 3½ percent to 5 percent, its highest level since 1921. The rate for acceptances was raised in steps from 3 percent to 4½ percent,[6] which helped to end the gold drain and gave impetus to a new capital inflow to the United States.

The tight policy induced by the Federal Reserve was damaging to European economies, but the policy goal of dampening the stock market boom was supported by many European central banks, including the Bank of England.[7] Nevertheless, the new policy aroused opposition at the time among those concerned about deflationary pressures. Cassel, for example, testified in congressional hearings in May 1928 against raising interest rates.[8] A recurrent question in the literature concerns whether deliberate action to slow the equities market was well advised. Friedman and Schwartz argue that the central bank ought to have maintained steady growth in monetary aggregates, hence "should not have made itself the 'arbiter of security speculation and values' and should have paid no direct attention to the stock market boom."[9] Eichengreen, Alexander Field, and Eugene White, too, are confident that deliberate contractionary action to block the stock market boom was ill-advised and triggered the initial downturn.[10]

Keynes argued the opposite view. The role that volatile expectations might have in destabilizing the level of investment is alluded to in Keynes's *Treatise on Money* and is central to the argument of the *General Theory*. This complicates the task of monetary management. Keynes wrote in the *Treatise* of "quick changes . . . in the spirit of enterprise."[11] He repeatedly vented doubt about the capacity of monetary authorities to avoid booms and downturns. In the *General Theory*, the behavior of financial asset prices appears as significantly independent of the usual tools of economic management. For example:

> A conventional [financial asset price] valuation which is established as the outcome of the mass psychology of a large number of ignorant individuals is liable to change violently as the result of a sudden fluctuation of opinion due to factors which do not really make much difference to the prospective yield; since there will be no strong roots of conviction to hold it steady.
>
> . . . It is by no means always the case that speculation predominates over enterprise. . . . [But] in one of the greatest investment markets in the world, New York, the influence of speculation is enormous. . . . Speculators may do no harm as bubbles on a steady stream of enterprise. But the position is serious when enterprise becomes a bubble on a whirlpool of speculation.[12]

If the American stock market had indeed become a "whirlpool of speculation" by 1928 and 1929, it may have contributed *independently* to economic instability.[13] If so, it was an appropriate focus of attention for the central bank — which is not to endorse specific subsequent action.

First, I want to consider evidence that there was indeed a speculative bubble in equity values. Second, I shall show that the financial bubble brought instability to the real economy and threatened to bring more. In this context I consider the extent to which this instability gave impetus to a domestic or world deflation or to both. Finally, I propose an alternative policy.

EVIDENCE FOR THE 1928–29 SPECULATIVE BUBBLE

A standard neoclassical view supposes that free markets tend naturally toward full-employment equilibrium, provided only that the money supply grows at a predictable rate and that government interference through taxes, regulations, and tariffs is minimized.[14] Monetarists conclude that the central bank should have ignored the equities boom. Friedman and Schwartz argue, based on the behavior of monetary aggregates, that there was no unusual credit expansion in the United States during the 1920s and certainly none at the end of the decade.[15] They do not deny evidence of asset price speculation, but they treat it as being of small import. In a monetarist framework, savings and investment reach equilibrium without having an impact upon either prices or output. This framework scarcely allows the possibility that stock speculation might generate an investment boom that would independently affect the second term of the fundamental price equation.[16]

In contrast to the monetarist denial that a credit expansion occurred, some Austrian School and French economists note the stock market–related expansion and attribute it to easy systemic monetary conditions in the late 1920s. Parallel to the monetarists' focus on balanced money supply growth, some Austrian School and French economists imagined that a rigorous gold standard automatically kept an economy close to a full-employment equilibrium. From the latter's point of view, the reason for the Wall Street boom was the inflation generated after the middle of the decade by the use of foreign exchange as an international reserve.[17] This conclusion implies that without the "inflationary" credit that heated the real economy, there would have been no unusual increase in equity prices. Indeed, this view of the role of easy credit in generating higher equity prices has become conventional.[18]

Evidence contradictory to the easy credit conclusion is that U.S. call rates, which were normally at levels close to other short-term domestic interest rates, rose repeatedly to levels several hundred basis points above both discount and commercial paper rates during 1928 and 1929.[19] The 1929 rates were themselves rising, which helped to reduce outstanding commercial paper from $600 million to $265 million;[20] corporations were disinclined to bid for expensive short-term money when the cost of issuing equity was declining. The independent rise in call rates suggests that they were forced upward by investor demand for equities — hence, that speculation was not accommodated by easy money or credit conditions. E. White tested data for 1926–30 and concludes,

> In the estimated demand equations, the variables for new issues and specula-
> tion on the stock market explained most of the variation in the demand for
> brokers' loans. However, it was impossible at even the 10 percent level to
> accept the hypothesis that the coefficient on the call rate was different from
> zero. *This apparent indifference of the borrowers to the interest rate is in
> accord with the claim that they were transfixed by the potential for capital
> gains and paid little heed to the interest rate.* [emphasis added]
>   . . . The coefficients on the dummy variables [in the equations to estimate
> the supply of credit], intended to capture any independent stimulus to the
> boom, had negative signs. It was not possible to reject the hypothesis that the
> coefficients were different from zero at the 10 percent level. This suggests that
> there was no "pushing" of funds into the stock market. If anything, lenders
> retreated a bit, *ceteris paribus,* from lending on the bull market.[21]

White's evidence suggests that volatile expectations in themselves contributed much to financial market instability in the late 1920s.[22]

Four other kinds of evidence make it likely that speculators drove the New York market of 1928–29 to levels disconnected from economic fundamentals. One is that stock price movements ceased to parallel those in dividend payments. From 1922 through 1927, increases in dividends and increases in stock prices moved nearly synchronously. From the beginning of 1928 through most of 1929, however, the Dow-Jones share index rose by some 70 percent while the dividend index gained no more than half of that.[23] (In an intriguing parallel nearly sixty years later, dividend increases failed to keep pace with the equities price index prior to the stock market crash of October 1987.)[24] Stock buyers were suddenly more bullish than corporate managers, who set dividend payment levels. One might conclude that active equity buyers were more bullish than long-standing owners — on whose behalf corporate managers are more likely to act; such divided opinion augured continued asset price instability.

A second type of data also points to a lack of market consensus. I offered evidence (in chapter 6) that rising share prices in France after 1926 facilitated a large increase in economy-wide real investment outlays. For the U.S. stock market boom of 1928 and 1929, this correlation is less clear. Gross private domestic investment rose from $14.1 billion in 1928 to $16.2 billion in 1929; but the increase reflected a $2.1 billion net increase in inventory accumulation, most of which was involuntary.[25] The lower cost of equity led to rapid growth in new shares during the last two years of the boom, from $1,474 million in 1927 to $5,914 million in 1929. This was somewhat offset by a decline in the issue of domestic bonds and notes, from \$3,183 million to \$2,078 million, and in foreign issues in the United States from \$1,338 million to \$678 million over the same period. Nevertheless, the overall volume of securities issues rose from \$5,995 million to \$8,670 million. Easy access to capital facilitated corporate issuers' investment in producer durables; industrial production rose 17 percent during the year ending July 1929.[26] Private construction, however, an activity more sensitive to the cost of debt, fell by a nearly offsetting amount.[27]

In a bull market with a consensus of opinion, bears would close or reduce their positions. This would be manifested by relative ease in call lending rates; indeed, a consensus bull market develops only when monetary conditions are fairly easy — that is, when the cost of capital is perceived as being lower than potential returns on investment. Proceeds from the sale of shares would return to "industrial" circulation, that is, where they might be held for investment or consumption transactions. But in a bull market characterized by a division of opinion, some proceeds from the sale of shares are moved from the industrial to the "financial" circulation, either to be loaned short-term (perhaps in the call market) or held as cash.[28] The division of opinion becomes well defined when monetary restraint drives short-term lending rates upward (indicating rising liquidity preference) while the bull market continues unabated. Monetary constraint forces a "two views" development.[29] In time, sufficiently high interest rates tempt some potential share buyers to become short-term lenders.

Field has identified a huge increase in the financial circulation in the late 1920s. Trading value on the New York Stock Exchange increased fiftyfold from less than \$2 billion annually in July 1921 to more than \$98 billion annually in October 1929. He estimates that 17 percent of total demand deposits in New York City during 1928 and 1929 represented holdings for securities transactions *additional* to those held in 1925 and traces the increased demand to the rise in trading volume.[30] That the volume of demand deposits for the United States was virtually flat from late 1925 through early 1930 indicates contraction of all circulation outside of the New York region and of the industrial circulation nationwide.[31] Keynes would almost certainly argue that Field exaggerates the transactions motive and overlooks the (bearish) speculative motive in the buildup of financial circulation;[32] one cannot separate one motive from the other in volume figures for demand deposits. Whichever of the two was more important, the buildup of nonindustrial circulation offers evidence that the rising stock market and the contracting monetary circulation were pulling in opposite directions. This is a third reason to doubt that equities were priced according to fundamentals; when bulls and bears stand in sharp opposition, both cannot be right.[33] When bullish sentiment nevertheless persists, it must digest rising call money rates.[34] At some point either (1) monetary conditions are relaxed and call rates decline, permitting a bullish consensus to return or (2) high call rates and a shrinking industrial circulation bring an equity market decline.

A fourth type of evidence that the U.S. stock market was overpriced is that it appears to have ignored crucial and specific information about an international deflation already under way during the last and most extravagant year of the bull market. Strong, Keynes, Cassel, and the *Economist* have been quoted in the context of the anticipated deflationary impact of the French Monetary Law of June 1928. Leffingwell anticipated the impact of an event comparable to the Monetary Law more than a year earlier, at the time the Bank of France began earmarking its gold in New York:

> By earmarking it, however, they take it out of our reserves as effectively as if they shipped it. Ben [Strong] welcomed this decision [because] he felt it would restore his control of the money market here. No doubt it is a good thing to do in moderation, but *if it were done on a large scale and abruptly there would be the devil to pay. The French have 7 or 8 hundred millions [of dollars] of valuta!* Anyway this is another step in the world wide return to gold, the tendency of which as I have pointed out is deflationary — to increase the value of gold and reduce commodity prices.[35] [emphasis added]

It soon became clear that the adoption of the de jure gold standard in June would not end the capital inflow to France, so that French policy would rapidly strain world reserves and aggravate systemic deflationary pressures. As the United States was linked to an international gold standard, the domestic price level could not for long diverge from trends elsewhere.

DAMAGE FROM THE SPECULATIVE BUBBLE

Somewhat contradictory arguments are advanced to explain the damage that may be associated with a soaring stock market. On one hand, higher equity prices make capital cheaper for issuers, which can give rise to overinvestment. This is most likely to occur when rising equity prices are matched with accommodative monetary policy and hence reflect a consensus of investor sentiment. When stock prices rise despite contractionary interest rates, however — that is, when two views develop — the financial circulation is likely to absorb resources from elsewhere, thereby boosting interest rates and reducing aggregate investment. Both effects can occur simultaneously, too, so as to have differing impacts upon different sectors of the economy. I said earlier that any boost to economy-wide investment from the rising U.S. stock market of 1928 and 1929 was countered by the contractionary impact of rising short-term interest rates.

If, contrary to what happened but in line with many contemporary and ex post facto recommendations, the Federal Reserve had turned its attention away from the stock market boom and adopted a more accommodative monetary policy in 1928 and 1929, the result might have been a surge in aggregate domestic investment. Given easier credit conditions and a continued equities boom, investment in producer durables would have been at least as strong as it was and construction would have decreased less or not at all.[36] A premise of this book is that the deflation after 1928 was disastrous because of the large volume of long-term, nonindexed contracts entered during the previous years of relative stability (see chapter 1). A speculation-driven boost in investment at the end of the decade would have increased this exposure. As it was, the heady atmosphere of the 1929 stock market boom led consumers to increase their debt (almost all of it unindexed) by more than 20 percent during that year alone.[37] When a speculative boom takes on a life of its own, it is not likely to be self-correcting in a manner that is stabilizing for the broader economy.

There is abundant evidence that the New York stock boom heightened systemic deflationary pressure by changing the pattern of international capital movements. While U.S. equity costs declined, most foreign stock indexes were approximately steady or posted only small gains from late 1927 through September 1929.[38] Diverging movements in equity price indexes implied higher expected returns or lower equity capital costs or both for domestic U.S. issuers relative to foreign issuers. One result was a spontaneous movement of international capital to the United States.[39] In conditions of systemic equilibrium, the higher demand for capital in the United States would have reflected growing American demand for foreign goods and services. But as I pointed out earlier, rising American interest rates blocked this demand response, so overall U.S. demand changed little. Also, higher U.S. rates forced parallel rises elsewhere and contributed to systemic contraction. Keynes noted in October 1929 that nothing had happened to enable foreign economies to support a higher rate of interest than before.[40]

Equilibrium might have been restored by easing U.S. monetary conditions — that is, through open-market purchases or lower discount rates — but perhaps at the cost of encouraging more speculation on stocks. More speculation would have added upward pressure to short-term rates, to some extent offsetting the effect of deliberate monetary ease.

The potentially destabilizing effect of a soaring stock market was evident in the late 1980s in Japan, where price-earnings ratios reached extraordinary heights. The Japanese equity bubble was accommodated for years by low short-term interest rates, approximately as Cassel, Friedman and Schwartz,

Eichengreen, E. White, and Field suggest would have been appropriate for the late 1920s in the United States. Easy access to capital in Japan led to over-capacity and distorted investment; two-thirds of the increase in the country's gross national product between late 1986 and early 1991 came from a capital spending spree. As a consequence, the Japanese economy has been hugely susceptible to debt-deflation, and the subsequent Japanese downturn was al-most certainly more painful than it otherwise would have been.[41]

POLICY ALTERNATIVES

The problem in the United States was that one instrument, monetary policy, was directed simultaneously toward two targets: stable general prices and stable financial asset prices. Starting about the end of 1927, the Federal Reserve focused increasingly upon the level of asset prices. The central bank needed a second policy lever, one that would slow the stock market boom without affecting the cost or availability of credit for other purposes. The Washington board of governors attempted to do this with its call for restrict-ing rediscount facilities used to extend so-called speculative loans.[42] However, selective controls on credit are a very blunt instrument, one probably not confined in its effects to the stock market. Leffingwell wrote in May 1929,

> The board in Washington is now hinting that a bank that makes loans on stocks and bonds may not be fit to borrow from the Reserve Banks even on eligible commercial paper. . . . It doesn't always do, though, to carry a ques-tionable position to its logical extremity. I suspect that in undertaking to deprive the holders of billions of dollars of stocks and bonds . . . of the right to borrow on them, by discriminating against the banks that lend on them, the Board in Washington have gone one step too far.
>
> . . . I am not without anxiety; for while dear money is burdensome, the threat of a denial of credit at any price to one great category of borrowers may be disastrous.[43]

The New York Federal Reserve Bank objected to the Washington policy and probably deliberately obstructed its implementation.[44] In retrospect, efforts to selectively restrict credit to call-market lenders in all likelihood pushed call rates higher than a simple rise in the discount rate would have.[45] If so, they increased both the drain of funds from the industrial circulation in the United States and the induced movement of capital from abroad.

Keynes doubted that easy credit was the problem. He proposed specifically to tame the stock market and suggested alternatives to both higher interest rates and credit restrictions: "A hint to banks to be cautious in allowing their names to appear on prospectuses, and to the Committee of the Stock Exchange to exercise discrimination in granting permission to deal would be more efficacious. And if necessary a temporary increase of a substantial amount in the stamp on contract-notes (as distinguished from transfers) in respect of transactions in ordinary shares would help to check an undue speculative activity."[46] The immediate conclusion is that when a bull market in stocks has become destabilizing it might be brought under control with a minimum of damage to the real economy and in a way that stabilizes output and employment. This is the second policy lever that the Federal Reserve might have used in 1928 or 1929. These proposals for bringing stock market speculation under control were closely related to a crucial argument in the *General Theory*. The stock market, Keynes argued — and this followed from his premise that volatile expectations could destabilize share prices — was often a poor guide to accurate calculation of the marginal efficiency of capital, hence a poor guide for the allocation of capital resources. He implied that the State, in the future, should "tak[e] an ever greater responsibility for directly organizing investment."[47]

Use of this lever might be applauded in instances in which the stock market is widely believed to be wrongly priced, but in which higher interest rates might cause serious domestic or international disequilibrium. For those less persuaded than was Keynes of the State's ability to calculate economic advantage, the close connection between proposals to tame speculative froth in the stock market and those to replace its allocative function will give pause.

If Keynes's more extreme conclusions in the *General Theory* about the instability of investment are correct, then much of the argument of my book is undermined. A broader gold reserve base or more successful efforts to economize in the use of gold would not have prevented the Great Depression if its deeper cause was financial markets that were chronically unstable. Keynes himself would probably have rejected this extreme conclusion, however. In 1928, he wrote that tight money might lead to underinvestment in the United States.[48] In early 1930 he noted that the recovery of investment in the United States and Britain was delayed by "the obstinate maintenance of misguided monetary policies."[49] Subsequent to the *General Theory*, Keynes continued to emphasize monetary policy as a tool for maintaining equilibrium. He wrote in 1937,

> The transition from a lower to a higher scale of activity involves an increased demand for liquid resources which cannot be met without a rise in the rate of interest, unless the banks are ready to lend more cash or the rest of the public to release more cash at the existing rate of interest. . . .
>
> This means that, in general, the banks hold the key position in the transition from a lower to a higher scale of activity.[50]

Even when profit deflation originates in an independent change in expectations (which might give rise to a collapse in equity values), expansionary banking policy might help restore equilibrium.

The speculative boom in U.S. equities was a spent force by the autumn of 1929. Total gold movements to the Federal Reserve during the first ten months of the year were only $228 million and were offset by an outflow of $109 million during the following two months.[51] From the standpoint of the world's gold reserves, which then exceeded $10 billion, this was but a minor disruptive factor. Other trends did not yet indicate the onset of a depression. Unemployment rose in Germany during 1929 but was fairly steady in most other countries; in France, the United States, the Netherlands, and the Scandinavian countries it declined slightly.[52] Discount rates rose in much of the world during the first few months of the year, perhaps by enough to trigger a cyclical downturn but not by enough to explain the depression. Neither the size of capital and reserve movements nor the timing of the Wall Street boom fits.

The Federal Reserve after the Stock Market Crash

The downturn in 1930 has been a persistent puzzle in the literature. The pressure from the return to gold convertibility by central banks in the middle 1920s induced a gradual deflation of world commodity and wholesale prices. High interest rates in 1929 associated with the capital movement to the United States and gold losses to France contributed to downturns late that year. By 1931, money supplies were falling rapidly in the United States, Germany, and elsewhere. Yet 1930, in spite of steep declines in nominal interest rates accompanied by only mild declines in money stocks, also saw real income fall sharply. Moreover, the 1929–30 real decline was far steeper in the United States than elsewhere. Whereas industrial production in Europe as a whole fell year-on-year by perhaps 7 percent, it declined by 19 percent in the United States.[53]

Kindleberger argues that the stock market crash led foreign investors to withdraw credit that had been extended at high rates in the call market and led American banks subsequently to rein in lending. Firms in the United States that had counted on access to equity finance were suddenly forced to curtail expansion and seek liquidity. Domestic consumers found it harder to obtain mortgage credits, while the stock market decline diminished the value of their assets and hence reduced their spending.[54] Continued stock market volatility in the months after October 1929 heightened consumer uncertainty, which reinforced the demand for liquid assets.[55] By these mechanisms, an increase in liquidity preference slowed the economy and brought lower prices, even absent any contraction in the money supply. The subsequent general decline in prices allowed nominal interest rates to fall notwithstanding the rise in real (deflation-adjusted) rates.[56] Here is a variation on the observation that financial market instability can damage real economic performance.[57] Here is an instance in which an unfettered market did not lead the economy back to full employment of people and other resources but instead (endogenously) amplified consequences of the initial shock.

Nevertheless, whatever deflationary impulses followed from the Wall Street debacle were soon aggravated by clumsy monetary policy. In the years after Strong became inactive in August 1928 (he died in October), the Federal Reserve made little effort to offset either the post–stock market crash credit contraction or the French-induced gold deflation. Power in the Federal Reserve shifted to Washington's board of governors. The Washington group was less sensitive to international concerns and less inclined to act decisively in this sphere than Strong had been. Harrison, in New York, was by both temperament and legal training a negotiator and compromiser.[58]

During the last quarter of 1929, the Federal Reserve undertook open-market purchases to the extent of trebling its holdings of government securities. It sought to relieve the short-period strain on the money market resulting from the stock market crash—but not, however, to maintain equilibrium in aggregate employment or output.[59] From the end of 1929 through mid-1930, declines in the U.S. discount rate (in steps, from 4½ percent to 2½ percent) always lagged behind declines in the call lending rate. Banks could earn as much or more and at lower risk by repaying borrowings as by extending new credit.[60] Beginning in October 1930, the United States suffered two waves of bank failures, and subsequently money supplies contracted sharply. Over a slightly longer period, aggregate demand deposits declined from $22.6 billion in December 1929 to $21.1 billion in December 1930, to $19.1 billion in September 1931, and then rapidly to $13.5 billion by March 1933. Aggregate currency holdings were steady at $3.8 billion to $3.9 billion through May 1931, after which they rose to $5.6 billion over the following twenty-one months—an increase much short of offsetting the concurrent decline in demand deposits.[61] From December 1929 through September 1931, the Federal Reserve's share of world monetary gold increased from 38 percent to 41 percent, in part owing to a collapse in U.S. demand for imported goods. Thus American monetary policy faced no external constraint and indeed imposed constraint elsewhere through its reserve absorption.

This conclusion offers additional perspective on the argument of the previous section. The postcrash stock market of 1930 and 1931 appears to have declined further because of deflationary pressure in the United States and in the world beyond and because this pressure was aggravated by the uncertainty engendered by misguided monetary policies. Investors did not irrationally remain bearish over this longer period. It is unlikely, therefore, that self-generated instability in the stock market *after* October 1929 made a large independent contribution to cooling the economy.

A look at the reigning monetary doctrine at the Federal Reserve reinforces the conclusion that deflation was its handiwork. The Reserve's defenders could not point to restrictions upon its open-market purchase authority (as have some defenders of the Bank of France)[62] to justify contractionary policies. It was widely believed that deflation and consequent liquidation were appropriate and necessary to undo the excesses of previous years' speculation and investment. A central bankers' corollary to this viewpoint is the procyclical real bills doctrine.[63]

The real bills doctrine was partially incorporated in sections 13 and 14d of the Federal Reserve Act of 1913. The first of these indicated that discounting should be linked to "notes, drafts and bills of exchange arising out of actual commercial transactions."[64] Not all U.S. central bankers accepted the doctrine as a guide to action. An exchange between Leffingwell and Strong in 1922 highlights the degree of contention. Leffingwell, a real bills advocate, wrote,

> Now it appears, however, that during the last six months [the Reserve Banks] have been actively engaged in making money cheap by the purchase of Government obligations for their own account. . . .
>
> I scarcely need to say to you that *inflation occurs quite as definitely and harmfully when currency and credit are prevented from contracting co-ordinately with the contraction in business and prices* as when currency and credit are expanded beyond the expansion of business and prices.[65] [emphasis added]

The influential *Tenth Annual Report* of the Federal Reserve Board, published in 1923, also embraced the real bills doctrine in its defense of "liquidationist" action carried out during 1920 and 1921.[66] Real bills advocates inferred that provision of credit in response to the needs of trade would not generate price inflation because a concomitant increase in the production of goods could be relied upon to bring prices downward. (This argument neglects the role that procyclical monetary policy might have in generating inflation through the second term of the price equation.) Strong rejected the real bills argument and urged that central banking should provide countercyclical weight.[67] He criticized Leffingwell for misunderstanding this function:

> Your view seems to be that the Federal Reserve System was designed for the purpose of providing the means by which credit and currency would expand

as trade demands increase and that when trade demands diminish the volume of credit and currency would automatically contract, without employing rate changes to influence either movement. This, I believe, is contrary to the experience of the world in central bank practice; and I would be most regretful to feel that we differed materially on such a fundamental matter as this.[68]

Leffingwell threatened to make this difference of opinion public two months later, but Strong dissuaded him.[69] Strong was not alone at the Federal Reserve in opposing the real bills doctrine. Randolph Burgess, an economist and deputy governor at the New York bank, argued that monetary policy should be countercyclical, hence that the discount rate should increase during booms and decrease during downswings.[70] Strong had sufficient clout to carry his views into policy, but he sought to do so without public confrontation.

The dispute was revisited after Strong's death. Harrison sought authority to continue open-market purchases during 1930.[71] He met opposition from the Washington board, of which Adolph Miller was the leading figure, and elsewhere. George W. Norris of the Philadelphia bank was a particularly insistent advocate of the real bills doctrine at the Open Market Conference in September 1930; most regional bank governors supported Norris in his liquidationist view.[72] As the year went on, Harrison came to doubt his own expansionist arguments, which in the event did not become policy. On July 31, 1930, in a letter to Moreau, he even described the Federal Reserve's policy as one of "easy money" — because nominal interest rates were low. This formulation implicitly accepted the real bills position.[73] As the depression gathered force, member banks became increasingly unwilling to show Federal Reserve borrowing on their balance sheets because it might be interpreted as an indication of financial weakness.[74] In 1931, Harrison joined with Norman in pressing a restrictive discounting upon the Reichsbank during the German banking crisis.

Here is where events might have turned out differently had Strong lived a few years longer and remained the dominant figure at the Federal Reserve. Strong presumably would have rejected the procyclical real bills views of Miller and Norris in 1930, just as he had earlier rejected theirs and Leffingwell's. Strong's propensity for countercyclical action is indicated by the fact that the relatively calm years of 1922, 1923, 1924, 1927, and 1928 saw more variation in the system's holdings of government securities (which suggests countercyclical discounting efforts) than did the turbulent years of 1930 and 1931.[75] He was specifically concerned by the potentially deflationary consequences of French gold absorption.[76] Following the 1929 break in the stock market and possibly earlier, a Strong-dominated Federal Reserve might have injected money into the banking system on a sustained basis. Parallel to his response to pressures upon sterling in 1924 and 1927, Strong might have tolerated sizable losses of U.S. gold in 1930 and 1931 in order to hinder deflationary advances elsewhere. (Looking ahead, one can anticipate that the diplomatically sensitive Strong would have denounced the Smoot-Hawley tariff of 1930, although it is hard to know what impact his opposition would have had.) Had expansive monetary measures been taken, the specifically American contribution to the post–October 1929 deflation would have been much less.

This is a long way from asserting that the depression would not have occurred had Strong lived. Earlier I noted Strong's skepticism regarding the gold exchange standard and his distaste for the views of Keynes, Cassel, and Fisher regarding potential international deflation. There is little reason to believe that a Strongian Federal Reserve after 1928 would have sought a systemic remedy for the world's gold shortage — a coordinated rise in the currency price of gold — insofar as Strong had often insisted that gold supplies were adequate. Strong's goals were more limited. The most likely scenario, had he lived, is that international deflation would have come more slowly, not that it would have been avoided.[77] The deflation's largest and most protracted impetus came from Paris, not New York or Washington.

Friedman and Schwartz indicate that the United States could directly control its money stock, and they hold the Federal Reserve responsible for not offsetting the internal drain (that is, the rise in the currency-to-deposit ratio) with open-market purchases.[78] They imply that the American deflation had almost exclusively domestic origins. They write, for example, that it "would be difficult indeed to attribute the sequence of bank failures to any major current influence from abroad."[79] In fact, however, given free movements of capital, the United States could increase (or maintain) its own money stock only by increasing (or maintaining) the world money stock, hence by issuing more currency even in the face of an outflow of gold reserves.[80] Causality ran both from and to the United States. Kindleberger answers Friedman and Schwartz:

> I find it easy [to attribute U.S. bank failures to influences from abroad]. Depreciation of the Argentine, Uruguayan, Australian, and New Zealand currencies in early 1930 helped push down wheat prices in the United States. Falling prices of grain were communicated to corn and other feeds, sowing bankruptcies among farmers, as well as failures among banks in farm communities, particularly in 1930 in Missouri, Indiana, Illinois, Iowa, Arkansas, and North Carolina.[81]

To overcome the international pressures causing agricultural price declines in the United States would have required a systemic cure. It is far from clear that the Federal Reserve was in a position to provide one in 1930 or 1931; already in late 1927 and 1928 the United States had large reserve losses. But American policy instead moved in the opposite direction: 1930 and the first eight months of 1931 comprised the period of the greatest American gold absorption.

After sterling was floated in September 1931, however, U.S. gold reserves declined by more than $1 billion to June 1932. These losses reflected almost entirely conversions of dollar holdings by France and other Gold Bloc countries. The wisest American action probably would have been to let the dollar decline, in step with the pound, after September 1931. But even in the context of maintaining the dollar's gold parity, it was a mistake to delay conversions by raising the American discount from 1½ percent to 3½ percent in October 1931 (see chapter 9). The Federal Reserve should have invited the French (the Swiss, Belgians, and Dutch had liquidated most of their U.S currency by the end of October) to convert all of their dollar holdings to gold at their pleasure and then have maintained the lower discount rate and undertaken open-market purchases. It would certainly have been preferable that France continue to hold dollars as a reserve, then expand the French credit-to-reserve ratio (by "monetizing" their reserves) as part of a coordinated effort with the Federal Reserve to reflate; the point here is that the Federal Reserve was not powerless to act alone.

The declining level of American free gold need not have been an obstacle. President Hoover presented the proposals that were later embodied in the Glass-Steagall Act, which expanded the range of securities eligible for collateral against Federal Reserve notes — thereby removing the free gold problem — in early October 1931. Even after passage of Glass-Steagall in February 1932, the Federal Reserve waited two months before beginning open-market operations. Elected members of the American government for the most part wanted a more expansionary monetary policy;[82] responsibility for the continued U.S. contribution to the world deflation sits with the central bank.

The Smoot-Hawley Tariff and Systemic Deflation

The Smoot-Hawley tariff was signed into law by President Hoover in June 1930. Its finished form was the product of a large amount of legislative logrolling. The tariff provided more across-the-board protection than any specific interest group desired, and it was certainly more protectionist than Hoover intended or than the Republican party had promised in the campaign of 1928. It was publicly denounced by 1,028 professional economists, an event reported on the front page of the *New York Times* on May 5, 1930.[83] In the popular understanding, it was and perhaps still is widely believed to have played an essential role in bringing about the world depression.[84]

From the standpoint of so-called real analysis (in which one leaves aside effects from monetary changes) a tariff can have two kinds of macroeconomic impacts. One of these is certainly negative, the other arguably positive — for the country imposing the tariff. Negatively, a tariff is equivalent to a tax on doing business for both firms and consumers. Inefficiencies result as goods and services become more expensive and less accessible; this is the flip side of the ubiquitous "comparative advantage" case for free trade. However, this argument scarcely appears in the literature on the Smoot-Hawley tariff as it related to the origins of the depression.[85] The damage from tariff-induced inefficiencies — like the benefits of free trade — are usually thought to be concentrated in the medium or long period.

The other real argument stresses macroeconomic shifts in demand. Higher American tariffs would somewhat shelter the U.S. economy from price drops elsewhere. Higher relative domestic prices would bring a comparative boon to U.S. production. On the other hand, foreign prices would presumably have declined more than otherwise, a consequence of the partial closing of the American market. Focus on these effects can explain the origins of the depression outside of the United States only if we presume that those origins were preponderantly American.[86]

Historical data offer little support for the conclusion that the Smoot-Hawley tariff raised relative prices or increased relative demand in the United States. From September 1930 through September 1931, U.S. wholesale prices declined by 17 percent, which exceeded declines in France, Britain, Germany, Italy, Canada, and Japan.[87] Similarly, the decline in the U.S. stock market and in industrial production and the rise in U.S. unemployment matched or exceeded that in most other countries during 1930 and 1931.[88] This is not to deny that a tariff could have raised relative domestic prices, but rather to observe that *this* tariff was not the dominant influence upon relative prices; although we cannot gainsay the possibility that relative U.S. prices would have fallen even more without Smoot-Hawley. In the case of the United States during 1930 and 1931, the deflationary influence of Federal Reserve monetary policy almost certainly outweighed any countervailing influence from trade policy.

Eichengreen, Rudiger Dornbusch and Jeffrey Frankel, and, in part, Jude Wanniski argue that the greater damage from the Smoot-Hawley tariff came not from relative price changes but from the undermining of the international adjustment mechanism through which debtor and reparation-paying countries exported goods and services.[89] Coming as it did after the slowdown in American lending in 1929, the tariff clogged one of the few remaining channels for balancing international accounts without gold movements. The United States absorbed gold during 1929 and 1930; in this sense the American situation was then opposite to that in Britain, where Keynes proposed partial closing of the British market in order to prevent gold outflows (see chapter 1). The Federal Reserve would have faced no reserve constraint had it chosen to pursue a more expansionary monetary policy.

On the terrain of economic theory, this argument against Smoot-Hawley is impeccable. But it does not demonstrate that the degree of practical damage to international adjustments from the new tariff — as opposed to that caused by Federal Reserve policy — was great. The effects of the Smoot-Hawley tariff are not directly evident in the trade balance. The American trade surplus declined from $841 million in 1929 to $782 million in 1930, then to $334 million in 1931.[90] An alternative explanation emphasizing trade movements might be that a relatively buoyant United States economy attracted relatively more imports — in spite of the new tariff. But this is implausible because price, production, and employment data indicate that the U.S. economy saw relative (as well as absolute) decline during most of 1929–32. An explanation more consistent with this evidence is that trade flows adjusted (in part) to capital flows, which were shifting toward America. Capital movements might have shifted because of fears of foreign bank failures, doubts about currencies aggravated by declining foreign central bank reserve ratios, or even concerns about political stability. (Foreign tariff barriers — whether retaliatory or erected independently of Smoot-Hawley — were in this context beneficial. They gave rise to a larger decline in the U.S. trade surplus than might have occurred in their absence and hence blocked a larger movement of gold to the Federal Reserve.)[91]

The issue of the extent to which Smoot-Hawley contributed to the relative shift in capital movements toward the United States remains. In theoretical terms, it is plausible that by reducing the resources of foreigners owing money to U.S. lenders the new tariff generated fears that led to capital flight. But this returns one to an earlier observation: higher U.S. tariffs (ceteris paribus) would bring a relative rise in U.S. prices and in relative U.S. prosperity — which in turn might generate a spontaneous capital in-movement. This boon to the U.S. economy would have been reinforced by monetary ease following a reserve inflow. Yet U.S. prices and production fell, even in relative terms. This suggests that trade policy was not the core problem; induced capital flows to the United States would have occurred even in the absence of Smoot-Hawley. The deflationary systemic effects of misguided trade policy, like those of reparation and war debt policies, might have been softened through more open-market purchases and more accommodative discounting in the United States during 1929–31 and in France during almost all of 1927–32.

Why Did the Great Depression Happen?

It has become almost a commonplace that the deflation of 1929–32 was a consequence of a malfunction of the interwar gold standard. But this essential agreement breaks down as soon as one shifts to details. Hawtrey, Cassel, and Keynes proposed that the gold standard be "managed" to avoid the monetary contraction that would otherwise result from inadequate reserves. Friedman and Schwartz argued that no international deflation would have occurred had exchange rates been allowed to float. Temin and Eichengreen more recently have linked the gold standard to deflationary policies adopted by various central banks, while either neglecting or denying any general reserve constraint.[1]

Keynes's analysis of economic disequilibrium provides an alternative to equilibrium-model accounts of the systemic effects of transfer payments, investment flows, and gold movements. His essential argument is that price declines after 1928 directly produced declines in output and employment— that is, profit deflation. In this way the effects of the post-1928 deflation differed from those of income deflations, including those of the 1870s and 1920–21. The conclusion that the 1929–32 price declines were unanticipated is reinforced by evidence that futures market speculators actually expected price increases during much of the period.

Keynes was also suggestive about the roles of Britain, France, and the

United States in his *Treatise on Money,* but he never provided a detailed narrative of events. His explanation suffers from his neglect of the undervaluation of gold as the underlying cause of the systemic gold shortage and the price declines. Friedman and Schwartz in their *Monetary History* similarly detect no large deflation in the works until restrictive Federal Reserve actions in 1928, and they largely dismiss factors external to the United States. Friedman has since revised his view to acknowledge that the Bank of France had a large systemic deflationary effect, but he has not offered a history of developments outside the United States. Temin emphasizes the role of the United States and Germany in inducing deflation but overlooks the role of the Bank of France. Eichengreen's stress upon the role of international cooperation (or its absence) leads him to emphasize crises to the point that he loses sight of underlying structural weaknesses in the interwar gold standard. Cassel offered narratives closest in spirit to this one, and he highlights the problem of inadequate reserves; but he offers little detail.[2]

A Historical Summary of the Deflation

One can summarize the sequence of events that brought the systemic deflation by reference to Thornton and reverse-Thornton effects. The outflow of European gold during World War I produced an inflationary Thornton effect, as belligerent governments ended convertibility rather than contract domestic money supplies or aggregate demand. Credit-to-gold ratios increased in Europe, while the exported gold provided a base for monetary expansion elsewhere. A rapid gold-backed inflation subsequently occurred in the United States. Because the gold/dollar price ratio was unchanged from its prewar level, the price increases of 1919 and early 1920 left the dollar's metallic reserve base with a sharply diminished real value. A partial reverse-Thornton effect occurred with the 1920–21 deflation. But even after 1921 the real value of gold remained near its historic low, and the systemic ratio of credit to the real value of the world's monetary gold was much higher than before 1914. Gold's undervaluation hampered both supply and demand responses to the reserve shortage. One demand response was a reverse-Thornton effect brought about by a spectacularly large flow of gold to India during several years of the first postwar decade.

The international restoration of gold convertibility during the 1920s increased demand for monetary gold. Wherever central banks adopted restrictive monetary policies to attract gold, further reverse-Thornton effects were produced, moving general currency price indexes toward their lower prewar levels. The German restoration in 1924 and the British restoration the following year were both accompanied by upward movements in domestic and international interest rates. The alternative to systemic deflation was the "economization" of monetary gold, either through reduced central bank reserve ratios or the supplemental use of foreign exchange as a reserve. The Federal Reserve adopted expansionary policies in 1924–25 and again in 1927 to aid the sterling restoration. The French inflation of 1924–26 gave impetus to a large export of capital that also eased conditions in London markets. American and French action alike expanded credit, which somewhat offset the contractionary reverse-Thornton effects of British and German policies.

The direct result of restoring sterling at too high a level against the dollar and gold was to make sterling-denominated goods more expensive than otherwise in international markets. This raised systemic prices somewhat, through arbitrage, which slightly aggravated the undervaluation of gold. But the more important effect of the overvaluation was that it weakened the Bank of England's ability to attract reserves without raising interest rates to a level unacceptably restrictive. This relinquished leverage to the Federal Reserve and the Bank of France; if either attracted an unusual amount of gold, the Bank of England would be unable to block or offset it. Thus British policy both aggravated the international gold shortage and weakened the central bank that would have been most inclined to counteract its effects.

Whereas the poststabilization capital inflows to Germany and Britain were induced by high interest rates, the subsequent flow to France was spontaneous, a result of an attractive investment climate consequent upon low taxes and an undervalued currency. This facilitated a sharp increase in gold and especially foreign exchange at the Bank of France. By early 1928 the bank was able to restructure its assets, replacing tens of billions of central bank "advances" with the new reserves. Following passage of a new reserve law, additional foreign exchange inflow — as well as a portion of the outstanding stock — was converted to gold. Further reduction in world reserves followed as this (and German) action delegitimized foreign exchange as a reserve for other central banks. High legal reserve ratios then forced worldwide reductions in credit money nearly in step with reserve losses outside of France. Through both its actual gold absorption and its ability to convert foreign exchange balances, the bank slowed the credit money creation supportable by gold held elsewhere. During 1927–32 the French share of the world's monetary gold rose from less than 10 percent to 28 percent, a large amount of which was directly sterilized; of the monetized portion, much was hoarded by individuals and banks. This generated a huge reverse-Thornton effect.

Over the medium period from 1926 through September 1931, the U.S. gold share as a portion of the world total declined somewhat, and the United States played no active role in the liquidation of foreign exchange reserves — Federal Reserve holdings of foreign exchange were always recorded as investments rather than reserves. A deflationary reverse-Thornton effect began, however, in late 1929 — when the volume of U.S. credit money declined slightly despite a rise in domestic gold reserves earlier in the year. (From the standpoint of the international economy, that nearly the same volume of U.S. reserves supported a smaller volume of credit than before represented sterilization as much as the failure of new reserves in France to support a proportionally expanded credit structure.) The New York stock market boom, in conjunction with the Federal Reserve's antispeculative tight money policy at the end of the 1920s, played an important role in raising world interest rates and inducing an international crisis in 1929; but it accounted for only a relatively small gold movement. The boom thus aggravated the broader contraction related to the world's reserve shortage — but it was largely distinct from that systemic problem. Some of the short-term damage stemming from the stock market–related crisis might have been reversed had the Federal Reserve sustained an easy money policy after October 1929. More damaging from the standpoint of reserve movements than anything that happened to equities prices was the central bank's adherence to a procyclical (hence, deflationary) real bills discounting rule over much of the following three years.

An expansive Federal Reserve policy would have maintained or increased the domestic currency-to-deposit and credit-to-gold ratios. The U.S. central bank might have attempted expansion even to the point of causing an export of gold, as it did at times during the 1920s under Strong's leadership. Had gold exported from New York after 1928 gone into the coffers of the Bank of France and been sterilized — and much of it would have, especially while French prices remained below the world level — this expansionary effort would have been thwarted. United States policy was at least partly hostage to the dynamics of the French gold absorption. After late 1930, when dollar and sterling prices on internationally traded goods had fallen to reach approximate parity with franc prices, it is plausible that Federal Reserve gold exports would have been more broadly distributed, hence generating an expansionary Thornton effect. It is unfortunate that Federal Reserve discounting practice during this period was at its most contractionary.

United States monetary policy again became hostage to decisions of the Bank of France after Britain left the gold standard in September 1931. French pressure then forced a rise in the U.S. discount rate from 1½ percent to 3½ percent exchange for delay in converting more than $500 million in dollar reserves to gold over the next nine months. The money and credit superstructure contracted further in the remaining gold standard countries, which brought large new increases in unemployment elsewhere. In 1932, French industrial unemployment more than doubled, a consequence of the world slowdown that French policy did so much to foster.

The reparations and war debt situation gave rise to only mild systemic disequilibrium for as long as payor countries (predominately Germany) could induce offsetting capital inflows. This required high German interest rates, which slowed domestic activity and probably pushed rates somewhat upward in other countries. Beginning in 1928 and 1929, the combination of conversions of French foreign exchange to gold and the flow of capital to Wall Street made it harder for Germany to attract capital. The international recycling mechanism bogged down, resulting in harsher systemic distress in the form of higher real interest rates, declining prices, aggravated profit deflation, and declining output and employment. The Smoot-Hawley tariff of 1930 reinforced the deflation by clogging another channel through which a strong currency might have been recirculated, although comparative price and output data suggest that the effects of the tariff were minor relative to those of monetary policy. These effects are neglected when it is assumed, as it often has been in the economic literature on transfers, that international output equilibrium is maintained during and after capital movements. The short-period damage to the "real" economy from transfers and tariffs resulted from their monetary consequences, that is, the consequences of the deflationary policies imposed by recipients France and the United States.

The crises of 1931 should be viewed in this broader context. The collapse of the Creditanstalt in May 1931 was met by standstill agreements, rather than by bailout lending. Standstill agreements typically ensure that trouble will spread to the next tier of creditors, thus sowing doubts among potential lenders. A frequent argument holds that more aggressive international lending in May and June to both Austria and Germany might have blocked further deflation, thereby preserving the gold standard. This argument, however, neglects domestically induced damage from the Reichsbank's restrictive discounting policy, particularly toward banks involved in public sector lending. Discount restrictions ushered in the German bank collapse of the summer and led to more capital flight. More broadly, restrictive discounting practices in 1930 and 1931 in France, Germany, and the United States led to higher liquidity demands in all three countries and hence had reverse-Thornton effects.

The argument that international lending in 1931 might have saved the international gold standard also brushes too lightly over the cumulative drag brought on by the string of reverse-Thornton effects outlined a moment ago. More aggressive lending in 1931 might merely have slowed or extended the deflation, without addressing its underlying cause. This argument also confuses action needed to maintain the gold standard with that suited to promoting economic recovery. An economic recovery under the interwar gold standard would have required effective gold economization measures, probably including a reversal of the French Monetary Law, and expansionary policies in France and the United States, including a combination of liberalized discounting rules and ongoing open-market purchases. Even this omits what could have been the most fundamental reform, an increase in the currency price of gold. By 1931 it may have been too late to save the interwar gold standard. If the underlying liquidity problem could not be alleviated, it was better for the world economy that the gold standard fail.

The Role of Separate National Policies

I turn now to a country-by-country summary. The huge Indian absorption of gold for nonmonetary uses in the 1920s illustrates the deflationary consequences that may follow from the undervaluation of gold. It offers strong evidence — yet it is virtually ignored in both the contemporary and in more recent literature — that the wrong real gold price can dramatically affect the nonmonetary demand for gold and impart systemic instability. When the international price deflation came at the end of the decade, thereby raising the real value of gold, the gold flow to India stopped abruptly. In this sense, Indian absorption was a response to international price fluctuations, not their cause.

In terms of economic effects, Germany was more a victim than a causal agent during the years leading up to the depression. After 1928, German transfer payments were largely sterilized in France and to a lesser extent in the United States. Henceforth, German reserve ratios were almost always under pressure. Nevertheless, German actions did contribute in three ways to systemic profit deflation. Anemic domestic economic performance during the middle Weimar years was a small drag on world growth; much of this is attributable to interest group distortions of the German political economy, rather than to external pressure. This did not, however, bring a separate impulse to systemic slowdown *after* 1928. Second, Schacht's abandonment of the gold exchange standard as early as 1925 made it easier for other countries, especially France, to abandon it later. Finally, restrictive Reichsbank discounting policies in 1930 and 1931 led to the German bank collapse in the summer of 1931, which then shifted pressure to sterling.

The United States contributed to the coming of the deflation at four points. The first was the failure to adjust the dollar price of gold after the postwar inflation, in order to set the systemic gold-to-currency price ratio at a sustainable level prior to restorations of convertibility. Second was the tight money policy imposed to break the stock market boom of 1928 and 1929. The third was the contractionary discounting policy pursued after the stock market crash of October 1929. Fourth was the Smoot-Hawley tariff. American policy set an unenviable standard for repeated bad judgment, although the pattern is balanced somewhat by Strong's and private bankers' contributions to currency stabilizations during the 1920s. That policy mistakes were frequent, however, does not in itself demonstrate the severity of their consequences.

The failure to revalue gold after the 1914–20 inflation had enormous consequences; limited but real support for Fisher's dollar-stabilization plan suggests that a more resourceful American leadership might have proposed revaluation. The obstacles were imposing, however. Systemic revaluation of gold by monetary authorities would have been inconsistent with maintaining the mystique of the gold standard — by which metallic supplies were to regulate prices independent of official action. Furthermore, mitigating the consequences of this American omission, the gold undervaluation and shortage left only an underlying tendency toward currency price deflation. It does not explain why the violent deflation came when it did, after 1928. (Conjecturally, had world prices on traded goods dropped by 40 percent over a full decade, rather than over the three years from 1929 to 1932, it is likely that business would have suffered. But some portion of the decline in output almost certainly was driven by the rapidity of the deflation.)

Although the American tight money policy of 1928 and 1929 had deflationary consequences for the world economy, an unchecked stock market boom might also have done damage. The Federal Reserve had to choose between letting short-term interest rates soar, driven by higher rates on call money, and reinforcing the stock of industrial circulation in a way that might have led to an unwanted surge of new investment. It followed the first course and generally drew international support for it. Keynes later offered a theoretical framework for understanding a stock market boom with a life of its own, and he proposed steps for bringing it under control without collaterally reducing the industrial circulation. His argument has since been received skeptically or rejected outright in decades of "efficient market" literature. Keynes's suggestion that stock transaction taxes might be used to dampen a boom has disturbing implications in a free-market economy and has seldom been attempted. Again, in the context of those times, it is difficult to criticize American decisions. Yet even if one concludes (along with many economists) that the Federal Reserve ought to have treated world price stabilization as a higher priority than stopping the Wall Street boom during 1928 and 1929, one should not exaggerate the systemic damage from high American short-term interest rates. The immediate flows of capital and gold to the United States at the end of

1928 and in 1929 were small against the scale of the longer-period world liquidity squeeze.

Deflationary central bank discounting policy after the stock market crash was an avoidable and unambiguous policy error. The Smoot-Hawley tariff, which aggravated the systemic deflationary consequences of concurrent monetary policy, is also not defensible. It lacks even the neomercantilist justification that an improved trade balance would have permitted domestic monetary ease — for the United States at that time had positive international account balances, a steady inflow of gold, and a large stock of free reserves. As a consequence of restrictive monetary and trade policies, the United States absorbed nearly $700 million of gold during 1930 and the first half of 1931, which made an important short-period contribution to systemic contraction.

British decisions also aggravated the systemic deflation. Hawtrey, who in 1922 called attention to the world's liquidity shortfall, nevertheless argued concurrently that Britain had little choice but to restore sterling's prewar parity. He noted that if parity "were changed once, it might be changed again. A return despite difficulties to the former parity is a pledge of stability."[3] The (retrospective) response to this is that the overvaluing of sterling weakened both the currency and the influence of the Bank of England upon world reserve movements and prices in the longer-period more than a devaluation would have.

The British decision was based upon misapprehension of the way the pre-1914 gold standard worked. British experts argued that most prewar central banks typically adjusted their discount rates to offset international gold movements. They misunderstood the exceptional prewar role of the Bank of England. In contrast, the Reichsbank ordinarily adjusted discount policy to moderate *internal* drains and refluxes of gold before 1914, and the Bank of France was usually passive in the face of gold accumulation. Before 1913 the United States did not have a central bank. Some hoped that the new Federal Reserve would assume an internationally stabilizing postwar role; in the event, it did so only sporadically. The post-1918 official British analysis also posited that other countries would avoid more than moderate accumulation of gold, hence that Bank of England reserves would not come under pressure. Faulty analysis led to inept policy.

Even had they understood more, British officials could not have directly redressed the systemic undervaluation of gold in the early 1920s, for only the dollar was then convertible. After their error of 1925, the British could only hope for effective economization of gold by the United States and France. Had sterling instead been devalued in 1925, the Bank of England might have had more influence upon the distribution of world reserves. This might have been enough to slow the descent of prices and output that occurred after 1928; almost certainly, the Bank of France would have drawn less gold. However, this argument will be too conjectural for most readers; no one writing in 1925 — and certainly no one in a decision-making role — showed that amount of prescience. To understand the depression one needs to explain the timing of the price plunge; identification of long-period causes is useful but not sufficient.

This brings me to France. France became a gold sink, beginning in 1928, just as it had been before 1914. The consequences would be different after 1928. In 1914 the real value of gold was slightly above its long-period average level, and the world's monetary gold stocks were abundant; by the 1920s, the real value of gold production and stocks was compressed. The postwar world monetary system could not sustain the reserve concentration typical before World War I. Whereas the flow of gold to India in the 1920s was an unambiguous consequence of its real undervaluation — and would cease as soon as the undervaluation ended — the movement to France at the end of the decade forced the real value of gold upward. At the same juncture, the French gold inflow brought international deflation and stopped the flow of nonmonetary gold to India.

French actions in the later 1920s were almost deliberately disequilibrating for world prices. The franc was stabilized at a level anywhere from 10 to 25 percent below world price parity, and the Bank of France acted to keep it undervalued. Incoming foreign exchange was used to retire Treasury advances, hence was sterilized. The French demand for money remained unsatisfied, which led to more reserve inflow.

Subsequent to the French Monetary Law of 1928, further accumulation of foreign exchange would be converted to gold. In addition, more than $400 million of sterling already held by the Bank of France (on deposit in London) was gradually converted between June 1928 and September 1931 — against typical Bank of England reserves in only the $700 million to $1 billion range during 1925–31. With the support of leading French economists, the Bank of France pursued a procyclical discounting policy even after the downturn began to affect conditions in France. This marked a near-reversal of prewar practice. After Britain floated the pound in September 1931, the French prevailed upon the Federal Reserve to raise its discount rate to make it worthwhile for them to delay converting their holdings of $600–$700 million to gold. The combination of higher interest rates and new conversions after September 1931 sharply worsened the world deflation.

The American and British central banks have the historical defense that at least some of their mistakes were overlooked by contemporaries. As argued earlier, even subsequent scholars have seldom identified key events, for example, the failure to adjust the dollar/gold exchange and the effect of overvaluing sterling upon the Bank of England's systemic influence. In contrast, actions of the Bank of France were roundly criticized at the time — by (usually foreign) economists, private sector bankers, the Bank of England, and the gold delegation of the League of Nations. In historical perspective, French errors were avoidable.

The decisions to liquidate Bank of France advances and to block a rise in internal prices were motivated by domestic politics. They reflected memories of the inflation associated with the 1924–26 collapse of the franc as well as the political clout of rentiers, small farmers, and even industrial workers. The franc was undervalued to prevent British-style stagnation, not to attract reserves for diplomatic advantage; the anti-German Alsatians who were politically close to Poincaré usually wanted a *higher* franc (to enhance national prestige) and were relatively unconcerned about the unemployment that this might bring among workers. The decision to abandon the gold exchange standard reflected doubts about the pound and concern that further accumulation of sterling would be inflationary, rather than a scheme for diplomatic advantage. Indeed, Schacht at the Reichsbank had parallel economic motives and reiterated his goal of establishing a pure gold standard a few months before the French Monetary Law was adopted in June 1928. Bank of France discounting was restricted both before and after the downturn began. What made French action most responsible for the depression was neither that France's economic policy was more benighted than that of other countries (although it was no less so), nor that its diplomacy was more self-serving, but that policies pursued in France had greater deflationary systemic consequences than the same policies pursued elsewhere. This happened essentially because the credit-to-gold ratio in France was lower than almost anywhere else and because active sterilization of incoming gold further shrank the superstructure of world credit.

The Role of Individuals

The world's leading economists deserve criticism, individually and collectively. An orthodox view, represented by Rist and von Mises, assumed that deflation would have manageable and perhaps even desirable consequences. Other economists, including Keynes, Hawtrey, and Cassel, did fear deflationary consequences but believed that world prices could be supported through central bank management of reserves. Neither opinion could adequately guide policy-makers in a world in which deflation would have large disequilibrating

consequences and in which the structural problem was the effort to recon-
struct an international gold standard with an inadequate reserve base. Heads
of State and central bankers during the 1920s were never presented with the
advice that the price of gold was too low and ought to be adjusted. Moreover,
most of the economic literature on the depression during the past several
decades has equally neglected this fundamental issue.

Keynes bears some responsibility. He did not identify the comparative success of the prewar gold standard with the relative abundance of new gold
supplies or the historically high level of gold's real value. He framed the 1925
sterling parity issue in terms of its cyclical impact upon the British economy,
rather than in the context of the postwar world liquidity shortage. This weakened his case against resumption of prewar parity. A lifelong advocate of
managed money, he publicly dismissed the importance of the world's supply of
gold in 1926 — which contradicted the better judgment of Cassel, Hawtrey,
and Rist. After passage of the French Monetary Law, he acknowledged that
Cassel had indeed been right in warning of a gold shortage. But his subsequent
writings emphasized instead the instability of expectations and irrational market behavior, often within a closed-economy framework. Keynes occasionally
observed that the supply of new gold is responsive to price signals, but this
insight was far from his usual concerns. Had his *Treatise* or *General Theory*
included discussion of the role of the undervaluation of gold in giving impetus
to the worldwide profit deflation, the economic literature on the depression in
the decades following might have been very different.

One's judgments about the role of individual policy-makers follow from the
country-by-country summary. In the cases of Britain and the United States,
critical decisions often mirrored broad consensus. The Cunliffe Committee in
1919 and the Bradbury Committee in 1924 both called for restoration of
sterling's prewar parity. Norman became governor of the Bank of England in
1921, and he, too, was committed to restoration. Churchill at the Exchequer
accepted the consensus. Keynes and Reginald McKenna, the chairman of the
Midland Bank, were the only significant visible opponents of this policy.

American banking opinion was broadly anti-inflationist and skeptical
about central bank management. The gold standard was often understood as a
mechanism for assuring national economic autonomy, rather than as a framework that would connect American policy to events in other countries. No
U.S. official showed any public awareness of the postwar undervaluation of
gold. Even Strong, who understood that the interwar gold standard should be
managed to avoid protracted deflation, failed to see the world liquidity shortage; and he seems not to have wanted to hear from those, for example, Cassel,
who did. The important conjectural question is how the post-stock-market-

crash deflation might have been addressed had Strong lived and remained the dominant figure at the Federal Reserve. His active role in earlier stabilizations and his opposition to procyclical restrictions in discounting suggest that a Strongian Federal Reserve would have attempted to organize countermeasures to French deflation; which is quite different from concluding that these would have succeeded in halting or reversing the downturn.

Had the Reichsbank acted as a domestic lender of last resort during the banking crisis of 1931, the German crisis might have been contained and sterling might have maintained parity for longer. This would have changed the course of the depression — perhaps moderating it, perhaps extending it by prolonging gold convertibility. Luther might divide responsibility for this ineptness with those who encouraged him — Norman and Harrison and his fellow Reserve Bankers.

Harrison and his associates also deserve historical censure for pursuing contractionary discounting policy in the United States after 1929. The Federal Reserve was the one central bank in a position to offset, at least in part, the effects of the Bank of France's gold hoarding. Instead, it aggravated the shortage. The deflationary impact of American policy was further accentuated by the Smoot-Hawley tariff of 1930, which hampered the global adjustment mechanism, forcing payment for American exports in the form of gold rather than goods. The bill was signed into law by the Republican president Hoover, who must take proportionate historical responsibility for its outcome.

Following years of currency weakness that gave rise to fears for French political stability, Moreau came to the Bank of France in June 1926 and Poincaré to the head of a coalition ministry in late July, each with a strong mandate for change. A Committee of Experts' *Report* recommended stabilization of the franc combined with a moderate course vis-à-vis domestic inflation, hence continued discounting of defense bons at the central bank and replacement of paid-down Treasury advances with commercial advances. Finance Minister Caillaux sought to implement the *Report*'s recommendations in early July but was denied his request for temporary decree powers; had his request been granted, the French-induced deflation might never have occurred. Poincaré instead presided over a rapid consolidation of floating debt and liquidation of advances as an anti-inflationary and confidence-building measure. Moreau felt that the bank could not control the domestic money market without a thoroughgoing restructuring of its balance sheet — a dubious premise — and he also set in place a restrictive discounting policy. These actions later brought sharp disequilibrium in international prices and profits. Poincaré and Moreau together delivered reduced taxes on capital accumulation, stable internal prices, a domestic investment boom, and rapidly growing gold and exchange reserves, all at a time when economies elsewhere were plateauing or declining. Their achievements left each able to leave office, Poincaré in 1929 and Moreau in 1930, with his public esteem and reputation at an unusually high level. They were — and in most historical accounts have continued to be — associated with the French recovery of the late 1920s rather than with the world deflation that followed. In a more balanced accounting, their names should be linked to both events.

Of the two, Moreau was more important in bringing the deflation. Only under pressure from Moreau did Poincaré agree to measures that would bring a liquidation of bank advances to the Treasury. Almost to the moment of de jure stabilization in June 1928, Poincaré wanted a higher franc, and only Moreau's threat to resign ensured that the franc would remain at a level below international purchasing parity, and hence at a level that would attract reserves to France. The deflationary consequences of rapid pay-down of advances would have been softened had Moreau practiced a more liberal discounting policy. Had French policy been different on any of these matters, the systemic disequilibrium that resulted from French monetary policy might not have occurred. It would be overdrawn to conclude that Moreau's four-year tenure as governor of the Bank of France caused the depression. The underlying liquidity problem predated Moreau and might have wrought havoc in another way. Narrow emphasis on Moreau's role would also treat too gently the climate of economic opinion in the world of the 1920s and especially in France. But without Moreau's tenure at the Bank of France, the timing and intensity of the deflation would almost certainly have been different.

Appendix: Gold in Central Banks and Treasuries, December 1926–June 1932 (millions of dollars)

(A) Basic Data

DECEMBER 1926

World total: 9,233
U.S.: 4,083 (44.2%)
France: 711 (7.7%)
Belgium, Netherlands, & Switzerland (BNS): 343 (3.7%)
All others: 4,096 (44.4%)

DECEMBER 1927

World total: 9,593
U.S.: 3,977 (41.5%)
France: 954 (9.9%)
BNS: 361 (3.8%)
All others: 4,301 (44.8%)
Total annual increase, world, December 1926–December 1927: 360
Proportions of annual increase:
 U.S.: (−29%)
 France: 67%
 BNS: 5.0%
 All others: 57%

JUNE 1928

World total: 9,749
U.S.: 3,732 (38.3%)
France: 1,136 (11.7%)
BNS: 372 (3.8%)
All others: 4,509 (46.3%)
Total semiannual increase, world, December 1927–June 1928: 156
Proportions of semiannual increase:
　U.S.: (−157%)
　France: 116%
　BNS: 7%
　All others: 133%

DECEMBER 1928

World total: 10,057
U.S.: 3,746 (37.2%)
France: 1,254 (12.4%)
BNS: 404 (4.0%)
All others: 4,653 (46.3%)
Total semiannual increase, world, June 1928–December 1928: 308
Proportions of semiannual increase:
　U.S.: 5%
　France: 38%
　BNS: 10%
　All others: 47%

JUNE 1929

World total: 10,126
U.S.: 3,956 (39.1%)
France: 1,436 (14.2%)
BNS: 411 (4.1%)
All others: 4,328 (42.7%)
Total semiannual increase, world, December 1928–June 1929: 69
Proportions of semiannual increase:
　U.S.: 304%
　France: 264%
　BNS: 10%
　All others: (−471%)

DECEMBER 1929

World total: 10,336
U.S.: 3,900 (37.7%)
France: 1,633 (15.8%)

BNS: 458 (4.4%)
All others: 4,345 (42.0%)
Total semiannual increase, world, June 1929–December 1929: 210
Proportions of semiannual increase:
  U.S.: (−27%)
  France: 94%
  BNS: 22%
  All others: 8%

JUNE 1930

World total: 10,671
U.S.: 4,178 (39.2%)
France: 1,727 (16.2%)
BNS: 453 (4.2%)
All others: 4,313 (40.4%)
Total semiannual increase, world, December 1929–June 1930: 335
Proportions of semiannual increase:
  U.S.: 83%
  France: 28%
  BNS: (−1%)
  All others: (−10%)

DECEMBER 1930

World total: 10,944
U.S.: 4,225 (38.7%)
France: 2,100 (19.2%)
BNS: 500 (4.6%)
All others: 4,119 (37.6%)
Total semiannual increase, world, June 1930–December 1930: 273
Proportions of semiannual increase:
  U.S.: 17%
  France: 137%
  BNS: 17%
  All others: (−71%)

JUNE 1931

World total: 11,264
U.S.: 4,593 (40.8%)
France: 2,212 (19.6%)
BNS: 581 (5.2%)
All others: 3,878 (34.4%)
Total semiannual increase, world, December 1930–June 1931: 320
Proportions of semiannual increase:
  U.S.: 115%

France: 35%
BNS: 25%
All others: (−75%)

DECEMBER 1931

World total: 11,323
U.S.: 4,051 (35.8%)
France: 2,699 (23.8%)
BNS: 1,164 (10.3%)
All others: 3,409 (30.1%)
Total semiannual increase, world, June 1931–December 1931: 59
Proportions of semiannual increase:
  U.S.: (−922%)
  France: 1,015%
  BNS: 988%
  All others: (−795%)

JUNE 1932

World total: 11,348
U.S.: 3,466 (30.5%)
France: 3,218 (28.4%)
BNS: 1,254 (11.1%)
All others: 3,410 (30.0%)

(B) Longer-period Proportion Changes

Total world increase, December 1928–June 1931: 1,207
Amounts and proportions of increase:
  U.S.: 847/70%
  France: 958/79%
  BNS: 177/15%
  All others: (−775)/(−64%)
Total world increase, December 1926–June 1931: 2,031
Amounts and proportions of increase:
  U.S.: 510/25%
  France: 1,501/74%
  BNS: 238/11%
  All others: (−217)/(−11%)
Total world increase, December 1926–June 1932: 2,115
Amounts and proportions of increase:
  U.S.: (−617)/(−29%)
  France: 2,507/119%
  BNS: 911/43%
  All others: (−686)/(−32%)

(C) Shares at a Glance

	U.S.	France*	BNS	All others
1926				
December	44.2%	7.7 (9.8%)	3.7%	44.4%
1927				
December	41.5	9.9 (11.0)	3.8	44.8
1928				
June	38.3	11.7 (12.7)	3.8	46.3
December	37.2	12.4	4.0	46.3
1929				
June	39.1	14.2	4.1	42.7
December	37.7	15.8	4.4	42.0
1930				
June	39.2	16.2	4.2	40.4
December	38.7	19.2	4.6	37.6
1931				
June	40.8	19.6	5.2	34.4
December	35.8	23.8	10.3	30.1
1932				
June	30.5	28.4	11.1	30.0

*Adjusted figures for France during 1926–28 include gold pledged to the Bank of England in 1917 ($90 million) and gold coins brought to the Bank of France during 1928 ($116). For these adjusted calculations, the world's total of gold in central banks and treasuries is lifted by $116 million, the amount of French gold later absorbed by the central bank; the proportions held by other countries are left unadjusted. See also discussion in chapter 9.

Because of rounding, proportions may not add to 100%.

Sources: All data derived from *Federal Reserve Bulletin,* various issues. Helpful tabulations appear in T. E. Gregory, *The Gold Standard and its Future* (1932), table IX; and in Nurkse (1944), appendixes I and II, reprinted in Eichengreen (1985).

Notes

Introduction

1. Eichengreen (1992a), table 9.1.

2. Kindleberger (1986), figure 10 and accompanying table.

3. Lewis (1949); Galbraith (1988); Rothbard (1963); also of the Austrian School, Anderson (1949); Friedman and Schwartz (1963); Clarke (1967); Néré (1968); Palyi (1972); and Temin (1976) and (1989). Kindleberger (1986) mentions the undervaluation of gold in a footnote: 47n.

4. Eichengreen (1990), 240–41; and (1992a), 198–200. Also see discussion in chapter 4, below.

5. Hawtrey (1922). Rist (1931a), 193–206; also, (1933), 325–43. Cassel (1925), 205–06; also (1936). Rueff (1971), esp. 63–64. Also, Mundell (1989), 366–72.

6. Fisher (1930), 269; Keynes [1928a], in Keynes (1989), 19:759; and Keynes [1929a], in Keynes (1989), 19:775–80. Fisher and Keynes noted the shortage of gold without mentioning its undervaluation. Nurkse (1944), however, causally linked depressed gold output after World War I to its real undervaluation; 27.

7. Among those who discuss the role of France, see Friedman and Schwartz (1963), 362; Eichengreen (1990), esp. 263–64; Clarke (1967), 137–38, 164–68. Also, Kindleberger (1985), chap. 7. Hamilton (1987) argues that French policy during 1927 and 1928 played a role in forcing contractionary U.S. policy in 1928 and 1929; 146–47. He backs away from suggesting that French policy itself had a large systemic deflationary impact.

8. Nurkse (1944), 39.

9. "Sterilization" refers to the practice by which changes in central bank reserves are not permitted to affect the quantity of money in the domestic economy.

10. Federal Reserve Bulletins, 1927–1933. Also, Nurkse (1944), appendixes I and II.

11. Hawtrey (1936) estimates the quantity of gold pledged to the Bank of England and the movement from French hoards; 63.

12. Among others, Galbraith (1988), Rothbard (1963), Friedman and Schwartz (1963), and Temin (1976) and (1989). Also, Mishkin (1978), almost every article in Brunner (1981); Bernanke (1983); and Romer (1990).

13. Inter alia, Rist (1931a) and (1933); Néré (1968); Rueff (1971); Marseille (1980); Sauvy (1984); St.-Etienne (1984); Bouvier (1989).

14. Schuker (1988), 12.

15. Kindleberger (1986), xv, 147, 152–53, 295. Eichengreen (1992a), 276f.

16. Moggridge (1982) suggests that, in the context of the French gold inflow, the overvaluation of sterling and American economic mismanagement, the issue of failed leadership as a cause of the depression should not be raised "so early in the argument"; 184.

Kindleberger (1986) notes that the difference between his view — that massive international lending in the spring and summer of 1931 could have halted the downturn and ushered in recovery — and that of Moggridge, above, is one of "assertion"; xv. In this book I move beyond assertion in analyzing the underlying postwar liquidity shortage and the role of the half-decade-long French gold absorption in aggravating that shortage.

17. Inter alia, Friedman and Schwartz (1963), Temin (1976) and (1989), Kindleberger (1986), and Eichengreen (1992a) offer not a single word on the massive flow of non-monetary gold to India during the 1920s.

18. Some commentators acknowledge a similar distinction. Galbraith (1954) writes, "It is easier to account for the boom and crash in the market than to explain their bearing on the depression which followed;" 171. Field (1984a) writes, "I am concerned here with why the downturn in real activity began in 1929, not primarily with why it was so long or so deep;" 490. Temin (1976) notes, "There is no evidence of any effective deflationary pressure from the banking system between the stock-market crash in October 1929 and the British abandonment of the gold standard in September 1931;" 169. In a later study, Temin (1989) nevertheless found the long-period roots of the depression in the workings of the international interwar gold standard. Field and Temin are sometimes interpreted to have offered as a medium- or long-period explanation what each specified as applicable only for a shorter period.

Chapter 1. Deflation and Depression

1. Eichengreen (1992b).

2. For a textbook treatment of the Phillips Curve, see McCallum (1989), 177–85.

3. Friedman and Schwartz (1963), chap. 7; and Schwartz (1981), 5–48.

4. *Equilibrium* is used in this book in the Walrasian sense, to indicate the condition in which all markets (i.e., markets for money, bonds, goods, labor, etc.) clear simultaneously; it is shorthand for *general equilibrium*.

5. Leijonhufvud (1981); inter alia, 108. Davidson (1982) stresses the incompatibility

of general equilibrium theory, and hence the notion that markets adjust so as to clear rapidly, with the workings of a monetary economy; 58–78.

6. This is Lucas's (1981) self-descriptive term.

7. Krugman (1994); 199–202.

8. Ibid., title of chap. 8: "In the Long Run Keynes Is Still Alive."

9. For iterations of the fundamental equation, see Keynes (1930), chap. 10. In one version, Ü = E/O + (I − S)/O, where Ü is the price level of output as a whole, E is total money income (excluding the divergence of profit from the equilibrium rate), O is total output, I is the increment in value of new investment goods, and S is savings. Keynes (1930), 1:137.

10. The terminology by which investment and savings can be unequal is usually absent in Keynes's *General Theory*. (For exceptions, see Keynes [1936a], 21, 100, 261.) In this later book, an upward or downward adjustment in national income brings the amount of aggregate savings into equilibrium with aggregate investment. E.g., ibid., 180–81. The difference, however, between this argument and that in the *Treatise* lies mostly in expository perspective. The earlier work focuses upon inequality in planned (or ex ante) savings and investment, which induces profit inflation or deflation and results in an adjustment in prices and income. The *General Theory* explains the (ex post) restoration of equality between savings and investment. Subsequent to the *General Theory*, Keynes explicitly observed that ex ante inequality was a common condition. Keynes (1989 [1937c]), 14: 216. Presumably aware that his terminology shifts sowed confusion, Keynes mentioned in 1937 "a future article which I intend to write dealing with the relation of the ex ante and ex post analysis in its entirety to the analysis in my *General Theory*"; ibid., 216.

11. Keynes (1989 [1931b]), 13:353.

12. Keynes used *equilibrium* in the *Treatise* to indicate what is usually understood as general equilibrium—i.e., where resources are fully employed. In the *General Theory*, *equilibrium* was specifically defined to apply to situations in which unemployment of resources existed; Keynes (1936a), 242–43. In this book, *equilibrium* is usually used in the former sense.

13. Hicks (1974) discusses the concept of "inflationary equilibrium," in which none of the change in prices is induced by changes in the second term of the fundamental equation; 75f.

14. This was what Keynes (1936a) had in mind in his criticism of Say's Law; 18, 26, 363; also Keynes (1989 [1937b]), 9:123. Essential texts on disequilibrium in economic theory include Davidson (1977); Walker (1984); and Leijonhufvud (1968) and (1981).

Marx was not a "classical" economist in this sense; indeed, he identified a close relation between price declines and depression. He wrote in *Capital*, i.e., Marx (1977), "Since certain price relationships are assumed in the reproduction process, and govern it, this process is thrown into stagnation and confusion by the general fall in prices. This disturbance and stagnation paralyzes the function of money as a means of payment, which is given along with the development of capital and depends on . . . presupposed price relations. . . . All this therefore leads to violent and acute crises, sudden forcible devaluations, an actual stagnation and disruption in the reproduction process and hence to an actual decline in production"; 3:363.

15. E.g., Bernanke (1983), 258.

16. Buiter (1989) has written, "The assumption that economic agents use the true model to make their (unbiased) forecasts suggests that Muth-rational expectations are likely to be most appropriate when the analysis is restricted to the tranquility of a long-run steady state." He notes, nevertheless, that rational expectations theory has had its major impact in its evaluation of short-term policy, in which steady-state assumptions are most likely to be violated; 60, 69.

17. Keynes (1989 [1937b]), 9:113–14.

18. Lucas (1981), 284.

19. Equity pricing models include variables for a risk-adjusted interest rate (or cost of capital), an anticipated rate of return on investment, and an estimated rate of growth in future earnings. The derivation of the value of any one of these depends on one's estimates for the other two. (One cannot, for example, determine a company's cost of equity capital simply by computing its earnings-to-share-price ratio.) See Copeland and Weston (1988), appendix A; or almost any textbook on financial economics.

20. Because it is difficult to obtain reliable price indexes for newly produced capital goods, I shall use wholesale price indexes throughout the text as an estimator for the denominator. The resulting divergence matters little, since the denominator of this term varies much less than the numerator.

21. For a review of the literature on capital market efficiency, see Copeland and Weston (1988), chaps. 10 and 11. For reservations regarding the frequent conclusion among financial economists that capital markets in the United States and other economically advanced countries are efficient, see Shiller (1989). Among economic historians, the assumption of market efficiency is often challenged; e.g., Kindleberger (1989), esp. chap. 3.

22. I prefer the terms *profit inflation* and *income inflation,* from Keynes (1930), 1:155, to the more recent *demand-pull inflation* and *cost-push inflation,* which mean nearly the same thing. For definitions of the latter, see Tobin (1987), 320–23. First, Keynes's "profit" language denotes the distributional issues more clearly than do the more recent terms. Second, Keynes intended—and this book requires—that the analysis of inflation apply inversely to deflation. *Profit deflation* and *income deflation* are reasonably clear and are preferable to such awkward neologisms as *declining-demand-pull deflation* and *shrinking-cost-push deflation.* Davidson (1977) reintroduces a portion of this *Treatise on Money* terminology when he uses "profit inflation (deflation)" and "wage inflation (deflation)"; 339–48.

23. Fisher (1923), 54–112, 64. Similarly, Keynes (1930) wrote of "considerations of social justice" that may argue against a deliberate policy of profit inflation; 1:295; also, 2:162.

24. Fisher (1923), 64.

25. Friedman and Schwartz (1963), 41–42.

26. E.g., Paul and Lehrman (1982), 98–99.

27. Friedman and Schwartz (1963), 27.

28. Gresham's law comes into play when a conversion rate is set legally. Typically, such a rate has been maintained through fixed offering prices at the mint. Silver coins were driven out of circulation during the Greenback period, as a nominal exchange rate between silver and greenbacks was maintained. Friedman and Schwartz (1963), 27n.

29. Ibid., 26–27.

30. See, inter alia, the *Commercial and Financial Chronicle,* July 5, 1873, 14–15, which briefly describes gold bonds issued by the Lamoille Valley, St. Johnsbury & Essex County Railroads, the Chesapeake and Ohio, and the Northern Pacific Railroad Co. Also see Macaulay (1940), charts 25 and 26, table 19, and appendix C.

31. Macaulay (1940), chart 26. Also, Friedman and Schwartz (1963), chart 6. The ratio of greenback prices to gold stood at about 135 : 100 in 1866 and about 116 : 100 in 1872. Parity was reached by the beginning of 1879.

Note on calculations: To derive the ratio of change in the gold value of greenbacks, subtract the later index number from the earlier index number to get the absolute change in price indexes. Then divide the difference by the earlier number to derive a ratio of change. E.g., to calculate the rate of greenback deflation form 1866 to 1879, take 100 − 135 = − 35. The ratio of change is then −35/135, or −26 percent.

32. Jastram (1977); figures calculated from tables 3 and 8. The American Civil War thus marks a divergence from the usual pattern in which the real value of gold declines during wartime — a consequence of the rise in demand for materiel relative to the demand for specie. A possible explanation is that value of gold was determined through international arbitrage, which was largely independent of the localized war.

33. *Historical Statistics* (1960), series X 348–54.

34. See Friedman and Schwartz (1963), 32f. for discussion of price measurement during post–Civil War period.

35. Ibid., table 11 and chart 62. Data compiled from worksheets underlying Kuznets (1961).

36. *Historical Statistics* (1960), series X 348–54.

37. Inter alia, the Board of Trade's wholesale price index for Britain dropped by 50 percent from 1920:2 to 1922:1. Keynes (1930), 2:178. Data for the United States are included in chapter 3 and for France in chapter 5, below.

38. Jastram (1977), tables 3 and 8. The year 1931 (rather than 1932) is used as the terminal year for the British comparison because that was when sterling was floated. Some of the rise in gold's real value in 1931 is misleading, as its cause after September was a rise in the sterling-to-gold ratio rather than a decline in general prices.

39. Department of Commerce (1973); data reprinted in Gordon, *Macroeconomics* (1978), table B-1. Actual index numbers are 1918, 32.66; 1919, 37.23; 1920, 42.21; 1921, 35.34; 1922, 32.49. (1972 = 100)

40. Eichengreen (1992a), figure 4.2.

41. Mourré (1921), 561.

42. Eichengreen (1990), 32.

43. Keynes (1930), 2:178–80. Sources are the Board of Trade Wholesale Price Index and Bowley's Wage Index.

44. Keynes (1989 [1931a]), 9:153.

45. Romer (1988); esp. table 5.

46. *Historical Statistics* (1960), series X 348–54, for annual common stock indexes. Eichengreen (1992a), figure 4.2, for wholesale price indexes. Also, see Macaulay (1940) for month-to-month stock index averages.

47. On farm mortgage foreclosures in the United States during the 1870s, see Bowman (1964); data summarized on 66.

48. Keynes (1930), 2:164–67. Keynes's wage data are from Bowley's index in the *Economic Journal*, 1904, 459.

49. Reynolds (1983), table 1. His sources include the United States Commission on the Role of Gold in the Domestic and International Monetary Systems (1982), vol. 1; and Warren and Pearson (1935), 14.

50. For hourly earnings during the 1890s, see *Historical Statistics* (1960), series D 603–17 and D 618–25. A recent study reinforces the conclusion that nominal wages became more rigid during the 1890s; see Hanes (1993). For wholesale and general price indexes, see Friedman and Schwartz (1963), chart 62.

51. Macaulay (1940), charts 22 and 23.

52. *Historical Statistics* (1960), series 348–54.

53. On the monetary situation in 1892, see Friedman and Schwartz (1963), 107.

54. A conceptually comparable process would take place in France in 1925–26. An international gold standard deflation combined with a lax French monetary policy led to a collapse of the then-floating franc. See chapter 6, below.

55. For discussion of the "anticipated" inflation in the middle 1890s, see Friedman and Schwartz (1983), 629. Also, Friedman (1992), 116.

56. Keynes (1936a) does mention the open-economy argument; see 262–63.

57. Eichengreen and Hatton (1988), table 1.1.

58. All stock index calculations are made from Kindleberger (1987), figure 6. Gordon (1978), table B1, shows only a 22 percent decline in the U.S. price deflator index from the 1929 average to the 1932 average; in context, a lower price deflation adjustment to the stock index decline increases the measured decline in Tobin's q. Some wholesale price indexes show a steeper decline; e.g. Jastram (1977), table 8.

59. For French wholesale price data, see Sauvy (1984), vol. 2, figures 19 and 24.

60. Keynes (1989 [1931b]), 13:345f., 361.

61. This argument is not specifically Keynesian. Fisher (1933) and Cassel (1932) made nearly identical observations.

62. The breakdown of par values in the European Monetary Union during 1992 and 1993 offers a more recent illustration of this conflict.

63. Keynes (1930), 2:379–81.

64. Ibid., 1:250–53.

65. Ibid., 2:370–72.

66. Friedman (1989) offers the seemingly misdirected argument that, because the demand for money is nearly constant in the long period, one can overlook variations in the short period. He also argues in this connection that Keynes said — or implied — that the demand for real balances could shift to a higher level over the "long run," which might produce "equilibrium" with high unemployment (20). I believe Friedman's argument inaccurate, in that Keynes sought to explain the persistence of general *dis*equilibrium, hence profit deflation, during the early 1930s. When Keynes (1936a) speaks of "equilibrium at less than full employment" (243), he has in mind a Marshallian partial equilibrium, not a Walrasian general equilibrium.

67. Keynes (1930), 2:370.

68. Ibid., 2:376.

69. Keynes was clear then and later that the objectives of public works spending would

be thwarted without monetary accommodation. See Keynes and Henderson (1929). Also, Keynes (1936a), 119–20.

70. Keynes (1936a) argues for fiscal measures in the theoretical context of a closed economy — unlike his argument in 1929 or 1930, which assumed an open international system.

71. Clarke (1967), 73. See also chapter 7, below.

72. Bernanke (1983), 258. He offers a similar argument in Bernanke (1993), esp. 264.

73. Hamilton (1987), 163–66.

74. Keynes (1936a), 263.

75. Cassel (1932), 78–79.

Chapter 2. The Prewar Gold Standard

1. David Hume's essay "Of the Balance of Trade" (1898) offers a classical statement of this view. The essay also contains, however, an early statement of the "law of one price," according to which price differences are eliminated through arbitrage and hence relative outputs adjust. Mundell (1989) finds it doubtful that Hume, Ricardo, and other classical economists understood the transfer adjustment mechanism to be based on changes in relative prices; 391f., 399f., 451f.

2. Strong to Andrew Mellon, Secretary of the Treasury, May 27, 1924; in Clarke (1967), 28.

3. Taussig (1927), 260–61.

4. On prewar price arbitrage, see McCloskey and Zecher (1976) and (1984). Also, see Friedman (1984), 158–62, for reemphasis of the role of the price-specie-flow mechanism as a partial determinant of price levels.

5. Bagehot (1873), 47–48.

6. Committee on Currency and Foreign Exchanges after the War (1919).

7. League of Nations (1931a), 12.

8. H. A. Siepmann, "Reply to some observations by M. Quesnay on the Gold Exchange Standard," November 8, 1927; Par. 4. Bank of England, OV48/1.

9. Keynes (1989 [1913]), 1:12–13.

10. Keynes (1989 [1925b]), 9:220.

11. Keynes (1930), 2:306.

12. Ibid., 2:306–07.

13. Cassel (1936), 3–5.

14. On the interwar gold standard, see Nurkse (1944), 66ff. On the prewar experience, see Bloomfield (1959), 48ff.

15. Bloomfield (1959) finds that for prewar observations of eleven central banks, in only 34 percent of cases (32 percent if the Bank of England is excluded) did changes in international and domestic assets move in the same direction. For the Bank of England, 48 percent of the observations showed changes in the same direction — the highest correlation for any central bank tested.

16. Sayers (1936), 136. Also, Eichengreen (1992a), 36–37.

17. On Britain, see United States National Monetary Commission (1911), 30. On France, see White (1933), 179f. (White later served as Treasury undersecretary and chief

U.S. negotiator at the Bretton Woods Conference in 1944.) On Germany, see Cassel (1936), 17.

18. Bloomfield (1959), 23–24, 37–38. Goodhart (1972) advances this interpretation of the behavior of the Bank of England.

19. McCloskey and Zecher (1976), 380f.

20. DeCecco (1973), 56–57. Also see British Treasury memorandum, "Gold Reserves," by Basil Blackett, February 1914. T 170 19; reprinted in De Cecco (1973), appendix A. Blackett concluded, "Our position as a lending nation gives us a power of attracting gold from abroad whenever we require it such as no other country, with the possible exception of France, can command"; par. 18.

21. Keynes (1989 [1913]), 1:13.

22. For evidence of contrasting correlations between international asset flows and changes in domestic money stocks for Britain and the United States, see McCloskey and Zecher (1976), table 16.2.

23. Eichengreen (1992a), 48.

24. McGouldrick (1984); 312, 332.

25. Sommariva and Tullio (1987), 110–11.

26. Total monetary gold in 1913 measured £392 million in the United States, £304 million in France, £211 million in Russia, £184 million in Germany, and £150 million in Great Britain; the world total was £1,579 million. Gold in central banks and treasuries totaled £266 million in the United States, £162 million in Russia, £140 million in France, between £52 and £57 million each in Germany, Italy, Austria-Hungary, and Argentina, and only £35 million at the Bank of England. The world total was £965 million. Circulating gold totaled £164 million in France, £127 million in Germany, £126 million in the United States, £115 million in Britain, £49 million in Russia, and much less elsewhere. Keynes (1930), 2:297.

27. Interview with M. Pallain, governor of the Bank of France. U.S. Monetary Commission (1911), 212, 215.

28. White (1933), 189.

29. Ibid., 187, 195.

30. Ibid., 194.

31. Ibid., table 31, which shows the level of French reserves relative to the note issue and to the quantities of various categories of deposits.

32. U.S. Monetary Commission (1911), 207, 213.

33. Keynes (1989 [1913]), 1:14–16.

34. McCloskey and Zecher (1976), 358–59.

35. Eichengreen (1987), 12–13.

36. Hawtrey's testimony, Macmillan Committee (1931a), par. 4174–76, 4201.

37. Ford (1962). Summarized in Bordo (1984), 83–86.

38. Eichengreen (1987) demonstrates that the asymmetry of sterling's reserve position relative to that of other important European currencies before 1914 provided a game-theoretic justification for the Bank of England to adopt a leadership role in setting world interest rates.

39. This effect is named after Henry Thornton (1760–1815), author of Thornton (1978). See also Mundell (1989), 423f.

40. Cassel (1936), 4–5.

41. Cassel (1932) emphasizes this difference; 69f.

42. Keynes (1930), 2:232.

43. Ibid., 2:287.

44. Ibid., 2:298.

45. Frenkel and Johnson (1976), esp. 25.

46. De Cecco (1973), appendix A, par. 38.

47. Ibid., 72–73. For evidence of the use nationalists wanted to make of the Gold Standard Reserve by the middle 1920s, see Royal Commission on Indian Currency and Finance (1926), Minute of Dissent, par. 30.

48. Royal Commission on Indian Currency and Finance (1926), par. 12.

49. Cassel (1936), 11. On the spread of the gold standard as inducing a reverse-Thornton effect, see Mundell (1989), 424–25.

50. DeCecco (1973), 120–21.

51. Friedman and Schwartz (1963), 168–69.

52. DeCecco (1973), 113–16.

53. Eichengreen (1992a), 48ff; Bloomfield (1959), 56–57.

54. For amounts of loans, see Eichengreen (1992a), 51, 52, 57.

55. Ibid., 275.

56. Data from Gordon (1978), table B-1, show the 1931 dollar bought 55 cents on the 1900 dollar. Jastram's (1977) index of the purchasing power of gold shows less inflation of dollar-denominated prices during this period. On his data, the purchasing power of both gold and the dollar—the mint price of gold at $20.67 per ounce was unchanged throughout—declined only from 154.3 to 118.6, or by about 23 percent; by this measure the later dollar bought 77 cents of the earlier one; table 8.

57. Keynes (1930), 1:346f.

58. Ibid., 2:281–82.

59. Rist (1951), 322–23.

60. Keynes (1930), 1:144, 147.

61. Keynes (1989 [1911]), 11:377; also Keynes (1989 [1936b]), 11:495–96.

62. Marjolin (1937), 133.

63. Bloomfield (1959), 37. He notes the depressant effect of short supplies during 1873–96, and the post-1896 increase in international liquidity; 17. Ford (1962) also argues that an expanding international supply of gold eased adjustments during the two decades before World War I; 24–26.

64. For annual world gold production measured in fine troy ounces, 1871–75, see J. Aron & Co. (1976), table III-F. J. Aron & Co.'s source is the U.S. Bureau of Mines.

65. The actual increase from 1896 to 1914, including both reserves and circulating gold, was from £852 million to £1,647 million; League of Nations (1930), table B, 84.

66. Jastram (1977), table 3. (1930 = 100.)

67. Friedman and Schwartz (1963), 106–11.

68. On the Sherman Act and its repeal and on Austria-Hungary and Russia, see De Cecco (1973), 51–56.

69. J. Aron & Co. (1976), table III-F.

70. Jastram (1977), table 3. Joseph Kitchen (1930), in the League of Nations (1930), annex XI, table B.

71. Cassel (1930), 76.

72. Keynes (1930), 2:165–69. Also on the Baring crisis, see De Cecco (1973), 88ff.

73. Keynes (1930), 2:164.

74. Ibid., 2:169–70.

75. E.g., Leffingwell wrote to Walter Lippmann on November 9, 1931, "There is a gold inflation in France." Leffingwell Papers, box 5, folder 108.

Chapter 3. *The Postwar Undervaluation of Gold*

1. Friedman and Schwartz (1963), chart 19.

2. The world's gold reserves increased from $5.3 billion to $7.1 billion over the same three-year period. Nurkse (1944), appendix I. Annual world production ranged from 20.05 to 22.65 million ounces per annum, or from $414 million to $468 million. J. Aron & Co. (1976), table III-F. The remainder of the increase in reserves came from coins previously in internal circulation.

3. Friedman and Schwartz (1963), 218–19. A similar pattern occurred during World War II.

4. The Kondratief price index. Cited in Mundell (1989), 366.

5. Jastram (1977), table 3. Jastram relies heavily upon price indexes for 170 different commodities compiled by Beveridge (1939), vol. 1.

6. Friedman and Schwartz (1963), 228–30.

7. Gordon (1978), table B-1. These figures are not directly comparable to those used elsewhere for unemployment rates "in industry," which reached 19.5 percent in the United States in 1921. For "industrial" unemployment rates, see Eichengreen and Hatton (1988), table 1.1.

8. Eichengreen (1985b), 147.

9. J. Aron & Co. (1976), table III-F. Also, Keynes (1930), 2:295, provides sterling-denominated amounts of gold production per annum during 1919–28.

10. Joseph Kitchen (1931), 57–58.

11. Memorandum by Robert Warren, "Conversation of August 25, 1926," attended by Strong, Rist, Quesnay, and Warren. Strong Papers 1000.7, p. 6.

12. Royal Commission on Indian Currency and Finance (1926), Wilson, appendix 89, 3:578.

13. Niemeyer (1931), 84–85. Brown (1940), 370, 838–39. Also, Keynes (1930), 2:295.

14. Gold use in the 1860s and 1870s is measured in sterling because the gold (and exchange) value of the dollar was inconstant during those two "greenback" decades. During the early 1920s the situation was reversed, as the pound's gold value was rising; a stable dollar measure is used for the later period.

15. Royal Commission on Indian Currency and Finance (1926), Kitchen, appendix 82, 3:520.

16. Royal Commission on Indian Currency and Finance (1926), Wilson, 3:578; also, Blackett, par. 435.

17. For annual amounts of gold output and monetary absorption during 1919–28, see Keynes (1930), 2:295.

18. Brown (1940), 844–46. Brown cites Samuel Montagu & Co., *Annual Bullion Letter, 1931,* 8.

19. Hawtrey (1931), 75–76. Also, Kitchen (1931), 62–63.

20. Kitchen (1931), 73. Kitchen's estimates are expressed in sterling.

21. De Litra et Cie: Monnaies d'or et Lingots (1951), 24–25.

22. Cassel (1920), 42.

23. Eichengreen (1990), 24. Also, Eichengreen (1992a), 198–200.

24. U.S. National Monetary Commission (1911), 30.

25. Cassel (1936), 17.

26. The committee chairman noted in October 1926, "Before the War large sums of gold were often drained from the Bank for internal circulation, which can no longer occur. For this reason, prewar cover requirements were somewhat more exacting than those at present. At times of specific payment demands during the prewar era we saw reductions of from 200 to 300 million marks in the Bank's gold stock, most of which was drained internally. . . . The 40 percent cover we have now is therefore no more stringent than the 33 percent cover that prevailed before the War." Reichsbank President Schacht then observed that this was also the case "in England as well as other countries that had not yet restored a gold circulation but remained limited to a gold bullion standard [under which gold is held only in the central bank]." Enquête-Ausschuß (1929), 155–56.

27. Felsenhardt (1922); Felsenhardt also remarks on the parallel role of circulating gold in Germany; 68–70.

28. White (1933), 175–80.

29. Kitchen (1931), 67.

30. Enquête-Ausschuß (1929), 155–56. Bank of France (1933), 150. The German Bank Law of 1924 set a 40 percent reserve requirement, one quarter of which could be held in foreign exchange; Governor Schacht made it Reichsbank policy to hold the full 40 percent in gold.

31. Kitchen (1931), 66. Also, Cassel (1930) estimates 2.8 percent per annum as a growth rate in the gold stock consistent with long-term price stability; 73. Cassel probably intended this as a provocative observation, not a hard conclusion for policy formation. See Mlynarski (1931), 37. Hawtrey challenges the logic of the 2.8 percent per annum figure, pointing out that most of the commercially advanced world switched from a silver to a gold standard during this sixty-year period, which surely disrupted "typical" demand growth. He also noted the widespread development of credit substitutes during the sixty-year period. Hawtrey (1931), 75–76. See also Nogaro (1931).

32. I.e., if one uses an index price level of 165 (in which 1914 = 100; figures calculated from GNP deflator index in Gordon [1978], table B1) as typical for the 1922–29 period in the United States, then gold's purchasing power is 100/165 = .61 of its historic level. (This actually somewhat understates the inflation-induced undervaluation of gold, for the 1896–1914 inflation already left gold below its average purchasing power for 1789–1914.) One then calculates the real value of gold output during 1924–29 by taking the physical amount of gold produced — 87 percent of the peak levels of 1912 and 1915 — multiplied by the commodity value equivalent per unit produced — 61 percent of the prewar level. Hence, $.87 \times .61 = .53$.

33. Jastram (1977), table 3.

34. Inter alia, see Miskimin (1987), 697–705.

35. Jastram (1977), table 3; this table is also the source of data in the following paragraph in the text.

36. Ibid., 178–79.

37. Blainey (1970); cited in Rockoff (1984), 626.

38. Rockoff (1984), 623–27.

39. Ibid., 630. This conclusion may be contrasted with Kindleberger's (1986) view that the discovery and flow of gold from the Rand were evidence of "a deus ex machina"; 290.

40. Rueff (1947), 349. Also, see Rothbard (1963), 37–38.

41. Leffingwell to Dwight Morrow, March 16, 1925; Leffingwell Papers, box 6, folder 130. Also, Brown (1929), 75–76.

42. J. Aron & Co. (1976), table III-F.

43. Brown (1940), 1310–11.

44. Jastram (1977), table 3.

45. Ibid., table 8, which lists annual indexes of the purchasing power of gold in the United States, 1800–1976. Triffin (1960) argued that at the established price of $35 per ounce, gold production could not meet the monetary need. Paul Volcker (who would be chairman of the Federal Reserve System from 1979 to 1987) accepts Triffin's conclusion. See Volcker and Gyohten (1992), 39.

46. Hawtrey (1922), 294.

47. Ibid., 293.

48. Hawtrey reiterated this years later at the Macmillan Committee (1931a) hearings; par. 4155. The argument that the United States might have inflated to ease sterling's return to prewar parity continues to be advanced, especially by economists who neglect the postwar gold shortage in their analysis. E.g., Schwartz (1981), 21.

49. Hawtrey (1922), esp. 293, 301, 303.

50. Cassel (1925), 206.

51. Cassel (1928), 44; also see Cassel (1920), 45.

52. Rist (1931a), 195f. and (1933), 331, 334f. Also, Warren, "Conversation of August 25, 1926," 6; Strong Papers, 1000.7. This point of view was common among French economists. E.g., Dieterlen (1930), esp. 1533; also Marjolin (1937).

53. Fisher (1920), 105.

54. Fisher wrote, "My own guess is that the price recession, while it will occur, will not be very great or very long continued. I would not be surprised if the upward course of prices would be soon reversed." Fisher to H. M. Sedgwick, May 26, 1920. Irving Fisher Papers, box 4, folder 49.

55. In "Probleme des Goldstandards: Zur New Yorker Bespechung der Noten-Präsidenten," unsigned, *Frankfurter Zeitung*, July 10, 1927, 4: "Experts are nearly at one in anticipating a gold shortage, even if they differ on how soon this shortage will arrive or how severe it will be. . . . While on one side the view persists that prices may be managed, and hence that the value of gold may be manipulated through central banking policies, experts — especially those from gold-producing countries — recommend an international regulation and coordination of gold production, and *a revaluation of gold,* in order to eliminate disturbances to the price level" (emphasis added).

Rist wrote nearly thirty years later that systemic revaluation of gold would have been the most effective action against systemic deflation, while acknowledging that he did not propose this during the 1920s. Rist (1955), 1022.

Jacques Rueff, a Bank of France economist during the 1920s and an adviser to Charles de Gaulle nearly four decades later, urged a systemic revaluation of gold during the 1960s, when years of currency price inflation had left gold undervalued at the fixed price of $35 per ounce. E.g., Hirsch and Rueff (1965). Paul Volcker, who was then undersecretary for monetary affairs in the Nixon Treasury, indicates that the "Gaullist" argument was taken seriously in 1969 — but rejected for diplomatic reasons. Volcker and Gyohten (1992), 67.

56. Mundell (1975), 143.

57. Schuker (1988), 62. Quesnay was previously an economist at the Bank of France.

58. Keynes proposed stabilizing the value of obligations with reference to an index number of commodity prices — precisely in order to avoid international wealth shifts that would have resulted from changes in the value of a gold *numéraire*. Keynes (1989 [1922]), 3:120–21.

59. Committee of Experts (1924), 360.

60. Schuker (1988), 91. In the same mode, Strong "observed that whenever a responsible statesman came out with a candid recognition of liability of the debt and expressed a willingness to effect a settlement and to do the utmost to make the payments provided under the settlement, the debt shrank in size, both in the debtor country and in the United States. On the other hand, when the liability was denied, it assumed at once an unusual magnitude in both countries." Memorandum by Robert Warren, "Conversation of August 31, 1926," Strong Papers, 1000.7

61. Strong to Gilbert, September 30, 1925, Strong Papers, 1012.1.

62. E.g., Rockoff (1984), 617.

63. Leffingwell, "To the Editor of the *Manchester Guardian Commercial*," July 28, 1922; Leffingwell Papers, box 9, folder 182.

64. Mises (1978), "The Causes of the Economic Crisis," 1931; 197–98. Perhaps as a result of observing the events of 1929–32, Mises subsequently changed his mind. He wrote later of the "debt aggravation" that can result from deflation; Mises (1949), 778. However, for more recent statements of the "liquidationist" view, see Anderson (1949); also, Rothbard (1963). This view is echoed by the popular historian Paul Johnson (1983), chap. 7.

65. Rist (1930), 41–42.

66. More exactly, Rist (1931a) surmised that "the demand for credit [was] insufficient to balance the credit which could be offered"; 199.

67. For Keynes's own summary of his views prior to 1928, see Keynes (1989 [1929a]), 19:775–76.

68. On Strong, see Warren, "Conversation of August 25, 1926," 6; Strong Papers 1000.7. Strong's views are discussed further in chapter 4, below. Keynes is quoted in Keynes (1989 [1926d]), 19:482. Also see Keynes (1989 [1923]), 4:134–35.

69. Cassel (1928), 70f. Also see Keynes (1930), chap. 35, for discussion of the differences between the prewar and postwar gold standards. Eichengreen (1992a), 161–62, 164, argues that Strong exaggerated the "automaticity" of the prewar standard. Also on Strong, see chapter 4, below.

70. Another possibility was a restoration of bimetallism. This would have raised the price of silver and had the undesirable consequence of depressing prices in countries with silver-based monetary systems. In fact, this price effect occurred a few years later follow-

ing American action in 1933 to support the price of silver, which caused a depression in China. Friedman (1992), chap. 7; also Cassel (1936), 166f.

71. Fisher (1920), 274–77.

72. Keynes (1930), 2:307.

73. Ibid., 2:292.

74. Jastram (1977), table 3.

75. Mundell (1989), 379–83. Also, see Coombs (1976), on pressure against the dollar in 1964 and 1965; 153ff. Given slow but persistent currency price inflation during much of the 1950s and 1960s, and its acceleration with the American military buildup in Vietnam, the real value of the $35 per ounce official gold price declined steadily. Consequently, nonofficial purchases of gold rose persistently relative to total production and, beginning in 1966, exceeded new production. (Jastram [1967], chart II.) The London Gold Pool allocation arrangement among central banks could be maintained henceforth only if the affiliated banks agreed to sell gold from their stocks at what they knew to be a submarket price. Rather than accept losses, and in part in pursuit of President de Gaulle's broader foreign policy objectives, France withdrew from the Gold Pool in June 1967.

Coombs notes that the $35 per ounce price of gold was maintained during most of 1961–65 with the adventitious support of official gold sales from South Africa, which was otherwise running a net deficit on current and capital accounts. Had South Africa not felt the payments pressure it would not have released metal, and the undervaluation of gold might have generated an international monetary crisis sooner.

76. Jastram (1977), table 8. Data for the United States rather than for Britain are used for 1929–32 because the end of sterling convertibility in 1931 makes the contemporary British index not strictly comparable.

Chapter 4. The Postwar Gold Exchange Standard

1. See Genoa Financial Commission Report (1922), 678–80.

2. Hawtrey (1922) wrote, "At the gold center countries some gold reserves must be maintained"; 294. This formulation implies that gold center countries would hold significant foreign exchange reserves. He was more explicit in testimony in April 1930: "[The Bank of England] should itself resort to the device recommended in the Genoa resolutions, the holding of a reserve of foreign exchange in place of gold whenever the world situation requires an economy of gold." Macmillan Committee (1931a), par. 61. In fact, the Bank of England typically held from 10 percent to 20 percent of its reserves in the form of foreign exchange during 1925–30. Eichengreen (1992a), figure 9.6.

3. Hawtrey (1922), 294–95.

4. See Strong-Salter Memorandum of Conversation, May 25, 1928, 1. Harrison Papers, box 15.

5. Niemeyer (1931), 90–92.

6. For Strong's concept of an "automatic" gold standard, see his congressional testimony in 1927; quoted in Keynes (1930) 2:305.

7. From Strong's letters to Norman, July 14, 1922, and February 22, 1923; quoted in Clarke (1967), 31.

8. See "Outline for Discussion about Gold," April 20, 1928, prepared by the Foreign

Information Division of the Federal Reserve. Harrison Papers, box 8. The outline approvingly quotes Cassel's remark that "the gold bullion standard is a real gold standard." The writer then mentions an "advantage" of this system as constituting "the only real safeguard against manipulation of currency for political purposes"; 2. "Political purposes" presumably include the furtherance of specifically domestic economic objectives.

9. Strong-Salter Memorandum of Conversation, op. cit.

10. Ibid., p. 5.

11. Strong to Gilbert, July 14, 1928, Strong Papers, 1012.2.

12. Cassel (1928), 73.

13. "Discussions with the Bank of France," May 27, 1928. FRBNY, C261.1.

14. Strong to Gilbert, July 14, 1928, op. cit.

15. Strong to Jay, July 21, 1927. Strong Papers, 1012.3.

16. Friedman and Schwartz (1963), 412–14. Friedman's judgment of Strong is much harsher in an essay of 1991: "It is a tragedy that the personal characteristics we admire so much in Strong and Moreau [governor of the Bank of France from 1926 to 1930] — adherence to principle and force of character — should have enabled them to follow policies that did so much harm to the rest of the world, and indirectly to their own countries as well." In Friedman (1991), xiii–xiv. In fact, much of the systemic damage caused by U.S. policy during 1930–32 resulted from the Federal Reserve System's adherence to the procyclical real bills doctrine — which Strong rejected. Hence, it seems unfair to hold him responsible for the results of that policy. See chapter 10, below.

17. Hawtrey (1946), 15.

18. See "Governor Strong: An Appreciation," *Economist,* October 20, 1928. Also Clarke (1967), 106–07.

19. Strong-Salter Memo of Conversation, May 25, 1928, op. cit., 8.

20. Moreau (1991), entry for May 23, 1928.

21. Mlynarski (1929), 73–74; and *Frankfurter Zeitung,* July 10, 1927, op. cit.

22. Genoa Financial Commission Report (1922); Currency Resolution 11 (1b); 679.

23. Sommariva and Tullio (1987), 87. Also, Enquête-Ausschuß (1929), 155–56.

24. Loveday (1930), 96f. Also, Ohlin (1927), 6.

25. Loveday (1930), 94, table IV.

26. Ibid., 94.

27. Eichengreen (1992a), 198–200.

28. On price deflation, the real cost of holding cash, and liquidity preference, see Mundell (1971), 14–22; also Keynes (1936a), 166–74.

29. Marjolin (1937), 128, 140–43.

30. Strong to Gilbert, September 30, 1925, 5. Strong Papers, 1012.1.

31. *Sight deposits* and *demand deposits* are used as synonyms.

32. Saint-Etienne (1983), appendix 2. Ratios calculated for 1926 : 3, 1928 : 2, and 1931 : 4. Also, Saint Marc (1983), 215, 229.

33. M1 (currency and sight deposits at the Bank of France and commercial banks) rose only from F140 billion at the end of 1928 to F166 billion at the end of 1932. Saint-Etienne (1983), appendix 2. The bank's gold stock rose from F31.3 billion to F81.4 billion over the same period. Nurkse (1944), appendix II.

34. Kindleberger (1986): "The British [at Genoa], under the inspiration of Montagu

Norman, worried about the world's gold supply. The prewar gold price remained fixed, but mining costs had risen because of wartime inflation. Moreover, the higher price level increased the demand for gold reserves by central banks"; 47. He does not return to this issue.

Also prominent in its emphasis on central bank diplomacy is the classic study by Clarke (1967). Clarke never asserts that a breakdown in cooperation (or lack of leadership) actually caused the depression. But because he discusses central bank diplomacy without first examining whether a gold shortage existed, he leaves many readers with the impression that the former factor was crucial.

35. Inter alia, see Royal Commission on Indian Currency and Finance (1926), Cassel, appendix 92, 3:597; also, Cassel (1931), 16, and (1936), 23.

36. James (1985a), 19–21.

37. Ibid., 29–30.

38. Chandler (1958), 68f., 94f.

39. Kindleberger (1986), 30.

40. Jones (1920), 171–72. Keynes (1930) cites part of this passage; 2:290. Keynes wrote in 1929 that the reason the amount of gold in the world might affect the price level was that gold was a "fetish"; Keynes (1989 [1929a]), 19:776.

Chapter 5. The French Inflation, 1921–26

1. Wolfe (1951) notes this expectation; 57.

2. Eichengreen (1990), 52.

3. Ibid., 33.

4. Ogburn and Jaffé (1929), 97–98.

5. Sauvy (1984), 2:188–89. See also chapter 1, above.

6. Ogburn and Jaffé (1929), 97–98, 158. Again in Eichengreen and Wyplosz (1988), undifferentiated figures for the 1921–27 period are used, which leaves the impression of more rapid growth in economic activity than actually occurred.

7. A Tobin's q of 100 refers here to the share-index-to-price-index relation of 1919, not to a hypothetical situation in which profits are at some steady-state level. In fact, 1919 was a year of rising prices, thus probably of profit inflation also. This suggests that data in the text, where 1919 = 100, may understate the level of profit inflation in the 1920s.

On the other hand, real share values in the early 1920s were well below their prewar level; Sauvy (1984). In the text, I concentrate on the direction of change in values of Tobin's q, rather than on their levels relative to another historical era. This is plausible because contextual factors, including the debt-equity mix, the distribution of tax burden, and real balance effects might change so as to make one era scarcely comparable to another. Also, the apparent correlation between the direction of change in Tobin's q and the rate of change in industrial production over the period suggests that it is a relevant indicator. Nevertheless, it should be used cautiously.

8. The stock index, wholesale price index, and industrial production index (for December of each year) are taken directly from Ogburn and Jaffé (1929), 88, 97–98. Tobin's q is then calculated from the stock and price indexes.

The monetary and tax environment changed significantly in late July, when Poincaré assumed power. However, the immediate trend in Tobin's q was scarcely affected. For this reason, year-end data can be used with little distortion. The stock index in December 1926 was approximately the same as in June. See Kindleberger (1986), figure 6. Between those two dates, French retail prices rose but wholesale prices declined. See Sauvy (1984), 2:188, 193. Industrial production reached a peak of 125 in July, then declined slightly.

9. Sauvy (1984), 2:189.

10. Eichengreen and Wyplosz (1988) also point to the correlation between Tobin's q and industrial production in France during the entire 1922–38 period; 275–78.

11. Data in the following table are from Ogburn and Jaffé (1929), 163–64; these appear to be the best comparative wage data available. Also, the average wages are compiled from data for thirty-seven trades, skilled and unskilled. Source: *Bulletin de la Statistique Générale de la France.* For similar conclusions, see Bérenger (1926), 644.

12. This is not strictly accurate. Stock prices measure the relation between the cost of equity capital and expected returns on investment. A rise in the stock index may reflect a change in either, or both, of the variables.

13. Ogburn and Jaffé (1929), 89, 120, 161, 180. In a period of high price volatility such as 1924–26, equity can become a less risky investment than debt — hence it becomes cheaper to issue. On differing perspectives of old and new industry regarding price inflation, see also Georg Bernhard, of Ludwig Bendix and Co., "My Impressions of the French Currency Problem," September 1926. Morrow Papers; series I, box 22, folder 87.

14. Ogburn and Jaffé (1929), 84–86.

15. Becker and Bernstein (1990), 297. Also, *Economist,* July 14, 1928, 68.

16. Sauvy (1984), 2:193. Keynes (1989 [1926a]), 9:81.

17. Ogburn and Jaffé (1929), 105.

18. François-Marsal (1927), 200–02. Generally on French taxes, see Haig (1929).

19. Keynes (1989 [1926b]), 19:456.

20. Moreau (1991), entry for July 29, 1926.

21. Prati (1991), table 3. These estimates include only national government expenditures.

22. Schuker (1976), 122–23.

23. Eichengreen (1992a), 173.

24. Frayssinet (1928), 62–63.

25. On capital levies in general, see Keynes (1930), 2:162, 175. For the case of France, see Keynes (1989 [1926a]), 9:77, 80–81. For a conceptually similar treatment of the pitfalls of imposing capital levies, see Barro (1989), 201–02. For Caillaux's reference to Keynes, see Bredin (1980), 357.

26. Keynes (1989 [1926a]), 9:81, for mention of underrewarded farmers.

27. H. A. Siepmann to Leith Ross, "The French Franc," November 30, 1926, 2. Bank of England, OV45/1.

28. Robert B. Warren (a senior Federal Reserve official), "Developments of July 7 and 8," July 9, 1926: "M. Blum concentrated upon the plan of stabilization [recommended in the just-issued *Report* of the Committee of Experts] at a level which would involve a rise in domestic prices. The program, Blum said, 'oozes inflation at every page'; he advocated deflation by means of a capital levy"; 2–3. Strong Papers, 1000.7.

29. E.g., see internal memorandum, Bank of England, "Monsieur Quesnay's opinion on the French Franc," December 7, 1926, (unsigned): "Monsieur Quesnay's personal opinion about any kind of capital levy is that (owing to export of capital and so on) it would in the end make it difficult to hold the franc at even 200 to the £, and that to hold it at 100 would certainly be more than twice as difficult still." Bank of England, OV45/1.

30. See Mundell (1968) on what has come to be known as the "policy mix" issue; chap. 16, "The Appropriate Use of Monetary and Fiscal Policy under Fixed Exchange Rates." For a textbook treatment, see Kenen (1994), 377–84.

31. Comité des experts (1926), 24.

32. Ibid., 25.

33. Ibid., 23.

34. The notion behind the Laffer Curve is that beyond a theoretically defined point of maximum intake, further increases in the marginal tax rate produce less revenue rather than more. For a formal treatment, see Barro (1989), 200–01. The experts noted, "General income taxes do not yield proportionate revenue when the nominal rate is increased to 60%." Comité des experts (1926), 23.

Similarly, the committee pointed to depreciation-induced bracket creep: "The Committee has commented that rates on the important progressive taxes, those on income and inheritance, are currently quite high. It must be observed that the effect of a declining value of money is to raise the rate of revenue collected where the real value of capital is unchanged, and thus to push capital into higher tax brackets." Ibid., appendix chap. 5, no. 4.

35. Warren, "Memorandum of Conversation of August 31, 1926," attended by Strong, Moreau, Rist, Quesnay, and Warren. Strong Papers, 1000.7. For evidence that Strong may have had in mind, see Calvin Coolidge's speech of February 12, 1924, quoted in Mellon (1924), 216–17; quoted also in Wanniski (1989), 131–32.

36. Jeanneney (1976), 215f., and (1977), 36–37.

37. E.g., see letter, Robineau to Finance Minister Etienne Clémentel, July 17, 1924; quoted in Philippe (1931), 61.

38. Eichengreen (1992a), figure 6.3.

39. Schuker (1976), chap. 1.

40. Ibid., 117–19; also, Rist (1928), 9, and (1955), 996.

41. A *bon* is a security interest, often used to designate a short-term security issued by the Treasury, i.e., roughly a Treasury bill. I will use the French term.

42. Moreau (1991), entry for June 26, 1926; also, Jeanneney (1976), 202–08; also, Patat and Lutfalla (1986), 47.

43. De Mouÿ's views are discussed in Schuker (1976), 43–44; in Jeanneney (1977), 38, 41; and in Philippe (1931), 60–61.

44. De Mouÿ's report, July 27, 1924; quoted in Jeanneney (1977), 38.

45. Clémentel's memorandum concerning meeting of December 16, 1924; cited in Jeanneney (1976), 214. Published and actual circulation totals are presented in Moreau (1991), entry for June 26, 1926.

46. Blum, *Journal Officiel*, July 7, 1926; quoted in Sédillot (1979), 131. See also "La situation monétaire de la France et le prélèvement du Sacrifice National: premier discours prononcé par Léon Blum à la Chambre des Députés, le 7 Juillet 1926," esp. 7–8; Auriol Papers, 1 Au 11, Dr 2.

47. Comité des experts (1926), 32. "La France économique, 1927," *Revue d'économie*

politique 41 (1927): 355, on threat of forced consolidation in late 1925. Also, Warren, "Paris Money Market," June 26, 1926, Strong Papers 1000.7, 2–3; Jeanneney (1976), 254; and Jeanneney (1977), 72.

48. As prime minister in 1911, Caillaux negotiated a settlement to the Morocco crisis that gave France a protectorate over North African territory in exchange for generous concessions to Germany in Central Africa. This settlement soon became so unpopular that he was forced to resign. Before and during World War I he advocated negotiations with Germany and maintained contacts with German agents. He was imprisoned in 1918 and convicted of committing "damage to the external security of France" — he was found innocent of the greater charge of treason — in 1920, at which time the rest of his sentence was commuted. He was granted an amnesty by a Cartel des gauches ministry in 1924. Caillaux also gained notoriety when his wife shot *Le Figaro* editor Gaston Calmette to death in March 1914. See Bredin (1980); also Berenson (1992), esp. chap. 2.

The journalist Robert Dell (1926) offered a representative British view: "[Caillaux] is now, as he was fifteen years ago, the only prominent French 'bourgeois' politician who sincerely believes in a peaceful and united Europe." Caillaux was one of the rare Frenchmen who had read Keynes's *Economic Consequences of the Peace* and shared that book's view of the Versailles Treaty; see Bredin (1980), 351. (Rist also shared Keynes's judgment; see chapter 6, below.)

49. Jeanneney (1976), 251ff.

50. See the Herriot-affiliated *Le Quotidien,* July 13, 1925. Quoted in parts in Jeanneney (1976), 259, and in Bredin (1980), 338.

51. The subscription figure is from Jeanneney (1976), 260. On the government's expectations, see letter, Leffingwell to Lamont; Lamont Papers, box 103, folder 111.

52. Robert de Rothschild, a relative of the bank regent Edouard de Rothschild, offered anecdotal evidence that wealthy bon-holders took advantage of the exchange offer, while *petits rentiers* rejected it. The issue contained tax exemptions that would have been worth more to those with high incomes than to most peasants. Jeanneney (1976), 261.

On a sterling basis, the exchange bonds issued in 1925 yielded between 4.3 and 4.4 percent; i.e., they were sold at 95 with a 4 percent coupon. Equivalent British bonds yielded 4.5 percent in 1925, despite the fact that they were almost certainly perceived to be less risky than French consols. The French government floated short-term sterling-denominated notes in Britain at 6 percent in 1924 — further evidence that the 1925 offering yielded too little. Makinen and Woodward (1989), 205–06. Prati (1991) accepts Makinen and Woodward's evidence that the sterling-indexed rate on Caillaux's exchange bonds was close to that for British consols, then concludes that the French rate was very attractive. But this holds only if French and British treasury bonds were perceived to be equally risky.

53. Jeanneney (1976), 261–63.

54. Ibid., 271–72.

55. See Prati (1991), 218–22, for a brief review of cartel ministries and tax proposals.

56. Jeanneney (1977), 71–72.

57. Makinen and Woodward (1989), figure 2. Eichengreen (1992a), table 6.3.

58. Leffingwell to Lamont, June 19, 1925; Leffingwell Papers, box 7, folder 92.

59. "Extracts of Letter from Mr. Warren to Gov. Strong," June 24, 1926; Strong Papers, 1000.7.

60. Rist, "Pour la stabilisation du franc," which appeared first as a series of eight articles in *Moniteur des intérêts*, from October 7, 1925, to February 16, 1926; included in Rist (1933), 17.

61. Makinen and Woodward (1989), table 1.

62. Prati (1991), 219. Makinen and Woodward (1989), 195.

63. Leffingwell to Lamont, April 23, 1926; Leffingwell Papers, box 4, folder 93. On Parmentier, see Schuker (1976), 39–42.

64. For total bon issue, see Makinen and Woodward (1989), table 2; their sources are Rogers (1929) and Haig (1929). Assuming bon rates were market-driven, higher interest payments might have been met through the issue of new bons, with no increase in either advances or the note issue.

65. Saint-Etienne (1983), appendix 2.

66. Eichengreen (1992a), figure 6.3.

67. Saint-Etienne (1983), appendix 2.

68. Warren, "Observations on the Role of the Bank of France in a Program of Financial Reconstruction," June 10, 1926, 2–3; also, Warren, "The Budget Position," June 11, 1926," 1–2. On the bank rate, see Warren, "The Paris Money Market," June 26, 1926, 4. All in Strong Papers, 1000.7.

69. Warren, June 26, 1926, 2–3.

70. Ibid., 4. Also, Rogers (1929), 59, 235. Rogers provides data for the Société Générale, the Comptoir d'Escompte, the Crédit Industriel, the Banque de Paris et des Pays-Bas, and the Banque de l'Union Parisienne.

71. Data are from Rogers (1929), chart 43. The report rate is the "contango" rate, or the rate at which a buyer of stock pays a seller to postpone transfer.

72. Rogers (1929), chart 43. Rogers, consistent with the explanation above, tied the lower commercial paper and report rates of late 1925 and early 1926 to the ease in French money markets consequent upon heavy bank advances; 232. Makinen and Woodward (1989) similarly argue that monetary ease made all French interest rates too low; 206–07.

73. Makinen and Woodward (1989), figure 2.

74. Memorandum (unsigned), "Impressions of a talk with Mr. Warren — 30 June, 1926," 3; Bank of England, OV45/1.

75. Eichengreen (1992a), 179, argues that soft commercial paper rates in France in late 1925 and early 1926 and declining British treasury bill rates in the second half of 1925 demonstrate that French bon rates were at a competitive market level. But if, as argued here, the demand for reimbursements was driven by fears for bon liquidity, one would expect rising demand and relatively declining rates for alternate investments, including placements in London, where liquidity was more certain. I shall point out again in chapter 8 that expatriated French capital permitted indeed some ease in London markets.

Eichengreen elsewhere appears to concede that higher bon rates might have slowed the reimbursements. E.g., Eichengreen (1986) argues, "When [from March 1924 onward] the maturity of an outstanding issue coincided with expectations of future deficits to be financed by additions to the stock of bons, the public became unwilling to purchase the existing stock *at prices consistent with the Treasury's debt management objectives*"; 61 (emphasis added).

76. Prati (1991), 231–34.

77. Ibid., table 6.

78. Keynes (1989 [1924a]), 4:xxii.

79. Jeanneney (1977), 72–75.

80. Makinen and Woodward (1990) generalize from the French funding crisis of 1925–26, as they note similar crises at about the same time in Belgium, Italy, Portugal, and Greece. The timing suggests an underlying systemic cause, probably the British and German stabilizations. Keynes wrote later, "The Bank [of England]'s pursui[t of] a policy of deflation in the years preceding Great Britain's return to the gold standard . . . was aggravating the problems of the rest of Europe." In Keynes (1930), 2:288.

81. Eichengreen and Hatton (1988), 6–7. The authors' data for France are less precise than those for the other two countries.

82. For estimates for 1924, 1925, and 1926, see Meynial (1927), 271. For earlier years' estimates, see Meynial (1925), 52. The French Committee of Experts noted the difficulty of correctly estimating this amount. Comité des experts (1926), 13–14. Keynes (1989 [1927b]) offered a roughly consistent estimate that the "increase in credits in London, partly attributable to the 'flight from the franc', is £100M from the beginning of 1925 to the middle of 1927"; 710–11. Not all expatriated francs went to London. A representative of the Irving Bank in New York told Moreau that French individuals had placed $1.5 billion in the United States, perhaps half of it between the end of March and the end of June 1926. Moreau (1991), entry for August 27, 1926.

83. Moreau (1991), entry for July 19, 1926.

84. Eichengreen (1990).

85. Eichengreen (1992a), figure 5.3.

86. James (1986), 129–30. Also, Colm and Neisser (1930); statement by Hans Ritzschl, 1:162.

87. Hardach (1976), 146. Also Sargent (1986), 94.

88. Krohne (1982), 419: "In each case, inflation undoubtedly worked to the advantage of investors, and permitted a rapid postwar reconstruction. Industrial capacity at the beginning of the stabilization [in 1924] had expanded over the 1913 level to an extent that astonished the reparations experts of the Dawes Commission."

89. Eichengreen and Hatton (1988), table 1.1.

90. Eichengreen (1990), figure 3.2.

91. Makinen and Woodward (1989), figure 2.

92. Galenson and Zellner (1957), 455; reproduced in Balderston (1982), 505.

93. Macmillan Committee (1931a), par. 3332.

94. Ibid., par. 3390.

95. Ibid., pars. 3360–62.

96. Tobin's q for 1926 and afterward derived from Kindleberger (1986), figure 6.

97. Eichengreen and Wyplosz (1988), figures 14.3 and 14.4.

98. Schuker (1976), 3.

Chapter 6. German and French Capital Inflows

1. Keynes (1930), 1:338f.

2. *Sterilization* is not a precise term. The *London Times* (February 15, 1938) defined it as "the Treasury's policy of limiting the expansion of credit which would follow if the imports of gold were used as a basis for the expansion of note issue or bank credits."

Mundell explains: "Sterilization (or neutralization) policy is a specific combination of monetary and exchange policy. When the central bank buys or sells foreign exchange the money supply increases or decreases. The purpose of sterilization policy is to offset this effect." Mundell (1968), 256. Both definitions are included in *A Supplement to the Oxford English Dictionary* (1987).

A complication in the meaning of *sterilization* comes when the amount of credit superstructure per unit of gold held in reserves differs among national economies. E.g., posit that Britain maintains three units of currency and six units of deposits for each unit of gold reserves, whereas for France the multipliers of currency and deposits are only two and four, respectively. Suppose reserves are then transferred from Britain to France, and each economy subsequently preserves its traditional reserve multipliers. The French could argue that they merely followed their usual practice. However, international contraction of currency and deposits — hence systemic sterilization — will have occurred.

3. This is implied by the title of Schuker's (1988) study, *American Reparations to Germany, 1919–33.*

4. Temin (1971); Temin (1976), 152–59; and Temin (1989), 34. Also, Schuker (1988), 84f.

5. The exchange rate was $1 = RM4.2. See Eichengreen and Hatton (1988), table 1.1, for unemployment data.

6. Schuker (1988), table 7; he cites the *Statistisches Reichsamt.*

7. Temin (1976), 153–58.

8. McNeil (1986), 112.

9. Temin (1976), 153.

10. See Falkus (1975) for a critique of Temin's argument, 456–57.

11. Schuker (1988) finds the decline in the German demand for funds in early 1929 causally unrelated to the simultaneous surge in lending to Wall Street in early 1929, despite the fact that interest rates then rose in Germany as elsewhere. He notes, "Neither long- nor short-term borrowers experienced overwhelming difficulty in obtaining money. . . . The American investment-banking community exhibited no little ingenuity in designing issues with an equity 'hook' for those German firms that still cared to borrow"; 46. This is the same analytical mistake Temin makes when he denies the connections among reserve flows, the trend in interest rates, and domestic demand.

12. Schuker (1988), 27–28.

13. Aftalion (1929), 16–17. Also, Rist (1933), 20.

14. Saint-Etienne (1983), appendix 2, on money stock totals. Sauvy (1884), vol. 2, figures 20, 22, and 23, for price indicators.

15. Cassel (1928), 15.

16. *Bulletin de la Statistique Générale de la France;* data tabulated in Sintenis (1934), 7. A wholesale price tabulation for 1925 shows purchasing power indexes of 137 in Germany, 158 in England, 162 in the United States, and only 127 in France. In 1929 the indexes stood at 135 in Germany, 132 in Britain, 147 in the United States, and 120 in France. See also Rist (1937), plate 6, for data on other countries.

17. Schuker (1988), 34. Balderston (1982) assembles corroborative evidence regarding the anemic profitability of German industry during 1925–29; table 4.

18. Kindleberger (1986), figure 6.

19. Borchardt (1990), table 6.1.

20. Galenson and Zellner (1957), 455; evidence reproduced in Balderston (1982), 505.

21. Falkus (1975), 455. Falkus cites the Reichs-Kredit Gesellschaft (1930). On comparison with British discount rates, see Schuker (1988), 51.

22. Falkus (1975), 454.

23. Hardach (1976), 160.

24. Keynes (1989 [1924a]), 18:259.

25. Balderston (1982), 507–10. Schuker (1988), 33–34.

26. The locus classicus of this argument is in Keynes (1920), 81ff. Also, Balderston (1982), 493. Rist concurred with Keynes's judgment that the expropriations were at the heart of the transfer complications. Rist (1955), 989.

Jèze also argued that transfer difficulties must limit the amount of German reparation payments, and he was pointedly critical of French politicians for ignoring or obscuring this. Warren, "Conversation of August 31, 1926," attended by Strong, Jèze, and Warren, 3; Strong Papers, 1000.7. Jèze and Rist were the only professional economists appointed to the Committee of Experts in 1926.

Schuker rejects the argument that Germany faced a burdensome "structural" trade deficit during the 1920s. However, his reasoning relies heavily on Temin's argument that the credit environment in Germany prior to the 1925–26 and 1928–29 downturns was "autonomous," i.e., independent of international monetary conditions. Schuker (1988), 83–84. Temin's argument is rejected above.

27. Kindleberger (1986), 61f. Demands for higher tariffs as well as preferential duties were spotlighted at Imperial Conferences of 1923 and 1926.

28. Rist (1923), 198.

29. Schuker (1988), table 1.

30. From the Committee of Experts (1924): "We estimate the amount which we think Germany can pay in gold marks by consideration of her budget possibilities; but we propose safeguards against such transfers of these mark payments into foreign exchange as would destroy stabilization and thereby endanger future reparation"; 360. For a different understanding of the Dawes Plan, see Balderston (1982), 490–91.

31. Gilbert to Norman, September 17, 1925; Strong Papers, 1012.5. Also, McNeil (1986), 121. See Hardach (1976), 42–48 on the Dawes Plan's stricture against "artificial maneuvers."

32. E.g., a Dr. Sering concluded, "The result of reparations is to block an ample formation of capital in Germany, because they hold industrial interest rates too high. In this way they block an expansion of production and exports." In Salin (1929), 1:145; also, inter alia, statements of Solmssen, 1:155; and of Hahn, 1:174, 178.

33. Schuker notes a decline in Germany's ex post savings ratio from 15.5 percent during 1899–1913 to 8.6 percent during 1925–29; Schuker (1988), 31.

34. Data from Balderston (1982), 492–93. Balderston's reserve data on reserves are taken from Hardach's dissertation. For reserve amounts, see Eichengreen (1992a), figure 9.5.

35. Balderston (1982), table 3, panel f.

36. Schuker (1988), tables 9 and 10. Also, Borchardt (1983), 130. However, for a viewpoint that wage increases were economically justified, see Krohn (1982), 417–18.

37. Schuker (1988), 84–85.

38. Holtfrerich (1990), 72–73.

39. Winkler (1988), 51–53.

40. This issue is discussed in chapter 2, above; see specifically Keynes (1989 [1979]), 29:99–100. In the case of labor's share of German national product in 1932, see Hoffmann (1965), 87–88; cited in Holtfrerich (1990), 76.

41. McNeil (1986), 213–16.

42. Berghahn (1982), table 19.

43. Von Kreudener (1990), 96–98; Borchardt (1990), 151. For a cautious statement of the role of agrarian leaders in the triumph of Nazism in 1933, see Turner (1985), 324–28.

44. On German cartelization, see Winkler (1988), 34–41. Hilferding's phrase, "demokratisch organisierte Wirtschaft," appears on 38.

45. The economist Emil Lederer, previously a Social Democrat, wrote in 1932, "The partial organization of production in cartels and trusts, and the fixing of the most important prices, hindered the development of manufacturing, the absorption of workers in new industries, and the growth of social product." Winkler (1988), 39.

46. McNeil (1986), 276.

47. Schuker (1988), 46.

48. Gilbert, "Memorandum for the German Government," October 20, 1927; 12–13. Strong Papers, 1012.2.

49. Ohlin (1928), March, 9–10.

50. James (1986), 131. On the United States, see chapter 5, above; on French reforms, see below in this chapter.

51. James (1986), 55.

52. Colm and Neisser (1930); statements of Bernard Harms (chairman), 1:385, 388; Gustav Stolper, 1:397.

53. Von Kreudener (1985), 376: "The increase in the social burden to include the introduction of unemployment insurance . . . was conditioned not merely by the exigencies of the economic situation, but was also an expression of the decision to establish a welfare state. It is hard to imagine how the new, undefended Republic, encircled by a phalanx of enemies—burdened also with the transfer requirements inherited from the Versailles Treaty—could otherwise have gained legitimacy in the eyes of its citizens."

54. McNeil (1986), 202.

55. Colm and Neisser (1930); statements of Salin, 1:209–10; and of Harms, 1:385.

56. James (1986), 49. Also, Feldman (1985b), 273; and McNeil (1986), 277.

57. Sargent (1986), 92f; James (1985b), 216; also, Borchardt (1990), 106.

58. James (1984), 78–79.

59. This estimate appears in a letter, Luther to Brüning, October 24, 1931; cited in James (1985a), 205.

60. James (1984), 74–75.

61. "Real" bills discounting, practiced by the Bank of France and the Federal Reserve during this period, permitted discounts on real commercial bills and restricted it only on financial bills. See chapters 9 and 10. The Reichsbank's discount restrictions on commercial bills exceeded even the real bills doctrine in the way they limited a central bank in carrying out its role as lender of last resort.

62. James (1985a), 203.

63. Bagehot (1873), 48, 51.

64. James (1985b), 223.

65. James (1984), 76–78. Although it is impossible to be precise about this, it is likely that a large portion of the "foreign" deposits withdrawn were in fact deposits held by German nationals that had previously left Germany as flight capital.

66. Bagehot (1873), 56.

67. Eichengreen and Hatton (1988), table 1.1. Industrial unemployment in Germany rose to 34 percent in 1931 and 44 percent in 1932.

68. Balderston (1983), 402–03.

69. Balderston (1982), 495–97.

70. James (1984), 79.

71. James (1985b), 223–25.

72. James (1985a), figure 6.

73. James (1984), 82.

74. James (1985a), 17, 215–18.

75. Ibid., 328–29.

76. Eichengreen and Hatton (1988), table 1.1.

77. Leffingwell to Lamont and Gilbert (who returned to Morgan in 1930), July 24, 1931; Leffingwell Papers, box 4, folder 95. See Kunz (1991) on the "Morgan ideology"; esp. 40–41. Leffingwell had urged Italian and French devaluations in 1926. Leffingwell to Lamont, October 25, 1926; Leffingwell Papers, box 4, folder 93.

78. Holtfrerich (1990), 66–68.

79. For a review of this literature, see Borchardt (1990) and Holtfrerich (1990). Holtfrerich draws attention to widespread calls in Germany for monetary and fiscal expansion during 1931 and 1932; however, he offers little evidence that those calling for expansion were prepared to violate the provisions of the 1924 Bank Law, devalue, or abandon the gold standard.

Chancellor Heinrich Brüning wanted an economic downturn to force foreign powers to end reparations. To some extent, his failure was broadly political and diplomatic (that is, reparations were canceled in the summer of 1932, as Brüning desired, but the National Socialists came to power anyway the following year), rather than a mistake of economic policy. Borchardt identifies pursuit of this diplomatic goal as one of the constraints upon Brüning, although he believes German options were also limited on purely economic grounds. E.g., Borchardt (1982), 171; and (1990), 104–05.

80. Skiba (1974), 193; cited in Schuker (1988), 88.

81. Makinen and Woodward (1989), figure 2.

82. "Confidential Minutes of Meeting of Friday, May 27, 1927," translated by O. E. Moore, 5; FRBNY, C2 61.1.

83. Ogburn and Jaffé (1929), 97–98.

84. Eichengreen and Hatton (1988), table 1.1.

85. Haig (1929), 149–64. *Economist,* August 7, 1926, 248. See also discussion in chapter 5, above.

86. E.g., Eichengreen and Wyplosz (1988), 259, 273–74; also, Sargent (1986), 117, 120. Eichengreen (1992a) again endorses this conclusion; 180f. The argument that the key to recovery of the franc was in balancing the budget rather than in making monetary

changes recalls the position of the more recalcitrant regents at the Bank of France during 1924–26. See Philippe (1931), 59–63; see also chapter 5, above. Rist (1955) called the regents' theory "absurd"; 998.

87. Keynes (1989 [1926a]), 9:78–79; and (1989 [1926c]), 19:564–65. The Bank of France economist Paul Ricard noted, "The repair of the damage had been practically completed by 1926 and from the point of view of the public finances had been paid for by a proportional tax on capital levied generally. The depreciation of the monetary unit had effected arbitrarily and blindly what the Government and the Parliament had not desired to do by other more correct means." Quoted from "The Characteristic Features of the French Monetary System," January 27, 1931 (translation). Bank of England OV45/4.

88. In 1926, more than 42 percent of the national budget was allocated to service on the national debt: F 15.9 billion of a total of F 37.2 billion. Comité des experts (1926), 85. The proportion of the national debt relative to national income declined from 2.5 times in 1922 to 1.7 in 1925 and to 1.0 in 1929. Sauvy (1984), vol. 3, figure 3.

89. Eichengreen and Wyplosz (1988), table 14.2.

90. Eichengreen and Wyplosz's (1988) conclusion that the 1926 budget resolution, which eliminated the deficit, was the key to the subsequent boom is weak on another ground. In theory, heavy interest payments on a national debt, when financed through borrowings, merely shift resources from new lenders to old lenders. The money never leaves the private sector, so to speak — it is not allocated to defense, administration, medical services, public works, etc. Those who receive interest payments may then apply them toward "consumption" or "investment" spending. It is misleading to lump these interest payments with "government" spending on a national income breakdown (as the authors' data do; table 14.2), as if further allocation to investment or consumption is precluded.

German government debt from World War I was practically wiped out by the inflation. Interest as a portion of the German public budget was a tiny fraction of the level in France and, especially, Britain. See data in James (1986), 48. This does not appear to have had any appreciable "crowding-in" effect on German investment, which aside from a robust year in 1927 did not really recover after the inflation.

91. I argue in chapter 9 that monetary non-neutrality in fact endured. Also, see Einzig (1931), on long-lasting undervaluation of the franc; 41. But Eichengreen and Wyplosz (1988) offer an opposing view; 280.

92. E.g., Eichengreen and Wyplosz (1988), table 14.1.

93. Eichengreen and Wyplosz (1988), figure 14.8. In chapter 10 I examine data during approximately the same time period for the United States; the correlation there between a rising Tobin's q and growing investment is much less clear.

94. Eichengreen and Hatton (1988), table 1.1.

95. Frayssinet (1928), 221, 224, 258; see also chapter 8, below.

96. Eichengreen (1992a), figure 8.6; Friedman and Schwartz (1963), chart 29.

97. Bank of France (1932), 163.

98. Bank of France (1931), 147.

99. Mouré (1991), figure 4.3.

100. Memorandum (unsigned), July 24, 1929; Bank of England, OV45/2.

101. Leffingwell to Lamont, June 24, 1927. Leffingwell Papers, box 4, folder 93. Also,

"Note sur la Trésorerie depuis le 1er janvier 1927," March 28, 1927, 6. Unsigned. Archives économiques et financières, B33179.

102. Robert Lacour-Gayet (financial attaché to the French embassy), Address to the Foreign Exchange Club of New York, November 22, 1927, 12–13. Lamont Collection, box 95, folder 4.

103. Memorandum, April 25, 1929. Bank of England, OV45/2.

104. *Economist,* July 14, 1928, 68.

105. M. Cheron, "Note pour le Ministre," November 13, 1928, 10–11. Archives économiques et financières, B33179.

106. Balderston (1983), table 7.

107. Eichengreen and Wyplosz (1988) are persuasive here; see data, 263–65. They also list previous studies that adopt the view that French growth during 1927–30 was export-led; 260.

108. Siepmann, "Note of Conversations held with Monsieur Quesnay in Paris on the 18th and 19th June, 1928" (labeled "Secret"), 4–5. Bank of England, OV45/2.

109. Leffingwell to Gilbert, May 22, 1928. Leffingwell Papers.

110. Keynes (1989 [1929b]), 11:458.

111. Keynes (1930), 1:340; also, 342.

112. Rueff (1929), 390.

113. Ohlin (1929), 177.

114. Ibid.

115. Mantoux (1952), 130–31.

116. Ibid., 123–25.

Chapter 7. The British and German Deflations, 1924–27

1. Keynes (1989 [1923]), 9:183, 186.

2. Keynes (1989 [1925a]), 9:198.

3. DeCecco (1973), 110–17. See also chapter 2, above.

4. Some evidence for the relative postwar rise in sterling costs appears in the sharp decline in the British trade balance during the 1920s relative to 1909–14. See Mitchell (1976), 497, 819, 826.

5. Cassel, who did recognize the gold shortage and the potential for systemic deflation, nevertheless, a decade later, defended the British decision to restore prewar parity. He thought economization of monetary gold possible, even in retrospect but evidently overlooked the contribution that a stronger Bank of England might have made toward achieving this. Cassel (1936), 40–41.

6. E.g., suppose one-third of world trade is conducted in sterling, and the international value of sterling (i.e., its gold or dollar value) rises by 10 percent. Then world prices would rise by $.10 \times x\,.33 = .033$, or 3.3 percent. By these numbers, and ceteris paribus, 6.7 percent of general sterling price deflation associated with stabilization would bring British prices to the world level. Hence restoring prewar parity would act as a drag on British industry and employment by racheting down domestic prices by 6.7 percent, yet at the same time aggravate the systemic undervaluation of gold by an additional 3.3 percent.

7. E.g., assume the exchange rate of sterling increases from $4.40 (before) to $4.86

(after), while Britain's stock of gold reserves was twenty-five million ounces. If the systemic price of gold was $20.67 per ounce, then Britain's gold stock was worth £117 million before revaluation, but only £106 million afterward.

8. For the sterling-dollar exchange, see Eichengreen (1992), figure 6.1. For gold wholesale price indexes, see *Bulletin de la Statistique Générale de la France;* reproduced in Sintenis (1934), 7. The 13 percent figure averages the rates of increase for Germany, France, Britain, and the United States without adjusting for the size of their respective economies. For a much lower estimate of British domestic wholesale price inflation, see *Federal Reserve Bulletin,* cited in Clarke (1967), chart 3.

9. Clarke (1967), 85–88. Brown (1940), 371–74.

10. Clarke (1967), chart 2, on discount rates; and Makinen and Woodward (1989), figure 2, on British market rates.

11. Clarke (1967), 100–01.

12. Eichengreen (1992a), chart 9.6.

13. Hawtrey's testimony, Macmillan Committee (1931a), pars. 4174–76.

14. Macmillan Committee (1931a), par. 4179. Also, Leffingwell argued that the return to sterling parity had been a prime factor in causing the world deflation, although he did not single out the effect of interest rates. Leffingwell to Lamont, June 24, 1927; Leffingwell Papers, box 4, folder 93. Keynes also identified the British restoration of parity as an important factor pushing world interest rates up and prices down in the middle and late 1920s. Keynes (1930), 2:379.

15. Macmillan Committee (1931a), par. 4256.

16. Brown (1940), 378.

17. Leffingwell to Lamont, October 16, 1925; Leffingwell Papers, box 4, folder 93. Also, Ohlin (1927), 13.

18. This argument is developed in Makinen and Woodward (1990). For more on submarket rates in Italy and Belgium, see letter, Leffingwell to Lamont, June 9, 1925; Leffingwell Papers, box 4, folder 92.

19. E.g., suppose one can sell dollars for francs at a current market rate of 1 : 30, where a rate two years earlier was 1 : 15. Assume further that the current purchasing power ratio is 1 : 22, reflecting the franc's greater loss of purchasing power externally than internally. A dollar's purchasing power in France would thus exceed that in the United States by 30 : 22. Because the price of gold is fixed in dollars, the commodity value of gold would be greater in France than in the United States by the same ratio — here, by 36 percent.

20. Even Keynes, the leading critic of the 1925 restoration, omitted any mention of the consequences of overvaluing sterling upon the Bank of England's systemic influence. E.g., see Keynes (1989 [1925b]).

21. H. A. Siepmann, head of the central banking section at the Bank of England, expressed concern as early as December 1926 that the Bank of France might reject sterling as a reserve; he hoped the United States would continue to pursue price stability, even if this required sterilizing large amounts of gold outflow. Siepmann to Quesnay, December 17, 1926; Quesnay Papers, 374 AP/9.

22. "Discount and Currency Policy of the Reichsbank" (translation), *Frankfurter Zeitung,* July 29, 1925. Strong Papers, 1135.0.

23. "The Reserve Policy of the Reichsbank: Gold instead of Devisen" (translation), *Frankfurter Zeitung,* August 1, 1925. Strong Papers, 1135.0.

24. Figures from Nurkse (1944), appendix II; in Eichengreen (1985), 221–23.

25. Berichterstattung der Reichsbank, April 13, 1928; cited in Hardach (1976), 93.

26. Schacht formally testified as follows in October 1926: "When gold exports become likely, and are realized as a newspaper reports 'A gold transfer has occurred'—then the whole world turns its attention to this singular and unusual occurrence.... This is not the case where only foreign exchange is affected." Enquête-Ausschuß (1929), 158.

27. Shepard Morgan to Strong, April 2, 1925. Strong Papers, 1012.4.

28. Lord Albernon's memo on conversation with Schacht (untitled), October 7, 1925. Strong Papers, 1012.5

29. On these grounds Schacht justified the Reichsbank's willingness to forego interest that it might otherwise earn on foreign exchange. Enquête-Ausschuß (1929), 158–59. See also discussion of German interest rates in chapter 6, above.

30. Keynes would suggest in 1930 that adjustment of gold point spreads was not then used anywhere to manage gold flows; Macmillan Committee (1931a), par. 5825. In fact, we know that the Reichsbank did use gold point spreads for this purpose at times during the later 1920s.

31. Shepard Morgan to Strong, Nov. 16, 1927; Strong Papers, 1012.4. Jay to Strong, June 22, 1927; Strong Papers, 1012.3. Also, Hardach (1976), 75–76.

32. Schacht's testimony, October 1926; Enquête-Ausschuß (1929), 168. Also, Hardach (1976), 85.

33. Brown (1940), 797 and chart 52.

34. Bureau of Labor wholesale price index, cited in Cassel (1928), 88.

35. League of Nations (1945). Charts reproduced in Kindleberger (1986), figure 2. However, evidence of declining commodity prices during 1925–28 should be interpreted cautiously. Commodity price indexes tend to over-weight agricultural products. During World War I, farm production expanded rapidly in North and South America and in Asia. When European production recovered in the 1920s, the world faced a glut. The commodity price decline thus to some extent reflected nonmonetary causes. Eichengreen (1989), 6–8.

36. Keynes (1930), 2:258.

37. Ohlin (1927), 7.

38. Ohlin (1929b), February, 5.

39. Keynes (1930), 2:188–89.

40. Ibid., 2:276–77.

41. Eichengreen et al. (1985) find evidence that British policy was "asymmetric in the sense that the Bank of England was more inclined to raise its discount rate upon losing reserves that to lower it upon gaining them." They argue that the bank violated the rules of the gold standard and conclude, "Such violations of the 'rules of the game' . . . may have contributed to the instability of the interwar financial system"; 740–41. However, the Bank of England did not apply rules in a symmetrical fashion before 1914, when the system was purportedly more stable. A Bank of England official indicated an asymmetrical application of prewar rules in testimony before the United States Monetary Commission in 1910: "The Bank rate is raised with the object either of preventing gold from

leaving the country, or of attracting gold to the country, and lowered when it is completely out of touch with the market rates and circumstances do not render it necessary to induce the import of gold." Quoted in Bloomfield (1959), 23n.

42. Cassel (1936), 43.

43. Kindleberger (1986), 94.

Chapter 8. The French Stabilization

1. Generally, see Haig (1929).

2. Leffingwell to Lamont, October 16, 1925; Leffingwell Papers, box 4, folder 93. Triffin (1968) drew an almost identical conclusion; 30.

3. Paul Ricard, "The Characteristic Features of the French Monetary System" (translation), Jan. 27, 1931. Bank of England, OV45/4.

4. Keynes (1989 [1926a].

5. Keynes (1989 [1926b]), 19:456, 464; and (1989 [1926c]), 19:563–64.

6. See Keynes (1989 [1923]), 4:22. See also chapter 5, above.

7. Leffingwell to Lamont and Harjes, May 10, 1926; Leffingwell Papers, box 4, folder 93.

8. These figures are monthly averages; Frayssinet (1928), 85.

9. Jeanneney (1977), 128.

10. Frayssinet (1928), 76.

11. Committee members are listed in Comité des experts (1926), 3.

12. Jeanneney (1976), 297.

13. Warren, "The New Cabinet," June 25, 1926, 2; Strong Papers, 1000.7.

14. Warren remarked of the committee's proposal to stabilize the franc but let internal prices rise that it "has a very familiar ring. It is in fact the very program which J. M. Keynes formulated for France about a year ago." Warren to Strong, July 8, 1926; Strong Papers, 1000.7. For Keynes's mostly favorable views on the experts' *Report,* see Keynes (1989 [1926c]), 19:563–65.

15. E.g., the committee wrote of the need to "reconstitute working capital . . . which had been partially destroyed by inflation." Comité des experts (1926), 50.

16. Ibid., 47.

17. Ibid., 35.

18. Ibid., 23.

19. Makinen and Woodward (1989), 202.

20. Comité des experts (1926), 16, and appendix to chap. 4. Also, Eichengreen (1992a), table 6.2.

21. For 1925 budget deficit, see Makinen and Woodward (1990), table 1; on bank advances, see chapter 5, above.

22. Frayssinet (1928), 137.

23. Jeanneney (1976), 307.

24. Ibid., 310–13.

25. Franc exchange levels are included in various diary entries in Moreau (1991).

26. Warren, "The New Ministry," June 19, 1926, 1; Strong Papers 1000.7. A Herriot ministry was envisaged and prematurely announced on June 19 but was not officially

appointed. Instead, the Briand-Caillaux ministry took office on June 23. A succeeding Herriot ministry was formally appointed on July 19. Warren's observations about a potential Herriot ministry in June would presumably remain applicable in July.

27. Moreau (1991), entry for July 29, 1926.

28. Frayssinet (1928) observed "disillusion caused by the ministerial declaration — when more had been expected than a simple fiscal package"; 221. It bears note again that Haig (1929), Prati (1991), and Eichengreen (1992a) emphasize Poincaré's fiscal changes — rather than subsequent monetary changes — in explaining the recovery of the franc after the summer of 1926. Rist (1931b) criticizes Haig's conclusions and ridicules his failure to mention the Law of August 7, 1926 (see below in text); 199.

29. Rist (1928), 13.

30. Moreau (1991), entry for July 30, 1926.

31. On the discount and advance rate, see Moreau (1991), entry for July 31, 1926; Frayssinet (1928), 153, 221. On bon rates, see Haig (1929), 240; reproduced in Eichengreen (1992a), table 6.3.

32. Philippe (1931), 121–23.

33. Moreau (1991), entry for July 30, 1926.

34. Jeanneney (1976), 339. Also Moreau (1991), entry for October 14, 1926.

35. Blum, "La situation monétaire de la France," July 7, 1926; 9, 12. Auriol Papers, 1 Au 11, Dr 2 (see chap. 5, n. 46).

36. Frayssinet (1928), 159.

37. Ibid., 156, 159–60.

38. "Note," June 25, 1927, 1; and "Note sur la circulation," 2; Archives économiques et financières, B33179.

39. Frayssinet (1928), 236.

40. Robert Lacour-Gayet "Address to the Foreign Exchange Club of New York," November 22, 1927, 7. Lamont Collection, box 95, folder 4. Also Frayssinet (1928), 257ff.

41. Moreau (1991), entries for July 26 and July 29, 1926.

42. Ibid., entry for August 30, 1926. See also entry for July 8, 1926.

43. On discontinuance of discounting real estate paper and Rothschild's support, see ibid., entry for October 14, 1926. On Wendel's support, see Jeanneney (1976), 346.

44. Siepmann to Leith-Ross, "The French Franc," November 30, 1926, 4; Bank of England, OV45/1.

45. "La Banque de France: son rôle dans la restauration financière," *L'Europe Nouvelle,* May 28, 1927. For a more detailed discussion of the "monetary circuit," see Frayssinet (1928), 233ff.

46. G. Royet, "La nouvelle convention avec la Banque de France," Feb. 1927. Quesnay Papers 374 AP/7, folder 12. For similar arguments (all in Quesnay Papers), see Projet de M. Quesnay pour le rapport Dausset, "Les finances publiques et la politique monétaire," 374 AP/6, folder 4; Quesnay, "Réponse à un article de M. Landry dans L'Information," 374 AP/7, folder 12; H. Lagarde, "La liquidité de la Banque de France," Aug., 1927, 374 AP/7, folder 22; etc.

47. "Note sur la mobilisation des bons du Tresor remis à la Banque en representation des avances à l'Etat," Dec. 1926 (unsigned). Quesnay Papers 374 AP/6, folder 4.

48. G. Royet, "Note sur la situation comparée de diverses banques d'émission," Feb. 1927. Quesnay Papers 374 AP/7, folder 12.

49. "Le nouveau régime monétaire et la Banque de France," June 21, 1928, 6; FRBNY, C261.1, "French Situation."

50. Quesnay, "Note sur la mobilisation des bons du Trésor remis à la Banque en représentation des avances à l'Etat," December 1926, 4–5; 374 AP/6, folder 4.

51. Nurkse (1944) similarly noted the effect of bank policy in sterilizing the effects of new foreign exchange and gold reserves; 38, 76–77.

52. Moreau (1991), entry for February 7, 1927. A Bank of England memorandum, "Note on conversations with Monsieur Rist in Paris on August 5th and 6th, 1927," probably by Siepmann, describes Moreau's position as "extreme"; 6. Bank of England OV45/2.

53. For discussion involving Moret, see Moreau (1991), journal entry for September 24, 1926, 112; also see entry for November 3, 1926, 152.

54. Poincaré (1928), 105. The text of the July 13, 1927, convention is reprinted in Moreau (1954), 347–48.

55. Siepmann, "Note of Conversations held with Monsieur Quesnay in Paris on the 18th and 19th June, 1928," 4; Bank of England, OV45/2.

56. Recounted by Rueff (1991), 4–5.

57. Sintenis (1934), 7.

58. *Economist,* April 7, 1928, 704.

59. Rist, "Taux théorique de la stabilisation du franc," Nov. 1926. Quesnay Papers, 374 AP/7, folder 12, 2, 3.

60. Poincaré (1928) emphasized this point later; 99–100.

61. "Note," unsigned, June 25, 1927, 3. Archives économiques et financières, B33179.

62. Poincaré (1928), 100.

63. Sicsic (1992). For earlier related studies, see Wolfe (1951); Sayers (1970); Jeanneney (1976), 321–54; and Mendès-France (1984).

64. "Procès-verbal de l'entretien de vendredi 27 Mai 1927: visite de M. Norman à Paris." (Translation included.) FRBNY, 261.1.

65. Ibid.

66. Inter alia, *Frankfurter Zeitung,* July 10, 1927.

67. Friedman (1991) makes a similar observation; xii–xiii.

68. Moreau (1991), entry for June 11, 1927.

69. Moreau (1991), entries for May 20 and 21, 1927. The final paragraph above is omitted from the 1991 translation; the French original is in Moreau (1954), entry for May 21, 317.

70. H. A. Siepmann, "Reply to some observations by M. Quesnay on the Gold Exchange Standard," November 8, 1927. Bank of England, OV48/1.

71. Ibid.

72. Strong to Moreau, June 20, 1927. FRBNY, 261.1 Special Conference.

73. Strong to Jay, August 4, 1927. Strong Papers, 1012.3.

74. Cassel (1928), 90.

75. Bank of France (1929), 202.

Chapter 9. The French Deflation, 1928–32

1. Saint-Etienne (1983), 363. The M1 figure includes total sight deposits, i.e., those in both the Bank of France and commercial banks.

2. Moreau to Strong, Sept. 21, 1927. FRBNY, C261.1 "French Situation." For evidence of the thin volume of British reserves, see Keynes (1930), 2:271, 277.

3. Nurkse (1944), appendixes I and II. World gold reserves at the end of 1928 were $10.1 billion, while foreign exchange reserves held by twenty-four Continental countries were $2.5 billion.

4. Robert Lacour-Gayet to E. A. Goldenweiser, Dec. 3, 1930. FRBNY, C261 "Bank of France": "Since June 25, 1928, the bank has felt that it would not be in accord with the intention of the laws prepared by the Government and passed by the Chambers at the time of the stabilization of the franc, for the bank to build up its reserves of foreign exchange by direct and systematic purchases."

5. Dr. J. Hans, "The Gold or Gold Exchange Standard: The Gold Policy of the Banks of Issue," *Frankfurter Zeitung*, January 20, 1929; translation at the Bank of England, OV 48/1.

6. Leffingwell to Lamont, July 12, 1927; Lamont Collection, box 103, folder 12. The above reverses the sequence of paragraphs in the original text.

7. "Probleme des Goldstandards," *Frankfurter Zeitung*, July 10, 1927, 4.

8. *Economist*, July 21, 1928, 121.

9. Keynes (1989 [1929a]), 19:779–80. Keynes also acknowledged that Cassel had been right in his earlier warnings of an impending gold shortage; 776.

10. Keynes (1930), 2:271; see also 298.

11. Cassel (1928), 44. Quoted in chapter 3, above.

12. Cassel (1936), 47. See also Cassel (1931), 16; and Cassel (1932), 68.

13. Hawtrey reemphasized this point in Hawtrey (1932), 251.

14. Regarding the central bank's opposition to a rise in the franc, see Bank of France (1929), 204. On the threat to resign, see Moreau (1991), chap. 18, opening summary.

15. See Mouré (1991), 139, for Moreau's concerns, expressed in the *Procès verbaux* of the Council of Regents, Jan. 23, 1930. See Bouvier (1989), 363, for Moreau's comments in *Procès verbaux* of Nov. 27, 1930. See Friedman and Schwartz (1963), 397n, for the position of the Bank of France representative in discussion with Governor Harrison of the New York Federal Reserve in October 1931.

16. Outstanding exceptions include Hawtrey (1932) and (1936), Nurkse (1944), and Eichengreen (1986); the last is discussed below. Inter alia, Friedman and Schwartz (1963), Temin (1976) and (1988), and Kindleberger (1986) do not mention the French Monetary Law. See the notes to the Introduction, above, for a more extensive bibliography on France and the Great Depression.

17. Sauvy (1984), 1:71.

18. Saint-Etienne (1983), appendix 2.

19. Sunday, June 24, 1928, second session. *Journal officiel, Sénat Débat, Session Ordinaire;* 108:1125, 1127.

20. Ibid., 108:1126.

21. Bank of France (1929), 202.

22. Sunday June 24, 1928, second session. *Journal officiel, Sénat Débat, Session Ordinaire;* 108:1131.

23. Jeanneney (1976), 393.

24. Ibid., 396.

25. Ibid., 399.

26. Moreau (1991), entry for May 31, 1928.

27. Ibid., entry for June 8, 1928.

28. Jeanneney (1976), 400; also Moreau (1991), entry for June 9, 1928; 582.

29. Einzig (1931), esp. 30–31. Einzig credits Poincaré with authorship of the policy to undervalue the franc. He mentions Moreau only to describe him — inaccurately — as a moderate; 18, 58.

30. Wheeler-Bennett (1933), 110–12.

31. "Note on conversations with Monsieur Rist in Paris on August 5 and 6th, 1927," 1; Bank of England, OV45/2.

32. Bank of France (1929), 207. Also, Mouré (1991), 48.

33. For data on gold pledged to the Bank of England, see Hawtrey (1936), 63. Also, Bank of France (1928), 190. Nurkse's (1944) frequently used data include this amount — and that for domestic gold exchanged for notes — as increases in the French totals; hence they overstate the in-movement to France during 1926–28; appendixes I and II.

34. Hawtrey (1932), 30. *Federal Reserve Bulletin*s, 1927–33; also, for French and world totals, see Nurkse (1944), appendixes I and II. For an estimate of French foreign exchange holdings in July of each year, 1928–31, see Mouré (1991), table 4.2.

F2.903 billion of gold from circulation was converted to notes at the Bank of France during the two and a half years after the Monetary Law came into effect. Data from Netter (unpublished), chap. 4, p. 41. Also see similar estimate in Bouvier (1989), 352.

35. Bouvier (1989), 353.

36. Stringent American monetary policy beginning in 1928 is routinely identified in the literature as the proximate cause of international monetary contraction. E.g., Friedman and Schwartz (1963), 359–62; McNeil (1986), esp. 218–19; Hamilton (1987); Eichengreen (1992a), 222f.

37. Macmillan Committee (1931a), par. 4367.

38. Rist (1931a), 194–95.

39. It is arithmetically accurate but possibly misleading to juxtapose a 4 percent increase in the U.S. share of the world total with an 8 percent increase in the French share during this thirty-two-month period. Because the U.S. share was larger at the outset, the U.S. stock had to grow more in absolute terms simply to maintain a constant relative share of a growing world stock.

The data nevertheless fly in the face of Friedman and Schwartz's influential conclusion: "*The clinching evidence* that the United States was in the van of the movement and not a follower *is the flow of gold.* If declines elsewhere were being transmitted to the United States, the transmission mechanism would be a balance of payments deficit in the United States as a result of a decline in prices and incomes elsewhere relative to prices and incomes in the United States. That decline would lead to a gold outflow from the United States which, in turn, would tend — if the United States followed gold-standard rules — to lower the stock of money and thereby income and prices in the United States. However, the U.S. gold stock rose during the first two years of the contraction and did not decline, demonstrating . . . that other countries were being forced to adapt to our monetary policies rather than the reverse" (emphasis added). Friedman and Schwartz (1963), 360.

Friedman (1991) amended this earlier judgment to note that France, too, "did not follow gold-standard rules"; xii. He added, "We [in 1963] attributed responsibility for the initiation of a worldwide contraction to the United States, and I would not alter that judgment now." But why not alter that judgment, if the volume of gold movements is "clinching evidence"?

40. For U.S. data, see *Federal Reserve Bulletin*s of 1927 through 1933. Semiannual and, for 1930 and most of 1931, monthly data are conveniently recapitulated in Gregory (1932), table IX. For conclusions similar to those in the text on the relative unimportance of gold flows to the United States, see Fremling (1985). For evidence regarding commodity prices and international trade, see Kindleberger (1986), table 16 and figure 10, respectively. On manufacturing volume, see Eichengreen (1992a), figure 9.1.

41. The French percentage of world "official" gold (i.e., gold in central banks and treasuries) for 1926 does not include gold in circulation or gold pledged to the Bank of England. If those amounts are included, the French share of non-U.S. reserves in 1926 rises to 19 percent. See also Appendix, below, for numerical comparisons.

42. Nurkse (1944), appendixes I and II; *Federal Reserve Bulletin*s, 1927 through 1933.

43. Hurst (1932), esp. 645ff.

44. Data from Nurkse (1944), appendix II.

45. Data from *Federal Reserve Bulletin*, various issues.

46. Cablegram, Harrison to Moreau, July 31, 1930, par. 5; FRBNY, C261, "Bank of France."

47. See Gregory (1932), table IX.

48. James (1984), 78.

49. Kennedy (1987), table 30.

50. See econometric study in Eichengreen (1990), 255ff. Eichengreen estimates the demand for reserves as a function of the import-to-GNP ratio, import variability, and the GNP. He concludes that during 1929–35, "U.S. gold reserves were fully 110 percent and French gold reserves 280 percent above levels that can be accounted for by their economic characteristics. . . . [I]n 1931 France and the United States possessed between them some 60 percent of the global stock of monetary gold. . . . [H]ad France and the United States adhered to the same patterns as other countries, their combined share would have been less than one-quarter"; 264. To assess more accurately the disruption caused by surplus holdings of gold in France and the United States, one would need not only seven-year averages but also a serial listing that shows changes in country surpluses.

51. For exchange reserve data in June 1931, see Brown (1940), table 59 (B). On amounts of sterling and dollars held at the Bank of France, see Bouvier (1989), 353.

52. Macmillan Committee (1931b), 149–50.

53. Discussed in Kunz (1985), 83ff.

54. Macmillan Committee (1931b), 75–76; also Eichengreen (1992a), table 9.6.

55. Hurst (1932), 642.

56. Moreau (1991), entry for May 27, 1927.

57. Data are from the League of Nations (1932), 66. World gold reserves increased by $1.280 billion from December 1928 through June 1931; see Appendix, below.

58. Ibid., 67.

59. Ibid., 66–67. The authors quote at length from Cassel (1932), 70–72.

60. *New York Times*, June 28, 1931, p. 10. Also see Sumner (unpublished).

61. Cassel (1931), 17–18: "In France, any criticism meets the response that they are not in a position to hinder the gold inflow. This defense is specious. Any central bank can bring its internal prices to a level that will block it from obtaining more gold. As France set its new gold parity in 1928 its internal prices were too low relatively to international prices. In other words, the French currency was undervalued. This brought a certain disruption to world commerce, and an increase in the internal French price level was much to be wished for."

62. Strakosch, cited in discussion, Royal Institute of International Affairs (1931), 214. The same pattern of price changes appears in Sauvy (1984), vol. 2, "Les Prix," esp. 188.

63. Memorandum, Harrison to Crane, Dec. 6, 1930. FRBNY C261. Figures from "L'Afflux d'or en France," a memorandum prepared by the Bank of France in late 1930 that used data from the *Bulletin de la Statistique Générale de la France*.

64. Bank of France (1930), 114.

65. Bank of France (1931), 149.

66. Rist (1931b), 1326. Rist leaves the misleading impression that the Bank of France did not import gold during the period of de facto stabilization. The Bank of France (1927) noted, "We have converted into gold a considerable part of our stock of foreign exchange"; 190. The extent of the gold inflow is estimated earlier in this chapter and in the Appendix, below. Rist's implication that France imported more gold after adoption of the Monetary Law was correct.

67. Board of Trade index figures, cited in Cassel (1936), 38. While sterling-denominated prices fell to parity with dollar prices, British unit wages did not. Gregory (1932), 41; also, Cassel (1936), 37.

68. *Bulletin de la Statistique Générale de la France;* in Sintenis (1934), 7. See also chapter 6, above.

69. Nurkse (1944), appendix II.

70. Sauvy (1984), vol. 1, figure 7.

71. Sauvy (1984), 2:188.

72. See Kindleberger (1986), figure 6, on stock prices. See Eichengreen and Wyplosz (1988), figures 14-7 and 14-8 for Tobin's q, and tables 14.2 and 14.6 on the levels and rates of change of investment in France. Figure 14.7 shows a close correlation during 1927–34 between Tobin's q and the rate of investment in France one year later.

73. On world trade, see Kindleberger (1986), figure 10; on money supplies, see Eichengreen (1992a), figures 10.5, 10.6.

74. Eichengreen (1992a), figure 10.3.

75. Eichengreen and Hatton (1988), table 1.1.

76. Cairncross and Eichengreen (1983), esp. 83–103. For the experience of Spain, Finland, Norway, and Denmark, countries that adopted partially or fully floating exchanges, see Choudhri and Kochin (1980).

77. Kindleberger (1986), 178–79.

78. For a list of the years that fifty-four countries were on the gold standard during 1919–37, see Eichengreen (1992a), table 7.1. For discussion of the effects of German exchange controls, see chapter 6.

79. Proportions compiled from Brown (1940), table 59.

80. On September 21, 1931, the Bank of France held F8 billion (about $320 million) in pounds and F18 billion (about $720 million) in dollars. Bouvier (1989), 353.

81. Friedman and Schwartz (1963), 402f.

82. Brown (1940), 1180–81.

83. Reynaud (1933), 253–54.

84. Reynaud's (1933) figure for the foreign exchange converted appears low. Mouré's data indicate that the Bank of France held F36 billion ($1.44 billion) in mid-1928; Mouré (1991), table 4.2. Nurkse's (1944) data indicate that the bank's foreign exchange holdings were reduced to only $176 million (F4.4 billion) by the end of 1932; appendix II. These figures suggest that of the F54 billion increase in official gold, conversion of foreign exchange accounted for F31 billion or F32 billion. See also, Eichengreen (1992a), table 10.7. Sicsic and Villeneuve (1993) offer an argument similar to Reynaud's.

85. Saint-Etienne (1983), appendix 2.

86. Bouvier (1989), 358ff. Netter, inter alia, also emphasizes the bank's low discount rate as evidence that it did nothing to attract capital during the three years after passage of the Monetary Law. Netter (unpublished), chap. 4, p. 48. See a nearly identical argument, offered as the interwar gold standard was collapsing, in Schneider (1933), 151.

87. Eichengreen (1986), 72; and (1992a), 254.

88. Bank of France (1932), 162–63.

89. Moreau (1991), entry for June 24, 1928.

90. From the June 23, 1928, convention between the Bank of France and the Amortization Fund; English text in Moreau (1991), chap. 18, notes.

91. Siepmann, "Note of Conversation in Paris on Saturday the 6th October, 1928," Oct. 9, 1928; Bank of England OV45/80. Cited in Mouré (1991), 139. Thomas Balogh noted a couple of years later that permission to purchase Amortization Fund bons was of no assistance toward easing deflationary pressure because the bank had never sold any of them. The bank's open-market authority was understood to have been limited to operations involving fund bons specifically placed with it in 1928. Balogh (1930); 456.

92. From the June 23, 1928, convention between the Bank of France and the Treasury; English translation in Moreau (1991), chap. 18, notes.

93. Balogh (1930), 458–60.

94. The Décret Impérial du 16 janvier 1808, article 8, stated, "The Bank may not in any case, or under any pretext, undertake any operations other than those permitted under the Laws and the present Statute." Banque de France (1931b), 34.

95. Siepmann, "Note on a Visit of B.C.G. and H.A.S. to Paris on the 31st July 1930," 15 Aug. 1930; Bank of England OV45/81. Quoted in Mouré (1991), 143.

96. Netter (unpublished), chap. 4, pp. 56–61. Also discussed in Mouré (1991), 139–40.

97. Netter (unpublished), chap. 4, p. 2.

98. Eichengreen (1986) concludes that lowering the discount rate, i.e., by 2 percent,

would have had little effect upon banks' demand for cash reserves; 77–78. The issue considered here, by contrast, is not the discount rate but what the central bank would discount (or rediscount).

99. U.S. National Monetary Commission (1911), 201.

100. Ibid., 197.

101. Schneider (1933), 146. See Goodhart (1988) regarding earlier discounting by the Bank of France during crises; 121.

102. Hawtrey (1932), 34–35.

103. Balogh (1930), 448–52.

104. Netter (unpublished), chap. 4, p. 87.

105. Hawtrey (1932), 35.

106. Banque de France (1931), 371.

107. Netter (unpublished), chap. 1, pp. 15–16.

108. Mouré (1991), 126–27. Mouré cites Moreau's testimony before the Oustric Commission; Netter (unpublished) also mentions this testimony; chap. 4, p. 94.

109. Jèze (1932), 527.

110. Ibid., 528.

111. Ibid., 529–30.

112. Bank of France (1931), 164. See similar language in Bank of France (1932), 148.

113. Quotation is from a M. Mollien; in Schneider (1933), 152–53.

114. Banque de France, *Délibérations du Conseil général,* March 17, 1932, 202; quoted in Bouvier (1984), 50.

115. Charpenay (1939), 95–114, 131f.

116. Louis Escallier (director of Mouvement générale des fonds, 1930–40), "Note for the Minister of Finance," January 13, 1931, translated; 4–5. Bank of England, OV45/4.

117. F. G. Conolly, "The Paris Money Market and the *Caisse des dépôts et consignations,*" 4. Bank of England OV45/4

118. Myers (1936), 67.

119. See debate in the Chamber of Deputies, *Journal officiel: Débats,* March 9, 1931; 1694f.

120. Siepmann to S. D. Waley, March 5, 1931; Bank of England, OV45/4.

121. Of F28 billion managed by the Deposit Fund at the end of 1929, F18 billion were held in *rentes,* F6 billion in bons, F2 billion on deposit at the Bank of France or the Treasury, and F2 billion elsewhere. Conolly, "The Paris Money Market," March 16, 1931; 1. Bank of England, OV45/4. On accessibility of deposits, see L. Rist (1933), 793.

122. Vergeot (1931), 656.

123. Vergeot (1932), table 10; and L. Rist (1933), table 4.

124. Caillaux, "L'Or," *Le Capital,* February 24, 1932. Copy in Joseph Caillaux— Emile Roche Papers 5, dr 2.

Chapter 10. The American Deflation, 1928–32

1. *Historical Statistics* (1960), series X 348–54. The figures indicate annual averages.

2. Strong to Norman, September 28, 1925; Strong Papers 1116.5.

3. For primary references, see Clarke (1967), 127.

4. FRBNY (1929), 7.

5. Friedman and Schwartz (1963), 412–14. Also, Chandler (1971), 26, 38f.

6. Hamilton (1987), esp. 147.

7. Eichengreen (1992a), 218.

8. Cassel (1932), 73–74. See also, inter alia, Schneider (1929), esp. 549–51.

9. Friedman and Schwartz (1963), 291–92.

10. Eichengreen (1992b), 213–14, 220; White (1990), 180; also, Field (1984a).

11. Keynes (1930), 2:360–62.

12. Keynes (1936), 154, 158–59.

13. George Soros offers general support for this view from his perspective as a successful investor. He notes, "A boom/bust process occurs only when market prices find a way to influence the so-called fundamentals that are supposed to be reflected in market prices. . . . The most common error is a failure to recognize that [during a boom] a so-called fundamental value is not really independent of the act of valuation." Soros (1995), 71.

14. Friedman rejected the view of an early guide, Henry Simons, according to which the depression was caused by changes in confidence that worked their way through an unstable credit system; Friedman emphasized instead unstable patterns of growth in the money supply. Kindleberger (1989), 80.

15. Friedman and Schwartz (1963); e.g., 298.

16. Leijonhufvud (1981), 132: "Use of the saving-investment approach to income fluctuations is predicated on the hypothesis that the interest rate mechanism fails to coordinate saving and investment decisions appropriately. This is where *all* the Wicksell Connection theories [including that of Keynes] differ from Monetarism. In Monetarist variants of the Quantity Theory, saving and investment have to do with the allocation of output but nothing to do with the determination of aggregate income or the price level. This is true because Monetarist theory assumes that the interest rate mechanism can be relied upon to coordinate the intertemporal decisions of households and firms. Some twenty years of IS-LM exercises and applied econometrics failed to spotlight this point as fundamental to the Monetarist controversy."

17. Inter alia, Rothbard (1963); Rueff (1971). Also, see letter, Leffingwell to Walter Lippmann, December 20, 1931. Leffingwell Papers.

18. Eichengreen (1992a) identifies this view as "conventional"; 213.

19. For comparative data on short-term interest rates, see White (1990), figure 9.

20. Ibid., 166.

21. Ibid., 164.

22. See Galbraith (1993) and Kindleberger (1989) for similar arguments.

23. White (1990), 153–58, especially figures 4 and 5.

24. The dividend-to-price ratio fell to less than 3 percent before the stock market crash of October 1987 (its decades-long range had been between 3 percent and 6 percent). *Economist,* Sept. 4, 1993, 18. The low yield ratio suggests that stock prices were higher than corporate managers thought sustainable.

25. Field (1984a), 497. Keynes (1930) notes a similar increase in inventories (a form of "working capital") during 1928–29 but (probably inaccurately) assumes the accumulation was voluntary; 2:192–93.

26. Data from National Bureau of Economic Research; cited in Meltzer (1976), 457. Similar evidence is cited in Keynes (1930), 2:193.

27. Field (1984a), 497–98.

28. For Keynes's definitions of *industrial* and *financial* circulation, see Keynes (1930), 1:47–48. See also Shackle (1967), 210–13.

29. The two views terminology is from Keynes (1930), 1:143, 251–52. A two views development refers to a simultaneous hardening of bullish and bearish sentiment.

30. Field (1984b), 50.

31. For monthly data on demand and time (savings) deposits in the United States, see Friedman and Schwartz (1963), table A-1.

32. Keynes (1930), 1:251–52.

33. This argument calls into question a premise of "efficient market" theory, at least as applied to the market of the 1920s. Efficient market theory requires that securities prices represent a *consensus* of bull and bear opinion; Copeland and Weston (1988) explain: "Asset prices are correct signals [assuming market efficiency] in the sense that they fully and instantaneously reflect all available information and are useful for directing the flow of funds from savers to investment projects that yield the highest return"; 331. This brushes over the possibility of a large divided opinion, in which case asset price levels reflect a *contested* interpretation of available information.

34. Keynes (1930) pointed to the growing *volume* of call loans in 1928 and 1929 as evidence for two views development; 2:195–96. However, call loan volume and the stock price index moved in close synchronization through all of 1926–30, not just during the frenzied bull phase of 1928–29; see White (1990), figure 6. Again during the bull market of 1982–87, call loan volume and stock price movements were closely synchronized; for margin credit figures, see *Federal Reserve Bulletin,* table 1.36, various issues. This repeated pattern makes it likely that a rising volume of broker lending may be correlated with any rising stock market, rather than specifically with one accompanied by a two views development.

When a two views situation develops, call rates rise because monetary policy does not accommodate the rising demand for financial circulation. If credit conditions are easier, margin credit may expand without a matching rise in call money rates, hence without betokening a rise in bear sentiment. Keynes's mistaken identification of call lending volume with the strength of a two views development parallels one for which he later chided others: i.e., attempting to measure liquidity preference by the economy-wide volume of hoarding rather than by the level of interest rates. Keynes (1936a), 174. Just as an increasing propensity to hoard may be manifested in rising interest rates, the strength of a two views development may reveal itself in the higher borrowing rates that bulls are willing to pay.

35. Leffingwell to Lamont, May 18, 1927; Leffingwell Papers, box 4, folder 93.

36. Keynes (1989 [1937a]), 387.

37. Mishkin (1978), 920–21.

38. The exceptions were the Canadian index, which moved nearly parallel to Wall Street's, and the French index, which rose even more rapidly before cresting in February 1929. Kindleberger (1986), figure 6.

39. Gregory (1931b), esp. 26. Spontaneous and induced capital movements are discussed in chapter 6, above.

40. Keynes (1989 [1929c]), 20:2; also (1930), 1:339.

41. See Wood (1992), 14f., 181f, 186f.

42. Eichengreen (1992a), 218; for month-to-month share index averages, see Kindleberger (1986), figure 5.

43. Leffingwell to Lamont, May 9, 1929; Leffingwell Papers, box 4, folder 94.

44. See Galbraith (1988), 37–38; also Friedman and Schwartz (1963), 260n.

45. Schneider (1929), 547.

46. Keynes (1989 [1937a]), 11:389–90. A contract note is a written statement indicating terms and conditions for a specific purchase or sale of securities.

47. Keynes (1936), 164.

48. Keynes (1989 [1928b]), 13:58. Also, letter, Keynes to C. Snyder, October 2, 1928; in Keynes (1989 [1928c]), 13:65.

49. Keynes (1930), 2:384.

50. Keynes (1989 [1937c]), 13:222.

51. Data from various *Federal Reserve Bulletins*.

52. Eichengreen and Hatton (1988), table 1.1.

53. Figures derived from Eichengreen (1992a), chart 12.8. See also Kindleberger (1986), figure 13, panel III. The common source for these comparisons is the League of Nations (1939).

54. Kindleberger (1986), 112–13.

55. Romer (1990).

56. Temin (1976) offers a different explanation for the nonmonetary downturn of 1930. He finds the distinctive development between the time of the New York stock market crash and Britain's abandonment of the gold standard to have been an unusual and autonomous decline in consumption; 171–72. A decline in consumption might be caused by an increase in liquidity preference (as in Kindleberger's argument, above), in which the demand for liquid assets increases relative to their supply. Temin's counterexplanation holds that liquidity preference actually *declined* following the stock market crash — as evidenced by the coincident decline in nominal interest rates.

Temin's focus upon nominal interest rates assumes that causality runs from higher liquidity demands to higher interest rates and then to lower prices. But if higher liquidity preference lowers prices directly — through reduced profit margins and distress sales — then Temin's chain of argument is broken, and the causal importance of increased liquidity preference may be reasserted. This weakens his case for an autonomous decline in consumption. See also Schwartz (1981), 19–21.

57. For a pessimistic summary, see Keynes (1936a), 316–20. Also, Minsky (1975).

58. Friedman and Schwartz (1963), 414.

59. Inter alia, Eichengreen (1992a), 249–50.

60. Ibid., 252–53.

61. Friedman and Schwartz (1963), table A-1.

62. On open-market operation authority in France, see chapter 9, above.

63. Meltzer (1976), 455. Also, on the real bills doctrine, see chapter 9, above.

64. Friedman and Schwartz (1963), 191.

65. Leffingwell to Strong, April 15, 1922; Leffingwell Papers, box 7, folder 92.

66. Eichengreen (1992a), 251.

67. Keynes (1930) offers perhaps the most extensive criticism of the real bills doctrine on record, although without mentioning the doctrine by name. What mattered was not the identity of the first borrower, but the effect of excess (or restrictive) money creation on the demand for money. Meltzer, (1976), 456n.

68. Strong to Leffingwell, October 8, 1919; attached to letter, Strong to Leffingwell, April 28, 1922. Leffingwell Papers, box 7, folder 92.

69. Leffingwell to Strong, June 30, 1922, and Strong to Leffingwell, July 7, 1922. Leffingwell Papers, box 7, folder 92.

70. Burgess (1927), 197–98. Meltzer (1976), 464–65, inaccurately identifies Burgess's and Strong's views with the real bills doctrine. The Riefler-Burgess-Strong analysis called for reduced Federal Reserve discounting in general, rather than specifically during periods of declining trade. They wanted to replace some discounting with expanded open-market operations. Real bills advocates urged opposite measures. E.g., George W. Norris of the Philadelphia Bank wrote to Harrison on July 8, 1930, "[Open-market purchases] created artificially low interest rates, and artificially high prices for government securities. . . . It *had resulted in making open market operations usurp the discount function*, and tends to foster the regrettable impression that there is some element of impropriety in borrowing by member banks. . . . We do not undertake to say how much Federal Reserve credit should be in use today, but we do hold to the belief that *a substantial part of it should be the result of a demand expressed in borrowing by member banks*, and used in cooperation with those banks" (emphasis added). Quoted in Friedman and Schwartz (1963), 373n.

71. Friedman and Schwartz (1963), 370–71.

72. Ibid., 372–73, for short and longer quotations from Norris; for views of other governors and board members, see 368–72.

73. Harrison to Moreau, July 31, 1930. FRBNY C261 "Bank of France." Also on Harrison's shifting views, see Eichengreen (1992a), 251–52.

74. Chandler (1971), 149.

75. Friedman and Schwartz (1963), 411.

76. See Leffingwell's letter to Lamont of July 12, 1927; the letter is quoted in chapter 9, above. Also, Moreau (1991); entry for May 21, 1928.

77. Proceeding from their somewhat narrow emphasis upon events in the United States, Friedman and Schwartz (1963) are inclined to overestimate the systemic importance of Strong's departure; esp. 411ff.

Temin (1989) argues the opposite view, that "the death of Strong was a minor event in the history of the Great Depression"; 35. Temin's (1989) argument about Strong's role follows from his analysis in Temin (1976). There he argues that interest rates in the United States were low during 1929–31, while the real (i.e., deflation-adjusted) money supply expanded. (He does not distinguish between nominal and real interest rate levels; in fact, the former were low but the latter—given deflation—very high.) He concludes that monetary policy was not contractionary. I counter that the fall in prices during this period implied rising liquidity preference. An excess supply of money—which Temin alleges — would have led, on the contrary, to price increases. (See Meltzer [1976], 461.) Temin's argument is akin to the real bills reasoning advanced by Strong's and Harrison's opponents. Temin replaces the real bills advocates' focus upon declining member bank borrowings from the Federal Reserve with attention to rising real money balances; both then draw the conclusion that the supply of money was adequate during 1929–31. It is more likely that member banks borrowed less and the public increased its real money holdings because both, frightened by the decline in economic activity, sought to avoid debt or enhance their own liquidity. Temin's failure to recognize the deflationary consequences of adherence to the real bills doctrine after the stock market crash leads him to underestimate the consequences of Strong's departure.

78. Friedman and Schwartz (1963), 311.

79. Ibid., 360.

80. Hawtrey proposed at about the same time that *Britain* ease world monetary conditions by selling gold for foreign exchange, with the intent of expanding world reserves to offset French contraction. Macmillan Committee (1931a), par. 4351. The Federal Reserve, with 38 percent of the world's gold reserves at the end of 1929, was in a far stronger position to do this than was the Bank of England, which had only 7 percent.

81. Kindleberger (1989), 133.

82. Friedman and Schwartz (1963), 403–04.

83. Eichengreen (1989) summarizes the political and legislative history of Smoot-Hawley and offers a critical review of the literature on its economic effects.

84. The Smoot-Hawley tariff again worked its way into American popular awareness in 1993 in connection with the proposed North America Free Trade Agreement. In a televised debate in November of that year, Vice President Albert Gore argued that the 1930 Tariff Act contributed in some essential (but not quite articulated) way to the coming of the interwar depression.

85. Dornbusch and Frenkel (1987), 82. Wanniski (1989) devotes more attention to tariff-induced welfare losses; 139–53. But his evidence fails to establish that this — rather than disruption to the international monetary system, which he also emphasizes — was the mechanism by which Smoot-Hawley did its damage. To my knowledge, no one has attempted an econometric analysis of the short-term inefficiency costs of the 1930 tariff.

86. E.g., Kindleberger (1984), 366; Meltzer (1976), 460.

87. Schwartz (1981), table 5. Schwartz's sources are the U.S. Bureau of the Census, the Librairie du Recueil Sirey, the U.K. Board of Trade, and the League of Nations. The wholesale price declines in the other six countries during this twelve-month period ranged from 12.3 percent to 16.9 percent. Metzler (1976), who asserts a relative increase in U.S. prices following passage of Smoot-Hawley, compares average wholesale price data for 1930 with data for 1929; table 1. On its face, this comparison is less likely to isolate the effects of an event that occurred in June 1930 than are Schwartz's data for the period beginning in September 1930. Metzler notes that "not until 1931 did the decline in U.S. wholesale prices [exceed] the declines abroad"; at most, Metzler's argument indicates that Smoot-Hawley delayed this development by a few months. Even Metzler's data show a decline of 9.2 percent in U.S. wholesale prices during 1930, against an unweighted average decline of 12.3 percent in the other six countries for the same year. This difference seems too small to deduce that an important amelioration of U.S. conditions oc-

curred; and certainly too small to identify a reason (that is, the new tariffs) for the relative (and short-term) U.S. buoyancy.

88. For comparative stock index and unemployment data, see chapter 1, above. For comparative data on industrial production, see Saint-Etienne (1984), tables 1.1–1.4; during 1929–31, industrial production fell by 31 percent in the United States, 16 percent in Britain, 12 percent in France, and 32 percent in Germany.

89. Eichengreen (1989), 30–31; Dornbusch and Frenkel (1987), 82; Wanniski (1989), esp. 139, 142. Metzler (1976) also stresses the effect of the new tariff upon the international adjustment mechanism but believes this effect worked through relative price changes; 460.

90. Schuker (1988), table II.

91. Eichengreen (1989) offers evidence that foreign tariff increases usually occurred independently of provocation from the Smoot-Hawley Tariff Act; 31– 35. Eichengreen also reaches the puzzling conclusion that "the argument that Smoot-Hawley disrupted both the smooth operation of the international monetary system and the normal functioning of international financial markets depends for its force on the presumption that the tariff elicited widespread retaliation"; 31. Metzler (1976) similarly argues that foreign retaliation contributed to the damage wrought by the tariff; 460. I argue the opposite, above.

Chapter 11. Why Did the Great Depression Happen?

1. Temin (1989); Eichengreen (1992a).
2. Cassel (1932) and (1936).
3. Hawtrey (1923), 389.

Glossary

Bracket creep: The phenomenon whereby a progressive tax schedule combined with general price inflation drives taxpayers into higher marginal brackets — absent any change in their real incomes. See *Marginal tax rate.*

Capital account: The change in a country's assets abroad and in foreign-owned assets domestically. The account has both long-term and short-term components. See also *Induced capital movement* and *Spontaneous capital movement.*

Ceteris paribus: "Assuming other things to be equal."

Clear: A market is said to "clear" when supply and demand are balanced so there is no excess of either. This is presumed to occur through a price adjustment.

Cost of capital: The weighted average of the costs of (long-term) debt and equity capital. The cost of capital varies among borrowers, contingent upon their market access and perceived riskiness. See also *Marginal efficiency of capital.*

Current account: This includes all sales and purchases of currently produced goods and services, income on foreign investments, and unilateral transfers (including aid, grants, private gifts).

Efficient market theory: The empirically testable claim that financial asset prices reflect a consensus understanding of available information. In its rigid form, efficient market theory implies that investor sentiment always responds to available information and does not itself affect market prices.

Endogenous variable: A variable determined inside the system at hand, by the relations that determine the model. Compare *Exogenous variable.*

Equilibrium: The term is used here in its Walrasian, "general" sense — as Keynes used it in the

Treatise on Money — in which all markets (money, bonds, goods, labor, etc.) *clear* simultaneously. This means that prices adjust so that supply and demand are balanced in each market. Marshall and Keynes in the *General Theory* used "equilibrium" differently, to describe a situation in which the system is stable even though some markets do not clear; this is often designated "partial equilibrium."

Exogenous variable: A variable determined outside the system at hand. See also *Endogenous variable.*

External drain: An international loss of central bank reserves; also called a "foreign" drain.

Financial circulation: Savings deposits and that portion of business deposits used for the holding and exchanging of existing titles to wealth. The size and content of the financial circulation can be sensitive to speculative temper, interest rates, and liquidity demands.

First Term: From the *Fundamental price equation*; it measures the degree of *income inflation (deflation).*

Fixed fiduciary system: This requires that the amount of the note issue not exceed the amount of gold reserves by more than a stated margin. See also *Fixed maximum* and *Percentage reserve system.*

Fixed maximum: This prescribes a maximum that the note issue should not exceed regardless of the amount of reserves. Compare *Fixed fiduciary system* and *Percentage reserve system.*

François-Marsal Convention: Agreement between the Bank of France and the French Treasury in April 1920 under which bank advances would be reimbursed at the rate of F2 billion annually.

French Monetary Law: The law adopted on June 25, 1928, that placed the country on a *percentage reserve system*, whereby gold held at the Bank of France could not fall below 35 percent of the sum of the note issue and its own sight deposits. This law formally removed France from the interwar *gold exchange standard* and ended the Bank of France's prior practice of increasing its foreign exchange holdings.

Fundamental price equation (sometimes called the *Price equation*): A series of closely related equations in Keynes (1930), intended to exhibit the causal process by which the price level is determined. In one iteration,

$$\pi = E/O + (I - S)/O,$$

where π is the price level of output as a whole, E is total money income (excluding the divergence of profit from the equilibrium rate), O is total output, I is the increment in value of new investment goods, and S is savings. In this iteration, E/O is the *first term* and $(I - S)/O$ is the *second term*. The equation distinguishes between *profit inflation (deflation)* and *income inflation (deflation).* The phrase has nearly disappeared from current literature. See also *First term* and *Second term.*

Genoa Resolutions: From the Genoa Conference of 1922; called for central banks to hold foreign exchange alongside gold as a reserve.

German Bank Law of 1924: Set required reserves at 40 percent of the note issue; the law permitted as much as one quarter of reserves to be held in foreign exchange. The law prohibited Reichsbank advances to the German Treasury and discounting of Treasury paper. It also required progressively higher discount rates when reserves fell below the minimum. The law granted some discretion to the Reichsbank concerning the qualitative and quantitative selection of private bills for discount.

Gold exchange standard: Similar to a *gold standard*, but central bank gold reserves are supplemented with reserves held in designated foreign exchange; the latter usually consisted of pounds and dollars during the 1920s and early 1930s.

Gold standard: The central bank of a gold standard country is committed to maintaining a constant currency price of gold. National monetary reserves are held exclusively in gold.

Income inflation (deflation): A change in the cost structure of enterprise, including especially labor cost, which results in parallel upward (downward) pressure on prices. See also *Fundamental price equation* and *Profit inflation (deflation)*.

Induced capital movement: The capital account changes in response to changes in interest rates, induced by the banking system. When a capital inflow is induced by rising interest rates, it may correlate with a decline in domestic investment. Compare *Spontaneous capital movement*. The phrase, from Keynes (1930), is usually absent from current literature.

Industrial circulation: That quantity of money (loosely defined) used for transactions, including income deposits and those business deposits held to maintain output, distribution, and exchange. Compare *Financial circulation*.

Internal drain: Refers here to the withdrawal of gold from a central bank for use in domestic circulation. The term can also refer to the aggregate withdrawal of deposits from the domestic banking system in favor of greater individual currency holdings.

Investment: Real outlays of cash or credit for the purchase of plant, equipment, or supplies for future commercial benefit. Compare with *Savings*.

Law of August 7 (1926): Authorized the Bank of France to buy foreign currency at market prices; this opened the way to stabilizing the franc at a devalued level. It also ended the *fixed maximum* régime that had theretofore restricted monetary management.

Liquidity preference: The concept that interest rates are determined by the desire of the public to retain cash or near-cash assets, rather than by a trade-off between immediate consumption and future consumption.

Marginal efficiency of capital: Always an abbreviated form of "schedule of marginal efficiencies of capital." It indicates both borrower- and firm-specific and economy-wide expected returns on incremental investment. Investment can be expected to occur when the marginal efficiency of capital exceeds the *cost of capital*.

Marginal tax rate: The rate of tax on individual or corporate income at the upper band (margin) of earnings; it may be contrasted with the average tax rate on income. See also *Bracket creep*.

M1: A commonly used measure of a national money supply, which includes currency and demand (sight) deposits.

Monetarism: A *neoclassical* framework closely associated with Milton Friedman which emphasizes the correlation between changes in the supply of money and changes in the rate of price inflation or deflation. Monetarists usually argue that monetary policy affects output and employment in the "short" period but not in the "long" period.

Monetary approach to the balance of payments: This term emphasizes that international reserves move in response to an excess or deficiency of money supply relative to money demand in specific countries. In this framework national price levels are determined by international arbitrage, rather than by country-specific factors. Contrast the *Price-specie-flow mechanism*.

Monetary neutrality: The hypothesis that changes in the quantity of money affect prices but do not affect the real economy. The idea is that all prices change proportionately in response to changes in the money supply. *Rational expectations* theory assumes monetary neutrality over all except the shortest time intervals.

Neoclassical economics: A framework that views economics as having scientific laws, parallel to those of mechanics. Generally assumes the premise that market operations move the economy toward *equilibrium.*

Paradox of the gold standard: If the world's money (including circulation and deposits) increases at a constant proportional rate, world gold production must increase in accelerating absolute amounts if there is to be a constant money-to-gold ratio.

Percentage reserve system: This system prescribes that gold and/or foreign exchange reserves (as specified) not fall below a certain percentage of the note issue or of the note issue combined with some portion of sight deposits (as specified). See also *Fixed fiduciary system* and *Fixed maximum.*

Phillips curve: Narrowly, the curve predicts a close correlation between changes in the nominal wage rate and the level of unemployment. As generally used, it connotes a predictable correlation between the rate of general price change and the unemployment rate, so that price inflation (deflation) brings with it less (more) unemployment.

Price equation: See *Fundamental price equation.*

Price-specie-flow mechanism: This is the hypothesis that international reserves move in response to national price differentials; contrast the *Monetary approach to the balance of payments.*

Profit inflation (deflation): A change in the profitability of enterprise from the steady-state norm, which results in inflationary (deflationary) pressure on prices. Rising profits (ceteris paribus) lead to an effort to invest more, declining profits to an effort to save more in liquid form. See also *Income inflation (deflation)* and *Fundamental price equation.*

Profit term: See *Second term.*

Rational expectations: Narrowly, this is the assumption that firms and individuals do not make predictable mistakes when faced with price changes. The underlying assumption is that markets always move toward *equilibrium,* in which resources are fully employed. A consequence is the conclusion that a persistent decline in prices should not have a sustained effect on output. This is an extreme version of *neoclassical economics.* See *Monetary neutrality.*

Real bills doctrine: Makes a distinction between "commercial" and "financial" bills and proposes that central banks should discount only the former. Because commercial bills are abundant during booms and scarce during downturns, the consequences of implementation tend to be procyclical.

Rules of the game: The notion that countries — or their central banks — should avoid *sterilization* of reserves, particularly gold reserves. Where a country lost gold reserves, the "rules" required that it raise interest rates or otherwise contract its money supply to staunch the drain. It was never clear that these rules applied in inverse fashion, so as to require that a country gaining gold must adopt expansionary policies.

Savings: Earnings not used for consumption. Savings may be placed in stocks and bonds, deposited in bank accounts, held in cash form, buried in the ground, etc. The act of saving does not necessarily lead to *investment,* either by the saver or anyone else. "Savings" is used here to mean savings (ex ante) or intended savings. When aggregate savings (ex ante) exceed (fall short of) aggregate investment outlays, savings (ex post) and investment are brought into equality through a decline (increase) in aggregate income. For example, if everyone attempts to increase savings without an offsetting increase in investment elsewhere in the system, then total spending, and hence aggregate income, must decline.

Second term: From the *Fundamental price equation*; it measures the degree of *profit inflation (deflation)*. Sometimes called the *profit term*.

Spontaneous capital movement: The national capital account changes due to a rising (or declining) trend in new domestic investment. The phrase, from Keynes (1930), is usually absent in current literature. Compare *Induced capital movement*.

Stagflation: A combination of price inflation with stagnation or decline of real output; also may be thought of as a combination of *income inflation* and *profit deflation*.

Steady-state: This is the state of *equilibrium* that, once reached, is postulated to continue indefinitely. It is often preceded by the modifier "long-term."

Sterilization: A state in which the inflow or outflow of monetary reserves (gold or foreign exchange) is not permitted to affect the quantity of domestic money. The effect of a reserve movement on the quantity of money can be offset by expansionary (contractionary) open market and/or discounting policies.

Systemic: Refers to the international economy as one integrated economic system.

Thornton effect: Substitution of credit for gold in the domestic money supply leads to export of gold and (ceteris paribus) causes inflation abroad. A "reverse Thornton effect" is the opposite; a substitution of gold for paper in the domestic money supply requires gold imports and causes deflation abroad. Named after Henry Thornton (1760–1815), author of Thornton (1802).

Tobin's q: The ratio of an equity share price index divided by the price level of newly produced capital goods. It is used here to approximate trends in the rate of *profit inflation (deflation)*.

Bibliography

Unpublished Sources

Archives économiques et financières (Ministère de l'économie)
Vincent Auriol Papers (Fondation nationale des sciences politiques; FNSP)
Bank of England Archives
Joseph Caillaux — Emile Roche Papers (FNSP)
Federal Reserve Archives (FRBNY)
Irving Fisher Papers (Yale University)
George Harrison Papers (Columbia University)
Thomas Lamont Collection (Historical Collections, Baker Library, School of Business Administration, Harvard University)
Russell Leffingwell Papers (Yale University)
Dwight W. Morrow Papers (Amherst College)
Pierre Quesnay Papers (Archives nationales)
Benjamin Strong Papers (FRBNY)

Other Unpublished Sources

Netter, Marcel. "La Banque de France entre les deux guerres." (Manuscript at the Bank of France).
Sumner, Scott. "News, Financial Markets, and the Collapse of the Gold Standard: 1931–1932" (written in 1995).

Newspapers and Periodicals

American Economic Review
Cato Journal
Commercial and Financial Chronicle
Economica
Economic History Review
Economic Journal
Economist
European Economic Review
Explorations in Economic History
Foreign Affairs
Geschichte und Gesellschaft
Index (Svenska Handelsbanken)
Journal of Economic History
Journal of European Economic History
Journal of International Money and Finance
Journal of Monetary Economics
L'Activité économique
Le Capital
L'Europe Nouvelle
Le Figaro
Le Quotidien
L'Information
London Times
Manchester Guardian Commercial
Moniteur des intérêts
Nation and the Athenaeum
New York Evening Post
New York Times
Revue d'économie politique
Revue économique
Rivista de Economica Politica
Quarterly Journal of Economics

Official Publications

Ausschuß zur Untersuchung der Erzeugungs- und Absatzbedingungen der deutschen Wirtschaft (i.e., "Enquête-Ausschuß") (1929). *Die Reichsbank. Verhandlungen und Berichte des Unterausschußes für Geld-, Kredit-, und Finanzewesen (5. Unterausschuß)*. Berlin: E. S. Mittler und Sohn.

Bank of France. *Annual Report,* various issues. Translated and reprinted annually in the March issue of the *Federal Reserve Bulletin.*

—— (1931b). *Lois et statuts qui régissent la Banque de France*. Paris: Imprimerie P. Dupont.

Bureau of the Census and the United States Department of Commerce (1960). *Historical Statistics. Historical Statistics of the United States: Colonial Times to 1957*. Washington: GPO.

Comité des Experts (1926). *Rapport du Comité des Experts*. Paris: Imprimerie Nationale.

Committee of Experts (1924). *Report to the Reparation Committee*. In *Federal Reserve Bulletin*, May 1924.

Committee on Currency and Foreign Exchange after the War (1919). *First Interim Report*, Cmd. 9182. London: HMSO. (I.e., Cunliffe Committee *Report*)

Committee on Finance and Industry (1931a) (a.k.a. Macmillan Committee). *Minutes of Evidence*, Cmd. 3879. London: HMSO.

——. *Report* (1931b), Cmd. 3879. London: HMSO.

Department of Commerce (1973). *Long-term Economic Growth, 1860–1970*. Washington: GPO.

Enquête-Ausschuß. See Ausschuß zur Untersuchung, etc.

Federal Reserve Bank of New York (FRBNY) (1929). *Annual Report*.

Federal Reserve Bulletin, various issues.

Genoa Financial Commission Report (1922); reprinted in Federal Reserve Bulletin (1922), 678–80.

Institute nationale de la statistique et des études économiques. *Bulletin de la Statistique Générale de la France*, various issues. Paris: L'Institute.

Journal officiel de la République française, annales de la Chambre des Députés: Débats parlementaires.

Journal officiel de la République française, annales de Sénat: Débats parlementaires.

League of Nations: Gold Delegation (1930). *Interim Report of the Financial Committee of the Gold Delegation*. Geneva: League of Nations.

—— (1931a). *Second Interim Report of the Gold Delegation*. Geneva: League of Nations.

—— (1931b). *Selected Documents Submitted to the Gold Delegation*. Geneva: League of Nations.

—— (1932). *Report of the Gold Delegation of the Financial Committee*, "Note of Dissent," by Albert Janssen, Reginald Mant, and Henry Strakosch. Geneva: League of Nations.

—— (1939). *World Economic Survey, 1938–1939*.

—— (1945). *Economic Instability in the Postwar World: Report of the Delegation on Economic Depression*. Geneva: League of Nations.

Macmillan Committee. See Committee on Finance and Industry.

Reichs-Kredit-Gesellschaft. *Deutschlands Wirtschaft Entwicklung im ersten Halbjahr, 1929* (1930). Berlin.

Royal Commission on Indian Currency and Finance (1926). *Report and Appendices*, Cmd. 2687. London: HMSO.

Statistique générale de la France, various issues.

Statistisches Reichsamt, various issues.

United States Commission on the Role of Gold in the Domestic and International Monetary Systems (1982). *Report to the Congress*, vol. 1. Washington: GPO.

United States National Monetary Commission (1911), vol. 1. *Interviews on Banking in*

England, Germany, France, Switzerland, and Italy, S. Doc. 405, 61st Congress, 2d Session. Washington: GPO.

Other Published Sources

Aftalion, Albert (1931). *Monnaie et Industrie: les grands problems de l'heure présent.* Paris: Recueil Sirey.

Anderson, Benjamin M. (1949). *Economics and the Public Welfare: Financial and Economic History of the United States 1914–1946.* Princeton: Princeton University Press.

Aron, J. & Co. (1976). *Gold Statistics and Analysis.* New York: J. Aron.

Bagehot, Walter (1873). *Lombard Street.* London: Henry S. King.

Balderston, Theodore (1982). "The Origins of Economic Instability in Germany, 1924–1930: Investment and the Capital Market." *Vierteljahrschrift für Sozial und Wirtschaftsgeschichte* 69:488–514.

——— (1983). "The Beginning of the Depression in Germany, 1927–1930: Investment and the Capital Market." *Economic History Review* 36:395–415.

Balogh, Thomas (1930). "The Import of Gold into France: An Analysis of the Technical Position." *Economic Journal* 40:442–60.

Barro, Robert J. (1989). *Modern Business Cycle Theory.* Cambridge: Harvard University Press.

Becker, Jean-Jacques, and Serge Bernstein (1990). *Victoire et Frustrations 1914–1929.* Paris: Editions du Seuil.

Bérenger, Henry (1926). "La capacité de paiement de la France." In *L'Europe Nouvelle,* May 8, 1926.

Berenson, Edward (1992). *The Trial of Madame Caillaux.* Berkeley and Los Angeles: University of California Press.

Berghahn, Volker (1982). *Modern Germany: Society, Economy and Politics in the Twentieth Century.* Cambridge and New York: Cambridge University Press.

Bernanke, Ben S. (1983). "Nonmonetary Effects of the Financial Crisis in the Propagation of the Great Depression." *American Economic Review* 73:257–76.

——— (1993). "The World on a Cross of Gold." *Journal of Monetary Economics* 31:251–67.

Beveridge, William Henry (1939). *Prices and Wages in England from the Twelfth to the Nineteenth Century,* vol. 1. London: Longmans, Green.

Blainey, Geoffrey (1970). "A Theory of Mineral Discovery: Australia in the Nineteenth Century." *Economic History Review* 23:298–313.

Bloomfield, Arthur I. (1959). *Monetary Policy under the International Gold Standard, 1880–1914.* New York: Federal Reserve Bank of New York.

Borchardt, Knut (1983). "Zum Scheitern eines produktiven Diskurses über das Scheitern der Weimarer Republik: Replik auf Carl-Dieter Krohnes Diskussionsbemerkungen." *Geschichte und Gesellschaft* 9:124–37.

——— (1990). "A Decade of Debate about Brüning's Economic Policy." In von Kreudener (1990).

Bordo, Michael D. (1984). "The Gold Standard: The Traditional Approach." In Bordo and Schwartz (1984).

Bordo, Michael D., and Anna J. Schwartz (1984) (Eds.). *A Retrospective on the Classical Gold Standard, 1821–1931*. Chicago: University of Chicago Press.

Bouvier, Jean (1989). "A propos de la stratégie de l'encaisse (or et devises) de la Banque de France de juin 1928 à l'été 1932." In *L'historien sur son métier: Etudes économiques XIXe-XXe siècles*. Paris: Editions des archives contemporaines.

Bowman, John (1964). "Trends in Midwestern Land Values." Phd diss., Yale.

Bredin, Jean-Denis (1980). *Joseph Caillaux*. Paris: Hachette.

Brown, William Adams, Jr. (1929). *England and the New Gold Standard, 1919–1926*. London: P. S. King.

——— (1940). *The International Gold Standard Reinterpreted, 1914–1934*. New York: NBER.

Brunner, Karl (1981) (Ed.). *The Great Depression Revisited*. The Hague: Martinus Nijhoff.

Buiter, Willem H. (1989). *Macroeconomic Theory and Stabilization Policy*. Ann Arbor: University of Michigan Press.

Buiter, Willem H., and Richard C. Marston (1985) (Eds.). *International Economic Policy Coordination*. Cambridge and New York: Cambridge University Press.

Burgess, W. Randolph (1927). *The Reserve Banks and the Money Market*. New York and London: Harper Brothers.

Cairncross, Alec, and Barry Eichengreen (1983). *Sterling in Decline*. Oxford: Blackwell.

Cassel, Gustav (1920). "Further Observations on the World's Monetary Problem." *Economic Journal* 30:39–45.

——— (1925). "The Restoration of Gold as a Universal Monetary Standard." In United States Senate, Commission of Gold and Silver Inquiry, John Parker Young (Ed.), *European Currency and Finance*, 205–06. Washington: GPO.

——— (1928). *Postwar Monetary Stabilization*. New York: Columbia University Press.

——— (1930). "The Supply of Gold." In League of Nations (1930), 71–78.

——— (1931). *Kapitalismus und Wirtschaftskrise*. Text of a lecture before the Hansabund, June 17, 1931, Berlin.

——— (1932). *The Crisis in the World's Monetary System*. Oxford: Clarendon Press.

——— (1936). *The Downfall of the Gold Standard*. Oxford: Clarendon Press.

Chandler, Lester V. (1958). *Benjamin Strong, Central Banker*. Washington: Brookings Institution.

——— (1971). *American Monetary Policy, 1928–1941*. New York: Harper and Row.

Charpenay, Guy (1939). *Les Banques régionalistes*. Paris: Nouvelle revue critique.

Choudri, Ehsan U., and Levis A. Kochin (1980). "The Exchange Rate and the International Transmission of Business Cycle Disturbances: Some Evidence from the Great Depression." *Journal of Money, Credit and Banking* 12:565–74.

Clarke, Stephen V. O. (1967). *Central Bank Cooperation, 1924–1931*. New York: Federal Reserve Bank of New York.

Colm, Gerhard, and Hans Neisser (1930) (Eds.). *Kapitalbildung und Steuersystem: Verhandlungen und Gutachten der Konferenz von Eilsen*. Berlin: R. Hobbing.

Coombs, Charles A. (1976). *The Arena of International Finance*. New York: Wiley and Sons.

Copeland, Thomas E., and Fred Weston (1988). *Financial Theory and Corporate Policy*. 3d ed. Reading, Mass.: Addison Wesley.

Davidson, Paul (1977 [1971]). *Money and the Real World*. 2d ed. New York: Wiley and Sons.

—— (1982). *Internatonal Money and the Real World*. New York: Wiley and Sons.

DeCecco, Marcello (1973). *Money and Empire: The International Gold Standard, 1890–1914*. Oxford: Blackwell.

De Litra et Cie: Monnaies d'or et Lingots (1951). *Le Marché des Monnaies d'or de 1900 à nos Jours*. Paris: de Litra et Cie.

Dell, Robert (1926). "The Return of M. Poincaré." *The Nation and Athenaeum*, August 7, 1926, 519–21.

Dieterlen, P. (1930). "La dépression des prix après 1875 et en 1930." *Revue d'économie politique* 44:1519–68.

Dornbusch, Rudiger, and Jeffrey Frankel (1987). "Macroeconomics and Protection." In Robert M. Stern (Ed.), *U.S. Trade Policies in a Changing World Economy*. Cambridge: MIT Press.

Eichengreen, Barry (1985a) (Ed.). *The Gold Standard in Theory and History*. New York: Methuen.

—— (1985b). "International Policy Coordination in Historical Perspective: A View from the Interwar Years." In Buiter and Marston (1985).

—— (1986). "The Bank of France and the Sterilization of Gold, 1926–1932." *Explorations in Economic History* 23:56–84.

—— (1987). "Conducting the International Orchestra: Bank of England Leadership under the Classical Gold Standard." *Journal of International Money and Finance* 6:5–29.

—— (1989). "The Political Economy of the Smoot-Hawley Tariff." *Research in Economic History* 11:1–44.

—— (1990). *Elusive Stability: Essays on the History of International Finance, 1919–1939*. Cambridge and New York: Cambridge University Press.

—— (1992a). *Golden Fetters: The Gold Standard and the Great Depression, 1919–1939*. New York: Oxford University Press.

—— (1992b). "The Origins and Nature of the Great Slump, Revisited." *Economic History Review* 45:213–39.

Eichengreen, Barry, Mark W. Watson, and Richard S. Grosman (1985). "Bank Rate Policy under the Interwar Gold Standard." *Economic Journal* 95:725–45.

Eichengreen, Barry, and T. J. Hatton (1988) (Eds.). *Interwar Unemployment in International Perspective*. Dordrecht and Boston: Martinus-Nijhoff.

Eichengreen, Barry, and Charles Wyplosz (1988). "The Economic Consequences of the Franc Poincaré." In E. Helpman, A. Razin, and E. Sadka (1988) (Eds.), *Economic Effects of the Government Budget*. Cambridge: MIT Press.

Einzig, Paul (1931). *Behind the Scenes in International Finance*. London: Macmillan.

Enquête-Ausschuß. See Ausschuß zur Untersuchung, etc.

Falkus, M. E. (1975). "The German Business Cycle in the 1920s." *Economic History Review* 28:451–65.

Feldman, Gerald (1985a). "Weimar from Inflation to Depression, Experiment or Gamble?" In Feldman (1985b).

—— (1985b) (Ed.). *Die Nackwirkung der deutschen Inflation auf die Geschichte, 1924–1933*. Munich: R. Oldenbourg.

Felsenhardt, William (1922). *La Banque de France de 1897 à nos jours.* Bourdeaux: L'Imprimerie de l'Université.

Field, Alexander (1984a). "A New Interpretation of the Onset of the Great Depression." *Journal of Economic History* 44:489–99.

—— (1984b). "Asset Exchanges and the Transactions Demand for Money." *American Economic Review* 74:43–59.

Fisher, Irving (1920). *Stabilizing the Dollar.* New York: Macmillan.

—— (1923). "Stabilizing the Dollar." In Lionel D. Edie (Ed.), *The Stabilization of Business.* New York: Macmillan.

—— (1933). "The Debt-Deflation Theory of Great Depressions." *Econometrica* 1, no. 4:337–57.

Flink, Salomon (1930). *The German Reichsbank and Economic Germany.* New York: Harper and Brothers.

Ford, A. G. (1962). *The Gold Standard, 1880–1914: Britain and Australia.* Oxford: Clarendon Press.

François-Marsal, Frédéric (1927). "French Finances and the Franc." In *Foreign Affairs* 5:189–204.

Frayssinet, Pierre (1928). *La politique monétaire de la France, 1924–1928.* Paris: Librairie de Recueil Sirey.

Fremling, Gertrude M. (1985). "Did the United States Transmit the Great Depression to the Rest of the World?" *American Economic Review* 75:1181–85.

Frenkel, Jacob A., and Harry G. Johnson (1976). *The Monetary Approach to the Balance of Payments.* London: Allen and Unwin.

Friedman, Milton (1984). "Comment." In Bordo and Schwartz (1984).

—— (1989). "The Quantity Theory of Money." In J. Eatwell, M. Milgate, and P. Newman (1989) (Eds.), *The New Palgrave: Money.* New York: Norton.

—— (1991). "Forward." In Moreau (1991).

—— (1992). *Money Mischief: Episodes in Monetary History.* New York: Harcourt, Brace, Jovanovich.

Friedman, Milton, and Anna Jacobson Schwartz (1963). *A Monetary History of the United States, 1867–1960.* Princeton: Princeton University Press.

—— (1983). *Monetary Trends in the United States and the United Kingdom, 1867–1975.* Chicago: University of Chicago Press.

Galbraith, John Kenneth (1954 [1988]). *The Great Crash, 1929.* Boston: Houghton Mifflin.

—— (1990 [1993]). *A Short History of Financial Euphoria.* New York: Whittle Books in association with Viking.

Galenson, Walter, and Arnold Zellner (1957). *The Measurement and Behavior of Unemployment.* Princeton: Princeton University Press.

Goodhart, Charles E. (1972). *The Business of Banking, 1891–1914.* London: Weidenfeld and Nicholson.

—— (1988). *The Evolution of Central Banks.* Cambridge: MIT Press.

Gordon, Robert J. (1978). *Macroeconomics.* Boston: Little, Brown.

Gregory, Theodor E. (1931). "The Causes of Gold Movements into and out of Great Britain, 1925–1929." In League of Nations (1931b), Geneva: League of Nations.

—— (1932). *The Gold Standard and Its Future.* London: Methuen.

Haig, Robert Murray (1929). *The Public Finances of Post-War France.* New York: Columbia University Press.

Hamilton, James D. (1987). "Monetary Factors in the Great Depression." *Journal of Monetary Economics* 19:145–69.

Hanes, Christopher (1993). "The Development of Nominal Wage Rigidity in the Late Nineteenth Century." *American Economic Review* 83:732–56.

Hardach, Gerd (1976). *Weltmarktorientierung und relative Stagnation.* Berlin: Dunker und Humblot.

Hawtrey, Ralph G. (1922). "The Genoa Resolutions on Currency." *Economic Journal* 31:291–304.

—— (1931). "Discussion." In Royal Institute of International Affairs (1931).

—— (1932). *The Art of Central Banking.* London: Longmans, Green.

—— (1936). "French Monetary Policy." *Economica* 6:61–71.

—— (1946). *Bretton Woods for Better or Worse.* London: Longmans, Green.

Hicks, John (1974). *The Crisis in Keynesian Economics.* New York: Basic Books.

Hirsch, Fred, and Jacques Rueff (1965). *The Role and Rule of Gold: An Argument.* Princeton University Studies in International Finance, no. 47, June 1965.

Historical Statistics. See Bureau of the Census.

Hoffmann, Walter G., et al. (1965). *Das Wachstum der deutschen Wirtschaft seit der Mitte des 19. Jahrhunderts.* Berlin: Springer Verlag.

Holtfrerich, Carl-Ludwig (1990). "Was the Policy of Deflation in Germany Unavoidable?" In von Kreudener (1990).

Hume, David (1898 [1752]). "On the Balance of Trade." In *Essays, Moral, Political, and Literary* 1:330–45, London: Longmans, Green.

Hurst, Willard (1932). "Holland, Switzerland, and Belgium and the English Gold Crisis of 1931." *Journal of Political Economy* 40:638–60.

James, Harold (1984). "The Causes of the German Banking Crisis of 1931." *Economic History Review* 37:68–87.

—— (1985a). *The Reichsbank and Public Finance in Germany.* Frankfurt am Main: Fritz Knapp Verlag.

—— (1985b). "Did the Reichsbank Draw the Right Conclusions from the Great Inflation?" In Feldman (1985b).

—— (1986). *The German Slump: Politics and Economics, 1924–1936.* Oxford: Clarendon Press.

Jastram, Roy (1977). *The Golden Constant.* New York: Wiley.

Jeanneney, Jean-Noël (1976). *François de Wendel en république: L'Argent et le pouvoir, 1914–1940.* Paris: Editions du Seuil.

—— (1977). *Leçon d'histoire pour une gauche au pouvoir: La faillite du Cartel, 1924–1926.* Paris: Editions du Seuil.

Jèze, Gaston (1932). "Stabilisation des monnaies." *Academy of International Law, The Hague. Recueil des Cours, 1931* 4:469–540. Paris: Librairie du Recueil Sirey.

Johnson, Paul (1983). *Modern Times: The World from the Twenties to the Eighties.* New York: Haper and Row.

Jones, Ernest (1920). *Papers on Psychoanalysis.* New York: W. Wood.

Kenen, Peter B. (1994). *The International Economy.* 3d ed. Cambridge and New York: Cambridge University Press.

Kennedy, Paul (1987). *The Rise and Fall of the Great Powers: Economic Change and Military Conflict from 1500 to 2000.* New York: Random House.

Keynes, John Maynard (1920). *The Economic Consequences of the Peace.* London: Macmillan. Also in Keynes (1989), vol. 2.

—— (1930). *A Treatise on Money.* London: Harcourt, Brace. Also in Keynes (1989), vols. 4 and 5.

—— (1936a). *The General Theory of Employment, Interest, and Money.* New York: Harcourt, Brace, Jovanovich. Also in Keynes (1989), vol. 7.

—— (1989). *The Collected Writings of John Maynard Keynes,* ed. Donald Moggridge. 30 vols. Cambridge: Cambridge University Press. The following are cited as "Keynes (1989)":

—— [1911]. "Review of Irving Fisher, *The Purchasing Power of Money.*" *Economic Journal* 20. 11:375–81.

—— [1913]. *Indian Currency and Finance.* Vol. 1.

—— [1922]. *A Revision of the Treaty.* Vol. 3.

—— [1923]. *A Tract on Monetary Reform.* Vol. 4, chap. 5, "Positive Suggestions for the Future Regulation of Money." 9:183–86.

—— [1924a]. "A Preface to the French Edition." 4:xvi–xxii.

—— [1924b]. "The Dawes Scheme and the German Loan." *The Nation and Athenaeum.* October 4. 18:254–61.

—— [1925a]. "The Return towards Gold." *The Nation and Athenaeum.* February 21. 9:192–200.

—— [1925b]. "The Economic Consequences of Mr. Churchill." *Evening Standard.* July 22, 23, and 24. 9:207–30.

—— [1926a]. "The French Franc: An Open Letter to the French Minister of Finance (whomever he is or may be)." *The Nation and Athenaeum.* January 9. 9:76–82.

—— [1926b]. "The French Franc: A Reply to Comments on an Open Letter." *The Nation and Athenaeum.* January 16. 19:455–60.

—— [1926c]. "The Franc Once More." *The Nation and Athenaeum.* July 10. 19:563–67.

—— [1926d]. "Keynes' Evidence." Royal Commission on Indian Currency and Finance. 19:476–524.

—— [1927]. "The British Balance of Trade." *Economic Journal* 36. 19:704–22.

—— [1928a]. "The French Stabilization Law." *Economic Journal* 37. 19:755–60.

—— [1928b]. *Is There Inflation in the United States?* September 1. 13:52–59.

—— [1928c]. Letter to C. Snyder, October 2. 13:62–65.

—— [1929a]. "Is There Enough Gold? The League of Nations Inquiry." *The Nation and Athenaeum.* January 19. 19:775–80.

—— [1929b]. "The German Transfer Problem." *Economic Journal* 38. 11:451–59.

—— [1929c]. "A British View of the Wall Street Slump." *New York Evening Post.* October 25. 20:1–3.

—— [1931a]. *Essays in Persuasion.* In vol. 9.

—— [1931b]. *Unemployment as a World Problem.* 13:343–67.

—— [1936b]. "The Supply of Gold." *Economic Journal.* September. 11:490–98.

—— [1937a]. "How to Avoid a Slump." *London Times.* January 12–14. 21:384–95.

—— [1937b]. "The General Theory of Employment." *The Quarterly Journal of Economics.* February. 9:109–23.

—— [1937c]. "The 'ex ante' Theory of the Rate of Interest." *Economic Journal 46.* 14:215–23.

—— [1979]. *The General Theory and After; A Supplement.* Vol. 29.

Keynes, John Maynard, and H. D. Henderson (1929). Pamphlet, "Can Lloyd George Do It?" In Keynes (1989) 9:86–125.

Kindleberger, Charles P. (1984). *A Financial History of Western Europe.* London: Allen and Unwin.

—— (1985). *Keynesianism and Monetarism and Other Essays in Financial History.* London: Allen and Unwin.

—— (1986 [1973]). *The World in Depression, 1929–1939.* Berkeley: University of California Press.

—— (1989 [1978]). *Manias, Panics, and Crashes: A History of Financial Crises.* New York: Basic Books.

Kitchen, Joseph (1930). "The Supply of Gold Compared with the Prices of Commodities." In League of Nations (1930).

—— (1931). "Gold Production." In Royal Institute of International Affairs (1931).

Kreudener, Juergen Baron von (1985). "Die Überforderung der Weimarer Republik als Sozialstaat." *Geschichte und Gesellschaft* 11:358–76.

—— (1990) (Ed.). *Economic Crisis and Political Collapse: The Weimar Republic 1924–1933.* New York: St. Martin's.

Krohne, Claus-Dieter (1982). "Ökonomische Zwangslagen und das Scheitern der Weimarer Republik." *Geschichte und Gesellschaft* 8:415–26.

Krugman, Paul (1994). *Peddling Prosperity: Economic Sense and Nonsense in the Age of Diminished Expectations.* New York: Norton.

Kunz, Diane B. (1985). *The Battle for Britain's Gold Standard.* London: Croom Helm.

—— (1991). "American Bankers and Britain's Fall from Gold." In H. James, H. Lindgren, and A. Teichova (1991) (Eds.), *The Role of Banks in the Interwar Economy.* Cambridge and New York: Cambridge University Press.

Kuznets, Simon (1961). *Capital in the American Economy.* Princeton: Princeton University Press for NBER.

Leijonhufvud, Axel (1968). *On Keynesian Economics and the Economics of Keynes.* New York: Oxford University Press.

—— (1969). *Keynes and the Classics.* London: Institute of Economic Affairs.

—— (1981). *Information and Coordination: Essays in Macroeconomic Theory.* New York: Oxford University Press.

Lewis, W. Arthur (1949). *Economic Survey, 1919–1939.* London: Allen and Unwin.

Loveday, A. (1930). "Gold Supply and Demand." In League of Nations (1930), 88–119.

Lucas, Robert E., Jr. (1981). *Studies in Business-Cycle Theory.* Cambridge, Mass., and London: MIT Press.

Macaulay, Frederick R. (1940). *Some Theoretical Problems Suggested by the Movements of Interest Rates, Bond Yields and Stock Prices in the United States since 1856.* New York: NBER.

Macmillan Committee. See Committee on Finance and Industry.

Makinen, Gail E., and Thomas G. Woodward (1989). "A Monetary Interpretation of the Poincaré Stabilization of 1926." *Southern Economic Journal* 56:191– 211.

—— (1990). "Funding Crises in the Aftermath of World War I." In Rudiger Dornbusch and Mario Draghi (1990) (Eds.), *Public Debt Management: Theory and History*. Cambridge: Cambridge University Press.

Mantoux, Etienne (1952 [1946]). *The Carthaginian Peace, or the Economic Consequences of Mr. Keynes*. New York: Scribner.

Marjolin, Robert (1937). "Mouvements de longue durée des prix et extraction des métaux précieux." *L'Activité économique* 2, no. 8:119–44.

Marseille, Jacques (1984). "Les origines 'inopportunes' de la crise de 1929 en France." *Revue économique* 4:648–84.

Marx, Karl (1977 [1867]). *Capital*. New York: Random House. Translated by Ben Fowkes.

McCallum, Bennett T. (1989). *Monetary Economics: Theory and Policy*. New York: Macmillan.

McCloskey, Donald N., and Richard Zecher (1976). "How the Gold Standard Worked, 1880–1913." In Frenkel and Johnson (1976).

—— (1984). "The Success of Purchasing-Power Parity: Historical Evidence and Its Implications for Macroeconomics." In Bordo and Schwartz (1984).

McGouldrick, Paul (1984). "Operations of the German Central Bank and the Rules of the Game, 1879–1913." In Bordo and Schwartz (1984).

McNeil, William (1986). *American Money and the Weimar Republic: Economics and Politics on the Eve of the Great Depression*. New York: Columbia University Press.

Mellon, Andrew (1924). *Taxation: The People's Business*. New York: Macmillan.

Meltzer, Allan H. (1976). "Monetary and Other Explanations of the Great Depression." *Journal of Monetary Economics* 2:455–72.

Mendès-France, Pierre (1984). "L'oeuvre financière du gouvernement Poincaré." Written in 1928. *Oeuvres complètes*. Paris: Gallimard.

Meynial, Pierre (1925). "La Balance des Comptes." *Revue d'économie politique* 39:5– 53.

—— (1927). "La Balance des Comptes." *Revue d'économie politique* 41:271–89.

Minsky, Hyman (1975). *John Maynard Keynes*. New York: Columbia University Press.

Mises, Ludwig von (1949). *Human Action*. Chicago: Regnery.

—— (1978). *On the Manipulation of Money and Credit*. Dobbs Ferry, N.Y.: Free Market Books.

Mishkin, Frederic S. (1978). "The Household Balance Sheet and the Great Depression." *Journal of Economic History* 38:918–37.

Miskimin, Harry A. (1987). "Money, the Law, and Legal Tender." In G. Depeyrot, T. Hackens, and G. Moucharte (Eds.), *Rhythmes de la production monétaire, de l'antiquité à nos jours,* 697–705. Louvain-la-Neuve: Publications d'histoire de l'art et d'archéologie de l'université catholique de Louvain.

Mitchell, B. R. (1976). *European Historical Statistics, 1750–1970*. Columbia University Press: New York.

Mlynarski, Feliks (1929). *Gold and Central Banks*. New York: Macmillan.

—— (1931). *The Functioning of the Gold Standard*. Geneva: League of Nations.

Moggridge, Donald (1982). "Policy in the Crises of 1920 and 1929." In Charles Kindleberger and J. P. Laffargue (1982) (Eds.), *Financial Crises: Theory, History and Policy.* Cambridge: Cambridge University Press.

Moreau, Emile (1954). *Souvenirs d'un Gouverneur de la Banque de France: Histoire de la Stabilisation du Franc (1926–1928).* Paris: Librairie des Médicis.

―― (1991). *The Golden Franc: Memoirs of a Governor of the Bank of France: The Stabilization of the Franc (1926–1928).* Translated by Stephen D. Stoller and Trevor C. Roberts. Boulder, Colo.: Westview Press.

Mouré, Kenneth (1991). *Managing the Franc Poincaré: Economic Understanding and Political Constraint in French Monetary Policy.* Cambridge and New York: Cambridge University Press.

Mourré, Baron (1921). "La crise de 1920–1921 et ses causes." *Révue d'économie politique* 35:544–67.

Mundell, Robert (1968). *International Economics.* New York: Macmillan.

―― (1971). *Monetary Policy: Inflation, Interest, and Growth in the World Economy.* Pacific Palisades, Calif.: Goodyear.

―― (1975). "Inflation from an International Viewpoint." In David Meiselman and Arthur Laffer (1975) (Eds.), *The Phenomenon of Worldwide Inflation.* Washington: American Enterprise Institute.

―― (1989). "The Global Adjustment Mechanism." *Rivista di Economica Politica* 79:351–464. Also available in Mario Baldessarri, John McCallum, and Robert Mundell (1992) (Eds.), *Disequilibrium in the Global Economy.* New York: St. Martin's.

Myers, Margaret (1936). *Paris as a Financial Center.* London: P. S. King.

Néré, Jacques (1968). *La Crise de 1929.* Paris: A. Colin.

Niemeyer, Otto (1931). "How to Economize Gold." In Royal Institute of International Affairs (1931).

Nogaro, Bernard (1931). "La question d'or devant la Société des Nations." *Revue d'économie politique* 45:1–36.

Nurkse, Ragnar (1944). *International Currency Experience.* Geneva: League of Nations. Reproduced in part, including appendixes I and II, in Eichengreen (1985).

Ogburn, William F., and William Jaffé (1929). *The Economic Development of Postwar France.* New York: Columbia University Press.

Ohlin, Bertil (1927). "The Causes of the European Depression." *Index.* March, no. 15:3–17.

―― (1928). "The Reparations Problem." Part I, *Index.* March, no. 27:2–13.

―― (1929a). "Transfer Difficulties: Real and Imagined." *Economic Journal* 39:172–78.

―― (1929b). "Gold Policy and the Distribution of the World's Gold." *Index.* February, no. 38:3–9.

Oxford English Dictionary: A Supplement to the Oxford English Dictionary (1987); Volume 3 of *The Compact Edition.* Oxford and New York: Clarendon Press.

Palyi, Melchior (1972). *The Twilight of Gold: Myths and Realities.* Chicago: Henry Regnery.

Patat, Jean-Pierre, and Michel Lutfalla (1986). *Histoire monétaire de la France au XXe siècle.* Paris: Economica.

Paul, Ron, and Lewis Lehrman (1982). *The Case for Gold: A Minority Report of the U.S. Gold Commission*. Washington: Cato Institute.

Philippe, Raymond (1931). *Le drame financier de la France de 1924 à 1928*. Paris: Gallimard.

Poincaré, Raymond (1928). *L'Oeuvre financière et économique du Gouvernment: Discours prononcé è la Chambre des Députés, les 2 et 3 Février 1928*. Paris: Payot.

Prati, Alessandro (1991). "Poincaré's Stabilization: Stopping a Run on Government Debt." *Journal of Monetary Economics* 27:213–39.

Rist, Charles (1923). "Les Réparations." *Revue d'économie politique* 37:181–202.

—— (1928). "La loi de 7 août 1926." *Revue d'économie politique* 42:5–24.

—— (1930). "La question de l'or." *Revue d'économie politique* 44:1489–1518.

—— (1931a). "The International Consequences of the Present Distribution of Gold Holdings." In Royal Institute of International Affairs (1931).

—— (1931b). "Comptes rendu critiques." *Revue d'économie politique* 45:198–201 and 1325–26.

—— (1933). *Essais sur quelques problèmes économiques et monétaires*. Paris: Librairie du Recueil Sirey.

—— (1937) (Ed.). *L'évolution de l'économie français, 1910–1932; Tableau Statistique*. Paris: L'Institute scientifique des récherches économiques et sociales.

—— (1955). "Notice Bibliographique." *Revue d'économie politique* 69:977–1045.

Rist, Léonard (1933). "Les caisses d'épargne'" *Revue d'économie politique* 47:788–800.

Rockoff, Hugh (1984). "Some Evidence on the Real Price of Gold, Its Costs of Production, and Commodity Prices." In Bordo and Schwartz (1984).

Rogers, James Harvey (1927). *The Process of Inflation in France, 1914–1927*. New York: Columbia University Press.

Romer, Cristina (1988). "World War I and the Postwar Recession." *Journal of Monetary Economics* 22:91–115.

—— (1990). "The Great Crash and the Onset of the Great Depression." *Quarterly Journal of Economics* 105:597–624.

Rothbard, Murray (1963). *America's Great Depression*. Kansas City: Sheed and Ward.

Royal Institute of International Affairs (1931). *The International Gold Problem*. London: Humphrey Milford.

Rueff, Jacques (1929). "A Criticism by M. Jacques Rueff." *Economic Journal* 39:388–99.

—— (1947). "The Fallacies of Lord Keynes' General Theory." *Quarterly Journal of Economics* 62:343–67.

—— (1991 [1954]), "Preface to the French Edition." In Moreau (1991).

—— (1971). *La péché monétaire de l'occident*. Paris: Plon.

Saint-Etienne, Christian (1983). "L'offre et la demande de monnaie dans la France de l'entre-deux-guerres (1920–1939)." *Revue économique* 34:344–67.

—— (1984). *The Great Depression, 1929–1938: Lessons for the 1980s*. Stanford: Hoover Institution.

Saint Marc, Michèle (1983). *Histoire monétaire de la France, 1800–1980*. Paris: Presses Universitaires de la France.

Salin, Edgar (1929) (Ed.). *Das Reparationsproblem*. Berlin: R. Hobbing.

Samuel Montagu and Co. (1931). *Annual Bullion Letter.* London.

Sargent, Thomas (1986). *Rational Expectations and Inflation.* New York: Harper and Row.

Sauvy, Albert (1984 [1965]), *Histoire économique de la France entre les deux guerres.* Paris: Economica.

Sayers, Richard S. (1936). *Bank of England Operations, 1890–1914.* London: P. S. King and Son, Ltd.

—— (1970). "The Return to Gold in 1925." In Sidney Pollard (1970) (Ed.), *The Gold Standard and Employment Policy between the Wars.* London: Methuen.

Scammell, W. M. (1965). "The Working of the Gold Standard." *Yorkshire Bulletin of Economic and Social Research,* May 1965, 32–45; also in Eichengreen (1985).

Schneider, Andrée (1933). *La Banque de France dépuis 1914.* Nancy: G. Thomas.

Schneider, Franz, Jr. (1929). "Federal Reserve Policy: Its International Implications." *Foreign Affairs* 7:543–55.

Schuker, Stephen A. (1976). *The End of French Predominance in Europe.* Chapel Hill: University of North Carolina Press.

—— (1988). *American "Reparations" to Germany, 1919–1933: Implications for the Third-World Debt Crisis.* Princeton Studies in International Finance, no. 61. Princeton: International Finance Section, Dept. of Economics.

Schwartz, Anna Jacobson (1981). "Understanding 1929–1933." In Brunner (1981).

Sedillot, Réné (1979). *Histoire du franc.* Paris: Sirey.

Shackle, G. L. S. (1967). *The Years of High Theory: Invention and Tradition in Economic Thought, 1926–1939.* Cambridge and New York : Cambridge University Press.

Shiller, Robert J. (1989). *Market Volatility.* Cambridge: MIT Press.

Sicsic, Pierre (1992). "Was the Franc Poincaré Deliberately Undervalued?" *Explorations in Economic History* 29:69–92.

Sicsic, Pierre, and Bertrand Villeneuve (1993). "L'afflux d'or en France de 1928 à 1934." Paris: Direction générale des études, Banque de France.

Sintenis, Wolfgang (1934). *Das franzözische Bankwesen und die Wirtschaftskrise.* Marlburger sozialökonomischen Forschungen, Leipzig: Leipzig University.

Skiba, Rainer (1974). *Das Westdeutsche Lohnniveau zwischen den beiden Weltkriegen und nach der Währungsreform.* Cologne: Bund-Verlag.

Sommariva, Andrea, and Giuseppe Tullio (1987). *German Macroeconomic History, 1880–1979: A Study of the Effects of Economic Policy on Inflation, Currency Depreciation and Growth.* New York: St. Martin's.

Soros, George (1995). *Soros on Soros: Staying Ahead of the Curve.* New York: Wiley.

Taussig, Frank W. (1927). *International Trade.* New York: Macmillan.

Temin, Peter (1971). "The Beginnings of the Great Depression in Germany." *Economic History Review* 24:240–48.

—— (1976). *Did Monetary Forces Cause the Great Depression?* New York: Norton.

—— (1989). *Lessons from the Great Depression.* Cambridge: MIT Press.

Thornton, Henry (1978 [1802]), *An Enquiry into the Nature and Effects of the Paper Credit of Great Britain.* Fairfield: Augustus M. Kelley.

Tobin, James (1987). *Policies for Prosperity: Essays in a Keynesian Mode.* Cambridge: MIT Press.

Triffin, Robert (1960). *Gold and the Dollar in Crisis*. New Haven: Yale University Press.

—— (1968). *Our International System: Yesterday, Today and Tomorrow*. New York: Random House.

Turner, Henry Ashby, Jr. (1985). *German Big Business and the Rise of Hitler*. Oxford and New York: Oxford University Press.

Vergeot, J. (1931). "Les caisses d'épargne." *Revue d'économie politique* 45:651–58.

—— (1932). "Les caisses d'épargne." *Revue d'économie politique* 46:724–35.

Vicarelli, Fausto (1984). *Keynes: The Instability of Capitalism* (translated). Philadelphia: University of Pennsylvania Press.

Volcker, Paul, and Toyoo Gyohten (1992). *Changing Fortunes: The World's Money and the Threat to American Leadership*. New York: Random House.

Walker, Donald A. (1984) (Ed.). *Money and Markets: Essays by Robert W. Clower*. Cambridge and New York: Cambridge University Press.

Wanniski, Jude (1989 [1978]). *The Way the World Works*. Morristown, N.J.: Polyconomics.

Warren, George, and Frank Pearson (1935). *Gold and Prices*. New York: Wiley.

Wheeler-Bennett, John (1933). *The Wreck of Reparations*. London: Allen and Unwin.

White, Eugene N. (1990). "When the Ticker Ran Late: The Stock Market Boom and Crash of 1929." In Eugene N. White (1990) (Ed.), *Crashes and Panics: The Lessons from History*, 143–87. New York: Dow-Jones-Irwin.

White, Harry Dexter (1933). *The French International Acounts, 1880–1914*. Cambridge: Harvard University Press.

Winkler, Heinrich Auguste (1988). *Der Schein der Normalität*. Berlin: J. H. W. Dietz.

Wolf, Martin (1951). *The French Franc between the Wars, 1919–1939*. New York: Columbia University Press.

Wood, Christopher (1992). *The Bubble Economy: Japan's Extraordinary Speculative Boom of the '80s and the Dramatic Bust of the '90s*. New York: Atlantic Monthly.

Index

Academy of International Law, 154

Agriculture, 75, 98, 119, 173, 223n35. *See also specific countries*

Alsace-Lorraine, 88

American Civil War, 18, 136, 198n32

Amortization Fund (Fund for Debt Amortization and Management of National Defense Bons), 123, 124, 125, 127, 152, 231n91

Arbitrage, 29, 34, 36, 94, 114, 129, 147–149, 179, 199n32, 201nn1,4

Argentina, 42, 145, 173

Asia, 50

Australia, 21, 42, 51, 67, 145, 173

Austria, 5, 41, 42, 65, 93, 100, 140, 154, 181

Austria-Hungary, 35, 41

Austrian School economists, 2, 58, 162

Bagehot, Walter, 29, 101–102

Balderston, Theodore, 97, 102

Balogh, Thomas, 152, 231n91

Banking crises, 142, 176; Australia, 42; Austria, 42, 143, 144; Central Europe, 143, 144; France, 153–156; Germany, 5, 8, 42, 100–103, 143, 144, 172, 181, 182, 188; U.S., 170. *See also specific banks*

Bank of England: capital inflows, 4, 14, 179; and convertibility, return to, 8; as creditor, 6, 101; discounting rates and policies of, 29, 31–32, 34–36, 45, 93, 105–106, 113, 118, 129, 145; and fixed fiduciary system, 66; floats sterling, 149, 185; and flow of monetary gold to France, 4; and German banking crisis, 8; influence of, 33–43, 115, 118, 140, 179, 184, 186; interest rates, 86, 88, 113, 114, 118, 145, 179; Keynes on, 34; and monetary gold, 49, 202n26; and pressure on, 8, 70, 129, 136, 145–146; prewar gold standard and, 29–31, 70; prewar role of, 6, 184; reserves of, 33, 40–41, 113, 118, 145,

Bank of England (*continued*)
222n7; rules of the game and, 29–30,
184, 223n41; sterilization of reserves,
6, 132. *See also* Britain; Sterling
Bank of France: *Annual Reports,* 138,
147, 151, 155; capital inflows, 4, 7, 8,
14, 104–108, 134, 135, 157, 179; capital outflow, 86; convention of *June 13,
1927,* 130; currency stabilization, 154;
discounting rates and policies of, 9,
31–34, 84, 86, 105–106, 125, 127,
128–129, 147, 151, 153–157, 158,
176, 182, 185, 186, 188, 189, 231n86;
exchange crisis of March *1924,* 79;
and fixed maximum system, 66, 78;
foreign exchange reserves, 9, 79, 135,
145, 150, 179, 188–189, 227n4; and
François-Marsal Convention, 70;
Friedman on, 178; gold convertibility,
restoration of, 70; and gold exchange
standard, 135–136; and gold inflows,
3, 4, 9, 33, 42, 64–65, 131, 135, 137,
141–145, 146, 150, 154, 155, 157,
159, 172, 179, 185, 196n16, 228n33;
and inflation of *1921–26,* 7, 78–81;
influence (loss of influence) of, 71, 72,
84, 179; interest rates, 8, 82–87, 104,
105, 106, 121, 122, 125, 129, 146,
157, 214n72; and interwar gold standard, 29–30; Keynes on, 34; as lender
of last resort, 153, 155, 156; and monetary gold, 49, 179, 202n26; monetary
policies, 189, 200n54; monetization,
150–151; and percentage reserve system, 66; pressures British reserve position, 8, 70, 145; prewar, 37, 38; profit-
seeking behavior, 33; real bills doctrine, 218n61; reserve ratios in, 7, 33,
65, 67–69, 129, 150, 151, 155, 179;
reserves of, 8, 9, 32, 40, 109, 188–189;
sterilization in, 4, 9, 32, 107, 128, 131,
134, 135, 141, 146, 150–152, 155,
179, 185, 186; and WWI, 70. *See also*
Franc; France; French Monetary Law;
Treasury: French

Bank of International Settlements, 57,
102, 152
Bank of Russia, 40
Bankruptcies, 2, 90, 95, 148, 173
Banks, commercial: French, 9, 68, 79,
85, 106, 153, 158; German, 8, 102
Banque d'Algérie, 122
Baring Brothers banking crisis, 38, 41
Belgium, 21, 57, 64, 82, 88, 94, 133,
143, 148, 150, 215n80, 222n18
Berliner Handelsgesellschaft, 100
Bernanke, Ben, 25
Bimetallism, 20–21, 87, 207n70
Blackett, Basil, 37, 202n20
Bloomfield, Arthur, 30–31, 32, 40,
201n15, 203n63
Blum, Léon, 76, 77, 80, 81, 123, 126,
211n28
Bonds. *See treasuries of specific countries*
Borchardt, Knut, 97, 219n79
Bouvier, Jean, 151
Bracket creep tax increases, 122, 212n34
Bradbury Committee, 187; *Report,* 71
Brazil, 143, 145
Briand, Aristide, 122, 124, 126, 225n26
Britain: agriculture, 75; convertibility, res-
toration of, 112–115, 117, 119, 120–
21, 178–179; and deflation of *1870s,*
18; and deflation of *1890s,* 20; and deflation of *1920–21,* 18–19, 74, 112,
114; and deflation of *1925–28,* 119;
and French diplomacy, 140; and Genoa
Conference, 63–64, 65–66; effect of
German economy on, 89; leaves gold
standard, 145–146, 150, 180, 235n56;
Post Office, 20; pound floated, 149; and
prewar gold standard, 27; prices in,
175; return to gold standard, 4, 8, 46,
88, 93, 112; savings vs. investment in,
59; stabilization in, 94, 95; unemployment in, 21, 42, 45, 79, 87, 88, 105,
149; wages, 97, 230n67; war debt, 57
Brüning, Heinrich, 5, 219n79
Bryan, William Jennings, 20
Burgess, Randolph, 172, 236n70

Caillaux, Joseph, 77, 81–82, 122, 124–127, 140, 188, 213n48, 225n26
Caillaux-Churchill Agreement, 123, 124
Canada, 143, 149, 175
Candace Resolution, 125
Capital: cost of, 13, 15, 22, 86, 90, 92, 109, 164, 198n19; movement of, 7, 14, 90–91, 166, 176; returns on, 90, 92. *See also* Induced capital inflow; Spontaneous capital inflow
Cartel des gauches, 76, 78, 105, 122, 123, 126, 213n48
Cassel, Gustav: on arbitrage, 94; on convertibility, resumption of, 119, 137; on depression, 26; on economization of gold, 55, 56, 137, 221n5; on Federal Reserve policy, 64, 117, 134, 161, 167; on French policies, 3; on French Monetary Law, 3, 165; on gold standard, 59, 60, 61, 177, 178, 209n8; on "gold standard paradox," 41, 61; on growth rate of gold stock, 205n31; on industrial use of gold, 48; on Bank of England, 35; on management of international reserves, 3, 69, 186; on prewar gold standard, 28, 30, 41; on shortage of gold, 3, 69, 187; Strong on, 65, 173; on undervaluation of franc, 230n61; on undervaluation of gold, 3, 55, 56
Central bankers, 2, 5, 7, 60, 64, 187. *See also specific bankers*
Central banks: and arbitrage, 34; cooperation among, 28, 37–39, 43, 63, 65, 69, 115; cyclical (countercyclical) policies, 40, 70; discount rates and policies of, 29, 31, 184; efforts of, to protect own gold stock, 23; failure of, to support Reichsbank, 5; fixed fiduciary system, 66; fixed maximum system, 66; foreign exchange in, 179, 227n3; and French gold inflow, 4; and gold supply, 2, 3, 49; influence of, in *1920s*, 69–72; interwar gold standard, 29, 177; Keynes on, 24, 36, 60; monetary policies of, 178; percentage reserve system,

66; postwar gold exchange standard, 64; prewar gold standard, 28–34, 184; prewar policies of, 33, 34; reserve management of, 31, 60, 69; reserve ratios of, 34, 49, 59, 176, 179; responsiveness of, to international gold movements, 6, 70; rules of the game and, 27, 29–30. *See also individual banks*
Chéron, Henri, 138
China, 48, 208n70
Churchill, Winston, 25, 71, 187
Clarke, Stephen, 2, 210n34
Classical economists and economic theory, 13–14
Clémentel, Etienne, 79, 80
Commerzbank, 100
Committee of Experts (Dawes Plan), 217n26
Committee of Experts (French), 8, 77–78, 80, 122–126, 129–130, 140, 215n82; on German reparations, 217n30; *Report*, 81, 105, 122, 124, 127, 130, 132–133, 188, 211n28
Creditanstalt, 5, 100, 144, 158, 181
Crédit Industriel et Commercial, 153
Crédit Lyonnais, 83, 153
Cunliffe Committee, 29, 32, 187; *Report* of, 29, 71
Currency. *See specific currencies*
Cyclical (countercyclical) policies, 40, 70

Darmstädter Bank, 100
Davidson, Paul, 198n22
Dawes Committee of Experts, 57, 215n88
Dawes Plan, 57, 70, 92, 96
Deflation: 1870s, 16–18, 10, 177; 1890s, 20–21; *1891–96*, 20–21, 41–42; *1920–21*, 16, 18–20, 177, 178; *1925–28*, 119, 148; Britain in *1920s*, 112; post-*1928*, 21–22; profit vs. income, 25–26
Denmark, 21, 149
Deposit Fund (Fund for Deposits and Consignations), 156, 157

Diplomacy, 4, 27, 56, 58, 63, 64, 144, 210n34; Britain and, 88; Eichengreen on, 69; French, 140, 186; German, 101, 219n79; Kindleberger on, 69; WWI and, 69

Disconto Gesellschaft, 100

Discount rates, 169; League of Nations on, 29. *See also specific central banks*

Disequilibrium, 6, 12, 23, 36; Keynes on, 39, 59

Dornbusch, Rudgier, and Jeffrey Frankel, 175

Dow-Jones, 146, 163

Dresdner Bank, 101

Economist, 20, 106, 131, 136, 165

Economization of gold, 55–56, 63, 65, 137

Efficient market theory, 9–10, 12, 15, 24, 159–169, 183, 187, 234n33

Eichengreen, Barry, 2; on failure to support Reichsbank, 5; on France, 151, 153, 214n75, 220n90, 225n28, 229n50, 231n98; on Germany, 87–88; *Golden Fetters,* 69; on interwar gold standard, 69, 177, 178, 223n41; on prewar gold standard, 27–28; on prewar monetary standard, 38; on reconstruction, 73–74; on reserve ratios, 67–68; on shortage of gold, 48–49, 67; on Smoot-Hawley Tariff, 175, 238n91; on sterling, 202n38; on stock market, 161; on Strong, 207n69; on U.S., 167, 229n50

Einzig, Paul, 140, 228n29

Equilibrium, 11–13, 36, 108–109, 129, 146, 196–197nn4–5, 197nn12,13, 198n16; and deflation, 59; employment and, 162; Keynes on, 168; and quantity of gold, 39–40

Ernest-Picard, Paul, 122

Federal Reserve Act of *1913,* 171

Federal Reserve Bank: *Annual Reports,* 160, 171; capital inflows, 4, 14, 91, 166, 167, 169, 183; Cassel on, 117; as creditor, 35, 101; contractionary policies of, 10; discounting rates and policies of, 45, 93, 105–106, 113, 134, 160–162, 167, 170, 172, 176, 180, 182–185, 187, 188, 236n70; expansionary policies, 179, 182; foreign exchange in, 180; free gold in, 150, 184; and German banking crisis, 8; gold inflows, 2, 3, 4, 38–39, 141–145, 146, 174, 176, 183, 184; gold outflows, 134, 160; Friedman and Schwartz on, 12; influence of, 8, 117–118, 134, 136, 179; interwar gold standard and, 29–30; interest rates, 9–10, 64, 65, 142, 146, 165, 166, 169, 183; Keynes on, 117; monetary gold in, 202n26; monetary policy, 160, 165–166, 167, 170, 171–172, 174, 176, 180, 182–183, 228n36, 236n77; offsets systemic contraction, 8; Open Market Conference, 172; Open Market Investment Committee, 113; Open Market Policy, 148; prewar, 38; real bills doctrine and, 171–172, 180, 218n61; reserves of, 9, 40, 66–67, 146, 170; sterilization in, 61, 103, 146, 180; Strong on, 64, 117; and undervaluation of gold, 69; and U.S. stock market boom, 9; use of gold reserves, 8; reserve ratio of, 135; sterilization, 9, 134; Washington board of governors, 167, 170, 172

Field, Alexander, 161, 164, 167, 196n18

Fisher, Irving, 3, 16, 56, 59–60, 65, 134, 173, 183, 195n6, 205n54

Fixed fiduciary system, 66

Fixed maximum system, 66

Fixed-payment contracts, 1

Ford, A. G., 35, 203n63

Franc: de facto stabilization of, 3, 84, 93, 131, 135, 147, 230n66; de jure stabilization of, 3–4, 68, 104, 106, 140, 147, 165, 185, 188, 189; and inflation of *1921–26,* 76, 78–79, 81; recovery of, 219n86; stabilization of, 88, 112,

120–134, 139, 140, 152, 154, 224n14; undervaluation of, 3–4, 76, 84, 86, 87, 89, 104, 105, 107, 131, 132, 140, 179, 185, 186

France: bankruptcies, 139, 155, 156; Bloc national, 76; capital levy, 77, 81, 82, 104, 122, 123, 211n28, 212n29; as cause of Depression, 4, 147; Chamber of Deputies, 77, 81, 124, 125, 156; closed-economy model of, 86; convertibility, restoration of, 137; as creditor, 35; deflation of *1920–21*, 18–19, 74; deflation of *1928–32*, 135–158; effects of British policies on, 114; Finance Ministry, 152; and Genoa Conference, 63–64, 65–66; and gold exchange standard, 7, 136, 186; gold standard adopted in, 35; industrial use of gold in, 48, 49; and inflations of *1920s*, 4; inflation of *1921–26*, 7, 73–89, 179; international gold movements and, 70; investment, 86, 87, 104, 105, 107, 148, 188; Ministry of National Union, 124, 126; Popular Front, 16; *post-1924* stagflation, 76–82; Post, Telegraph, and Telephone service, 87; prewar gold standard and, 31; prices in, 175; price stabilization in, 8; real estate, 75, 85; reconstruction in, 74–75, 76; rentiers, 76, 77, 80–81, 105, 123–124, 127, 139, 157, 186; revalorization, 78, 122, 125, 139–141; reverse-Thornton effects of policies of, 149; Ruhr occupation, 76, 79; savings, 86; savings banks, 157–158; Senate, 138; Socialist party, 76, 77, 124; speculation in, 78; stagflation of *1924–26*, 70–71, 73–89, 139; stocks in, 75; taxes, 8, 68, 76–78, 79, 82, 87, 104, 107, 120, 122, 123, 124, 127, 179, 188, 220n87; unemployment in, 21, 87, 104, 105, 139, 149, 169, 181, 186; wages, 97; war debt, 57, 76, 81, 124, 125, 126, 140. *See also* Bank of France

François-Marsal Convention (1920), 70, 78, 80, 130

Franco-Prussian War, 67, 109, 136

Frankfurter Zeitung, 115, 136, 206n55

Frayssinet, Pierre, 125, 225n28

French Monetary Law, 3, 9, 116, 136–142, 150, 179, 182, 185, 187, 227n16; Cassell on, 3; Keynes on, 3; effects of, 9, 93, 106, 107, 228n34, 230n66, 231n86; and gold exchange standard, 3, 68, 136, 186; Nurkse on, 3; and sterling, 135

Friedman, Milton, 178, 200n66, 209n16, 233n14

Friedman, Milton, and Anna Jacobson Schwartz, 2; on cause of Depression, 177; on central banking policy, 12, 24, 161, 167, 173; on equilibrium, 162; on flow of gold, 228–229n39; on *1870s* deflation, 17, 18; *Monetary History,* 178; on Strong, 65, 236n77

Fundamental price equation, 13, 36, 197n9; and *1870s* deflation, 18; and *1890s* deflation, 20, 21; first term, 13, 15; second term, 13, 15, 16, 23, 39, 42, 88, 108, 162, 171. *See also* Profit deflation; Profit inflation

Fund for Debt Amortization and Management of National Defense Bons. *See* Amortization Fund

Fund for Deposits and Consignation. *See* Deposit Fund

Galbraith, Kenneth, 2, 196n18

Gaulle, Charles de, 206–207n55, 208n75

Genoa Conference, 54, 57, 63–64, 65, 135, 137, 208n2, 209–210n34

Germain, M., 153

German-Austrian Customs Union, 144

German Bank Law (1924), 65, 100, 115, 205n30, 219n79

German Labor Front, 103

Germany: agriculture, 98; banking crisis in, 5, 8, 42, 100–103, 143, 144, 172, 181, 182, 188; bankruptcies in, 95; cost of capital, 92, 94, 98, 99; effect of

Germany (*continued*)

British policies on, 95; effect of French policies on, 95, 132; effect of U.S. policies on, 95; and French diplomacy, 140; convertibility, restoration of, 71, 119, 178–179; and gold exchange standard, 7, 115; gold standard in, 35, 96, 110; hyperinflation in, 87–88, 93, 95, 100, 116; international gold movements and, 70; and investment, 8, 92, 93, 94, 99, 102, 220n90; monetary gold supply in, 202n26; National Socialists, 16, 101, 103, 219n79; and postwar reconstruction, 78, 79; prewar gold standard and, 31; prices in, 148; profit deflation of *1924–29*, 99, 103; returns on capital, 92, 94, 98, 99; Ruhr occupation, 76, 79; savings, 96; social welfare, 98–99; stabilization in, 8, 94, 95, 115–117; taxes, 87–88, 97, 98–99; Temin on, 178; unemployment in, 1, 21, 87, 88, 92, 95, 99, 102, 105, 149, 169, 218n53, 219n67; wages, 97, 99. *See also* Reichsbank; War debt and reparation

Gilbert, Parker, 96, 98

Glass-Steagall Act, 174

Gold: concentration of, in central banks, 3, 190–194, 230n57; currency price of, 58–60, 182; and cyanide process, 46, 53; discoveries of, 39, 51, 53, 67, 206n39; dollar price of, 2, 45, 57; economization of, 55, 137, 182, 184; exchange value of, 18–19; as fetish, 71–72, 210n40; industrial uses of, 48, 49, 50; movement of, 7; nonmonetary uses of, 62, 182; production of, 20, 39–40, 41, 45–46, 50–54, 56, 109, 204n2; real price of, 2, 116; undervaluation of, 2–3, 7, 44–62, 112, 114, 178, 179, 182, 183, 184, 185, 187

Gold, monetary: demand for, 41, 144, 178; economization of, 63, 137, 179; flow of, into France, 4; German policies regarding, 117; postwar supply of, 45, 48; prewar supply of, 6, 28, 40, 202n26; prewar distribution of, 6; shortage of, 61, 69

Gold, real quantity of: increase in, 45, 50, 54; and interwar gold standard, 2; in prewar years, 6, 28, 40, 41, 119; price-sensitivity of, 51, 53, 187; shortage of, 2–3, 4, 7, 50, 56, 65, 69, 112, 119, 142, 179, 183; supply of, 185, 204n2, 210n34, 227n3. *See also* Gold, production

Gold Bloc countries, 143, 149, 174

Gold convertibility: breakdown of, 51; Britain ends, 22; British return to, 8; Cassel on, 55, 137; during WWI, 2, 44; and effect of efforts to restore, 7, 45; French actions threaten, 8–9, 137; Germany and, 188; and Genoa Conference, 63, 65–66; Hawtrey on, 54–55; Keynes on, 22; and percentage reserve system, 66; return to, 18, 55–56, 57, 70, 112–115, 117–118, 169, 178; spread of, 42, 50; suspended in U.S., 17

Gold exchange standard: defined, 3; economization and, 63, 137; France and, 7, 133; and French Monetary Law, 3, 136; Germany and, 7, 115, 116; Hawtrey on, 55; postwar, 63–72; Rist on, 136; Strong on, 136; U.S. and, 7

Gold standard: and currency price of gold, 58–60; automaticity of, 28–33, 60, 64; end of, 142, 145–146, 149; feasibility of, 149; French actions threated, 133, 136; international lending and, 181; interwar, 2, 27, 29, 130, 155, 159, 177–178, 181, 187, 196n18; mystique of, 71–72, 183; prewar, 2, 6, 27–43, 60, 70, 118; reestablishment of, 2, 4, 45, 136, 187; return to, 133–134; spread of, in *1870s* and *1880s*, 35, 41, 42; understanding of, 58, 59, 184, 187; William Jennings Bryan on, 20. *See also* Gold convertibility

"Gold standard paradox," 41, 61
Gold Standard Reserve, 37
Greenback Era, 17–18, 198n28, 199n31, 204n14
Gresham's law, 17, 198n28

Hamilton, James, 25, 195n7
Hardach, Gerd, 88
Harrison, George, 101, 143, 170, 172, 188
Hawtrey, Ralph: on Bank of England, 34, 113, 237n80; on foreign exchange, 208n2; on France, 3; and Genoa Conference, 63, 208n2; on gold movements, 142, 196n11; on gold standard, 61, 177; on gold stock, 205n31; on management of international reserves, 3, 186; on shortage of gold, 3, 187; on stabilization of franc, 121; on sterling, 184; on Strong, 65; on undervaluation of gold, 3, 54–55, 56, 64
Herriot, Edouard, 76, 79–82, 123, 124, 139, 224–225n26
Hilferding, Rudolf, 98
Hitler, Adolf, 103
Holtfrerich, Carl-Ludwig, 97, 219n79
Hoover, Herbert, 102, 174, 188
Hoover Moratorium, 146
Hungary, 41, 65, 93

India: absorption of gold, 7, 46, 48, 56, 178, 182, 185, 196n17; currency, status of, 42; economic relationship of, with England, 37
Induced capital inflows, 90–91, 144, 167, 176
Interest rates: availability of data for, 15; and capital movement, 14; during Depression, 24, 181; and French inflation of 1921–26, 86–87; and induced capital flow, 90, 91; Keynes on, 36; Keynes on Depression and, 22, 23; sterling devaluation and, 150; U.S. and, 180. *See also specific central banks*
International Monetary Fund, 54

Investment: and capital movement, 14; and deflation of 1890s, 20; and German economy, 8; Keynes on Depression and, 22; under prewar gold standard, 2; reduction of, during Depression, 2. *See also specific countries*
Italy, 35, 73, 114, 140, 175, 215n80, 219n77, 222n18

Jacobson Schwartz, Anna. *See* Friedman, Milton
James, Harold, 102
Japan, 35, 143, 148, 160, 166–167, 175
Japy, Gaston, 139
Jastram, Roy, 17–18, 51
Jastram's index, 18, 40, 51, 203n56
Jèze, Gaston, 122, 152, 154–155, 217n26
Jones, Ernest, 71–72
Jouhaux, Léon, 130, 140

Keynes, John Maynard: on Bank of England, 34; on Bank of France, 34; on Britain, 39, 111–112, 118, 176, 215n80; on capital levy, 77; on capital movements, 90; on central banks, 24, 36; on deflation of 1920–21, 19; on Depression, 22–23, 102; on disequilibrium, 6, 177; *Economic Consequences of the Peace*, 213n48; on economization, 168; on equilibrium, 200n66; and Federal Reserve, 111, 117, 168; on France, 3, 75, 76, 86, 105, 123, 129–130; on French Monetary Law, 3, 136–137, 165; *General Theory*, 21, 110, 161, 168, 187, 197nn10,12; on German reparations, 108–109; on gold as fetish, 71–72, 210n40; on gold standard, 60, 61, 111–112, 177; on gold supply, 3, 39–40, 59, 112, 178, 187, 187, 195n6; on government intervention, 99, 200n69; *Indian Currency and Finance*, 30; on management of international reserves, 3, 186; on marginal efficiency of capital, 168; on

Keynes, John Maynard (*continued*)
monetary policy, 168, 234n34; on prewar gold standard, 36, 112, 187; proposals of, 23–25, 207n58; on quantity
theory, 42; on real bills doctrine,
236n67; on real value of gold, 59; on
reserve ratios, 59; on savings vs. investment, 59; on Say's Law, 197n14; on
speculation, 161; on stabilization of
franc, 121; on stock market, 167–168,
183, 234n34; Strong on, 65, 173;
Tract on Monetary Reform, 111;
Treatise on Money, 13–14, 21, 30, 77,
90, 99, 108, 137, 161, 178, 187,
197nn10,12, 198n22; on undervaluation of gold, 3, 178, 187; on U.S., 166;
and volatile expectations, 161; on war
debt, 217n26. *See also* Fundamental
price equation
Keynesian economics, 6, 11, 53, 99
Kindleberger, Charles, 2, 5, 27, 69, 119,
169, 173, 196n16, 206n39, 209–
210n34
Köhler, Heinrich, 99
Kreudener, Juergen Baron von, 99,
218n53
Krohne, Claus-Dieter, 88, 215n88
Krugman, Paul, 12

Laffer Curve, 78, 212n34
Laval, Pierre, 140
Law of *December 20, 1918,* 154
Law of *August 7, 1926,* 125, 126, 136,
138, 225n28
Lazard Frères, 79
League of Nations, 65, 66, 186; Execu-
tive Consultative Committee of the,
63; *Report* (1932), 146; *Second In-
terim Report of the Gold Delegation,*
29, 32
Leffingwell, Russell: on Britain, 114,
222n14; on France, 82, 83, 107, 120,
121–122, 204n75, 219n77; and
French Monetary Law, 165; on Ger-
many, 103; on gold standard, 58, 61;
on Italy, 219n77; on real bills doctrine,
171–172; on restoration of gold stan-
dard, 136; on supply of gold, 53; on
U.S., 45, 167
Lending, 5, 181
Lewis, W. Arthur, 2
Lombard Street, 29
London Times, 122, 215n2
Lucas, Robert, 14
Luther, Hans, 38, 70, 101, 102, 188

Macmillan Committee, 142, 206n48; *Re-
port,* 145
Mantoux, Etienne, 109, 110
Marginal efficiency of capital, 13, 14, 15,
109, 159; decline in, 23, 24; Keynes
on, 22, 26, 36, 168; spontaneous capi-
tal flow and, 90
Marin, Louis, 126
Marjolin, Robert, 40
Marx, Karl, 197n14
May Committee *Report,* 145
McCloskey, Donald, and Richard
Zecher, 34–36
McKenna, Reginald, 187
McNeil, William, 98
Mellon-Bérenger Agreement, 123, 124
Midland Bank, 187
Miller, Adolph, 172
Mises, Ludwig von, 58–59, 61, 186,
207n64
Moggridge, Donald, 196n16
Monetarists and monetarism, 13, 36,
108, 162, 233n16
Monetary approach to the balance of
payments, 31, 34, 36
Monetary Law. *See* French Monetary
Law
Monetary non-neutrality, 13–14
Monetary policy. *See specific central
banks*
Monzie, Anatole de, 124
Moreau, Emile, 8, 71, 72; at Bank of
France, 124–133, 138, 143, 152, 154,
157, 188–189; and Committee of Ex-

perts, 122; on Poincaré, 125; meeting with Strong, 76, 78; Friedman on, 209n16; on sterling, 135; threatens to resign, 137, 139, 189; on undervaluation of franc, 87; on weakness of gold standard in Britain, 145–146

Moret, Clement, 130, 139, 157

Morgan Bank, 53, 79, 103

Morocco, 81, 213n48

Mouré, Kenneth, 152

Mouÿ, Pierre de, 80, 83, 122

Mundell, Robert, ix, 3, 28, 57, 216n2

Napoleonic Wars, 51, 61, 68

Nationale d'Escompte, 153

National Socialists (Nazis), 16, 101, 103, 219n79

Neoclassical economic theory, 4, 11, 12, 162

Néré, Jacques, and Peter Temin, 2

Netherlands, 21, 94, 143, 148, 149, 150, 169

New Deal, 16

New York Times, 146, 175

New Zealand, 51, 173

1960s, 51, 61, 207n55

Norman, Montagu, 25, 64, 70, 71, 88, 101; and Bank of England, 113, 133; on France, 104, 132; and Genoa Conference, 209–210n34; and Germany, 172, 188; on sterling, 187; on U.S., 134

Norris, George W., 172, 236n70

North America Free Trade Agreement, 237n84

Norway, 21

Nurkse, Ragnar: on French Monetary Law, 3; on gold shortage, 3; on interwar gold standard, 30; on prewar gold standard, 30; on rules of the game, 30, 32; on undervaluation of gold, 3, 195n6

Ohlin, Bertil, 98, 108–109, 117–118

Office for Reparations Payments, 116

Oustric Bank, 154

Painlevé, Paul, 81, 82, 139

Pallain, George, 153

Parmentier, Jean, 83

Percentage reserve system, 66

Peret, Raoul, 122

Philippe, Raymond, 122

Phillips Curve, 11, 12, 13

Poincaré, Raymond, 8, 76, 87, 105, 123–133, 138–140, 152, 186, 188–189, 211n8, 228n29, 225n28

Populism, 16

Portugal, 215n80

Prati, Alessandro, 85, 86, 225n28

Price-specie flow mechanism, 6, 27–30, 201n4

Profit deflation, 13–16, 20–23, 25, 42, 88, 89, 159, 198n22; in Britain, 118; in Germany, 99, 100, 103. *See also* Fundamental price equation

Profit inflation, 13–16, 25, 36, 39, 40, 159, 198n22; in France, 74–76; in Germany, 87, 88. *See also* Fundamental price equation

Purchasing power parity, 148

Puritan Wars, 51, 61

Quesnay, Pierre, 57, 124, 152, 207n57, 212n29

Rational expectations theory, 12, 13–14, 25, 36, 108, 198n16

Real analysis, 175

"Real bills" doctrine: France and, 154–155, 156; Germany and, 218n61; Keynes on, 236nn67,70; U.S. and, 171–172, 237n77

Real distribution, 2

Real output growth, 2

Recession of *1920–21,* 45

Reconstruction, 73–75, 76, 78, 79

Reichsbank: advances to Treasury, 100; capital inflows, 4, 7–8, 14, 91–99, 179; capital outflows, 99; countercyclical (procyclical) policies of, 70, 100, 101; discounting rates and policies of,

Reichsbank (*continued*)
   5, 8, 31–32, 34, 70, 93, 95, 97, 100,
   101, 103, 105–106, 172, 181, 182;
   failure of central banks to support, 5;
   foreign exchange in, 65; and Genoa
   Conference, 64; and German Bank
   Law, 65, 70; and gold exchange standard, 71, 115, 116, 182; gold point
   spreads, 223n30; gold reserves of, 33,
   103; and gold standard, 116; interest
   rates, 86, 92–97, 98, 101, 113, 116,
   117, 146, 179, 181, 216n11, 217n32;
   as lender of last resort, 101, 188,
   218n61; and monetary gold, 49; pressure on, 129; pressures British reserve
   system, 70; prewar, 38–39; reserve
   ratios in, 7, 32, 68–69, 70, 96–97,
   100, 102, 115–117, 182; reserve rules,
   32, 66; reserves of, 5, 7, 8, 40, 49–50,
   96–97, 115–116, 132; statutes, 65;
   sterilization, 132
Reparations. *See* War debt and reparations
Reserves, 7–8, 14, 22, 56, 146, 179;
   ratios, 7, 55, 59, 66–69; shortage of, 3,
   115, 117, 178, 180, 187. *See also specific central banks*
Reynaud, Paul, 137, 150
Rist, Charles, 225n28; at Bank of France,
   124, 130; and Committee of Experts,
   122, 140; on deflation, 3, 147–148,
   186; on gold exchange standard, 116;
   on gold movement, 142, 230n66; on
   gold production, 39; on gold shortage,
   3, 112, 187; on gold standard, 28, 61,
   136; on interest rates, 83; meeting with
   Strong, 78; and reserve shortage, 3; on
   revaluation of gold, 206n55; on undervaluation of franc, 131; on undervaluation of gold, 3, 55–56, 59, 62; on war
   debt and reparations, 95, 217n26
Robineau, Georges, 78, 79, 80, 81, 124
Rockoff, Hugh, 53
Roosevelt, Franklin, 57
Rothbard, Murray, 2

Rothschild, Eduoard de, 78, 128
Rueff, Jacques, 3, 53, 108, 206n55
Ruhr occupation, 76, 79
Russia, 32, 35, 41, 202n26

Sauvy, Albert, 74, 137, 148
Scandinavia, 35, 94, 148, 169
Schacht, Hjalmar, 68, 70–71, 93, 96,
   101, 103, 115–116, 182, 186
   205nn26,30, 223n29
Schedule of marginal efficiency of capital.
   See Marginal efficiency of capital
Schuker, Stephen, 5, 91, 93, 94, 97, 98,
   216n11, 217n26
Sherman Silver Purchase Act (1890), 41
Siepmann, H. A., 130, 133, 152, 157,
   222n21
Silver, 48, 60
Sixteenth-century price revolution, 50–
   51
Smoot-Hawley Tariff Act, 9, 144, 160,
   174–176, 181, 183, 184, 188,
   237nn84,87, 238nn89,91
Socialism, 16
Société Générale, 153
Soros, George, 233n13
South Africa, 46, 53, 206n39, 208n75
Spain, 145
Speculators and speculation, 16, 19, 22–
   23, 64, 65, 101, 116, 133, 138, 144,
   160–163
Spontaneous capital inflows, 90, 91, 144,
   176, 179
Stagflation, 12, 15. *See also* France
Statistique Générale, 131
Steady-state. *See* Equilibrium
Sterilization: defined, 3, 196n9, 215–
   216n2; and depression of *1891–96*, 6;
   and spontaneous capital inflows, 91.
   See also specific central banks
Sterling, 4, 7–9, 17, 25, 54, 88, 89; de-
   valuation of, 142, 148, 149–150, 151,
   154; end of convertibility, 141, 149;
   floated, 149, 174, 185; overvaluation
   of, 118, 148, 179, 184

Stock market, U.S.: boom and crash of, 4, 42, 97, 134, 142, 145–146, 160–167, 169, 180, 183–184, 196n18, 233n24; decline in, 175; and demand for margin credit, 9; effects of, on Germany, 93; and efficient market theory, 9–10, 15, 183; post-crash, 171; speculation and, 65; Temin on, 235n56; volatile behavior of, 9–10

Stock markets, 23, 74, 119, 147, 159–160, 183, 234n34; Britain, 22; Canada, 22, 234n38; France, 21–22, 148, 211n, 234n38; Germany, 22, 93; Japan, 160, 166–167; Netherlands, 22; Sweden, 22; Switzerland, 22

Stresemann, Gustav, 70

Strong, Benjamin, 28, 46, 57, 59, 61, 64–65, 170; on automaticity of gold standard, 65, 207n69; and currency stabilization, 183, 188; on Federal Reserve, 117; on France, 134, 172; on French Monetary Law, 165; Friedman on, 209n16; on Germany, 68; on gold exchange standard, 65, 173; importance of, 71, 187–188, 236n77; leadership of, 180; on "real bills" doctrine, 65, 171–172, 209n16, 236n70; on shortage of gold, 65, 134, 173; on Smoot-Hawley Tariff, 173; on stock market, 160; on taxes, 76, 78; on war debt, 207n60

Sweden, 21, 22

Switzerland, 94, 143, 148, 150

Tariffs, 175, 181. *See also* Smoot-Hawley Tariff

Taussig, Frank, 28

Temin, Peter, 91–94, 177, 178, 196n18, 216n11, 235n56, 236–237n77. *See also* Néré, Jacques

Thornton, Henry, 35

Thornton effect (reverse-Thornton effect): defined, 35; and causes of Depression, 178–182; France and, 149; in postwar years, 69; in prewar years, 42;

and spontaneous capital inflows, 91; U.S. and, 145; WWI and, 44

Tobin's q, 15, 18–19, 21–22, 74–75, 87–88, 94, 105, 148, 200n58, 210n7, 230n72

Transvaal, 46

Treasuries: British, 85, 156; cooperation among, 28; German, 49, 70, 100, 102, 106; U.S., 38, 40, 106

Treasury, French: bank advances to, 8, 78, 79, 81, 122–125, 128–129, 132, 154, 188, 214n72; bank advances to, liquidation of, 128–130, 133, 134, 138, 179, 185, 186, 188, 189; bonds, 75, 106, 215, 128, 213n52; *bon* consolidations, 128, 130, 131; *bon* rates, 157, 214nn64,75; *bon registration*, 123, 127; *bon* reimbursements, 125; *bons*, 79–85, 104, 121, 123, 127, 131–132, 156, 188, 212n41; convention of *June 13, 1927*, 130; and François-Marsal Convention, 70; and *1921–26* inflation, 7; policies of, 8, 151; rates, 85–86, 121, 125, 127; and sterilization, 128. *See also* Amortization Fund; Bank of France

Treaty of Versailles, 95, 213n48, 218n53

Unemployment: economic theory and, 11–12; and deflations of *1870s* and *1920–21,* 20; in Germany during Depression, 1, 21; increase of, during Depression, 2, 181; and price deflation, 2; and profit deflation, 16. *See also specific countries*

Uruguay, 173

United States: agriculture, 75; bank failures in, 170, 173; as cause of Depression, 4–5, 9; currency, status of, 42; cyclical recovery of, 93; and deflation of *1870s*, 17–18; deflation of *1890s*, 20–21; deflation of *1920–21*, 18–19, 74; deflation of *1928–32*, 159–176; and Fordney-McCumber tariff, 95; and French diplomacy, 140; and Genoa

United States (*continued*)
  Conference, 63, 65–66; gold discoveries in, 51, 53, 67; and gold exchange standard, 7, 64–65; gold reserves of, 32, 109; gold standard adopted in, 35; industrial production in, 149; industrial use of gold in, 48; and inflation of *1914–1920,* 183; international gold movements and, 70; investment, 164, 183; leadership role of, 64; and maintenance of gold convertibility, 2; Panic of *1893,* 41; and prewar gold standard, 27, 38; prices in, 148, 175; Republican party, 174; reserve inflows, 9; reserves of, 40, 66–67; taxes, 76; Temin on, 178; trade policy, 160; unemployment in, 1, 10, 21, 45, 149, 169, 175, 204n7; wages, 97; war debts and reparations, 81, 109, 124. *See also* Federal Reserve; Greenback Era
U.S. National Monetary Commission, 153, 223n41
U.S. World War Foreign Debt Commission, 57
Upper Silesia, 88

Vietnam War, 61, 208n75
Volcker, Paul, 206n45, 207n55

Wanniski, Jude, 175
War debt and reparations, 4, 5, 7, 9, 57, 176, 181; American Civil War and, 18; France and, 76, 81, 123, 146; Germany and, 5, 76, 79–81, 87, 91–92, 95–96, 99, 101, 108–110, 116–117, 132, 146, 182, 217nn26,30,32, 218n53, 219n79; Keynes on, 22, 23, 108–110; and postwar gold exchange standard, 64, 65; Rist on, 95; Smoot-Hawley Tariff and, 175; systemic consequences of, 146; U.S. and, 102, 146. *See also* Hoover Moratorium
Warren, Robert, 82, 84, 224n14, 225n26
Wendel, François de, 78, 81, 122, 124, 126, 128, 139, 140
White, Eugene, 161, 162, 167
White, Harry Dexter, 49
Winkler, Heinrich Auguste, 97
World War I, 4, 51, 53, 54, 69, 109, 118, 178
World War II, 54, 57, 204n3

Young Plan, 100

Zecher, Richard. *See* McCloskey, Donald, and Richard Zecher